FAMILY FINANCE

A STUDY IN THE ECONOMICS OF CONSUMPTION

BY

HOWARD F. BIGELOW

FAMILY FINANCE

A STUDY IN THE ECONOMICS OF CONSUMPTION

By

HOWARD F. BIGELOW

Professor of Economics
Western State Teachers College, Kalamazoo, Mich.

EDITED BY BENJAMIN R. ANDREWS
TEACHERS COLLEGE, COLUMBIA UNIVERSITY

81856

J. B. LIPPINCOTT COMPANY

CHICAGO   PHILADELPHIA   NEW YORK

PRINTED IN THE UNITED STATES OF AMERICA

TO

BARBARA, MARY, JAMES, AND JOHN

WHO PROVIDED THE LABORATORY AND THE INCENTIVE
FOR WORKING OUT MUCH OF THE MATERIAL
THIS BOOK CONTAINS

PREFACE

Family Finance is a study in the economics of consumption, written from the point of view of the individual family. This approach was chosen for a number of reasons. In the first place, the American family is the biggest business in the United States. Every year it handles the entire national income, and in addition it turns out billions of dollars' worth of goods and services that statisticians have never discovered. The family serves more meals than all our restaurants, makes more beds than all our hotels, washes more clothes than all our laundries, grows more flowers than all our florists, and provides more man-hours of leisure-time activity than all our movies.

Even today, in a highly specialized, highly industrialized society, the family, not the individual, is the economic unit. It is true, of course, that in business we are accustomed to think in terms of individuals. Business hires individual workers. It borrows money from individual bondholders, pays dividends to individual stockholders, and sells its products to individual buyers. At the same time, many fallacies in our thinking about economic problems, many errors in business judgment, have come from the failure to realize that even though in business the individual appears to be acting for himself alone, his behavior can only be understood in connection with his family status. It is possible to think clearly about business and economic problems, only if we think in terms of the family as the fundamental economic unit.

In any unregimented economic order, the family as the consuming unit is the supreme authority which by its purchases controls the course of production. The success of any business is determined by its ability to anticipate and to provide effectively and economically for the wants of American families, in the way in which the family and not the business man decides to satisfy those wants.

It is because there are whole groups of families that have not been able to adjust their personal affairs successfully to the changes in their environment that we are faced with many economic and social problems. These broader economic and social problems seem remote to most of us. Or if they are near at hand, they seem so complex that we do not know where to take hold of them. The place for most of us to attack them is in our own homes. For by improving our own manner of living, each one of us, here and now, is doing something definitely to make the world a better place in which to live.

In improving our manner of living, there is, of course, a definite place for social action. The individual family cannot ignore its relation to other families. It should not overlook the benefits of collective action. It must not fail in its responsibilities to a larger social group. But no group activities can actually result in better living unless they make it possible for individual families to provide more adequately for the wants of their members. For it is as individuals that we experience all the satisfactions of life.

This book, therefore, is designed to suggest in considerable detail methods and devices by which the individual family may immediately go about improving its way of living. And since we can solve our personal problems only if we become intelligently aware of the social and economic situation outside the home, a second purpose is to help families develop a point of view and work out a technique of planning and management which will facilitate continuous and satisfactory adjustment to the constantly changing conditions in the world around them.

Of necessity this book deals largely with the material side of family life. But it is concerned with the problems of raising material levels of living, not because material things are an end in themselves, but because they are an effective means by which the family can provide a well-rounded and abundantly satisfying life for all its members.

It would require too much space to trace the intellectual heritage of this book. Footnotes and bibliographies acknowledge some small part of the author's personal indebtedness to other authors in this field. Special acknowledgment should be made to Mrs. Ruth V. Schumacher of the Home Economics Department, Western State Teachers College, for much help with material from the field of home economics; to Dr. Benjamin R. Andrews for his encouraging comment and intelligent and friendly criticism; to the Administration and my colleagues at Western State Teachers College for help in ways too numerous to mention; and to Agnes Wedaae and Eleanor

Embs for painstaking work in the preparation of the manuscript. I wish especially to express to my wife my appreciation for her constant encouragement, her many hours of work on the details of the book, her helpful advice, her straight thinking about family problems, and most of all for her insistence upon enjoying to the full, even among the uncertainties of recent years, a sane and fearless and happy family life.

Howard F. Bigelow

CONTENTS

xi

PART I

THE FAMILY: ITS WANTS AND ITS RESOURCES

CHAPTER I

THE MODERN AMERICAN FAMILY

The adaptable family. The family is a most adaptable institution. In the course of human history it has assumed many forms. There have been polygamous families, in which each man had several wives; polyandrous families, in which each wife had several husbands; and monogamous families, in which each man had only one wife, and each wife only one husband. There have been patriarchal families, in which the oldest male was recognized as the head, and all his sons and grandsons, and sometimes more distant kin as well, were subject to his authority. And there have been matriarchal families, in which the authority was centered in a female head. There have been autocratic families, which some one individual ruled with an iron hand; and there have been democratic families, in which all the members of the family were consulted on all major decisions.

All these forms of the family represent developments suited to the time and the conditions under which the families lived. The polygamous family developed among peoples in which the females in the population greatly outnumbered the males. A warlike people frequently lost heavily of its men in battle. The successful warriors who survived, were, however, able to provide amply for a number of wives, who in turn bore children to replace the war-time losses. On the other hand, a peaceful people with only a few of the well-to-do able to support more than one wife, when faced with a surplus of females, practiced exposure of girl babies in sufficient numbers to keep the population within the bounds of its resources. The polyandrous family developed among peoples in which the males greatly outnumbered the females. In some cases polyandry was perpetuated because living conditions were so difficult that it took the work of several husbands to provide the livelihood for one woman and her children.

Present diversity in family organization. The diversity of family organization in the past is paralleled by the diversity of family organization at the present time. Today in most Western countries the monogamous family is the accepted type, but there are parts of the world in which polygamy and polyandry still survive. Even within the limits of the monogamous family, we find great variety—in the consciousness of the importance of the family; in the scope of the family responsibility, not only for the immediate family group, but also for its more distant relations; in the strength of family ties; and in the centralization or decentralization of authority.

Even today, many families are autocratic in their organization, and many are democratic. There are still many families under the domination of a single strong personality. Of these, some are patriarchal and some are matriarchal in their internal organization. In other families there is definite division of responsibility and authority; each member of the family has certain duties to perform and certain decisions to make, and is given full control in his field. In others, all important decisions and many minor ones are made in family council.

In all probability some one or two of these forms of organization are better suited to present conditions than are the rest. A number of writers have made a strong case for the democratically organized monogamous family. But there is considerable difference of opinion as to how far children should be allowed to participate in family councils, and how much weight should be given to individual preferences in making major decisions. After all, no one form of family organization is necessarily best. The very diversity of family organization today is in itself evidence of the continued adaptability of the family as an institution to the widely varying conditions under which individual families must live.

The changing functions of the family. The exact form of organization to use in any particular case depends upon the functions which that individual family must perform for its members. The functions of the family, like its organization, change from time to time, and vary from place to place. In studying the problems of family finance we are not much concerned with the more general functions which, more or less in spite of itself, the family as an institution performs for society. Rather we are concerned with the types of service which the family may render to its members.

These types of service may be classified as economic, religious, protective, educational, recreational, status defining, and affectional.[1] For many years there has been an apparent trend of most of these functions away from the home. The economic function of production has been going from the home to the factory and specialized farm. The religious function has been largely turned over to the church. The protective function has been left to the public health service, the army and the navy, the city police and fire departments, the sheriff's office, and the state police. Recreation has gone to the playground, the theater, the golf course, the hotel, the dance hall, and the night club. With people moving frequently from place to place, even the status-defining function of the family has become less important than it used to be. For many people, social position has come to depend much more upon the job they hold, the neighborhood they live in, and the clubs they join, than upon the family to which they belong. Only the affectional function of the family has been free from the competition of institutions outside the home.

In the early 1930's some evidence of a reversing of this apparent trend of functions away from the family began to appear. As the depression deepened, more and more production went back into the home. With the rather general adoption by employers of the policy of discharging married women whose husbands were employed, and retaining married men, in order to provide the largest possible number of families with an income, women began to do for their families in their own homes many things they formerly paid others to do for them with the money they earned working outside the home. They began to buy the goods they needed in less fully processed forms. They bought flour and did their own baking. They bought fresh fruit and did their own canning. They bought piece goods and made more and more of their own clothing. They went back to doing their own laundering. And as their incomes were further curtailed, they substituted inexpensive types of home recreation for commercial amusements.

For some years Ralph Borsodi,[2] Consulting Economist for the Dayton Subsistence Homestead Project, has been insisting that there are obvious improvements in our way of life that can be secured by

---

[1] For a discussion of these see W. F. Ogburn, "The Family and Its Functions," Ch. XIII, especially pp. 661-679, in *Recent Social Trends in the United States*. McGraw-Hill Book Co., Inc., New York, 1933.
[2] Ralph Borsodi, *Flight from the City*, Harper and Bros., New York, 1933; and *This Ugly Civilization*, Simon and Schuster, New York, 1929.

bringing back a great deal of our factory production to the home. He maintains that what some people consider to be but a temporary break in the continued industrialization of our productive processes should mark the beginning of a new trend which will carry back to the home much that has left it. He believes that the subsistence type of homestead, when properly organized and adequately financed, will bring not only an increase in the importance of the economic function of the family, but also the economic security and close personal association in common tasks which will make for a strengthening of the affectional side of family life.

Family problems are difficult to discuss. For our present purpose we are not so much interested in trends which frequently turn out not to be trends at all as we are in understanding the diversity of the problems which present-day families face, and the variety of ways in which they are attempting to solve their problems. When we come to study them, however, we find that the problems which the family faces are difficult to discuss because of the great diversity in the make-up of family groups. Families vary widely in their personnel and organization, from time to time and from place to place, and at any given time and place. Families vary in size, in the age of their members, in the amount of their income and other resources, and in the ways in which they make their living.

The small family living in a city apartment, dependent upon employment for its income, dependent upon its income for the purchase of everything its members need, faces a problem entirely different from that of the farm family with a larger number of children and some dependent relatives, all, however, engaged literally in making their living from the land on which they live. Families in small towns face problems which contain elements of the problems of both farm and city families, and yet are unlike either. And among the farm families themselves the problems of the family engaged in general farming are decidedly different from those of the family engaged in truck gardening, fruit growing, or cotton planting, which must depend for the things it needs upon the income it receives from the sale of a money crop.

Family problems are difficult to discuss because each of us is given to thinking in terms of his own experience, of his own immediate family problems. If we live in the country we think in terms of the farm. If we live in the city we think in terms of apartments and subways and money to spend for all the apparent necessities of city life. If we live in a middle-sized city we have still a different situation in mind.

Our first problem, therefore, is to get a definite conception of modern American families, what they are like and into what types they may be classified. We need to know much about their diversity in size, in membership, and in organization. We need to know about the differences in their environment, their income, and their other resources. We need to understand the whole range of their immediate problems. We need to learn as much as we can about the variety of methods by which they are trying to solve these problems. For then, and only then, can we see our own families and their problems in proper perspective.

The size of the family. It is common knowledge that in 1930 the average American family was smaller than it was at the time of the first census. In 1790, the average size of the private household in the United States was 5.7 persons; in 1900, 4.6 persons; and in 1930, 4.0 persons. The size of the family remained fairly constant until about 1850. Since 1850, the average number of persons per family has declined with every successive census. The following table shows the changes which have taken place in the total population, the number of families, and the number of persons per family, from 1850 to 1930.

TOTAL POPULATION, NUMBER OF FAMILIES, AND NUMBER OF PERSONS PER HOUSEHOLD IN THE UNITED STATES, 1850-1930 [3]

Year	Total Population	Number of Families	Persons per Household
1850	23,191,876	4,197,914	5.6
1860	31,443,321	5,959,752	5.3
1870	38,558,371	7,579,363	5.1
1880	50,155,783	9,945,916	5.0
1890	62,622,250	12,690,152	4.9
1900	75,994,575	16,187,715	4.7
1910	91,972,266	20,255,555	4.5
1920	105,710,120	24,357,675	4.3
1930	122,775,046	29,979,841	4.1

For purposes of comparison with earlier census returns it is necessary to use statistics for "census families." The 1900 and 1930 census analyzed the family statistics in terms of private families,

---

[3] Compiled from U. S. Census Reports. In this table the family is the "census family" which includes institutions and hotels as well as "private families." Total population and number of families 1850 and 1860 corrected to include slave as well as free population.

which exclude hotels and institutions but include lodgers and servants living in a single household. The following table shows the difference in returns for "census families" and for "private families" in 1900 and 1930.

PRIVATE FAMILIES IN THE UNITED STATES, 1900 AND 1930

Year	Population Living in Private Families	Number of Private Families	Persons per Private Family
1900	73,410,992	15,963,965	4.6
1930	119,812,185	29,904,663	4.0

But averages tell little about actual families. The next table, showing the percentage distribution of families classified according to size, gives a more definite idea of the change that takes place in the size of individual families when the average size of the family changes from 5.7 to 4.0. According to this table, in 1790 two-thirds of the families in the United States had 5 or more members. In 1930, more than two-thirds had less than 5 members.

FAMILIES IN THE UNITED STATES CLASSIFIED ACCORDING TO SIZE IN 1790, 1900, AND 1930 [4]

SIZE OF FAMILY	PERCENTAGE DISTRIBUTION OF FAMILIES		
	1790	1900	1930
One person..................................	3.7	5.1	7.9
Two persons.................................	7.8	15.0	23.4
Three persons...............................	11.7	17.6	20.8
Four persons................................	13.8	16.9	17.5
Five persons................................	13.9	14.2	12.0
Six persons.................................	13.2	10.9	7.6
Seven persons...............................	11.2	7.7	4.7
Eight persons...............................	9.0	5.2	2.8
Nine persons................................	6.5	3.2	1.6
Ten persons.................................	4.2	1.9	0.9
Eleven persons and over.....................	4.9	2.2	0.9
All families................................	100.0	100.0	100.0

There are a number of factors which have been operative in bringing about a decline in the size of the family. Part of the decrease has been due to a decline in the birth rate. Even more has been due to a reduction in the number of servants, relations, lodgers, and boarders, of whom, as late as 1900, there were 63 for every 100

[4] U. S. Bureau of the Census, *A Century of Population Growth, 1790-1900*, Washington, 1909, p. 98; Fifteenth Census of the United States (1930), *Population*, Vol. VI, "Families," Table 4, p. 7.

households, and in 1930 only 44 for every 100 households, of whom 33 were relatives.[5]

During this thirty-year period a great many families have substituted machines for maid-servants. Many of the relatives have been going to housekeeping for themselves. In 1930 there were, out of 29,904,663 families, 2,357,463 families of one person listed in the census.[6]

These changes in the size of the family have not been uniformly operative, however. The decline in the size of the family is most noticeable in metropolitan centers. It is not so noticeable in cities and in small towns. In rural areas there is little indication of a

DISTRIBUTION OF POPULATION IN THE UNITED STATES [7]

	1930	1920	1910	1900	1890
Urban territory	56.2	51.4	45.8	40.0	35.4
Places of 1,000,000 or more.............	12.3	9.6	9.2	8.5	5.8
Places of 500,000 to 1,000,000.........	4.7	5.9	3.3	2.2	1.3
Places of 250,000 to 500,000..........	6.5	4.3	4.3	3.8	3.9
Places of 100,000 to 250,000..........	6.1	6.2	5.3	4.3	4.4
Places of 50,000 to 100,000..........	5.3	5.0	4.5	3.6	3.2
Places of 25,000 to 50,000..........	5.2	4.8	4.4	3.7	3.6
Places of 10,000 to 25,000..........	7.4	6.6	6.0	5.7	5.4
Places of 5,000 to 10,000..........	4.8	4.7	4.6	4.2	3.8
Places of 2,500 to 5,000..........	3.8	4.3	4.2	4.1	4.0
Rural................................	43.8	48.6	54.2	60.0	64.6
Rural non-farm.......................	7.4	8.5	8.9	8.3	7.6
Rural farm...........................	36.4	40.1	45.3	51.7	57.0

PERCENTAGE DISTRIBUTION OF FAMILIES BY SIZE IN THE URBAN, RURAL NON-FARM, AND RURAL FARM AREAS OF THE UNITED STATES, 1930 [8]

Size of Family	Urban	Rural Non-farm	Rural Farm
One person..................................	8.0	10.4	5.2
Two persons.................................	25.1	23.8	18.3
Three persons...............................	22.1	20.2	18.0
Four persons................................	18.1	16.6	16.6
Five persons................................	11.6	11.4	13.3
Six persons.................................	6.8	7.3	10.0
Seven persons...............................	3.8	4.5	7.1
Eight persons...............................	2.1	2.7	4.8
Nine persons................................	1.1	1.5	3.1
Ten persons.................................	0.6	0.8	1.8
Eleven persons..............................	0.3	0.4	1.0
Twelve or more persons......................	0.2	0.3	0.8
All families................................	100.0	100.0	100.0

[5] From *Recent Social Trends in the United States*, Report of the President's Research Committee on Social Trends; by permission of the publishers, McGraw-Hill Book Co., Inc. W. F. Ogburn, "The Family and Its Functions," Ch. XIII, pp. 682-683. New York, 1933.
[6] Fifteenth Census of the United States (1930), *Population*, Vol. VI, "Families," Table 4, p. 7.
[7] Fifteenth Census of the United States (1930), *Population*, Vol. I, Table 8, p. 14.
[8] Fifteenth Census of the United States (1930), *Population*, Vol. VI, "Families," Table 20, pp. 14 and 1-

decrease in the size of the family. One study,[9] which counted only the parents and children who are members of the immediate family circle, excluding other relatives, boarders, lodgers, visitors, and servants, found the following variations in the size of families: In 1930 farm families averaged 4.32 members; small town families, 3.72 members; urban families (cities of about 100,000 population), 3.43 persons; and metropolitan families (of which Chicago was taken as an example), 2.85 members.

In this same study it was found that in 1930, in the unbroken families in rural districts, only one family in six was without children living at home. In small towns there were no children living at home in one family out of four; in cities, in one family out of three; in metropolitan areas, half the families had no children living at home.

The tables on page 9 show the rate of urban drift in our population in the last forty years, the proportion of the population now living in communities of various sizes, and the proportion of families of various sizes in the urban, rural non-farm, and rural farm population.

The table on page 11 shows the number and percentage of families having a specified number of children under ten and under twenty-one years of age. This table shows that urban families have fewer children than rural families. Over 40 per cent of the urban families have no children, and 22 per cent more have only one child under 21. Only 30 per cent of the rural families have no children, while half the rural families have two or more children under twenty-one.

This does not mean, of course, that 30 per cent of the rural families and 40 per cent of the urban families never have children. There are many families that have finished rearing their children, and many younger couples that have not yet begun to rear their children. If we were to find out what proportion of the families of the country never have children, it would be necessary to make a study of families in which the wife is past the child-bearing age. The classifications of families having a specified number of children simply gives a cross section of the families of the country at the time of the 1930 census. It serves, however, to emphasize the diversity of problems which American families face.

---

[9] From *Recent Social Trends in the United States*, Report of the President's Research Committee on Social Trends; by permission of the publishers, McGraw-Hill Book Co., Inc. W. F. Ogburn, "The Family and Its Functions," Ch. XIII, p. 683. New York, 1933.

PERCENTAGE OF FAMILIES HAVING A SPECIFIED NUMBER OF CHILDREN UNDER 10 AND 21 YEARS OF AGE IN DIFFERENT TYPES OF COMMUNITIES IN THE UNITED STATES, 1930 [10]

Number of Children	All Classes		Urban		Rural Non-farm		Rural Farm	
	Number	Per Cent	Number	Per Cent	Number	Per Cent	Number	Per Cent
All families	29,904,663	100.0	17,372,524	100.0	5,927,502	100.0	6,604,637	100.0
Families having								
No children under 10	17,587,354	58.8	10,841,237	62.4	3,400,704	57.4	3,345,413	50.7
1 child under 10	5,745,158	19.2	3,368,013	19.4	1,112,999	18.8	1,264,146	19.1
2 children under 10	3,525,307	11.8	1,890,912	10.9	730,777	12.3	903,618	13.7
3 children under 10	1,787,690	6.0	805,889	4.6	399,059	6.7	582,742	8.8
4 children under 10	851,974	2.8	325,022	1.9	194,558	3.3	332,394	5.0
5 children under 10	311,074	1.0	108,827	0.6	69,043	1.2	133,204	2.0
6 or more under 10	96,106	0.3	32,624	0.2	20,362	0.3	43,120	0.7
Families having								
No children under 21	11,593,871	38.8	7,237,813	41.7	2,354,257	39.7	2,001,801	30.3
1 child under 21	6,226,861	20.8	3,843,472	22.1	1,185,444	20.0	1,197,945	18.1
2 children under 21	4,844,821	16.2	2,868,208	16.5	933,521	15.7	1,043,092	15.8
3 children under 21	3,008,129	10.1	1,616,073	9.3	601,652	10.2	790,404	12.0
4 children under 21	1,817,519	6.1	870,160	5.0	372,221	6.3	575,138	8.7
5 children under 21	1,081,620	3.6	460,863	2.7	222,431	3.8	398,326	6.0
6 or more under 21	1,331,842	4.5	475,935	2.7	257,976	4.4	597,931	9.0

[10] Fifteenth Census of the United States (1930), op. cit., Table 27, pp. 19 and 20, and Table 29, pp. 21 and 22. Children related in any way to the head of the family were counted, whether sons or daughters, grandchildren, nephews, nieces, or with other relationships.

Sectional differences in the size of the family. The size of the family varies also in different sections of the country. Both the average and the median for the New England and Middle Atlantic states are approximately the same as for the country as a whole. Families are a little smaller than the average for the whole country in the North Central and Mountain states; they are much larger in the Southern and decidedly smaller in the Pacific states. The following tables show the sectional differences in the median and mean size of families in the United States and the sectional differences in the median size of urban, rural farm, and rural non-farm families.

MEDIAN AND MEAN SIZE OF FAMILIES BY GEOGRAPHICAL DIVISIONS, UNITED STATES, 1930 [11]

Geographical Division	Median	Mean
South Atlantic	3.76	4.41
East South Central	3.69	4.29
West South Central	3.57	4.18
Middle Atlantic	3.43	4.01
New England	3.39	4.00
West North Central	3.34	3.92
Mountain	3.33	3.92
East North Central	3.32	3.88
Pacific	2.83	3.38
United States	3.40	4.01

MEDIAN SIZE OF URBAN, RURAL FARM, AND RURAL NON-FARM FAMILIES BY GEOGRAPHICAL DIVISIONS, 1930 [12]

Geographical Division	Total	Urban	Rural Farm	Rural Non-farm
New England	3.39	3.44	3.45	3.15
Middle Atlantic	3.43	3.42	3.71	3.38
East North Central	3.32	3.27	3.75	3.11
West North Central	3.34	3.14	3.91	3.02
South Atlantic	3.76	3.28	4.56	3.66
East South Central	3.69	3.22	4.15	3.52
West South Central	3.57	3.23	4.14	3.38
Mountain	3.33	3.13	3.86	3.23
Pacific	2.83	2.75	3.31	2.87
United States	3.40	3.26	4.02	3.28

Occupational differences in the size of the family. Figures showing the average size of families classified according to occupation are also interesting. In 1930, the average size of professional families was 3.01 persons, and of clerical employees, 3.04. The

---

[11] Fifteenth Census of the United States (1930), *op. cit.* Median, Table 44, p. 37; Mean, Table 61, p. 54.
[12] Fifteenth Census of the United States (1930), *op. cit.*, Table 44, p. 37.

average size of families in the proprietary group, the owners of stores, business managers and the like, was 3.25. The average size of the families of semi-skilled workers was 3.47 persons; of skilled workers, 3.51 persons; and of unskilled workers, 3.91 persons. The average size of the families of farm laborers was 4.32 persons, and of farm owners and renters, 4.48 persons.[13]

The relative advantage of the large and the small family. All these figures show clearly that there is a great diversity in the make-up and composition of American families. Can we, from this mass of figures, gain any idea as to the best size for the ordinary American family? What seem to be the relative advantages of the large and the small family? Why do we have small families in the city and large families in the open country? Why do professional families, with incomes well above the average, have small families, while unskilled workers and farm laborers, with small incomes, have large families?

It seems clear that in the large city the advantage is with the small family. Living costs, especially rents, are high. A family with a number of growing children finds city apartments decidedly inadequate. Everything the family needs must be purchased with money. The larger the number of individuals in the family, the smaller is the money income available for each one. And there is comparatively little that can be done in the home by the members of the family to supplement their money income.

In the small town, on the other hand, a larger family has fewer disadvantages. Living costs are lower, rents are moderate, and ample shelter is available. In the smaller communities it is possible for large families to do for themselves many things which small metropolitan families must pay to have done or do without.

In rural districts, children at a comparatively early age may become an economic asset. On the farm, when labor is difficult to secure, the children may begin serving their apprenticeship performing tasks suited to their years, at an age when city boys and girls are barred by law from seeking any employment.

In the smaller communities and in the open country, even if families do not look upon their children as economic assets, they find

---

[13] From *Recent Social Trends in the United States,* Report of the President's Research Committee on Social Trends; by permission of the publishers, McGraw-Hill Book Co., Inc. W. F. Ogburn, "The Family and Its Functions," Ch. XIII, p. 685. New York, 1932.

them by no means as much of a liability as they are in the city. In the small town and open country the enjoyment and satisfaction of parenthood can be secured at a reasonable cost.

Similarly, families are smaller in those occupational groups which have standards of living that call for a large amount of the sort of goods and services which must be bought with money. Families are larger in those groups in which occupation and standard of living allow the sort of living that can be had for a moderate money outlay.

Families are smaller in the professional group, in part because professional training necessitates later marriage, but even more because of the large money outlay which the maintenance of professional living standards entails. The professional family must spend enough money to maintain its social position in the community. It plans to provide professional training for its children. In all probability each child will cost such a family money for not less than twenty-five years.

The white-collared clerical employee is barred from practicing the economies either in shelter or in clothing which are available to the industrial worker. The clerical employee must provide a high school, and, if possible, a college education for his children. He must limit his family to the number he can support properly on his usually moderate salary. For he is expected to take care of all his current needs, to pay in full for all his medical care, and in addition to set up adequate financial reserves against old age and unemployment.

The industrial worker, on the other hand, has a standard which calls for a minimum of money outlay. His family is able to live in inexpensive neighborhoods, to wear inexpensive clothes, and to do many things for itself. And in many cases the industrial worker possesses the manual skill necessary for the performance of most of the common household tasks. As far as education is concerned, he expects his boys and girls to complete the required public school courses. If they want to go on to college, or even in some cases, if they want to finish high school, they must do so at their own expense. At the same time, his inconsiderable money income makes it almost impossible for the industrial worker to save enough to provide adequately either for unemployment or old age. He finds that if he can rear a good-sized family, they will provide him with the cheapest form of old-age and unemployment insurance it is possible for a poor man to buy.

To a very large extent, then, the size of the American family seems to be determined by the principle of pecuniary outlay. If the family's standard of living can be maintained only by generous money outlay, the advantage is clearly with the small family. If, on the other hand, its standard of living, occupation, and location make it possible for the family to secure many of the essential elements of its standard of living by its own efforts, and the rest with moderate money income, the advantage is with the larger family.

Not all the factors determining the size of the family are economic in character. Some families who could afford children, prefer to be free from the limitations upon social life which children involve. Some families refuse to rear children in the social situation in which they are forced to live. Some families limit the number of children in order to be able to give one, or two at most, careful social training and meticulous care.

There are a number of generally recognized social and psychological advantages of the large family. Nursery schools at best provide a necessary but inevitably artificial situation in which the only child can learn from contact with his fellows what the child in a large family learns in his own family group. Large families provide more opportunity for the development of well-rounded personalities. They offer more safeguards against personalities warped by forced loneliness or by too great parental dominance. Further, two children born within two or three years of each other do not restrict the social activities of the homemaker twice as much as does an only child. It usually requires less attention on the part of the mother to care for two children who can play together than to provide less desirable adult companionship for one. Large families provide more adequate insurance for the perpetuation of the family itself down through the ages. It is the larger families in this generation that will have most to do in determining the character of the next. Social as well as economic considerations, therefore, help to determine the size of families.

The family life cycle. In addition to the fact that the average size of families varies from time to time, from place to place, and from occupation to occupation, it is necessary to remember that the individual family changes in size from time to time.

Families everywhere pass through the same round of marriage, birth, schooling, adolescence, maturity and departure of the children, a few quieter years in later middle life, old age, and death. The same family varies in size with the passage of the years. And as its size varies, so its functions vary. Every family passes through a series of clearly defined stages, each of which brings with it a number of characteristic problems.

First comes the establishment of the family. During the first few years of family life, expenses for food and clothing and other current necessities are at a minimum. There is then the possibility of saving money for investment in securities to supplement income in later years, in durable household equipment, or perhaps even in the home itself.

Next comes the child-bearing and pre-school period. Current expenses will begin to increase gradually during this period. The outstanding expenses will be for medical attendance and hospital bills—the acquisition cost of the children—and extra expenditures for household service necessary while the children are small.

Then comes the elementary school period. Current expenses continue to increase gradually during this period but are still far from their peak. Food costs are increasing somewhat; clothing costs are increasing decidedly. While actual educational expenses are moderate, the children are beginning to bring pressure for higher standards at home in order that they may come up to the standards set by the other children in school who come from families with larger incomes.

For most families the high school period brings the largest demand upon the family income. Current expenses for food, clothing, books, and entertainment absorb a larger portion of the family income. In addition, social pressure on the family both at school and at home calls for improved standards at a time when it is most difficult to provide them.

If the standard of the family calls for a college education, the next period will entail even heavier expenditures. Some assistance from the children's earnings may be looked for here as a result of vacation employment with definite educational value. But even with some aid from this source, during this period comparatively few families are able to provide for current expenditures entirely from current income. Maintenance costs for the children are at their maximum. These expenses are increased if it is necessary for the boy or girl to live away from home. Frequently, educational expenses form the largest single item in the budget. In most cases the father and the mother are spending more on each one of their children during this period than they are spending on themselves.

Of necessity a period of recovery follows. As one by one the children finish high school or college and become self-supporting, current expenses drop rapidly; but there is a great deal to be done by way of recouping the family fortunes. The family's original supply of furniture is worn out. If it owns its home, the old house is usually too big and almost always out of repair. Savings are depleted, and old age is not so very many years ahead. In this period, for the second time in the life cycle of the family, accumulation for the future both in the form of investments and of equipment should take a large share of the family income.

Finally, there is a period of retirement. In this period current expenses are usually moderate and by necessity are scaled to what the individual fortune will permit. Travel and winters in Florida or California are desirable, but the longing for new thrills may have passed. Food needs and wear and tear on clothing are low. Usually a small, convenient apartment will provide more desirable housing than the large house which was necessary while the family was growing up. Adequate provision for personal service is the single item of expense which may run very high in elderly families.

AVERAGE NUMBER OF PERSONS IN HOUSEHOLDS, CLASSIFIED BY AGE OF WIFE
UNBROKEN WHITE FAMILIES, CHICAGO, 1920 [14]

Age of Wife	Average Number of Persons per Household
Under 25	3.1
25 and under 35	3.9
35 and under 45	4.6
45 and under 55	4.2
55 and under 65	3.5
65 and over	2.7
All ages	4.0

The number of years an individual family spends in each of these stages varies somewhat with the number of children and the interval between births. The table above shows the average size of a group of unbroken white families in Chicago in 1920, classified by the age of the wife. In this table the increase and decrease in the size of families is clearly in evidence.

The next table gives the number of children under sixteen years

[14] Day Monroe, *Chicago Families*, p. 38. University of Chicago Press, Chicago, 1932.

of age for this same group of families, also classified by the age of the
wife. This table shows the most usual child-bearing and child-rear-
ing period.

NUMBER OF DEPENDENT CHILDREN IN FAMILIES CLASSIFIED BY AGE OF WIFE
UNBROKEN WHITE FAMILIES, CHICAGO, 1920 [15]

AGE OF WIFE	FAMILIES HAVING SPECIFIED NUMBER OF CHILDREN UNDER 16 YEARS OF AGE					
	None	One	Two	Three	Four	Total
Under 25 years.................	43.0	35.9	15.8	4.4	0.9	100.0
25 and under 35 years...........	24.2	25.6	24.7	14.1	11.4	100.0
35 and under 45 years..........	30.8	18.7	18.3	12.9	19.3	100.0
45 and under 55 years..........	61.2	18.6	10.8	5.6	3.8	100.0
55 and under 65 years..........	92.3	5.9	1.4	0.3	0.1	100.0
65 years and over..............	99.6	0.4	....	....	....	100.0
All ages......................	41.2	21.6	17.3	9.9	10.0	100.0

Differences in family income and other resources. It is
impossible to get an adequate idea of the problems facing American
families without some consideration of the sources from which they
secure their income, and of the types of homes and the sort of home
equipment and other resources which are available for them in different types of communities.[16]

Some of the differences in the sources of family incomes are indicated by the following tables, showing the gainful employment of
family members. The first of these tables shows that almost one-
third of the families in the United States in 1930 had income from
the earnings of more than one member. The second shows the
extent to which homemakers, in addition to carrying their responsibility for the management of the home, are sharing in the earning
of its money income.[17] If in addition we take into account the rather
large number of families that have some income from invested savings, it seems safe to assume that a majority of the families in the
United States, while they may not be able to live upon the income
from their investments, still are not entirely dependent upon the
earnings of a single wage earner. And at the same time, it is equally
true that there are many families, especially the families with small

---

[15] *Ibid.*, p. 119. University of Chicago Press, Chicago, 1932.
[16] A detailed discussion of the amount and distribution of family incomes will be found in
Ch. III.
[17] For a detailed analysis of the gainful employment of members of a typical group of urban
families in 1920, see Day Monroe, *Chicago Families*, Chs. VII-VIII. University of Chicago Press,
Chicago, 1932.

children, that must depend almost entirely upon the earnings of one bread winner.

FAMILIES CLASSIFIED ACCORDING TO NUMBER OF GAINFULLY EMPLOYED WORKERS, UNITED STATES, 1930 [18]

Number of Gainful Workers	Number	Per Cent
All families..	29,904,663	100.0
Families having		
No gainful workers...................................	1,803,871	6.0
1 gainful worker......................................	18,568,705	62.1
2 gainful workers.....................................	6,321,816	21.1
3 gainful workers.....................................	2,140,386	7.2
4 or more..	1,069,885	3.6

FAMILIES CLASSIFIED ACCORDING TO THE EMPLOYMENT STATUS OF THE HOMEMAKER, UNITED STATES, 1930 [19]

Employment Status of Homemaker	Number	Per Cent
Families having homemaker..............................	28,405,294	100.0
Not gainfully employed................................	24,481,778	86.2
Gainfully employed....................................	3,923,516	13.8
Gainfully employed homemakers..........................	3,923,516	100.0
Employed at home.....................................	761,435	19.4
Agricultural occupations.............................	396,102	10.1
Other occupations at home............................	365,333	9.3
Employed away from home..............................	3,153,758	80.4
Professional workers.................................	387,618	9.9
Office workers.......................................	500,968	12.8
Industrial workers...................................	737,044	18.8
Servants, waitresses, etc.............................	957,963	24.4
Saleswomen...	271,857	6.9
Other occupations away from home.....................	298,308	7.6
Employed, place not specified..........................	8,323	0.2

Home ownership in the United States.

One of the most common ways by which families attempt to reduce the constantly continuing demands upon their money income is the purchase of a home. When the home is fully paid for, they are relieved of the necessity of regular payments for rent. In recent years we have been hearing a great deal about the advantages a family can secure by owning its home. Much concern has been expressed because of the apparent decline in home ownership.

A careful analysis of the census reports on home ownership shows that the decline in home ownership since 1890 has been a decline in the ownership of farm homes. In 1890, almost two-thirds of the farm families owned their own homes. In 1930, ownership of

[18] Fifteenth Census of the United States (1930). *Population*. Vol. VI, "Families," Table 7, p. 8.
[19] *Ibid.*, Table 10, p. 9.

farm homes had declined to 52.5 per cent. This decline is not an indication of the increasing difficulty farm families have had in securing a place in which to live. For farm families, owning a home is

TENURE OF HOMES OF THE UNITED STATES, 1890-1930 [20]

CENSUS YEAR	TOTAL NUMBER OF HOMES	OWNED		RENTED		TENURE UNKNOWN	
		Number	Per Cent	Number	Per Cent	Number	Per Cent
All homes							
1930.........	29,904,663	14,002,074	46.8	15,319,817	51.2	582,772	1.9
1920.........	24,351,676	10,866,960	44.6	12,943,598	53.2	541,118	2.2
1910.........	20,255,555	9,083,711	44.8	10,697,895	52.8	473,949	2.3
1900.........	15,963,965	7,205,212	45.1	8,223,775	51.5	534,978	3.4
1890.........	12,690,152	6,066,417	47.8	6,623,735	52.2	......	...
Farm homes							
1930.........	6,668,681	3,498,688	52.5	2,968,268	44.5	201,725	3.0
1920.........	6,751,204	3,825,677	56.7	2,755,487	40.8	170,040	2.5
1910.........	6,123,610	3,838,331	62.7	2,271,231	37.1	14,048	0.2
1900.........	5,689,838	3,638,403	63.9	2,010,605	35.3	40,830	0.7
1890.........	4,767,179	3,142,746	65.9	1,624,433	34.1	......	...
Non-farm homes							
1930.........	23,235,982	10,503,386	45.2	12,351,549	53.2	381,047	1.6
1920.........	17,600,472	7,041,283	40.0	10,188,111	57.9	371,078	2.1
1910.........	14,131,945	5,245,380	37.1	8,426,664	59.6	459,901	3.3
1900.........	10,274,127	3,566,809	34.7	6,213,170	60.5	494,148	4.8
1890.........	7,922,973	2,923,671	36.9	4,999,302	63.1	......	...

incidental to owning a farm. The decline in farm home ownership is a reflection of the increasing difficulty families have had in securing the capital necessary to go into farming.

Since 1900, the percentage of owned non-farm homes has been steadily increasing. In 1900, only a little over one-third of the

MEDIAN VALUE OR RENTAL OF NON-FARM HOMES, BY COLOR AND NATIVITY OF HEAD FOR THE UNITED STATES, 1930 [21]

Color and Nativity of Head	Median Value of Owned Non-farm Homes	Median Monthly Rental of Rented Non-farm Homes
All classes.....................	$4,778	$27.15
Native white.................	4,766	27.92
Foreign-born white...........	5,576	33.00
Negro.......................	1,341	13.04
Other races..................	Less than $1,000	12.28

non-farm homes were owned, and almost two-thirds were rented. In 1930, however, ownership of non-farm homes had increased to more than 45 per cent. In the decade from 1920 to 1930, the

[20] *Ibid.*, Table 16, p. 11.
[21] *Ibid.*, Table 26, p. 18.

increase in ownership of non-farm homes more than offset the decline in farm home ownership. In 1930, then, a little more than half the farm families, and only a little less than half the non-farm families, owned their homes.

Another tendency which has seriously concerned some students of family life has been the increase in construction of multiple-family dwellings. In spite of the large number of apartments built in our larger cities in the last twenty years, the 1930 census showed that more than three-fourths of the families in the United States live in single houses. It is well to keep in mind, however, the difference in the situation of families living in single houses and those living in multiple-family dwellings. Families living in single houses usually have more privacy, more light, more air, and more yard space than do families living in apartments. On the other hand, the single payment for rent for an apartment frequently includes water, heat, light, gas for cooking, often furniture, and sometimes even telephone and maid service, all of which the family living in the unfurnished single house usually must provide for itself.

DWELLINGS AND FAMILIES, BY CLASS OF DWELLING, UNITED STATES, 1930 [22]

AREA AND CLASS	DWELLINGS		FAMILIES	
	Number	Per Cent	Number	Per Cent
Total............................	25,204,976	100.0	29,904,663	100.0
1-family dwellings.............	22,833,110	90.6	22,833,110	76.4
2-family dwellings.............	1,728,087	6.9	3,456,174	11.6
3-or-more-family dwellings.....	643,779	2.6	3,615,379	12.1
Urban.........................	13,046,699	100.0	17,372,524	100.0
1-family dwellings.............	11,001,861	84.3	11,001,861	63.3
2-family dwellings.............	1,430,570	11.0	2,861,140	16.5
3-or-more-family dwellings.....	614,268	4.7	3,509,523	20.2
Rural.........................	12,158,277	100.0	12,532,139	100.0
1-family dwellings.............	11,831,249	97.3	11,821,249	94.4
2-family dwellings.............	297,517	2.4	595,034	4.7
3-or-more-family dwellings.....	29,511	0.2	105,856	0.8

Public utilities and home equipment. No picture of present-day American families would be complete without some consideration of the public utilities and home equipment at their disposal. Facilities vary greatly from community to community. The following table shows the extent to which a number of typical facilities were used in communities of various sizes in the middle 1920's.

[22] *Ibid.*, Table 13, p. 10.

FACILITIES AVAILABLE TO FAMILIES IN COMMUNITIES OF VARIOUS SIZES [23]

SIZE OF COMMUNITY	PERCENTAGE OF FAMILIES HAVING							
	Public Garbage Collection	Water Piped into House	Gas	Stationary Bathtub	Stationary Kitchen Sink	Flush Toilet	Electric Lights	Electric Irons
Under 1,000 inhabitants..	10.1	52.7	3.6	26.1	42.7	26.3	72.1	49.2
1,000-2,500 inhabitants..	17.3	87.3	11.9	40.6	57.1	44.2	77.3	55.0
2,500-5,000 inhabitants..	39.9	97.2	34.4	51.0	66.6	61.0	77.3	57.0
5,000-10,000 inhabitants.	48.9	100.0	74.0	61.0	72.3	72.3	79.3	58.9
10,000-25,000 inhabitants.	56.3	100.0	95.6	66.9	79.1	78.1	78.6	61.2
25,000-50,000 inhabitants.	88.4	100.0	98.8	70.5	81.5	80.8	78.4	60.2
50,000-100,000 inhabitants	88.1	100.0	100.0	74.5	79.9	85.7	77.0	54.7
Over 100,000 inhabitants.	95.3	100.0	100.0	75.5	93.7	90.3	81.5	67.8

Existing statistics are far from adequate. Any study made in the middle twenties probably underestimates the extent to which the more recently introduced of these facilities are now in use.

It is hard to realize how long it takes for the general adoption of any piece of equipment, and how many families are still getting along without the more common devices at a time when manufacturers are sure the market saturation point has been reached. The 1930 census shows (see the following table) that even the radio, which has been introduced more rapidly than almost any other single device, was in use in only 40 per cent of the homes in the country in 1930.

FAMILIES HAVING RADIO SETS, 1930 [24]

AREA	TOTAL NUMBER OF FAMILIES	FAMILIES HAVING RADIO SETS	
		Number	Per Cent
All families......................	29,904,663	12,048,762	40.3
Urban families..................	17,372,524	8,682,176	50.0
Urban farm families..............	64,044	28,422	44.4
Rural farm families..............	6,604,637	1,371,073	20.8
Rural non-farm families..........	5,927,502	1,995,513	33.7
All farm families................	6,668,681	1,399,495	21.0

The table on page 23 shows the rate at which three common facilities, bathtubs, telephones, and electricity, have come into use. The number per 1,000 non-farm population indicates the proportion of non-farm families for which these facilities are available. Even if we assume that urban families have an average of 4 members,

---

[23] Unpublished Survey by General Federation of Women's Clubs, quoted in Hazel Kyrk, *Economic Problems of the Family*, Table II, p. 5. Harper and Bros., New York, 1933.
[24] Fifteenth Census of the United States (1930), *Population*, Vol. VI, "Families," Table 12, p. 10.

then 200 bathtubs and 200 wired homes per 1,000 non-farm population means a bathtub and electric lights for only 80 per cent of the families in the non-farm group. Ninety-two telephones per 1,000 non-farm families means that there were telephones in use in less than 40 per cent of the non-farm homes in the country in 1928.

NUMBER OF SANITARY BATHTUBS, TELEPHONES, AND WIRED HOMES COMPARED WITH TOTAL NON-FARM POPULATION, 1913-1928 [25]

YEAR (JAN. 1)	ESTI-MATED NON-FARM POPULA-TION	HOMES EQUIPPED WITH STATIONARY BATHTUBS		RESIDENCE TELEPHONES BELL SYSTEM		WIRED HOMES (DOMESTIC ELECTRIC LIGHT AND POWER CUSTOMERS)	
		Total Number	Number per Thousand Non-farm Population	Total Number	Number per Thousand Non-farm Population	Total Number	Number per Thousand Non-farm Population
	Thousands	*Thousands*		*Thousands*		*Thousands*	
1913	64,545	7,066	109.5	2,800	43.4	3,101	48.0
1914	66,534	7,520	113.0	3,050	45.8	......	......
1915	68,021	8,004	117.7	3,275	48.1	......	......
1916	69,376	8,540	123.1	3,500	50.4	......	......
1917	70,941	9,123	128.6	3,864	54.5	5,260	74.1
1918	72,223	9,501	131.6	4,148	57.4	5,800	80.3
1919	72,905	9,722	133.4	4,228	58.0	6,900	94.6
1920	74,097	10,116	136.5	4,545	61.3	8,010	108.1
1921	75,832	10,702	141.1	4,903	64.7	8,700	114.7
1922	77,615	11,175	144.0	5,260	67.8	9,430	121.5
1923	79,238	12,028	151.8	5,653	71.3	10,211	128.9
1924	81,316	13,059	160.6	6,230	76.6	11,819	145.3
1925	83,055	14,150	170.4	6,798	81.8	13,567	163.3
1926	84,704	15,410	181.9	7,306	86.3	14,965	176.7
1927	86,297	16,545	191.7	7,875	91.3	16,359	189.6
1928	87,910	17,591	200.1	8,333	94.8	17,596	200.2

According to this table, even stationary bathtubs and electric lights, which are perhaps as common as any single type of facility, have come into general use only since the beginning of the World War. In 1913 and 1914, there were bathtubs in less than half of the non-farm homes, while not over 20 per cent of these same homes were equipped with electric lights. It is hard for us to realize that forty years were required for the general adoption of the stationary bathtub even in cities with running water. It seems almost unbelievable that more than twenty years after Edison built his first successful electric light plant, only one home in five was wired for electric lights, and that fifteen years more were required to make electricity available for even 80 per cent of the non-farm families. For farm

[25] Leo Wolman, "Consumption and the Standard of Living," *Recent Economic Changes in the United States*, Ch. I, Table 28, p. 67. McGraw-Hill Book Co., Inc., New York, 1929.

families electric lights are becoming available in the more densely populated rural areas. But in 1928, farm families, which constituted more than a third of the population of the United States, numbered only 2 per cent of the domestic users of electricity.

If we are to have an accurate picture of modern American families, it is essential that we have a definite idea of the variety of equipment and utilities that are available, and the extent to which each of these has come into use. It is equally essential that we realize clearly that satisfactory living is possible with a minimum number of comparatively inexpensive devices. This does not mean that we should minimize the desirability of all the conveniences invention has made available for the modern American family. Rather we should see these devices as something worth while, not in themselves, but only to the extent that they make for comfortable and convenient living, free the members of the family from daily routine, and facilitate the attainment of fundamental human values.

The personal nature of spending problems. It is highly important at the beginning of our study of family finance that we become familiar with the great variety existing in the make-up and resources of the modern American family. Because of the variety in the conditions under which families live, differences in environment, in income, in available equipment, in other social and personal resources, and because of the wide differences in the make-up of the families themselves in size, in membership, in the stage of the family in the family life cycle, it is clear that there is no single, simple solution for the problem of good living.

Providing ourselves with better living is a peculiarly personal problem. It is a problem in the solution of which there may be many right answers. In so far as it is possible to summarize the problem, however, its common elements reduce to this: The problem facing the modern American family is to adapt itself to changing conditions both within and without the home in whatever manner will make available through the years the richest possible life for all its members. For any given family the answer to its problem is the right answer if with the means at its disposal, by careful management, it provides the largest possible amount of satisfaction for all its members. The family must always remember that quality of satisfaction is just as important as the quantity of satisfaction enjoyed. It must keep material things in their proper place as tools to be used in developing to their utmost fundamental human values.

QUESTIONS

1. Make a list of changes in the world outside the home which would make it necessary for your family to change its ways of living or of spending its income. Describe a number of ways in which families of your acquaintance have adapted themselves to similar changes.

2. Read a detailed description of the way families lived in Colonial times. Compare the way in which they provided for the various wants of their members with the way in which these same wants are cared for today: (a) in the farm family; (b) in the small city family; and (c) in the family living in a great metropolitan center.

3. Is your family a democratic family, or does some one person or small group of persons dominate family affairs?

4. In a family in which there are children, how old should the children be before they are given a chance to have a voice in decisions affecting the whole family? About what matters do father and mother know best? What decisions are the younger and less experienced members of the family qualified to make? Just how should the authority be distributed in a modern American family?

5. Work out a family tree showing the size of the families in your immediate line for three or four generations. How do the changes in the size of your family compare with the changes in the average size of the family in the United States during the same period? How do you account for the difference in the size of these families in each generation?

6. List the advantages and disadvantages of living in large families and of living in small families. What is the best size for a family in your community? What are the problems that are faced by families you consider to be too large? What are the problems that are faced by families that are too small? How large is too large? How small is too small? Why?

7. If you were to plan in advance upon the size and make-up of your family, taking into account all the advantages and disadvantages of both large and small families, how large would your own family be? What factors other than economic factors must be taken into account in making such a decision?

8. How would you describe the position of each of the following families in the family life cycle? To what extent would a knowledge of the family life cycle theory help the heads of each of these families in working out their peculiar problems of family management and finance?

   (a) Husband, a carpenter, age 45; wife, age 43; boy, age 15; and girl, age 12.

(b) Husband, a lawyer, age 60; wife, age 55. They have brought up two children who are now married and established with homes of their own.

(c) Husband, a bookkeeper, age 25; wife, age 23, is employed as a stenographer.

(d) Husband, a bank teller, age 25; wife, age 23; and boy, age 2.

(e) Husband, a salesman, age 40; wife, age 35; boy, age 15; and girl, age 3.

(f) Husband, a doctor, age 48; wife, age 40; boy, age 10; girl, age 8; and boy, age 3. Father's father, a retired farmer, age 73, and father's mother, age 70, also live in this home.

(g) A widowed mother, age 40; son, age 14, and daughter, age 10, entirely dependent upon her for support.

(h) Living on a New England farm just before the Civil War. Husband, age 50, is married to his third wife. The oldest boy, age 25, son of his first wife, is married and established in a home of his own. The second son, also by the first wife, is now 22, living at home but engaged to be married within a year. Then there are a boy, age 16, and two girls, ages 14 and 11, children of the second wife; and three girls, ages 9, 7, and 1, children of the third wife. The paternal grandmother, now in her 70's, completes the family group.

9. A young couple is just setting up housekeeping. They plan to have two children. They hope sometime to own their own home. They wish to give their children a high school education, and if possible to give one of them a college education. They wish to accumulate enough to be independent in their old age, and to be able to leave to their children an estate of at least $5,000 in addition to their home. Indicate what they should try to accomplish during each of the stages of the life cycle. When should they plan to buy their home? When should they accumulate money for the college education? When should they make provision for their old age? When should they plan to set aside the savings necessary to the accumulation of their estate?

10. How many families of your acquaintance live entirely upon income from investments? How many are entirely dependent upon the earnings of the husband? In how many families does the wife work regularly for money outside the home? Occasionally? Part time? How many families dependent for most of their income upon their earnings supplement their earnings with income from investments? With income from other sources?

11. Make a list of the types of home equipment you would consider typical for families of your acquaintance. Compare with other members of your class. Do the families represented by your group have more or less

in the way of home equipment than the tables in the chapter would lead you to expect?

12. List the ways in which your family seems to be a typical American family, and the ways in which its problems differ clearly from the average. To what extent can individual differences be explained by the position of your family in the family life cycle? To what extent are these due to purely personal factors?

REFERENCES

Binkley, R. C. and F. W., *What Is Right with Marriage?* D. Appleton-Century Co., New York, 1929.

An excellent discussion of the functions and organization of the family from the personal viewpoint. The authors call their book "an outline of domestic theory."

Fifteenth Census of the United States (1930). (1) *Population*, Vol. VI, "Families," or (2) Population Bulletin, *Families*, U. S. Summary.

The 1930 census made the first comprehensive study of families in the United States since 1900. The summary contains most of the general data. The larger volume has much of the detail from which the summaries were derived.

Groves, E. R., *The American Family.* J. B. Lippincott Co., Chicago, 1934.

Groves, E. R., and Brooks, L. M., *Readings in the Family.* J. B. Lippincott Co., Chicago, 1934.

This book and *The American Family* provide the basis for an understanding of all the varied problems of family life, which is fundamental to successful family management and finance.

Kyrk, Hazel, *Economic Problems of the Family*, Chs. I and II. Harper and Bros., New York, 1933.

These two chapters present the facts about the modern American family, its present set-up and historical background, which are significant if the reader is to have a clear understanding of the economic problems of the family.

Sait, U. B., *New Horizons for the Family.* The Macmillan Co., New York, 1938.

A well-rounded, comprehensive, philosophical presentation of present-day living, showing clearly the importance of the economic problems of the family, and their relationship to the whole of family living.

Recent Social Trends in the United States, Ch. XIII, "The Family and Its Functions." McGraw-Hill Book Co., Inc., New York, 1933.

A thorough discussion of the effect of recent social changes upon the American family.

CHAPTER II

THE FAMILY'S WANTS

We take our wants for granted. Because our wants are always with us, we are inclined to take them for granted. But if we are to work out for ourselves the richest sort of a life possible with the means at our disposal, we must spend some time analyzing wants themselves in order that we may determine what sort of satisfactions are absolutely essential to the maintenance of life and health, and what sort of satisfactions add most to the richness of living.

We have in common a number of fundamental wants. It is fairly easy to list our wants in general terms. All of us want food and clothing and shelter. These we consider to be the very fundamentals of existence. All of us want some means of transportation, and facilities for communication with our fellows. We want recreation and whatever is necessary to maintain good health. And in addition to these tangible wants we want certain intangibles. We want security in the present and in the future. We want freedom from arbitrary domination by others, which only security can bring. We want companionship and affection. We want social position and the respect of others which it implies; and we want to maintain our own self-respect.

We satisfy these wants in many ways. Individuals and families usually think of these general groups of wants in terms of wants for a long list of specific goods and services, items which experience has proved to be, if not the best available, at least reasonably workable means of satisfying their fundamental underlying wants. Instead of wanting food in general, people want the specific foods that suit their palates. Instead of wanting transportation, they want an automobile. Instead of wanting some means of communication, they want frequent mail deliveries and a telephone and a radio. Even their want for security turns out to be a want for a bank account, some life insurance, and a few reasonably safe investments. And their want for social position, and the recognition and respect of others that it implies, in many cases becomes a want for a house on a certain street, a want for evening clothes, a want for an up-to-the-minute car, or a want for membership in a certain country club. It is the confusing and often apparently meaningless variety of these specific wants that makes an analysis of our wants seem such a hopeless task.

In our discussion of wants we must use words that in common parlance have a variety of meanings. In order that there may be no misunderstanding in our discussion in this chapter, we are going to use the following words with the following shades of meaning:

Interests are those objects and activities that stimulate pleasant feelings in the individual. The opposite of *interests* is *aversions*. Between interests and aversions there is a whole group of objects and activities which stimulate neither pleasant nor unpleasant feelings. For want of a better term we will call these *indifferences*.

Traits are tendencies to react in certain ways to certain stimuli. It is in these reactions of the individual that his peculiar quality of mind or character is ordinarily displayed.

A *desire* concerns an object worth having, which is near at hand, and is viewed as being attainable. A *wish*, on the other hand, concerns something remote, something viewed as difficult to attain or impossible of attainment. Desires grow out of our interests. An object is worth having because we are interested in it, because it stimulates pleasant feelings.

Taste is the ability to discern and appreciate what is beautiful and appropriate. A person is said to have developed a taste for something if he regards the object as worth having, and if he has had some first-hand experience of satisfaction from the use of the object in the past. A person develops a taste for a certain kind of food only after he has enjoyed eating it a number of times. He develops a taste for good literature only if he has read enough books to come to appreciate what is beautiful and appropriate in the books he is reading—only if the experience has been so pleasant that he desires to repeat it.

A *want* is the present lack of some satisfaction. A want is primarily an emotional attitude. Intellectual calculations are involved only in considering how to satisfy a want. A want is ordinarily considered to be stronger than a desire. It has been defined as desire plus the impulse to act.

Effective wants are those wants we decide to satisfy. Everyone leaves some of his wants unsatisfied. The impulse to act leads to action only in a few of the many possible situations in which a lack is felt. We may use the term "effective wants" for those wants in which the impulse to act is followed by action.

Individual demand is the willingness and ability of the individual to purchase what he wants for a price in the market. Only that part of his wants which he decides to satisfy by purchase in the market results in demand.

The *demand in the market* consists of the sum of these individual demands. A producer is primarily interested in consumers who are willing and able to pay as much as or more than the current market price. They form the *effective demand* for his commodity. But in fixing the price he will charge, he must also take into account the *potential demand*, which includes the individual demands of those consumers who are willing and able to pay a price, but a price lower than the price at which the article is selling currently in the market.

It is important also to distinguish clearly between wants and needs. A *need* is a lack of something, to be without which in the present will cause a felt lack at some time in the future. We want a new car, but we need to put some coal in the cellar so as to avoid a felt lack for heat later on in the winter. We are conscious of our wants. We may or may not be conscious of our needs. In some cases our wants and our needs are identical. In other cases there are things we need that we do not want. And there are many things we want that we do not need.

A family's specific wants are determined by various factors.

The analysis of our wants is further complicated by the fact that no two families agree upon the relative importance of these groups of underlying wants. No two families resolve their fundamental wants into exactly the same list of commodities and services. And no two families should.

The way in which any family resolves its underlying wants into wants for specific commodities and services depends upon a number of factors. The interests and background of the individual members of the family are involved. The family must consider its geographical environment, having regard for the climate, the topography, and the natural resources of the region in which it lives. The specific commodities that are available for the satisfaction of these more general wants, and the means by which a family can acquire them, depend in large degree upon the present stage of economic and technological development in the community in which the family lives. And, in addition, the specific wants which a family develops depend upon its social environment. Wants are determined to a very large degree by the standards of living of the groups among whom the members of the family are thrown.

Families must adapt themselves to their present environment.

Most families find themselves in a predetermined physical environment with a given set of climatic, topographic, and natural resources to which they must adapt. Most families must provide for their wants as best they may with the facilities available at the present stage of economic and technological development. Their immediate problem, therefore, is largely one of adapting themselves to their present environment. For this reason we will confine most of our analysis to the personal and social factors which are to a greater or less degree within the control of the family, the factors which they can change or adjust in the process of securing the most satisfying living from their physical environment.

The effect of individual interests upon wants. We are surrounded by stimuli of all kinds. Our senses are being hammered continually by a countless number of stimuli giving rise to sights, sounds, smells, flavors, and feelings. We cannot possibly pay attention to all of them. We are inclined to concentrate upon the pleasurable experiences and to force any unpleasant sensations into the background. And there are very many stimuli to which we are completely indifferent. They never register at all. In everyday life, then, we perceive that in which we are interested.

The psychologist explains the acquisition of individual interests in part in terms of the tendencies of nerve ends to establish connections which carry impulses from without to the cerebral connections in the brain. Every time we react to a certain stimulus, every time contact of the nerve ends is established, it becomes easier to re-establish the contact. As a result, we come to react more readily to familiar stimuli. We are inclined to seek satisfaction in accustomed ways.

Further, we can train ourselves to react to certain stimuli and to tune out others. A mother may pay no attention to the roar of traffic outside the house, but may hear the faintest cry of her child. An experienced motorist becomes oblivious to the hum of his motor, but hears the faintest click of a loosened tappet. We can, then, consciously direct our attention, tuning in or out, concentrating on what we want to see, hear, feel, touch, or smell.

But for the most part we follow our usual interests in accustomed ways. By repeated reactions to familiar stimuli, we develop certain traits or tendencies to action which become the peculiar characteristics of our own personalities. Some of these traits seem to be present at birth, while others appear very soon after. A young person finds it entirely possible to develop certain desirable traits and to eliminate to a very large degree other undesirable traits from his personality. The older he grows, the more firmly fixed do his traits become.

Out of this background of interests and traits there develops in each individual a set of desires for objects that his interests tell him are worth having, and that his past experience tells him are possible of attainment. But just as his interests shade off into indifferences, so some of his desires seem hardly worth bothering about. Other desires are strong enough to impel him to do something about them. It is these desires accompanied by this urge to action that develop into wants.

The effect of individual differences upon wants. Individuals vary widely in both the range and the intensity of their interests. Some persons have a deep and abiding interest in a few fundamental activities; others have a superficial interest in a wide variety of objects. Some individuals, because of their physical make-up, feel both pleasantness and unpleasantness keenly. They develop intense interests and strong aversions. There are other individuals who are for the most part indifferent to what is going on around them. There is much in their environment of which they are completely unaware.

Although there is inevitably this wide range in the sensitivity of individuals, it is entirely possible for any individual consciously to broaden the range of his interest and to deepen his appreciation of the significance of the stimuli he receives. Securing satisfaction is only in part a problem of achieving desirable and pleasurable experiences; it is just as much a problem of knowing how to get the most from experiences when they are received. To secure the maximum of satisfaction from a pleasurable experience, it is necessary to concentrate upon it, to consider consciously the significance of its various phases, and to analyze and relate it to past experience.

An individual, then, can improve the quality of his living by consciously broadening the range of his interests, by consciously seeking broadening experiences, in order that he may have a wide background from which to select the wants he is to satisfy. He can further improve the quality of his living by deliberately developing his capacity for the appreciation of what is intrinsically beautiful and appropriate. And then, as a result of the development of taste which this deepening appreciation implies, he can still further improve the quality of his living by selecting for satisfaction a harmonious and well-integrated group of wants which represent his fundamental interests, and which satisfy the peculiar traits in his personality.

The effect of physical environment upon wants. Interests are not entirely subjective in their origin. Many of the stimuli from which they spring come from without. Even though there are general and fundamental tendencies within each individual, the specific ways in which interests develop, and the specific wants into which they are resolved, depend to a large degree upon his physical and economic and social environment. The problem of adaptation to environment is largely a problem of selecting the ways and means for satisfying fundamental and underlying wants which are most easily to be secured in the existing environment. The specific wants which emerge are the result of the interaction of the individual and his environment.

Families everywhere want food, but the specific kinds of food which they want are determined very largely by what is available in the communities in which they live. All families want shelter. In a northern climate shelter involves primarily protection against the winter's cold. In a southern climate the family wants protection from the heat of the midday sun and from the heavy tropical shower. In the northern climate fuel assumes considerable importance, while refrigeration is a want which is satisfied only if there is means available. In the southern climate, where there are only a few cool days each year, refrigeration is a necessity, but only people of means allow themselves the luxury of central heating.

The effect of economic and technological development upon wants. Similarly, the specific commodities and services which we want depend to a large extent upon economic and technological development. Not so many years ago the want for light in the evening was a want for tallow candles and whale oil lamps. Then kerosene replaced the whale oil in the lamps, and in the cities gas was piped into the homes to provide light. In the 1890's Edison invented the electric light and the central power station. Today, in the city, the want for light is synonymous with the want for electric lights. In many of the rural districts, however, electricity is not even yet available. Here the want for light is still largely a want for kerosene lamps, although highly efficient incandescent mantle lamps are gradually replacing the less expensive but relatively inefficient wick lamps.

One of the most interesting problems in family management is the problem of keeping up-to-date in the ways and means we use to satisfy our fundamental wants. Some of the most difficult problems in financing the family arise when we must decide how long to continue to use a method or a means of satisfying our wants which industrial progress has rendered obsolete, or how soon to make the additional expenditure necessary to bring the family into line with the latest technological advances.

The effect of social environment upon wants. For most of us, our social environment is fully as effective in determining the specific ways in which our wants develop as is either our physical environment or the stage of economic and technological development. It is from others that we learn of the variety of ways to satisfy our wants. It is natural that we should imitate [1] those about us who seem to be doing a good job of satisfying their wants in our common environment.

The effect of custom and convention upon wants. Many of our specific wants grow out of the customs and conventions of the social groups among which we are thrown. There is an old saying, "When in Rome, do as the Romans do." It is usually wise to work out our fundamental interests in accordance with the customs and conventions of the groups in which we move. Custom ordinarily embodies the successes of the past. Convention includes the ways of doing which work best in the existing situation. The members of a social group form the habit of doing certain things in certain ways because experience has shown that, for this particular group at least, doing these things in these ways will lead to certain fundamental satisfactions which, it is assumed, all the members of the group desire to attain.

It is worth while, then, for the individual or the family to observe the customs and conventions of the social groups in which they move. Custom and convention facilitate social intercourse. Their observation makes it easy for an individual or a family to gain social recognition. And what is even more important in daily living, the observation of custom and convention reduces much of the detailed routine of daily living to a habitual basis, leaving the individual or the family

---

[1] *Imitation* is the transmission of acts or ideas from person to person either consciously or unconsciously through the mechanism of the mind. *Tradition* is an attitude of mind or a way of thinking which has come down from past generations. *Custom* is a socially accepted way of doing which has come down to us from past generations. *Convention* is a socially accepted way of doing which has originated in the present.

free to devote more time and energy to current problems involving conscious decisions, and to the satisfaction of wants in which purely personal preferences are involved.

Of course there can be too great adherence to custom and convention. Like any habitual activity, custom and convention may delay progress by perpetuating useless and inefficient ways of living. Custom and convention may come to contain some empty values. There is the same danger in the habitual observance of custom and convention as with any form of habitual action. The habit often continues after the need for the habit has passed. There are still buttons upon the sleeves of a man's coat though it has long ceased to be necessary to have the sleeves open to the elbow to allow him to roll them up when he must engage in manual toil or defend himself with his sword.

Slavish observance of custom and convention sets unnecessarily narrow limits upon the freedom of individuals to do as they please. And yet conventional hours for employment, for the opening of the theater, and for the holding of church services have developed, not because there is any desire to create an artificial or inconvenient amount of uniformity in the activities of the individual, but because on the whole they represent the most convenient hours for the majority of people in the group.

If the members of a family are to get the maximum benefit from the observance of custom and convention, and are, at the same time, to avoid empty values, they must try to understand clearly the reasons why a particular custom or convention has developed. They must analyze the values which it is supposed to contain. They must consider whether or not the original need still holds. It is wise for a family to follow custom and convention to the extent which seems at present advantageous, and to break away from the customs and conventions of a group when there is no longer any good reason for them. It is important in this connection to distinguish between the essential points in a custom without which easy social intercourse would be impossible, and the non-essentials which a family can violate with impunity. It is also particularly essential for the impetuous, freedom-loving individual who is frequently irked by seemingly unnecessary minor restrictions to decide what in his case are the essentials that are involved in satisfying his fundamental wants. He should break away from custom and convention when they definitely hamper the following out of his fundamental interests. On the other hand, he can well observe the non-essentials which, while meaningless to him, are simply not important enough to make a fuss about.

The effect of social classes upon wants. In our discussion of custom and convention, we have taken it for granted that each individual and each family is a member of one or more rather definite social groups. In this country we prefer the term "social groups" to the European "social classes," and yet in the interests of straight thinking we may as well recognize that even in a democracy these social groups arrange themselves into a rather definitely determined hierarchy of social classes. It is inherent in our nature that individuals do derive some very real satisfaction from social recognition, and social recognition implies membership in a group which in some way or other is considered to be superior to those about it.

Social classes in this country differ in a number of important respects from those in the older European countries. Here membership in a social class is not hereditary, and yet family membership helps to determine our social position. Membership in a social group is not always determined by wealth or income, although people with plenty of money find it easier to move into the so-called higher social circles. In this country, an individual may move either up or down the social scale from the group into which he was born. It is entirely possible to progress from one group to another by earning more money, by receiving promotion to better employment, by adding to one's education, even by such a simple device as moving to a better neighborhood. There are no hard-and-fast lines drawn between the social groups. The same individual may be a member of one occupational group, of a second neighborhood group, of a third religious group, of a fourth recreational group, and of a fifth educational group. Special talent in music or dramatics makes it possible for a worker, an employer, and a professional man to associate on common terms in a church choir, in a community orchestra, or in a Little Theater. Athletic ability makes a man with little money and no family background a welcome member of an athletic club. A high degree of artistic appreciation, a taste for good literature, a background of wide reading, and the inherent sensibilities of a gentleman make a man welcome among cultured people regardless of his birth, his income, or his employment. Every family must work out for itself a combination of social contacts which will satisfy the fundamental interests of its members, and at the same time will offer the fewest complications because of differences in wealth and income and family background.

The effect of emulation upon wants. In the United States few families settle at once into an accustomed niche in a familiar social situation. Almost every family at some time feels the urge to move to a higher social level, or to secure such a position of leadership in its present social group that its children may easily move up in the social scale.

Without question most of our wants spring from this desire to imitate the leaders in our present group or the members of some group we consider above us. We feel that by living like our leaders we may in time attain for ourselves a position of leadership. We feel that if we observe in our living the more obvious social characteristics of the higher social group we may in time secure recognition either as members of that group, or as their social equals. This type of imitation is known as emulation.

Emulation is a powerful social force which must be taken into consideration in any analysis of a family's wants. Each family must decide for itself how far and in what ways it will allow itself to be influenced by this natural tendency to emulation.

Pecuniary emulation. There are three generally recognized types of emulation. The first is pecuniary emulation. This involves spending as much or, if possible, a little more money than do our neighbors. In pecuniary emulation we imitate those whom we consider above us because they have more generous money incomes. Pecuniary emulation has caught the imagination of the rank and file of the American people for several reasons. In the first place, a person of generous means obviously is living well in his existing environment. He is the man who has been able to make a success out of life. To live as he does is an indication that we are equally successful. Again, we are inclined to assume that because an article is expensive it must necessarily be of high quality. If we would get the best, we must pay the most. Then, too, pecuniary emulation is perhaps the easiest type of emulation for the ordinary individual to follow. By this standard, equaling or excelling others is simply a matter of arithmetic; anyone who can read price tags is able to measure the extent of his success.

Emulation in novelty. Many people, however, do not have the money income necessary for purely pecuniary emulation, and yet they, too, are anxious to equal and, if possible, in some way excel those around them. They are attracted by the possibility of emulation in novelty. By giving thought to the current fashion, by studying style changes, by changing their habits a little more promptly than do those around them, it is possible for them to obtain a position of leadership in up-to-dateness.

To maintain a position of leadership where novelty is involved, it is necessary for the leaders themselves to be constantly pushing forward lest they lose their position of leadership to some of their more aggressive followers. Emulation in novelty places emphasis upon temporary satisfactions. The continued enjoyment of any position secured by emulation in novelty requires constant effort, and involves much expense. However, a moderate degree of emulation in fashion does bring the increased satisfaction which a reasonable amount of variety affords.

Emulation in taste. Many people become wearied of the constant effort emulation in fashion requires. They soon tire of the meaningless vagaries of changing styles. They see about them people of obvious culture, people with inherently good taste, who seem to be getting a larger amount of satisfaction out of living with considerably less expense and effort. There is a growing tendency, then, for people who are weary of the constant struggle which emulation in fashion requires, as well as for people who have tired of the empty values involved in much purely pecuniary emulation, to try instead to excel in the exercise of good taste. They set out definitely to acquire credit for an appreciation of what cultured people with a keen discrimination believe to be beautiful and appropriate. And, in so doing, they sometimes really do acquire good taste or good judgment in the process, since continued contacts with and attempts to develop an appreciation of the beautiful and a feeling for the suitable do stimulate and deepen the capacity for enjoyment of the permanent and enduring satisfactions of life.

Emulation in taste is, however, the most difficult of the three types of emulation to attain. For this reason it is the type of emulation which leads to a position most secure from social competition. And at the same time, it is the type of emulation which adds most to the quality of our living.

The effect of standards of living upon wants. In a familiar environment we take a great deal for granted. We are used to thinking in terms of the limitations of our physical environment and of the facilities provided by present economic and technological development. We are so accustomed to the ways of living of our own group that we hardly realize that we are imitating those about us, or that we are observing custom and convention. It is only when we attempt to gain admittance to a group above us or when we are forced to accept a position in a group below us that we become conscious of the standards which each group sets up. Nevertheless, group standards play a decisive part in the determination of our wants.

Every social group sets up standards to guide its members. Standards are necessary if there is to be sufficient uniformity to facilitate easy social intercourse among the members of the group. They are necessary if the members of the group are to know which customs and conventions are of fundamental importance and which are of minor importance to the group as a whole. They are essential if the members of the group are to advance together to higher levels of living. Incidentally, the insistence upon these standards protects the members of the group from unwanted invasion of those in other social levels.

These group standards are of many sorts. They include moral standards, standards of living, standards of taste, and standards of etiquette. In our study of family management and finance we are primarily concerned with the standards which each group sets up to guide its members in the selection of the wants they are to satisfy. These are known as standards of living.

For our purposes we may define a *standard of living* as consisting of those goods and services which an individual, a family, or a social group is accustomed to enjoy and which it considers so essential to respectable existence that it is willing to make any reasonable sacrifice to obtain them, such as postponing marriage, limiting the size of the family after marriage, or working longer hours.

In any discussion of standards of living it is important to distinguish clearly between a family's standard of living and its manner or scale or plane of living. A *manner of living, scale of living,* or *plane of living* is the way the family actually does live. The manner of living may include more or less than the standard of living calls for. The standard of living of an individual or of a family is usually judged by the manner of living. It is also important to understand clearly the difference between a family's standard of living and its ideal manner of living. An *ideal manner of living* is the best possible way of material living. It is the way in which an individual, a family, or a social group would live, the goods and the services it would enjoy if there were no limit to the means at its disposal. This is sometimes spoken of as an *ideal standard of living*. It is clearly a concept entirely different from the *actual standard* defined above, which an individual or a family must maintain if it is to associate here and now with its accustomed companions.

There are available a number of descriptions of standards typical of the more usual income levels. (See references at the end of this chapter.) These vary in the exact terminology they use, but most of them include a description of the following levels of living: poverty, subsistence, health and decency, comfort, moderately well-to-do, and well-to-do. In so far as these are stated in terms of quantities and qualities of goods and services, they suggest the order in which items are added as families move up the social scale. When they are set up in terms of the money it takes to maintain a certain standard, changes in prices soon make them out of date. And, in recent years, there have been so many changes in our ways of living that even standards formulated in terms of goods and services become obsolete in a few years.

Most of these descriptions of living standards are made in terms of the way people live in a large city. Such studies as are available for the larger centers indicate that there are considerable differences in the details which are included in the various levels, even in the larger cities in different sections of the country. If a family uses these standards as a guide in working out its own standard of living, they should be re-stated in terms of the ways of living and the current prices in the community in which the family lives.

What standards of living include. Standards of living usually include a list of required goods and services, and, in addition, the way or ways by which the members of the group are expected to provide them. In so far as goods are to be purchased in the market, standards tend to be expressed in pecuniary terms—$10 hats, $60 suits of clothes, $10,000 homes, $1,000 automobiles.

For some items, and in some groups, the emphasis is primarily upon the provision of a given list of items of a certain quality. How the goods are secured is left entirely to the individual or the family. In other cases, it is absolutely essential not only that the article be provided, but also that it be secured in a certain way from a certain source. For example, most standards include baked goods as part of the diet of the group. It is assumed that fresh bread will be purchased in the market. It is entirely a matter of indifference, as far as the standard of the group is concerned, whether cake and cookies and pie are bought at the bakery or baked at home. Many standards call for an attractive lawn about the home. In some standards it is assumed that the man of the house will take care of his own lawn. In others he must hire the work done. In still others, it is permissible for him to have flower gardening for a hobby, but he must never mow the grass or rake the lawn.

High standards, low standards, expensive standards. Standards of living are ordinarily classified on the basis of the amount of money it takes to maintain them. The type of standard a family can maintain with a low money income is called a low standard of living, and the type of standard that can be maintained only with a more generous expenditure is called a high standard of living. A standard of living which involves the expenditure of a generous money income is ordinarily considered to be more desirable than a standard which can be maintained with a small money outlay. This is not because there is any value in the expenditure of money as such, but because with a meager money income it is usually impossible for a family to provide for its members many of the things they would like to be able to enjoy.

Characteristics of a low standard of living. The outstanding characteristic of a low standard of living is the expenditure of the majority of the family's available resources for a meager supply of physical necessities. No provision for emergencies is possible. There is little opportunity for the individual members of the family to satisfy their purely personal preferences. There is little or no provision for the intangibles involving security, personal freedom, and self-respect. There are available for the members of the family only a minimum of social contacts. In many cases suitable clothing and occasional expenditure for recreation can be had only by inadequate provision for food or by neglect of health.

Characteristics of a high standard of living. A high standard of living, on the other hand, is characterized by the comparatively small proportion of the income which is used for physical necessities, and by its large emphasis upon the intangible elements of security, individual freedom, and self-respect. There is provision for a wide range of social contacts. Both clothing and shelter are selected with due regard to social demands. There is adequate provision for the care of health, with emphasis upon preventive rather than merely remedial measures. The individual members of the family are allowed considerable freedom in their personal expenditures. They are able to follow out a wide range of personal interests. There is careful consideration of future needs, and provision of adequate reserves for emergencies. A high standard places emphasis upon the importance of balanced spending. It assumes that the family will, in so far as its resources permit, provide for the wants of all its members in the order of their importance, sacrificing neither the future to the present, nor the present to the future. The high standard always emphasizes intrinsic rather than pecuniary values, enduring rather than temporary satisfactions, quality rather than quantity in living.

In the past there has been much criticism of the American tendency to insist upon too high standards of living. In particular, this criticism has been directed against people who have set for themselves standards more expensive than they could maintain with the income at their disposal. Most of this criticism has been due to the failure to distinguish between high and expensive standards.

Characteristics of an expensive standard of living. The expensive standard measures everything in pecuniary terms. It emphasizes temporary values. It is characterized by expenditure of a large proportion of the income upon highly conspicuous items designed to secure social recognition. The expensive standard is set up with more regard to what other people think than to the personal preferences of the individual members of the family. Because it concentrates upon heavy expenditures designed to secure social recognition, the expensive standard usually satisfies only a narrow range of immediate individual interests. The expensive standard overemphasizes pecuniary emulation in the present. It places immediate social recognition above both individual freedom and security. Many families have mortgaged their future and made themselves slaves to instalment payments in order to have as good a car and just a little better house than their neighbors. Then, when their income declined, they lost everything they had agreed to pay for. It is impossible to maintain an expensive standard without the expenditure of large sums of money. A family with an expensive standard, unless it is possessed of very large means, finds itself continually under pressure to live beyond its income.

The essential difference between a high standard and a low standard is the difference between a standard which will provide only meagerly for current necessities and a standard which will allow provision for fundamental underlying intangible wants. The essential difference between a high standard and an expensive standard is the difference between a standard which places emphasis upon the satisfaction of the fundamental underlying wants of the members of the family, and a standard which is concerned primarily with social recognition secured by heavy pecuniary expenditure.

It is true that a high standard of living requires the expenditure of more money than does a low standard of living, but a truly desirable standard of living is not necessarily expensive. It is entirely possible to maintain a high standard of living on a rather modest money income provided that the means which are used are adjusted in such a way as to make possible the satisfaction of the fundamental wants of the family.

Standards of living are family standards. Ordinarily standards of living are set up in terms of what is necessary to maintain a family. The members of a given group are not supposed to assume the responsibilities for family support which marriage entails until they are able to provide for their family the goods and services which their standard calls for. There are many single men and single women who continue to live for a long time in a manner which is equal to, and in some cases clearly above, the family standard set for their group. They would like to marry, but their income, while it will provide one with somewhat more than the standard calls for, will not provide what is necessary for two.

Ordinarily, the standard of any group is set up on the assumption that the members of the group have an income adequate to bring up one or more children in the style which the group demands. The family with a smaller income frequently finds it essential to limit the number of its children. The family that decides to have more children than the standard of the group includes may be forced to adjust

itself to the standard of living of another group, at least for a few
years at the peak of its expenditures.

At the same time, a group sometimes sets somewhat different
standards to be observed by the single individual, by the childless
couple, and by the family at the peak of the burden of rearing its
children.   The childless couple, or the family whose children have
attained maturity, usually is expected to meet demands from which
the family with a number of growing children is, for the time at
least, exempt.   When mothers of small children entertain, they are
expected to conserve their strength as well as their financial resources
by serving simple meals and by omitting unnecessary elaborations in
decorations and entertainment.   Furthermore, many women without children maintain that they are expected to provide more extensive meals and more elaborate service, to dress less simply, to keep
their houses more meticulously, to give more generously, and to spend
more time on community activities which take the housewife away
from home than are the mothers of small children.

How a family's standard of living is determined.   We are
inclined to assume that every family must accept without question a
standard of living set up for it by the group to which it belongs.   For
the family with very small income, for the family whose members
have a narrow range of interests, for the family whose major social
contacts are with a single group, this is usually true.   The details of
standards of living are enforced rigidly upon the members of the
lower income groups, not only because of the narrow range of their
social contacts, but also because in a group with limited resources,
minor distinctions are the only means of determining a family's position in the social scale.

It is sometimes difficult to realize how important these minor distinctions can be.   Whiting Williams in his interesting book, *Mainsprings of Men,*[2] emphasizes the importance of the distinction between
the man who works with a shovel and the man who works with a
wrench.   There may be very little difference in income, but there
is a difference in the way in which he is expected to live and in the
way he is regarded by his fellows.   A young minister working in a
rather poor parish found that the family of a garbage wagon driver
who worked at night when no one could see him moved on a higher
social level than did the family of the garbage wagon driver with

---

[2] Whiting Williams. *Mainsprings of Men*, pp. 56 ff. Charles Scribner's Sons, New York, 1925.

nearly the same income who had to work collecting garbage in the daytime.

On the other hand, the family whose members have a wide range of interests, a good education, and enough income to gain admittance to a variety of social groups can have considerable freedom in working out its own standards. In case the members do not care to observe closely the standard of some one of the groups with which they might associate, they can find some other worth while association to take its place. In the upper income levels it is customary for individuals to move in many groups. Each group usually insists upon conformity only in major essentials, recognizing individual freedom in minor details as an essential part of a high standard of living.

How a family determines its standard of living. There are two ways by which a family can determine its own standard of living. In the first place (and this is possible even in most of the lower income groups), the family can choose the group or groups with which its members are to associate. In the second place, if its members have contacts with several groups, the family can choose elements from the standards of each of these groups out of which to build its own standard. The only requirement is that the completed standard shall conform sufficiently to the standards of the various groups to make the family welcome in all of them.

For most families, then, the determination of the standard desired ought not to be the simple task of conforming to the standard of some one group. As far as possible, every family should work out for itself an individualized standard of living which will satisfy the fundamental requirements of the various groups with which the family is identified, and which at the same time will enable the members of the family to follow out their particular interests.

Ordinarily, standards of living include three sets of fundamental values: physiological necessities, selected for their survival value; conventional necessities, selected for their prestige value, or their social survival value; and elements representing the predominant interests of the members of the group, selected for their intrinsic or welfare value.

Physiological necessities include a minimum amount of inexpensive food, clothing, and shelter, necessary for mere physical subsistence. Conventional necessities include many articles of food, served not because people like them particularly but because it is the accepted thing to do so; clothing, designed not primarily to provide adequate protection from the cold, but rather to attract attention and secure social recognition; a house, built according to the latest style, located in the proper street; amusements, selected not for the fun there is in them, but because they represent the thing the social set is doing. Conventional necessities are selected because they indicate exactly the superior group to which the individual or the family belongs. They have social survival value in so far as they protect the members of the group from the competition of outsiders.

Elements representing the interests of the group vary greatly. Most standards include some sort of an automobile, various household conveniences, a radio, a newspaper, a few magazines, and the like, not because they are necessary either to physical well-being or to social success, but because the people are interested in them for their own sakes.

There are two main types of prestige values—those which represent purely formal values, and those which are incidental to the working out of the fundamental interests of the group. The purely formal values are common in groups engaged in pecuniary emulation. The insistence upon custom-built automobiles and uniformed chauffeurs, the purchase of the most expensive seats in the theater, the patronizing of the one exclusive shop, are examples of this sort of thing.

On the other hand, attendance at a certain school or college may be an indication of social position. Here, however, the social superiority is usually the result of the superiority of training which the particular school or university affords.

Planning a standard for a new family. It is especially important for a young couple planning to be married to work out deliberately the standard which their new family is to follow. The standard of the new family should be a blend of the standards of the man and woman who make it up. If they both come from the same social group, they will have similar standards and the task will be comparatively easy. If they come from widely different social levels, there will be more points upon which they will have to compromise. Even a couple coming from the same group frequently get into difficulties early in their family life because they assume too great a degree of similarity in their standards.

In planning their family affairs, particularly in working out a long-time plan for their family, the young married couple must keep in mind the fact that it is much more pleasant to raise than it is to lower the family standard. It is well enough to aim high as far as the future is concerned, but it is important not to start more than the family can finish. On the whole, the family will get more satisfaction out of life if it can live throughout its forty or fifty years as a family on a steadily rising standard than it will if it starts out on a higher level than it can maintain.

Keeping family standards up-to-date. There are two major forces, experience and emulation, at work in every family to raise its level of living. Young married people are influenced by what they formerly enjoyed in the homes of their parents at a time when the family income was much larger than young people just starting out can hope to earn. They work to attain as soon as possible for their family the living levels which they could afford as single individuals when they were both earning. Families everywhere at all stages of the family life cycle are influenced by what they see others about them enjoying.

The function of the standard of living is to keep the members of the group from falling below the level of living which the group considers essential. Whenever the majority of individuals in a group have been able to attain a level of living somewhat higher than their standard and to live upon that level for some time, it is the function of the standard to help the members of the group retain the ground which they have gained through experience or emulation. Furthermore, it is the function of the standard to strengthen those habits of living which the group considers desirable, and to weaken resistance to change in the direction which the group considers to represent improvement in its living. While, therefore, the forces working toward raising living levels are something distinct from the standards of living of the group, the standard itself facilitates change in the direction which the group considers to represent progress and, by its tendency to constant expansion, helps to retain as a part of a constantly expanding standard the new experiences which the group finds to be desirable.

Although, in general, the tendency is for a family or a group to advance toward higher levels of living, there are a number of conditions under which the members of the family, or the members of a whole social group for that matter, may consent to depart from their accustomed standard. They may accept a reduction in their standard of living if they believe the reduction will be only temporary. They will accept it under the stimulus of some strong religious or patriotic or other emotional appeal. They will reduce their standard of living more readily if the change is voluntary than they will if it is imposed upon them from without. And they will accept a reduction in their standard of living with much less reluctance in case a great many other people are adopting the same change. During the World War people voluntarily accepted the restrictions of gasless Sundays and wheatless Mondays and meatless Wednesdays, partly because they knew the restrictions were temporary, partly because they were under the stimulus of a strong emotional appeal. A family going on a camping trip in the summer voluntarily lowers its standard of living. If a number of families of its acquaintance are doing the same sort of thing, the family calls it fun, in spite of the fact that, under other circumstances, they would resist bitterly any similar forced lowering of their standard of living. Fur coats were accepted as necessary in the late 1920's. In the early 1930's furriers were left with large stocks of unsold coats on hand because many considered it to be in poor taste to flaunt a fur coat before less fortunate friends.

It is important for the family to examine its standards frequently. Too often a family retains in its standard elements which are no longer of value. Too often it neglects the opportunity to add new elements which will definitely increase the satisfaction which the family can get out of life. During prosperity, economic development makes new things available. The family must be alert to adopt such of these as will further the development of the interests of its members. On the other hand, business depression removes the means for securing much to which we have become accustomed. When from force of necessity we do without some of the things to which we have become accustomed, it is highly essential that we eliminate first the least necessary and that we continue for as long as possible to provide as many as possible of the items which are of fundamental importance to the family.

Conditions have been changing rapidly, particularly since 1914. Changes due to the World War, changes in the post-war period, changes due to the depression of 1929, have made it necessary for most families from time to time to revise their standards. It is highly essential in a period of uncertainty that every family work out for itself in terms of its current situation the most satisfactory standard which it can maintain.

In a period of rapid change, when business conditions are unsettled, when it is hard to see far into the future, the family working out its standard of living should begin by deciding what are the essentials of good living. Since prices and incomes change from time to time, the family should state its standard in terms of quantities and qualities of goods and services rather than in terms of prices. It should think in terms of quality of living rather than in terms of quantities of commodities, in terms of what is intrinsically worth while rather than in terms of pecuniary outlay. The family should place less emphasis upon the quantities of goods that it owns and more upon the quality of satisfaction these goods and services can render. While it must place sufficient emphasis upon the tangible elements in its manner of living, it must not neglect adequate provision for the absolutely fundamental intangibles of security and leisure and self-respect. Finally, it must remember that after all it is not the quantity of goods the family can command, not the social position it can attain, but the quality of satisfaction it can secure for the individual interests of its members that is of fundamental importance in determining what the family should want.

Wanted: a pattern for living. In a changing world we cannot safely take our wants for granted. We cannot hold rigidly to the old, nor can we drift aimlessly with the new. The first problem to be solved in connection with family finance is the selection of the wants we are to try to satisfy. This means that we must select for satisfaction a group of specific wants—wants for stylish, well-made, fashionable dresses, three of them, no more, no less; wants for three quarts of milk, not two or four; a want for a stylish, de luxe model automobile, or for a low-priced second-hand car. And when we have finished, our long list of specific wants must be those which represent and resolve our underlying wants into a rich and varied pattern of living—a pattern which represents us and which is entirely in harmony with the situation in which we find ourselves.

It is only by taking continued thought of our wants, it is only by deliberate, hard-headed, and at the same time sympathetic analysis, that we can work out such a pattern, changing the detail from time to time to keep it in harmony with the changing background of a changing world. We can plan intelligently only if we know not only what we want but also why we want it, only if we can distinguish clearly between incidentals and fundamentals. But the effort is worth while if it will provide a basis for intelligent selection of the goods and services and of the methods for securing them which will give us what may be the richest and most satisfactory life possible with the means at our disposal.

QUESTIONS

1. (a) List your fundamental wants in the order of their importance to you. (b) List a number of specific wants under each of these general headings. Arrange each group of specific wants in the order of their relative importance. (c) For three of these specific wants indicate all the factors—personal, geographical, economic, and social—which had anything to do with their development.

2. (a) How can a college student deliberately develop his capacity for the appreciation of what is intrinsically beautiful and appropriate? A teacher in a rural community? A hardware dealer in a small town? (b) How can you, by taking thought, increase your enjoyment of a radio program, a vacation trip, a trip to the theater?

3. There are two families, each made up of husband, wife, a boy, age 12, and a girl, age 9. One lives in Minneapolis, Minn. The other lives in Los Angeles, Calif. Point out the differences you would expect to find in their specific wants for food, clothing, shelter, fuel, and refrigeration.

4. Point out the effect of economic and technological development upon your wants for means of transportation; for entertainment; for shelter.

5. How have the customs and conventions of college life changed your wants since you came to college? Do you know of any college customs or conventions which tend to perpetuate useless and inefficient ways of getting an education? Can you as an individual student safely ignore them? Why or why not?

6. Give examples from your own experience of the practice of each of the three types of emulation. What were the benefits derived in each case?

7. Compare the influence of standards of living and of moral standards upon the conduct of the individual.

8. "There are really as many standards of living in the world as there are people." "A standard of living is a group phenomenon, the product of the interaction of many minds, imposed upon the individual from without." How do you reconcile these two statements?

9. Write a detailed description of your own or your family's present standard of living. Is it a high standard? A low standard? An expensive standard? How do you determine this?

10. After reading the suggested references to Andrews, Nystrom, and Atkins,

formulate for yourself in terms of the present situation in your own home community a detailed description of each of the following levels of living: poverty, subsistence, comfort, moderately well-to-do. How much do you estimate it would cost for a family consisting of a man and wife, and for a family consisting of a man, wife, and two boys, ages 9 and 12, to live for a year in your community on each of these levels as you have described them?

11. Under what conditions will an individual consent to depart from his accepted standard of living? Give examples from your own observation.

12. Some economists define standards of living as those items in one's accustomed manner of living which are put ahead of marriage or the rearing of a family after marriage. Nystrom suggests that marriage and children may be an alternative within a given standard. With which point of view do you agree and why?

13. Said a business man, "I don't see that it costs me any more for my family of three children than it does my friend A, who has only a wife to support. Both of us manage to spend all we can spare from the demands of our business." Said Mrs. A, "So much more is expected of the women without children in the way of social activities that it really costs us more to keep up the social position that is expected of us than if we had children." Are these statements consistent with Nystrom's statement that it is ordinarily assumed that the addition of a child to the family means the sacrifice of some part of the customary or habitual standard of living for the parent? Do the groups with which you are familiar set one standard for childless families and another for families with children? If so, give specific examples of the differences in these standards.

14. People live very differently today than they did forty or fifty years ago. Even in the last fifteen years there have been great changes in the standard of living of the great majority of the American people. What are the factors which have made possible these changes? To what extent do you think that present standards are more desirable, and to what extent less desirable, than those of fifty years ago?

15. A newly married couple come to you for advice as to the sort of standard they should attempt to maintain. On the basis of the material in this chapter, what suggestions would you make to them? How would you make clear the nature and importance of a harmonious pattern of living?

REFERENCES

Andrews, B. R., *Economics of the Household*. The Macmillan Co., New York, 1923; Revised Edition, 1935.

Contains among other things a description of the usual levels of living.

Compare especially the description in the 1923 edition, pp. 85-87, with the 1935 edition, pp. 118-121.

Gordon, L. J., *Economics for Consumers*, especially Chs. 2 and 5-11. American Book Co., New York, 1939.

An analysis of how wants are determined, with much interesting material describing the origin of a great variety of specific wants.

Hoyt, Elizabeth E., *The Consumption of Wealth*, especially Parts II, III, and V. The Macmillan Co., New York, 1928.

The whole book is worth reading, both for its point of view and for the wealth of material it contains. It not only provides an enlightening analysis of what we want and why we want it, but also a great deal of illuminating material on a wide variety of consumer problems.

Hoyt, Elizabeth E., *Consumption in Our Society*, especially Part I, the chapters on standards of living in Part III, and Part IV. McGraw-Hill Book Co., Inc., New York, 1938.

Adds more detail on interests and standards of living, and a significant discussion in Part IV of the possibility of maximizing satisfactions by expanding appreciations as well as by increased production, more effective use, and wiser choice.

Kyrk, Hazel, *A Theory of Consumption*, especially Chs. VIII to XI. Houghton Mifflin Co., Boston, 1923.

A thorough and scholarly discussion of the theory of standards of living and their significance in our present economic order.

Kyrk, Hazel, *Economic Problems of the Family*, Ch. XIX, pp. 372-397. Harper and Bros., New York, 1933.

A somewhat briefer discussion of standards of living, dealing specifically with the part they play in the economic problems of the family.

Nystrom, P. H., *Economic Principles of Consumption*, pp. 241-312. The Ronald Press Co., New York, 1929.

Ch. XII contains an excellent and much-quoted description of the characteristic details of the various levels of living, together with estimates of the amount of income required to maintain them in 1929 by families of various sizes living under urban conditions. It is interesting to compare Nystrom's description of the minimum of comfort standard with the *Tentative Quantity and Cost Budget for Government Employees in Washington, D. C.*, worked out by the Bureau of Labor Statistics just at the close of the World War. Here the changes in clothing and in miscellaneous commodities are especially significant.

CHAPTER III

THE FAMILY'S INCOME

We know little about family incomes. Each of us knows the extent of his income more accurately than that of his wants. We know definitely how much or how little we have available to spend. No matter what its amount may be, it hardly ever is enough to provide us with everything we feel we need. As we look about us it seems to us that our friends must have more to do with than do we ourselves.

But most of us have no accurate or comprehensive knowledge of other people's incomes. We have only fragmentary knowledge of the incomes of the families of our immediate acquaintance. And in most cases, our ideas of the amount of their incomes are exaggerated. If we are to check on the standards we set for ourselves, if we are to keep our wants well within the range possible of attainment, it is clearly important that we analyze our own and others' incomes. We must understand and evaluate the sources of our money income. We must have a clear idea of the other resources at our disposal.

Money, real, and psychic income. Whenever income is mentioned, we are inclined to think first of money income. Money plays so important a part in our present market economy that it is hard for us to realize that families satisfied their wants for many years before our present monetary system was invented. If we are to get down to the fundamentals of our problems as consumers, we must guard against our present pecuniary bias in regard to income. Suppose, then, that we begin with a more inclusive definition. *Income* consists of the benefits or services received during a given period of time from wealth or free persons.

We must consider this flow of benefits in three ways. In the first place, we must take account of the family's *money income*—its monetary receipts during a given period of time. In the second place, we must analyze its *real income*—the goods and services which are available for its use during a given period. In the third place, we must consider its *psychic income*—the flow of satisfactions actually received during a given period by the members of the family. No two families want exactly the same list of goods. Because prices vary from place to place and from time to time, a given money income will not always buy the same amount of goods. Not everything a family has available to use is bought with current money income. Therefore, even though two families have the same money income, their real incomes may be decidedly different. Similarly, because individuals receive varying amounts of satisfaction from the use of identical goods or services, two families with the same amount of real income may find that the psychic income received by their members is decidedly different. For example, the members of one family may get a great deal of satisfaction from listening to their radio, while the members of another family may get little or no enjoyment out of theirs.

It is entirely possible to measure definitely a family's money income. It is also possible, though by no means so easy, to determine the amount and the quality of the goods and services which a family has available for its consumption. It is difficult even for the members of a family, and almost impossible for any outsider, to determine the amount of satisfaction the members of the family obtain from the use of the goods and services at their disposal. And yet, in the final analysis, it is the maximizing of psychic income, it is the increasing to the greatest possible extent the sum total of satisfactions enjoyed by the members of the family, that is the ultimate objective of all family finance.

Because psychic income is so peculiarly personal in its nature, each member of the family must work out for himself his own problem of increasing the amount of satisfaction he receives from the goods and services the family can make available. It is necessary for the family to concentrate primarily upon money income and real income. Keeping individual interests and personal preferences always in mind, it is the problem of the family to provide, with the money income and other resources that are available, the list of goods and services from which the members of the family can secure the largest total of personal satisfaction.

Statistics of money income. Every family can measure accurately in dollars its own current money income. It is hard, however, to find satisfactory statistics of the money incomes of American families. Most of the income statistics that are easily available deal with national income and with individual incomes, rather than with family incomes. Except for the estimates of national income, most of the income figures are two or three years old before they are available. However, if we study the relationship between national income, individual incomes, and family incomes for the years for which such figures are available, we may be able to get some idea of current changes in family income from the current statistics of individual and of national income. If we know about the increase or the decrease in the national income, and the increase or decrease in the number of individuals who share in this income, we can get an idea as to the direction and the amount of the change we should expect in individual incomes.

Sources of information about money income. For many years the chief sources of information about national income and its distribution came from income tax figures compiled by the federal government. During the World War, and for several years thereafter, people in the middle income brackets filed returns in sufficient quantities to give a fairly adequate idea of the amount and distribution of individual incomes. In the later 1920's, minimum exemptions were raised until not over 20 per cent of the people of the country, all of them in the upper income brackets, were filing returns. With the reduction of these minimum exemptions in the 1930's, federal income tax returns may again present a comprehensive picture of the incomes of the majority of the American people.

Ever since its establishment in the years following the war, the National Bureau of Economic Research has been studying both national and individual incomes. It has published a number of volumes containing the results of its research. In 1930, the Bureau published Willford I. King's comprehensive study of the amount, sources, and distribution of the national income under the title *The National Income and Its Purchasing Power*. This is the best single source of material on incomes available for the period. This study brings the statistics of income down to 1926 and 1927, and in a few cases to 1928, giving a detailed picture of incomes and their distribution at the peak of the Coolidge prosperity.

Most of the statistics used in this chapter will be drawn either from government figures or from the studies of the National Bureau of Economic Research.

The national income. The national income is ordinarily considered to be the sum of the monetary receipts of individuals during a given period of time. But in the study of family finance we cannot stop simply with money incomes, for there are many things from which individuals receive income through personal use rather than in the form of money. One individual owns a house which he rents to a tenant. He receives rent for the use of his house. The money which changes hands counts as part of the national income. Another individual owns a house but instead of renting it to another he lives in it himself. He charges himself no rent; there is no money income which can be counted for statistical purposes. A woman does housework in another woman's home. She receives money wages which count as part of the national income. A housewife does her own work; she receives no money income for her services, and' therefore her contribution cannot be counted in statistics of money income.

Some estimates of the national income include only actual money

ESTIMATED REALIZED INCOME OF THE PEOPLE OF THE CONTINENTAL
UNITED STATES [1]

YEAR	POPULA-TION (MILLIONS)	TOTAL INCLUDING IMPUTED INCOME		TOTAL EXCLUDING IMPUTED INCOME		IMPUTED INCOME	
		Millions of Current Dollars	Millions of 1913 Dollars	Millions of Current Dollars	Millions of 1913 Dollars	Millions of Current Dollars	Millions of 1913 Dollars
1909	90	$29,605	$31,300	$27,661	$29,221	$1,944	$2,079
1910	92	31,430	32,380	29,345	30,207	2,085	2,173
1911	93	31,858	32,920	29,660	30,634	2,198	2,286
1912	95	33,977	34,656	31,755	32,373	2,222	2,283
1913	97	35,723	35,756	33,393	33,413	2,330	2,343
1914	99	35,647	35,250	33,227	32,841	2,420	2,409
1915	100	37,205	36,636	34,690	34,137	2,515	2,499
1916	101	43,288	39,559	40,585	36,996	2,703	2,563
1917	103	51,331	40,242	48,314	37,613	3,017	2,629
1918	104	60,408	40,150	56,658	37,261	3,750	2,889
1919	105	65,949	38,017	61,628	35,098	4,321	2,919
1920	106	73,999	37,573	68,442	34,348	5,557	3,225
1921	108	63,371	36,710	58,271	33,638	5,100	3,072
1922	109	65,925	40,565	61,187	37,623	4,738	2,942
1923	111	74,337	45,164	69,295	42,072	5,042	3,092
1924	113	77,135	46,758	71,905	43,577	5,230	3,181
1925	115	81,931	48,412	76,561	45,191	5,370	3,221
1926	116	85,548	50,421	80,284	47,261	5,264	3,160
1927	117	88,205	52,892	82,921	49,655	5,284	3,237
1928	119	89,419	54,022	84,119	50,692	5,300	3,330

[1] W. I. King, *The National Income and Its Purchasing Power.* National Bureau of Economic Research, New York, 1930. Population figures from Table I, p. 47. Estimates in current dollars from Table VIII, p. 74. Estimates in 1913 dollars from Table IX, p. 77.

payments. Other estimates include, in addition to money income, an estimate of the money value which may be imputed to the use of homes, furniture, and other durable goods which families own and use themselves. No estimates of national income include any estimates of the value of housewives' services. The table on page 56 gives a summary of Willford I. King's estimates of national income for twenty years, from 1909 to 1928, both including and excluding imputed income from the use of commodities.

In order to determine the relative importance to the family of money income and of income received directly from the use of goods owned by the family and of services performed by members of the family within the home, Hazel Kyrk [2] worked out an estimate in which she added to estimates of money income, the imputed income from owned homes, other durable consumers' goods, and housewives' services which she put down arbitrarily at $750 per year. Miss Kyrk's estimate showed nearly 2 billion dollars of net rental value from owned homes, 3 billion dollars of imputed income from other durable consumers' goods, and more than 18 billion dollars of imputed income from housewives' services. Since in 1925 the national income in terms of money amounted to not far from 75 billions, her estimates indicate that in 1925 the money value which could conservatively be imputed to the use of consumers' goods and to housewives' services added about one-third to the nation's money income.

Incomes at the peak of post-war prosperity. But most consumers are unaccustomed to thinking in terms of billions of dollars. They are more interested in what the national income means when it is split up into individual or family incomes. King's figures for 1926, 1927, or 1928 are very similar. (See page 58.) Suppose we take 1928 as typical of incomes at the peak of our post-war prosperity. In 1928 the national income amounted to approximately 89 billion dollars. If this income had been equally divided among all the people in the country there would have been $749 for every man, woman, and child in the continental United States. If the money had been divided evenly among all the gainfully employed workers, there would have been $1,920 for every gainfully employed worker. If this 89 billions had been divided evenly among

[2] Hazel Kyrk, *Economic Problems of the Family*, Table XIX, p. 124, and discussion accompanying table. Harper and Bros., New York, 1933.

all the families in the country, there would have been available for each family $3,105.

ESTIMATED PER CAPITA RECEIPTS FOR VARIOUS CLASSES OF INDIVIDUALS [3]

YEAR	CURRENT DOLLARS				DOLLARS OF 1913			
	REALIZED INCOME		AVERAGE ANNUAL EARNINGS		REALIZED INCOME		AVERAGE ANNUAL EARNINGS	
	Per Capita†	Per Person Gainfully Occupied	Per Salaried Employee*	Per Wage Worker*	Per Capita†	Per Person Gainfully Occupied	Per Salaried Employee*	Per Wage Worker*
1909	$327	$ 864	$ 976	$ 527	$346	$ 914	$1,034	$556
1910	340	895	1,002	552	350	923	1,035	568
1911	339	892	1,022	540	351	922	1,055	557
1912	357	938	1,045	568	364	956	1,064	578
1913	368	965	1,066	594	368	966	1,066	594
1914	360	943	1,088	552	356	933	1,071	544
1915	371	980	1,096	582	365	965	1,064	564
1916	425	1,120	1,148	679	389	1,024	1,034	610
1917	497	1,304	1,204	771	390	1,022	930	594
1918	579	1,496	1,265	940	385	994	813	601
1919	628	1,637	1,453	1,029	362	944	804	563
1920	695	1,850	1,740	1,273	353	939	846	612
1921	585	1,552	1,696	983	339	899	950	550
1922	601	1,595	1,715	1,012	370	981	1,031	610
1923	667	1,763	1,831	1,150	405	1,071	1,082	679
1924	680	1,789	1,896	1,134	412	1,084	1,120	669
1925	712	1,869	1,950	1,176	421	1,104	1,126	680
1926	735‡	1,920‡	2,025‡	1,217‡	433‡	1,132‡	1,162‡	699‡
1927	748‡	1,928‡	2,084‡	1,205‡	448‡	1,156‡	1,220‡	705‡
1928	749‡	1,920‡	.....	.....	452‡	1,160‡	.....	.....

* These averages would be materially higher in bad years were they based upon the numbers actually employed rather than upon the numbers attached to industries.
† For entire population of the continental United States.
‡ Preliminary estimate.

But the national income is not divided in any such way. Part of the national income goes to owners of property in the form of rent or interest or dividends. Part of it goes to workers in wages and salaries. In 1928 approximately 60 per cent of the national income went to labor in wages and salaries, and approximately 40 per cent went to property owners in rent, interest, and profits.[4]

Most families receive income from both labor and property. Families in the upper income groups receive a much larger proportion of their incomes from property than do families in the lower income groups. In the lower income groups most, though by no means all, of the family incomes come from wages or salaries.

[3] W. I. King, op. cit., Table XII, p. 87.
[4] Ibid., Table X, p. 80; Chart 6, p. 81, and accompanying discussion.

Wage earnings at the peak of post-war prosperity. The preceding table gives King's estimates of the average annual earnings of salaried employees and of wage workers for the years 1909-1927. These average annual earnings for 1928 would not vary materially from the estimates for 1927. In 1927, at the peak of prosperity, the average annual earnings of wage workers attached to industry, including wage workers in agriculture, was in round numbers $1,200. The average earnings of salaried workers during this same period was perhaps 80 per cent higher, or between $2,000 and $2,100. These estimates were secured by dividing the total wage payments by the average number of workers employed during the year. They make allowance for unemployment, and so represent approximately the amount received by workers during the year.

If a worker received wages higher than the average in his industry, if he had steady employment during a year when a number of workers in his line were unemployed, his wage income would run considerably above the average. If, on the other hand, he were employed less than the average amount for his group, or at less than average wages, his income would fall below these estimates. But, while there are, of course, many individual exceptions, these figures give a fair picture of the earnings of the wage earning group in the United States at the peak of prosperity. Average annual earnings do vary somewhat from occupation to occupation; but in the industries for which King gives separate figures, only the average earnings in agriculture and in the construction industry vary as much as $400 from the average wages for all industries. The average annual earnings in agriculture were $533. This is, as we would expect, much lower than for urban employment, because, in addition to money income, farm workers secure a considerable part of their living. The average annual earnings in the construction industry, on the other hand, were $1,644, or nearly $450 above the all industry average.[5]

Similarly, studies of wage rates and employment indicate that while wage rates are higher in industries in which employment is irregular, and lower in industries in which workers can count on steady employment, and while there is considerable difference in hourly rates and weekly wages, nevertheless there is a tendency for

---

[5] *Ibid.*, pp. 146 ff.

yearly earnings to remain surprisingly uniform. The yearly earnings of the individual workers within a given group seem to vary much more than do the average earnings of the groups themselves. These actual yearly money earnings are most important, because actual yearly earnings determine the way the family can live.

Salaried incomes at the peak of post-war prosperity. King's estimates of average earnings of salaried employees, on the other hand, show much more variation from occupation to occupation than do the average earnings of the wage workers. Such few salaries as are paid in agriculture are very low. The average is only $1,242. The average earnings of salaried employees in mercantile and in government positions is also less than the average. The 1927 average was $1,844 for mercantile, and $1,771 for government employees. Salaries in manufacturing and mining ran well ahead of the average, being a little over $2,400.[6]

Family incomes at the peak of prosperity. But all these figures tell us very little about family incomes. We spend our incomes as families, not as individuals. Suppose we complete our picture of prosperity incomes with a few figures about family incomes. The following table shows one estimate of the distribution of families according to the amount of their annual income for the year 1928.

ESTIMATED DISTRIBUTION OF FAMILIES ACCORDING TO AMOUNT OF ANNUAL INCOME, 1928 [7]

1928 Income	Number of Families	Per Cent	Cumulative Per Cent
All incomes..........................	29,000,000	100.0	....
Under $1,000..........................	4,060,000	14.0	14.0
$1,000- 1,200..........................	2,117,000	7.3	21.3
1,200- 1,400..........................	2,610,000	9.0	30.3
1,400- 1,600..........................	2,784,000	9.6	39.9
1,600- 1,800..........................	2,407,000	8.3	48.2
1,800- 2,000..........................	2,059,000	7.1	55.3
2,000- 2,500..........................	3,712,000	12.8	68.1
2,500- 3,000..........................	2,523,000	8.7	76.8
3,000- 4,000..........................	3,074,000	10.6	87.4
4,000- 5,000..........................	986,000	3.4	90.8
5,000-10,000..........................	1,885,000	6.5	97.3
10,000 and over..........................	783,000	2.7	100.0

[6] *Ibid.*, pp. 157 ff.

[7] Louis H. Reed, *The Ability to Pay for Medical Care*, p. 14, Abstract of Publication No. 25, The Committee on the Costs of Medical Care; University of Chicago Press. This estimate was made by Dr. Maurice Leven. The families are census families, and include approximately 2,286,000 households of one person. In addition to the families distributed here, there were in 1928 approximately 6,400,000 gainful workers outside the family units as designated by the census.

According to this table, in 1928 more than half the families in the United States had incomes of less than $2,000, three-fourths of the families had incomes of less than $3,000, only 10 per cent had incomes over $5,000, and less than 3 per cent had incomes of $10,000 and over. It is interesting to speculate upon how far above $10,000 some few of these incomes must have gone to offset the three-fourths of the families with less than the average family income.

The majority of American families are middle-class families. We cannot ignore the obvious problems presented by the glaring inequalities in the distribution of family incomes. It is clearly impossible for some families in the lowest income groups to secure even a bare subsistence with the money incomes at their disposal. On the other hand, the families with the largest incomes find difficulty in securing a living that is intrinsically worth while. It is much more difficult to get a dollar's worth for every dollar of a large income than it is to get a dollar's worth for every dollar of a small income. In spending a large income it is difficult to avoid the purchase of many empty values. It is especially difficult to spend a large income so as to fulfill all the social responsibilities which the receipt of a large income involves.

It is of fundamental importance that we do not allow our interest in these obvious problems of poverty and riches to blind us to the fundamentally significant fact that the great majority of families in the United States are neither very rich nor very poor.

In 1928, according to Leven's estimates, less than one-tenth of the families in the United States had incomes over $5,000, and less than one-seventh had incomes under $1,000. At the peak of prosperity, three-fourths of the families in the United States, including farm as well as city families, had incomes between $1,000 and $5,000. And more than half the families had incomes between $1,500 and $4,000. The distribution of family incomes in the United States clearly indicates that the fundamental problem of the majority of American families is the typically middle-class problem of how to live just a little better in the future than they have been able to live in the past on the modest money incomes at their disposal.

How much is an income worth? How well a family can live upon a given money income depends upon a number of factors. In the first place, the significance of a given income depends upon the range of incomes in the community. Wealth tends to concentrate in the larger metropolitan centers. There are many more large incomes in the big cities than in the smaller communities. As a result, a $6,000 salary may not represent as high a ranking in the income scale in a city of half a million as does a $4,000 salary in a middle-western city of moderate size, or a $2,500 salary in a small town.

The following table shows the distribution of incomes in Appleton, Wis., a middle-western industrial and college town of 25,000 population, representing 6,000 families. It is interesting to compare this table with the estimated distribution of family incomes for the country as a whole.

THE INCOMES OF THE FAMILIES OF APPLETON, WIS. [8]

		Per Cent
4,444	families with incomes under $2,000	71.7
978	families with incomes between $2,000 and $3,000	15.8
438	families with incomes between $3,000 and $5,000	7.0
220	families with incomes between $5,000 and $10,000	3.5
119	families with incomes of $10,000 and over	2.0

How well a family can live upon a given income depends a great deal upon what that amount of money will buy at the time in the community. Although there are no comprehensive statistics to measure accurately differences in living costs, it is commonly assumed that there is a tendency for living costs to be somewhat higher in the large urban centers in the industrialized northeastern section of the country, and somewhat lower in the small towns and country districts in the more definitely agricultural sections of the country. It is entirely possible that an income of $2,500 or $3,000 may provide as much in the way of comfortable living for a family in a small community as will $5,000 or $6,000 in a metropolitan center.

The significance of a given money income depends upon the amount of goods and services in the family's standard that must be purchased with money, and upon the possibility of supplementing these goods and services with real income from other sources. In the larger cities it is necessary to purchase with money almost everything the family uses. Most urban standards assume that food and clothing will be purchased in very near to finally processed form. Entertainment and, in many cases, even exercise must be paid for. In a smaller community, there are fewer things for the family to buy, and more that it is permissible and possible for the family to do for itself. There are fewer opportunities for expenditures for commercial entertainment. Food can be bought in less fully processed forms. There are fewer marketing charges to be paid for. Expenses for local transportation are negligible.

How well a family can live upon a given money income depends upon the number of members in the family dependent upon that income for support. Other things being equal, a family of one or two persons can live rather comfortably upon an income which would be entirely inadequate for a family of four or five or six.

The middle-class nature of our spending problems is further emphasized by the fact that in the large centers high living costs tend to decrease the purchasing power of the large incomes, while in the smaller communities and the rural districts lower living costs and the possibility of supplementing money income with real incomes from other sources makes the lower incomes count for more in the way of actual living. On the other hand, these same facts cannot but drive home the difficult nature of the spending problems faced by larger-than-average families with smaller-than-average incomes in the large cities with their higher-than-average living costs.

Family incomes since 1930. The picture of family incomes which 1928 statistics give us represents the largest money incomes which American families have ever had at their disposal. There are as yet (1936) no similarly comprehensive statistics of family income for the years since 1930. The figures in the tables on pages 65 to 67 are typical of the statistics available from which to estimate current trends in family income. They are taken from material in a report on the national income compiled by the Secretary of Commerce for the use of the Senate of the United States.[9] Similar material becomes available from time to time in other government publications and in the bulletins of the National Bureau of Economic Research.

The first of these tables shows the changes in the total national income, both produced and paid out, and the changes in wages and

[9] *National Income, 1929-1932.* Senate Document No. 124, 73rd Congress, 2d Session. United States Government Printing Office, Washington, D. C., 1934. A summary of this material is now available in Bull. 49, National Bureau of Economic Research, Inc., New York, June 7, 1934.

salaries, in dividends and interest payments, in rents and entrepreneurial withdrawals, from 1929 to 1932. The next table shows
the income received by each of these income recipients expressed as
percentages of total income paid out, and of total income produced.
These figures indicate that a considerable part of the property income and entrepreneurial income received by individuals during the
depression was not current income at all, but rather the return to
them of part of their capital.

The third of these tables shows the changes in the number of
people employed from 1929 to 1932. The fourth table shows the
changes which took place in the per capita income of various groups
of employees, and compares these changes with the changes in living
costs during this same period.

In using these figures as a basis for estimating changes in family
incomes we must keep in mind the fact that during a depression the
incomes of families in the upper income groups are usually reduced
more severely by reductions in dividend payments, rents, and entrepreneurial withdrawals than are the incomes of families in the middle
groups.

On the other hand, during a period of prolonged depression, many
families at the lower end of the income scale have their incomes very
severely curtailed or entirely wiped out by unemployment. Families
in the middle income groups usually find their incomes do not rise
as high during prosperity as do those of people above them, nor do
they fall as low as do the incomes of people below them during the
succeeding periods of depression. This again emphasizes the decidedly middle-class nature of the problem of the three-fourths of
the families in the country whose members manage to retain their
jobs, and who continue to receive some supplementary income from
their investments.

The family's real income. But if families even at the peak
of prosperity have had no larger incomes than these figures indicate,
how have they managed to live as well as they have seemed to? Have
they been using up some of their capital accumulations? Have they
been using credit and mortgaging their future incomes? Or have
they been doing for themselves, even during periods of prosperity,
many things that other people assumed that they were paying for?
There are probably many cases in which families have resorted to
each of these means of improving their manner of living. There is

National Income Produced and Paid Out, by Types of Payment, 1929-1932 [10]

	Millions of Dollars				Percentages of 1929			
	1929	1930	1931	1932	1929	1930	1931	1932
Salaries (selected industries)*	5,702	5,661	4,738	3,383	100.0	99.3	83.1	59.3
Wages (selected industries)*	17,179	14,210	10,542	6,840	100.0	82.7	61.4	39.8
Salaries and wages (all other industries)	29,052	27,794	24,622	20,302	100.0	95.7	84.8	69.9
Total labor income†	52,793	48,582	40,896	31,533	100.0	92.0	77.5	59.7
Dividends	5,964	5,795	4,313	2,588	100.0	97.2	72.3	43.4
Interest	5,677	5,815	5,649	5,491	100.0	102.4	99.5	96.7
Total property income‡	12,206	12,226	10,498	8,472	100.0	100.2	86.0	69.4
Net rents and royalties	4,116	3,475	2,752	1,865	100.0	84.4	66.9	45.3
Entrepreneurial withdrawals	12,020	11,127	9,102	7,024	100.0	92.6	75.7	58.4
Total entrepreneurial income	16,136	14,602	11,853	8,890	100.0	90.5	73.5	55.1
Total income paid out	81,136	75,410	63,247	48,894	100.0	92.9	78.0	60.3
Business savings§	1,896	−5,065	−8,604	−9,529	....	....	....	....
Total income produced§	83,032	70,345	54,643	39,365	100.0	84.7	65.8	47.4

* Includes mining, manufacturing, construction, steam railroads, Pullman, railway express, and water transportation.
† Includes also employee's pensions and compensation for injury.
‡ Includes also net balance of international flow of property incomes.
§ Items so marked are from Table 1, p. 3, of the bulletin referred to in the footnote.

10 National Bureau of Economic Research, Inc., Bull. 49, Table 1, p. 3; and Table 2, p. 5. New York, June 7, 1934. The grand totals in this and the following tables are obtained by an addition of the totals for each industrial field. The income subtotals by industrial fields are primarily in thousands of dollars, while the subtotals of gainfully engaged are usually in actual numbers. But the subtotals entered in Tables 2 to 10 are either in millions of dollars (for income) or in thousands of persons (for numbers engaged). These subtotals do not, therefore, add up exactly to the grand totals given.

PERCENTAGE DISTRIBUTION OF NATIONAL INCOME PRODUCED AND PAID OUT, BY TYPES OF PAYMENT, 1929-1932 [11]

INCOME	PERCENTAGES OF TOTAL INCOME PAID OUT				PERCENTAGES OF TOTAL INCOME PRODUCED			
	1929	1930	1931	1932	1929	1930	1931	1932
Salaries (selected industries)*	7.0	7.5	7.5	6.9	6.9	8.0	8.7	8.6
Wages (same as in line 1)*	21.2	18.8	16.7	14.0	20.7	20.2	19.3	17.4
Salaries or wages (all other industries)	35.8	36.9	38.9	41.5	35.0	39.5	45.1	51.6
Total labor income†	65.1	64.4	64.7	64.5	63.6	69.1	74.8	80.1
Dividends	7.4	7.7	6.8	5.3	7.2	8.2	7.9	6.6
Interest	7.0	7.7	8.9	11.2	6.8	8.3	10.3	13.9
Total property income‡	15.0	16.2	16.6	17.3	14.7	17.4	19.2	21.5
Net rents and royalties	5.1	4.6	4.4	3.8	5.0	4.9	5.0	4.7
Entrepreneurial withdrawals	14.8	14.8	14.4	14.4	14.5	15.8	16.7	17.8
Total entrepreneurial income	19.9	19.4	18.7	18.2	19.4	20.8	21.7	22.6
Total income paid out	100.0	100.0	100.0	100.0	97.7	107.2	115.7	124.2
Business savings	....	....	....	....	2.3	−7.2	−15.7	−24.2
Total income produced	....	....	....	....	100.0	100.0	100.0	100.0

* Includes mining, manufacturing, construction, steam railroads, Pullman, railway express, and water transportation.
† Includes also employees' pensions and compensation for injury.
‡ Includes also net balance of international flow of property incomes.

[11] *Ibid.*, Table 3, p. 7.

NUMBER OF PEOPLE ENGAGED IN GAINFUL EMPLOYMENT, 1929-1932 [12]

	ABSOLUTE NUMBERS (THOUSANDS)				PERCENTAGES OF 1929			
	1929	1930	1931	1932	1929	1930	1931	1932
Salaried employees (selected industries)*.....	2,221	2,187	1,915	1,556	100.0	98.4	86.2	70.0
Wage earners (same industries as in line 1)*...	12,219	10,677	8,890	7,131	100.0	87.4	72.8	58.4
Salaried employees or wage earners (all other industries)	20,765	20,057	18,544	16,767	100.0	96.6	89.3	80.7
All employees.....	35,205	32,921	29,349	25,453	100.0	93.5	83.4	72.3
Entrepreneurs.....	9,020	8,889	8,704	8,677	100.0	98.5	96.5	96.2
All gainfully employed.....	44,225	41,809	38,053	34,131	100.0	94.5	86.0	77.2

PER CAPITA INCOME OF EMPLOYEES AND THE COST OF LIVING, 1929-1932 [12]

	ABSOLUTE NUMBERS				PERCENTAGES OF 1929			
	1929	1930	1931	1932	1929	1930	1931	1932
Salaried employees (selected industries)*.....	$2,507	$2,589	$2,474	$2,175	100.0	100.9	96.4	84.7
Wage earners (same industries as in line 1)*...	1,406	1,331	1,186	959	100.0	94.7	84.4	68.2
Salaried employees or wage earners (all other industries)	1,399	1,386	1,328	1,211	100.0	99.1	94.9	86.6
All employees.....	1,475	1,448	1,360	1,199	100.0	98.2	92.2	81.3
Bureau of Labor Statistics cost of living index.....	....	....	....	....	100.0	97.4	88.9	80.4

* Includes mining, manufacturing, construction, steam railroads, Pullman, railway express, and water transportation.

[12] *National Income, 1929-1932*. Senate Document No. 124, pp. 18, 19. United States Government Printing Office, Washington, D. C., 1934. In this table and in all subsequent tables relating to the number of people employed or engaged, the annual estimates are averages for the calendar year. The numbers represent, in some industries, a full-time equivalent.

no question but that many people counted gains in the value of their invested capital as income and used it for current expenses; also, many families undoubtedly used credit extensively when times were good and they felt sure of continued employment. Franklin Ryan has estimated that at the end of 1929 there were outstanding some 11 billions of dollars of obligations incurred by consumers.

The following table shows the items which Ryan included in his estimate of outstanding consumer credit obligations.

CURRENT FAMILY FINANCING IN THE UNITED STATES, 1929 [13]

Class of Indebtedness	Total Amount Outstanding
Open-account debts	$4,500,000,000
Instalment debts	2,500,000,000
Short-term cash credit	1,500,000,000
Life insurance policy loans	2,200,000,000
Real estate mortgages *	1,000,000,000
Total current family debts	$11,700,000,000

* Ryan does not include this item in his table, but in a footnote to the table he concludes that fully $1,000,000,000 or more of the real estate mortgages on homes in the United States have been incurred on account of current household needs.

But even this enormous debt, which if it had been liquidated in a single year would have required more than one-eighth of the next year's national income, is much less than Miss Kyrk's conservative estimate of the annual value of housewives' services.[14]

After all, the best explanation of our ability to live as well as we have upon as little money income as these statistics indicate can be found in the fact that all of us have been doing for ourselves many things that other people have assumed we have been paying for with our money incomes. For, while money income is, for many families, the chief source upon which they must rely for the goods and services at their disposal, money is, after all, only one means of securing the benefits which result in want satisfaction. The significant thing in determining the well-being of the family is not the money income which it has available to spend, but its real income—the goods and services which are available for its use during a given period.

[13] Franklin W. Ryan, "Family Finance in the United States," in the *Journal of Business of the University of Chicago*, October, 1930, Vol. III, p. 417. Reprinted in *Recent Social Trends in the United States*, Ch. V, "Trends in Economic Organization," p. 257, published by McGraw-Hill Book Co., Inc., New York, 1933.

[14] See p. 57.

Sources of the family's real income.   The family's real income ordinarily is secured from a number of sources.   Andrews [15] classifies these sources of real income as follows:

    I. Outside money income
        a. Outside labor income
        b. Outside management income
        c. Outside capital or investment income

    II. Household production income
        a. Household labor income
        b. Household management income
        c. Household capital income, or use income

    III. Social use income

Most of the family's real income comes from goods and services purchased with the family's money income.   But real income is secured also from services performed for the family by its own members, either in the form of work done about the house or in planning, supervising, and buying.   Real income is secured also from the use of what the economist calls "durable goods," purchased in the past but still available for the use of the family.   Furniture, various articles of household equipment such as a radio or a vacuum cleaner, the dishes in the cupboard, the pots and pans in the kitchen, the automobile, and even the house in which the family lives, all are sources of real income, even though they were not purchased out of current funds, even though they bring in no current money income.   Finally, some real income is secured from the use of goods and services provided by the community.   The public schools, parks and playgrounds, highways, police protection, inspection of weights and measures, the enforcement of pure-food regulations, public libraries, municipal band concerts, all to a greater or lesser degree add to the real income of the family.

If all these sources of real income are reduced to their lowest terms, there are three underlying sources from which a family can secure real income.   They are: first, the earning power and personal abilities of its members; second, the earning power and serviceability of the property it owns; and third, the resources of the community in which it lives.

[15] From B. R. Andrews, *Economics of the Household*, pp. 40-73.   Revised edition, 1935, pp. 67-86.   By permission of The Macmillan Co., publishers.

The significance of household management income. It is important that we understand clearly the essential difference between household labor income and household management income. Household labor income includes any benefits received from work done within the home by members of the family. Washing dishes, cooking food, making beds, tending the furnace, mowing the yard, washing the car, all are examples of household labor. The benefits which they provide are household labor income. Household management income, on the other hand, includes any benefits secured from planning and supervising the activities of the home, including the planning and buying that is involved in the spending of the family's money income. The benefits which can be secured from careful management are too often taken as a matter of course. Careful planning is essential to the smooth operation of any household. If their activities are properly planned and co-ordinated, the members of the family can make greater contributions to the family's labor income. Careful buying can make available for the family from a given money income a larger number of goods and services than is possible if less time is spent in shopping.

The contribution of the husband. In most families, with the exception of those with very small children, it is usually possible for every member of the family to make some contribution to its real income. In the majority of families it is the husband who provides with his earnings the major part of the family's money income.[16]

It is frequently assumed that it is the husband's job to earn the money income, and that it is his wife's task to spend it. In most families, however, the work of family management is divided between the husband and the wife. While there is no hard-and-fast division which is universally followed, there are a number of items for which the husband is ordinarily responsible. It may be his duty to provide the family with a place to live, to see that the house is kept in repair, and to provide for heat and light and other public utilities. Usually the husband is responsible for the care of the family car. He must plan for its purchase and maintenance, and either he must take care of it himself, or he must supervise the work which is done upon it.

In addition, in most families the husband, as well as the wife, makes substantial contributions in the form of household labor income.

---

16 See table on p. 19, "Families Classified According to Number of Gainfully Employed Workers."

The husband may mow the yard, spade the garden, tend the furnace, clean the walks, repair the back steps, paint the kitchen, replace burned-out light bulbs, wash and grease the car, and mend the children's toys. And if his hours of work are limited, and his wife's home duties are unusually heavy, he may even take his turn washing dishes, helping with the heavy housecleaning, running the washing machine, or taking care of the children.

The contribution of the wife. In the majority of families, the wife makes her contribution in the form of household management and household labor income. It is not easy to distinguish sharply between her contributions to management and to labor income. She carries on many of these activities simultaneously. She plans the meals, purchases the food, and prepares it for the table. She plans, purchases, and cares for the clothing, at least for herself and the children. She cares for the interior of the home, purchases supplies and furnishings, makes the beds, cleans and orders the house, and does the thousand and one little tasks involved in "housekeeping." She looks after the children. She cares for their physical needs, dresses and undresses them, feeds them, and washes their faces, until they are able to take care of themselves. She orders their coming and going, supervises their school work, sees that they practice their music lessons, and that they wear their coats and hats and rubbers when it rains. And, in many families, she keeps the family books, pays the family bills, and supervises the operation of the family's budget.

In addition to all this, in a large number of cases, she makes a substantial contribution to the family's money income.[17] There are two periods in the life of the family in which the wife is frequently found to be gainfully employed. In the first place, it is not uncommon for her to continue to work for some time soon after her marriage, helping to earn the money which is necessary to establish the family upon a firm financial foundation and to buy the family's initial supply of furniture and equipment. In the United States, the earnings of the wife, either just before or more frequently just after marriage, take the place of the dowry system common in some European countries. In the second place, during the high school and college period, the wife, now freed from the care of small children

---

[17] The table on p. 19, "Families Classified According to the Employment Status of the Homemaker," shows the proportion of housewives who are employed outside the home, earning some part of the family's money income.

See also Day Monroe, *Chicago Families*, Chs. VII and VIII, pp. 141-225. University of Chicago Press, Chicago, 1932.

in the home, again may make her contribution in the form of regular money earnings, in order to help defray the unusually heavy expenses which come at the peak of the family's financial cycle. And, in addition to these two periods in which it is rather usual for the wife to be employed outside the home, in case of emergency, when the husband is disabled or out of a job, she may for a time take his place earning the family's money income.

The contribution of the children. It is ordinarily assumed that children make no contribution to the family's money income until they have finished their formal education. The age at which they begin to earn varies from time to time, with the standard of living of the family, and with the locality in which the family lives. Day Monroe, in her study of Chicago families, found that in these families in 1920, 80 per cent of the boys and girls over sixteen years old living at home were gainfully employed and were making some contribution to the family's money income.[18] In the 1930's, however, the combination of depressed business conditions and of legislation closed almost all opportunities for the employment of boys and girls under eighteen. While they are still in school, the most they can usually do is to earn a little spending money, the boys by mowing lawns, selling papers, or running errands, and the girls by taking care of the neighbors' children.

But while it is in many cases legally impossible, and while it is generally considered undesirable for the children to make any considerable contribution to the family's money income, there are a number of ways by which the children may add definitely to the family's household labor income. In the country there is so much for the members of the family to do that it is easy to find plenty of worth while work for the children in the home. Under most circumstances it is assumed that boys and girls at a comparatively early age will take over simple tasks suited to their capacities. If a family lives under conditions in which this is impracticable, it is still possible for the children to contribute something in the way of real income by providing themselves with wholesome recreation.

While the work that the children can do may seem to be hardly worth while, very frequently just the little extra help they can provide makes it possible for the family to do a number of things for

[18] Day Monroe, *op. cit.*, p. 173.

which it has almost but not quite enough time and money. A girl ten years old wants a party dress. The family has only money enough to buy the materials. The mother does not have the time she needs to make it. If the girl takes over the making of the beds, the relief from this one task may add enough to the mother's time to enable her to make her daughter the party dress. Or, in the time the daughter saves by setting the table, her mother can bake a three-layer cake with fancy frosting instead of a plain loaf cake. And if the daughter helps by taking care of the younger children, she will give her mother time enough to make arrangements for a birthday party. Similarly, if the boys help their father by mowing the yard, raking the lawn, or tending the furnace, he will have time to spend painting the kitchen, or fixing the back steps, or perhaps building a basement playroom, fitting up a gymnasium in the garage, or putting up a swing in the back yard.

Securing constructive contributions from the children is largely a managerial problem. The work which is selected must be within their capabilities. It must be something that the family needs to have done. It must, if possible, be work which has definite educational value. If it is necessary for the children to take over routine tasks, they should see clearly that the work they are doing is not simply to relieve others of drudgery, but that there are other tangible and rather immediate benefits which they as well as the rest of the family secure from their faithful performance of their daily tasks. It sometimes seems as if the children's contribution costs their mother more in supervision than it saves in labor. But if the tasks are properly selected, the educational by-products alone may entirely justify the effort that is involved.

Contributions of other members of the family. In many families there are one or more older people attached to the family group. In some cases these are older children who are now fully employed, in some cases grandparents, uncles, aunts, cousins, or even friends who live in the family. Members of this group usually make some contribution to the family's money income even if it is no more than payment for board and room. And they may supplement their money payments by some work around the house. Here again making good use of their abilities is largely a managerial problem. The work they do must be worth doing, it must be something that they can do, and something that they get satisfaction from doing well. Here, as in all other cases of household labor income, there is no justification of activity for its own sake. "Busy" work adds nothing to the family's real income. The results in every case must be greater than the effort involved. However, it is possible to add a surprising amount to the real income of the family simply by making use of the varying abilities of its members. It is highly essential that every family realize the importance of taking stock of, and making maximum use of, the personal resources of its members.

Contributions of property to the real income of the family. Just as there are two ways in which the members of the family contribute to the family's real income, so there are two ways in which the property the family owns can add to the goods and services available for its use. Families ordinarily think of income from property as a money return from investments. They recognize clearly the fundamental importance of the security against the hazards of unemployment, accident, illness, and old age which such a source of money income can give. At the same time, in taking stock of the sources of real income from the property at their disposal, they must not overlook the use income which can be secured from the household equipment and other goods in which they have invested part of the family's capital. It is often possible for a family to add more to its real income over a period of years by investing money in equipment which will pay dividends in use than by investing the same amount in money-earning securities. The family faced by a period of heavy expense or of curtailed income can often provide for its needs more adequately by investing part of its savings in needed and durable equipment, than by investing all of its surplus in interest-bearing securities. This is true especially if the period of financial strain is near at hand.

For example, many families find that the investment of $150 in home laundry equipment, such as a washing machine, a power ironer, some tubs, clothesline, clothespins, and other necessary supplies, will make available a much larger amount of laundry service than could be purchased with both the principal and the accumulated interest of a similar investment in interest-bearing securities. Many families will get a much larger amount of enjoyment from money invested in a radio than they could from tickets to concerts and baseball games which both the interest and principal of the same amount of savings would buy. In taking stock of the contributions of property to the family's real income, we must include both the security provided by money income from investments, and the services to be secured from properly selected, well-made, really durable consumers' goods.

Contributions of the community to the family's real income. Finally, no family can afford to overlook the contributions which the community can make to its real income. The number and quality of these services varies from place to place. There is usually a greater variety of facilities available in the larger communities. The quality of services they can render depends upon the extent to which their value is recognized and used, and upon the extent to which families in the community are willing and able to pay for their support.

In almost every community there are churches, hospitals, and a number of fraternal and social organizations, lodges, country clubs, dancing clubs, bridge clubs, and study clubs. In most communities there are branches of some one or more national organizations such as the Boy Scouts, the Girl Scouts, the Y.M.C.A., and the Y.W.C.A. In a growing number of communities opportunities for physical development are provided by community athletic programs, church basket-ball leagues, factory baseball leagues, business bowling leagues, and the like. There are opportunities for cultural development provided by church choirs, community choral organizations, amateur and professional community bands, and symphony orchestras. There are little theaters, book review clubs, night school and university extension classes, art museums, and writer's clubs. Many of these facilities are maintained by private organizations for the benefit of their members. Others are provided voluntarily out of private funds for the benefit of all the members of the community.

And finally there is the long list of services provided by public funds for the members of the community: police and fire protection, a good water supply, sewage and garbage disposal, public schools, parks and playgrounds, libraries and museums, and state-supported colleges and universities. Every family is paying its share for the provision of these facilities when it pays its taxes. Every family, therefore, by making the fullest possible use of the facilities the community provides, can increase the return from its tax payments.

Dividing up vs. building up. Every period of business depression, and every period of prosperity, too, for that matter, brings with it a number of suggestions for increasing family incomes for the great majority by redistributing existing incomes. One of the most common proposals is that we limit the amount going to any one individual and redistribute all he receives over that amount among families with lower incomes. The only difficulty with this plan is that there is so little to divide. In 1928 any individual with an income of $8,309 and above was in the upper 1 per cent of income receivers in the country. And the upper 1 per cent received 14 per cent of the national income. Had we confiscated all their income and supported them by charity, we would have been able to add only one-seventh to the incomes of the other 99 per cent of recipients of the national income. And had we left them $8,309 for their own use, we could have added only one-eleventh to the income of the lower 99 per cent.[19]

Another common suggestion is that, since most families in the lower income groups receive most of their income from wages and salaries, we should increase the proportion of the national income going to labor and decrease the proportion going to capital. This tendency is already at work. As we increase the proportion of capital we use in production, the return per unit of capital declines and the return per unit of labor increases. This the economist calls the *law of proportionality*. The figures for the years from 1909 to 1928 indicate that this tendency is working out. During this twenty-year period, the proportion of the national income going to labor has increased from 50 to 60 per cent and the proportion going to capital has decreased from 50 to 40 per cent.[20]

This tendency continued to be operative throughout the first few years of the secondary post-war depression. For 1930, 1931, and 1932, Department of Commerce figures indicate that 65 per cent of the income paid out went to labor, and 35 per cent to capital. But during these years, much of the payment to capital was in the form of deferred payments from prosperity earnings. The items in the table on page 66, giving the relationship between payments to labor and income produced, show that during this period the proportion going to labor increased until in 1932 labor was receiving more than 80 per cent of the income actually produced during that year.

---

[19] W. I. King, *The National Income and Its Purchasing Power*, pp. 176 ff., especially p. 178. National Bureau of Economic Research, New York, 1930.
[20] *Ibid.*, Table X, p. 80; Chart 6, p. 81, and accompanying discussion.

A third method of increasing the incomes of families in the lowest income groups is by enforced sharing of work. But whether this is done by blanket rules limiting hours or by voluntary sharing of existing employment, this sharing of work only takes away from workers with small incomes to give to those who have no incomes. If present employees are required to work fewer hours at the same hourly rates, this is obvious enough. It is not so obvious if workers work fewer hours per week for the same weekly incomes. This means they are getting higher hourly rates. But higher hourly rates mean either more work per hour with no increase in employment, or higher labor costs which in turn necessitate higher prices. Actually in many cases a worker would be better off to divide up the work at present wage rates and be able to buy what he needs at present prices than to accept present wages for less work and pay the higher costs such a program involves.

The great majority of families in this country have but little to gain by a comprehensive program of dividing up. If totals of national income in the tables in this chapter are anywhere nearly correct, in 1932 any family with an income of $1,700 or over would have had its income reduced for the benefit of those with smaller incomes.[21]

The fundamental importance of real income. There is, however, another alternative. Instead of dividing up what we have, we can go to work building up the stock of goods and services available for the consumer. Instead of limiting production until we find ourselves once more in a situation of serious scarcity, we can go back to work producing more of the goods and services we need for comfortable living. The test of well-being, after all, is found not in money income but in real income. The only way to increase real income is to increase the amount of goods and services families have available for their use.

But during depressions it seems impossible to get our economic machinery to function so as to let every family procure the goods that it needs. Not even during periods of so-called prosperity can

[21] In 1932, Department of Commerce estimates of national income were in round numbers 38 billions of dollars for income produced, and 49 billions of dollars for income paid out. If, in 1932, 38 billions of dollars had been divided equally among 29 millions of families, each family would have had $1,310.34 to spend from income produced during the year. If the larger amount, 49 billions of dollars, had been divided evenly among the 29 millions of families, there would have been $1,696.55 for each family. Even a national income of 58 billions of dollars will provide only $2,000 per family for the more than 29 million families in the United States.

most families secure enough money income to buy everything they need. A family is not, however, limited to the use of what it can buy in the market with its money income. When hours of employment are limited, either by the maladjustment of industry or by legislative fiat, the members of the family always have open to them the alternative of doing for themselves much that they formerly paid for. As long as there is opportunity for increasing the family's money income by increased employment or by wise investment of the family's funds, they can put their personal and financial resources to work for money in the market. When, however, there is no longer opportunity for profitable employment, either of men or money, the family can always put its resources to work at home. Home production is not always as efficient as industrial production, but it is better than no production at all. And with modern electrical equipment it is frequently possible to equal average industrial efficiency with only a moderate capital investment.

Increasing the family's real income. The family's problem of securing the largest amount of real income, the largest amount of goods and services for the use of its members, may be summed up as follows: First, the family must consider how to secure a moderate amount of money income from a reasonably secure source. From time to time it must canvass the possibilities for increasing both the amount and the security of its money income.

Second, the family must consider how to spend its money so as to secure the largest amount of goods and services that it is possible to buy in the market with the money income at its disposal. Increasing efficiency in buying will frequently add more to the real income of a family than would a program of redistribution of the larger incomes.

Third, the family must consider what it can add to its real income by production for its own use. Even in times of prosperity housewives are, according to Miss Kyrk's estimate,[22] adding between 15 and 20 billions of dollars' worth of goods and services to our real income. In periods of depression, the proportion of production for use to purchase in the market is greatly increased. Each family must consider just what in its individual situation can best be bought in the market and what can best be produced at home.

Fourth, the family must consider what it can add to its real income

---
[22] See p. 57.

by increasing the amount of social use income available in the community. It must, of course, remember that even the government cannot give something for nothing. But it may be that in some cases it will be possible to get much more in the way of efficient service by spending together than families can secure by spending alone. Two examples will suffice. By spending together for good roads a little of the money we pay for gasoline for our automobiles, we can ride more miles for less money than we could if we spent it all for gasoline and bumped along over unimproved highways. By spending money together for public schools, it is entirely possible to get efficient, well-rounded education for our children at a cost much lower than many families are accustomed to pay for a couple of hours of music or dancing lessons. The family must not overlook social use income in considering ways and means of increasing real income. But here, as in the market, it must not expect something for nothing. Everything must be paid for.

And, finally, we must always remember that income is the means, not the end, of family finance. We must be sure that everything we buy and everything we do is worth the cost. The problem, then, resolves itself to this: How can we get the most of what we want for a reasonable cost either in money or in time and effort? The rest of this book will be devoted to the problems involved in securing for the family the largest possible amount of satisfaction with the means at its disposal.

QUESTIONS

1. Give some examples from your own experience to show the importance in family finance of the distinction between money income, real income, and psychic income.

2. To what extent is it possible to compare the real incomes of different families? What do we need to know besides the money income of a family if we are to determine its real income?

3. Show why the same real income may yield different amounts of psychic income to different individuals; to the same individual at different times. To what extent is it possible to compare the psychic incomes of different individuals? To what extent is it possible for an individual to measure his own psychic income?

4. How do incomes of the people of your acquaintance compare with the statistics given in the text for the country as a whole?

5. How do you account for the existing differences in the incomes of fam-

ilies of your acquaintance? Which is more striking, the differences in their money income or the differences in their real income?

6. How well can a family consisting of a man, age 45, his wife, age 42, a boy, age 15, and a girl, age 12, live in your community if the husband earns $300, $200, $150, $100 a month? What is the smallest income on which such a family could live above the poverty level? How do you know?

7. (a) Compare the adequacy of the following money incomes for family support. (b) Compare the amount of goods and services and social use income you would expect each of these families to have available to supplement their money incomes.

Family A: An oil station attendant, married, no children, owns a car. His wife has the use of an 8-room house by paying repairs and taxes. His salary is $75 a month.

Family B: A retired school teacher, age 70, living on a pension of $50 a month. Works for part of room and board. Earns $50 a year knitting hand-made sweaters. Has an income from investments of $100 a year.

Family C: A bookkeeper in a brokerage house. Has a salary of $1,800 a year with which to support his wife, a boy, age 15, and a girl, age 11.

Family D: A woman, age 35, private secretary to a bank president. Salary $200 a month. Independent income from investments is $1,000 a year.

8. On the basis of the statistics in this chapter, how did each of the following families fare compared with the average in the first four years of the secondary post-war depression?

Family A: In 1929 this family had an income of $4,460 from the following sources: husband's salary, $2,500; wife's salary, $1,200; interest on $5,000 first mortgage public utility bonds, bearing interest at 5 per cent, $250; interest on $5,000 first mortgage real estate bonds, bearing interest at 7 per cent, $350; dividends on bank stock, par value $1,000, $80; dividends on stock in a local manufacturing plant, par value $1,000, dividends 2 per cent quarterly, $80.

In 1932, the wife had lost her job. Her husband had had his salary cut 20 per cent. Their 7 per cent bonds were in default. The bank failed. Their 5 per cent bonds were still paying the interest regularly, and selling slightly above par. Their stock in the manufacturing company was earning dividends of 1 per cent per quarter.

Family B: In 1929 the husband was employed at a salary of $3,000. The family had additional income from investments as follows: interest on $10,000 utility bonds at 5 per cent, $500, and dividends on stock with a par value of $10,000 paying 8 per cent, $800.

In 1932 the family income had been reduced as follows: The salary was cut 10 per cent, and $2,000 worth of bonds were in default. The stocks which had been paying on an average of 8 per cent dividends in 1929 were averaging 6 per cent, bringing in $600 money income.

Family C: In 1929 the husband was employed as a carpenter drawing a dollar an hour for a 44-hour week. He was able to find employment for 40 weeks out of the year. The family had savings to the amount of $500 in the local savings bank paying 3 per cent interest, and $2,500 worth of stock in the local building and loan association paying 6 per cent.

In 1932 he was able to secure 20 weeks of work, 40 hours a week, at 50 cents an hour. The building and loan had reduced its interest rate to 3 per cent and was allowing no withdrawals of principal. The family had used up its savings deposit shortly before the bank moratorium. The wife in this family was able to secure part-time employment washing dishes in a restaurant 3 hours a day for 50 cents a day and 1 meal. Her work lasts 10 months out of the year.

9. During a period of marked business recovery the total of factory pay rolls was increased several billion dollars. During this same period the average wages of the individual workers in manufacturing remained approximately the same. Which is most significant from the point of view of family finance, the increase in the amount going to wage workers as a group, or the amount of the pay check of the individual worker? Why?

10. (a) Compare in detail the money incomes of the following families. (b) If they lived in your community, what social-use income would be available with which to supplement their other incomes?

Family A: A man, age 26, and his wife, age 25, have been married 3 years. The husband is a college graduate. His wife attended a teachers college for 3 years, receiving a life certificate entitling her to teach home economics in the state of Michigan. He is employed as a teller in a bank at a salary of $1,800 a year. His wife taught for some years in the junior high school but was dropped from her position when the school board passed a ruling barring married teachers from the schools.

They are living in a 4-room furnished apartment, for which they are paying $35 a month. This includes water, gas, electricity, heat, hot water, telephone, garbage removal, and a garage for their car. The family owns a light coupe 5 years old, which they purchased 3 years ago for $300. Operating expenses on the car, including license and insurance, run not far from $15 a month.

They have no investments, other than a savings account amounting to $200, to which they have been adding about $50 a year. The husband is carrying $2,500 of ordinary life insurance, on which the premium is $50 a year.

Family B: A man and his wife, age 27 and 25 years, have been married for 2 years. Both are college graduates. The husband is a salesman, earning about $2,400 a year. The company furnishes him with a car. The family does not own its own home or furniture. They have been planning to buy furniture and a home of their own as soon as they are able. They have no other income or investments except the expectation that the husband will eventually inherit a half interest in a farm assessed at a value of $18,000, which is yielding no net income at the present time.

Family C: A man, age 47, his wife, age 45, and 4 children—2 boys, age 16 and 12, and 2 girls, age 18 and 13. The father and mother are both high school graduates. The father is employed as a bookkeeper at a salary of $2,200 a year. His salary is supplemented by the earnings of the older boy, which amount to $200 a year. The family owns its own home, which it purchased 20 years ago for $2,500. It is now worth about $3,000. The head of the family is carrying $3,000 worth of life insurance, and sickness and accident insurance paying $25 a week. The house and furnishings are insured for $1,500. They have a savings account of $400 drawing 3 per cent interest.

Family D: A man and his wife, each a little over 50 years of age. The head of the family is a college professor with a Ph.D. degree, and his wife is a college graduate. His salary is $4,500 a year. They have a son and daughter, both of whom have graduated from college. The son has a law degree, and has just passed the bar examinations and accepted a position with a law firm in a neighboring city. The daughter is teaching in a high school in another town. This family owns its own home, worth $7,500, subject to mortgage for $2,500 incurred to provide funds for the education of the children. They own a car 4 years old, purchased 3 years ago for $700. The man is carrying an ordinary life insurance policy for $10,000.

11. Summarize briefly all the possible ways for increasing the real income of the members of the ordinary family. What costs are incurred in each case? How far is it wise for a family to go in increasing its real income by each of these means?

REFERENCES

Andrews, B. R., *Economics of the Household*, Ch. II, pp. 33-73 in 1923 edition; Ch. IV, in 1935 edition. The Macmillan Co., New York, 1923 and 1935.

An excellent analysis of the sources of the family's real income.

King, W. I., *The National Income and Its Purchasing Power*. National Bureau of Economic Research, New York, 1930.

A comprehensive analysis of the sources and distribution of the national income. One of a series of publications of the National Bureau of Economic Research, growing out of their study of the national income. The student of family management and finance should keep in touch with their current publications on incomes.

Kyrk, Hazel, *Economic Problems of the Family*, Chs. VII-XII, pp. 108-227. Harper and Bros., New York, 1933.

An excellent analysis of the family income. A consideration of the advantages and objections to contribution to the family's money income by the wife and by the children, and a thorough analysis of the adequacy of family incomes for the support of a desirable standard for American families.

Monroe, Day, *Chicago Families*, Chs. VII and VIII, and Ch. IX, pp. 244 ff. University of Chicago Press, Chicago, 1932.

Miss Monroe's study of Chicago families, based upon the 1920 census, contains some excellent analyses of the sources of family income, and some interesting observations concerning the adequacy of these incomes for family support.

National Income, 1929-1932. A Report on the National Income by the Department of Commerce, published as 73rd Congress, 2nd Session, Senate Document No. 124. United States Government Printing Office, Washington, D. C., 1934.

A comprehensive analysis of the national income, its sources and its distribution for the years 1929-1932. Available at the Government Printing Office at low cost.

Nystrom, P. H., *Economic Principles of Consumption*, Chs. VII and VIII, pp. 128-184. The Ronald Press Co., New York, 1929.

An interesting analysis of the amount and distribution of wealth and income in the United States.

Waite, W. C., *Economics of Consumption*, Ch. III, pp. 21-34. McGraw-Hill Book Co., Inc., New York, 1928.

A concise but stimulating discussion. Contains an interesting analysis of the causes and results of the inequalities of money income.

Recent Statistics

For later statistics on *national income* see *The Statistical Abstract of the United States* for the current year, the latest available publication of the Department of Commerce entitled *National Income 1929-(to date)*, and recent publications of the National Bureau of Economic Research.

For later statistics on *family income:* for 1929, see Leven, M., Moulton, H. G., and Warburton, C., *America's Capacity to Consume,* The Brookings Institution, Washington, D. C., 1934.

For 1935-36, see National Resources Committee, *Consumer Incomes in the United States,* United States Government Printing Office, Washington, D. C., 1938. The estimates in this report have been developed from data gathered in connection with the Consumer Purchase Study conducted in 1935 and 1936. For more detailed analysis of the Consumer Purchase Study material, see publications of the Bureau of Labor Statistics (for families living in cities of 8,000 and over) and of the Bureau of Home Economics (for families living in cities of less than 8,000, in villages and in the open country).

No two studies of national income agree exactly on their estimates. In part this is due to the unwieldy nature of the material involved, and in part to differences in definition of income.

No two studies of family income agree exactly on their estimates, for the same reason. In using estimates of family income from any source it is important to check the author's definition of both *families* and *family income*.

PART II

MAKING THE MOST OF THE FAMILY'S RESOURCES

CHAPTER IV

THE IMPORTANCE OF CHOICE IN THE AMERICAN ECONOMY

Scarcity or abundance? Much has been written and said in recent years about the impending change from an economy of scarcity to an economy of abundance. Since the close of the World War, agriculture has been plagued with surplus. In the early 1930's, we found ourselves possessed of an apparent surplus of millions of bushels of wheat and thousands of bales of cotton. We had an automobile industry with a productive capacity of over five million cars a year, though we ordinarily needed to buy only a little over four millions. We had shoe factories enough to make more shoes than we had ever worn out in one year. "No wonder," said the pessimists, "that we are confronted with business without a buyer."

And yet, for most of us, there has been no surplus. Even at the peak of our productive efforts there has never been available for everyone even a reasonable abundance of the very things of which we are said to have too much. In the face of the existence of all this potential productive capacity there are too many families without enough to eat, too many families without enough to wear, too many families trying to make the old car do one more year. There are too many families living in scarcely habitable homes, and too many families with long lists of essential and desirable commodities they are unable to buy.

For many years, then, we have been struggling with the problem of personal scarcity in the face of potential surplus. How has this situation developed? And how can we resolve our dilemma?

The situation has developed because all of us, producers and consumers alike, are yet given to thinking in terms of a situation of scarcity. We have been trying to work out our problems from the point of view of what is good for business, forgetting that even in an economy of scarcity, the only reason business developed was because it could satisfy the wants of the consumer better than he could satisfy them for himself. We have not as yet, either as producers or consumers, realized the strategic position which the consumer is coming to hold as we enter into a situation of abundance.

And how can we resolve our dilemma? On the one hand, as producers, we must realize clearly that if we are to remain in business, either as employers or as workers, it is our job to satisfy as completely and as economically as we can the wants of consumers. On the other hand, as consumers, we must all of us develop as rapidly as we can the capacity for intelligent choice, so that by our selection from the variety of products offered us by producers, we may direct industry into those channels which will make possible the satisfaction of the largest number of the most important of consumers' wants.

This is no easy task. Nor is it a task capable of early accomplishment. Nevertheless, to whatever extent we are able to move in this direction, to that extent are we making available some part of our ultimate democratic ideal, the good life for all.

The new problem of the producer. In a situation of abundance, the problem of the producer is no longer primarily technological. He is no longer in a position in which he can concentrate entirely upon the development of improved means of turning out commodities without thought as to their market. Today his primary problem is to estimate consumer demand, and then to direct his productive facilities toward the maximizing of the satisfaction of consumers' wants. His problem is no longer only "What can I do best as a producer?"; rather, it is "What can I do which will satisfy a consumer's wants better and more economically than either he or someone else can satisfy them for him?"

For many years following the Industrial Revolution, a manufacturer could concentrate upon the technological problems of production. If he could turn out a satisfactory product he was sure of a market for it. If he could produce it at any reasonable cost, he could sell it at a profit. The problem of the merchant in these early years was more that of finding and financing the purchase of merchandise of reasonably good quality which could be sold at a fair price than it was of finding out the personal preferences of his customers.

By the late 1880's and early 1890's the productive capacity of the country in many basic industries had increased to the point which marked the beginning of the shift from the seller's market of the nineteenth century to the buyer's market of the twentieth century.

Since that time, it has been increasingly true that as the technical problems of production become easier to solve, the problem of finding a market becomes more difficult. Every recurring business depression makes it increasingly evident that the permanently successful business concern not only must be able to produce efficiently, but also must be able to estimate accurately and satisfy effectively and economically the wants of large bodies of consumers. In order that they may have always available in the market a reasonably generous selection of the goods and services consumers demand, alert and progressive business concerns are already devoting an increasing amount of time and money to the analysis of the market for their product.

If producers are to be able to satisfy the great variety of wants of the great variety of American consumers, they must add to their present technical training in production methods and efficient management, more through training in the technique of demand prediction. And since accuracy in the prediction of consumer demand depends in large degree upon the regularity and dependability of consumer choice, it is highly important that, at the same time, all of us as consumers develop as rapidly as possible the capacity for intelligent choice.

What is intelligent consumer choice? By intelligent choice, ordinarily we mean reasoned choice. Reasoned choice involves: (1) accurate and adequate information as to all available alternatives; (2) the weighing of the advantages and disadvantages of all possible courses of procedure; and (3) decision on the basis of the evidence at hand.

But not all choice is reasoned choice. There is not time for the individual consumer to make all his decisions only after careful consideration of all possible alternatives. Nor would his wants be best satisfied if he did. Wants are emotional in character, rather than rational. Intelligent choice must make allowance for the emotional as well as for the reasoned elements in want satisfaction. There is a place for instinct, for emotion, and even for habit in intelligent choice. Intelligent choice involves the decision as to what should be decided upon a reasoned basis, what upon an emotional basis, and what upon a habitual basis. Choice is intelligent if it decides upon a reasoned basis that which is best decided by reason, and decides upon an emotional or instinctive basis that which involves primarily instinctive and emotional elements. Intelligent choice involves primarily keeping each basis for choice in its proper place.

The place for choice on an emotional basis. There are many cases in which it is legitimate for a person to want what he wants just because he wants it. One prefers his roast beef well done, another prefers it rare, and another, being a conservative soul, prefers it medium. One person prefers a gaily colored automobile. Another prefers his to be the conventional black. One person prefers a garden full of old-fashioned flowers. Another prefers the more sedate green of sweeping lawns and ordered shrubbery.

Books, pictures, art objects of all kinds, even many articles of furniture and food and clothing, are purchased largely for their emotional values. Wherever taste and appreciation are significant elements in the satisfaction to be secured, there is a legitimate place for choice on an emotional basis. Choice is intelligent if it recognizes that such choices are being made upon an emotional or instinctive basis. Choice is intelligent if reason indicates that in this case or in that case emotional appeal is a legitimate basis for choice.

The danger of rationalization. It is, however, important to guard against the rationalization of these emotional preferences. There is a fundamental distinction between reason and rationalization. Reason considers all possible alternatives first, and decides upon a course of action only after all the evidence bearing on the case is in. Rationalization, on the other hand, decides what is to be done on a purely emotional basis, and after the decision is made, seeks what seem to be good reasons to support the already determined decision. Rationalization admits only the favorable evidence. Arguments to the contrary are not given a hearing.

Intelligent choice should be deliberately reasoned or deliberately emotional. In some cases it should be deliberately reasoned, but with proper allowance for the instinctive and emotional factors as well as the reasonable elements that are involved. Choice is not intelligent if it is made, even unknowingly, on some basis other than the reasons which are advanced.

For example, buying a dress on the basis of intelligent choice might proceed something like this: A woman decides she needs a new dress. Her sister is to be married in June, and she will be invited to many afternoon functions. She must have suitable clothing to wear. With the money she has available for clothing, she can spend not more than $25 for her afternoon outfit. This must provide dress, hat, shoes, and all the necessary accessories. She canvasses the possibilities of her present wardrobe, makes a list of what she must buy, and then sets out to select a dress which must cost not more than $10. Keeping in mind the number of times she must wear the dress and the amount she can afford to pay, she selects the dress on the basis of her personal preferences. Even though she passes by one dress made of unusually good material and selects another of less durable goods and only reasonably good workmanship, because it has just the color which appeals to her color sense and a style which seems to her to be in unusually good taste, she is still choosing her dress intelligently.

Suppose, however, she is down town shopping with a friend. She sees a dress and decides she must have it, not because she needs it particularly, but simply because she likes it. She then thinks of several reasons why she ought to buy it, giving no thought to other things she might buy with her money. In this case she is choosing on the basis of rationalization.

Clever merchandising in many cases deliberately stimulates rationalization. Goods are presented so as to give them the greatest possible emotional appeal. By display, by advertising, and by clever salesmanship, the favorable arguments are so presented that the consumer buys without realizing that he has considered only part of the facts and that his decision is being made on the basis of rationalization, rather than of reasoned choice.

The consumer who would choose intelligently must always be on his guard against such attempts to stimulate choice on an unconsidered emotional basis. He should make many purely emotional choices, but he can do so safely only if he sets for himself definite limits within which he recognizes the legitimacy of emotional choice.

The place of fashion in choice. Fashion has been defined as the prevailing style. Fashion passes through recurrent cycles. A new style catches the interest of the consumer. First the curious and the daring, then the more conservative, adopt the new style. It reaches the peak of its popularity. Then the more original, those who want to be distinctive, and those who were first to adopt it, tiring of the present style, look for something different, find a satisfactory substitute, and the decline of the old fashion and the rise of a new are soon under way.

Some styles remain in fashion a long time, and others for a comparatively short period. But whether in the field of clothing, where fashions may change four or five times a year, or in the field of housing, where a style may remain current for as much as a decade, fashion implies change. What is predominantly in favor today will give place to something else predominantly in favor tomorrow.

Our discussion of fashion will be more intelligent if we have clearly in mind a few definitions of terms which are sometimes confused with fashion. *Style* is a characteristic or distinctive method of expression, presentation, or conception in the field of some art. *Mode* is a synonym for fashion. *Fad* is a miniature fashion in some unimportant matter or detail. If a fad becomes important or far-reaching, it becomes a fashion. *Craze* is a fad or fashion that is accompanied by much excitement or emotion. *Taste* is the ability to discern and appreciate what is beautiful and appropriate. *Good taste* is, essentially, making the most artistic use of current fashions. *Fashion cycle* is the rise, culmination, and decline of the popular acceptance of a style.[1]

Why fashion is desirable. From the consumer's viewpoint, the continuing change in styles which fashion brings has a number of advantages. Fashion relieves monotony, provides variety, lifts life above dull routine. Following the current fashion relieves the individual of the necessity of deciding along just what lines variety can best be secured. The constantly recurring fashion cycle facilitates the introduction of new and improved means of satisfying wants. Observation of the current fashion is an aid to social recognition. It gives evidence of up-to-dateness and of conformity to the standards of a social group.

Some criticisms of fashion. On the other hand, fashion is frequently criticized because it results in the adoption of many styles which are ugly, impractical, or in poor taste. Fashion is said to be expensive and wasteful. It is criticized because it leads to the discarding of many things before they are worn out, and because it adds unnecessarily to production costs by necessitating frequent changes of models.

Why fashion is expensive. It is true that in many cases fashion is expensive. It is the nature of fashion to place more em-

---

[1] For further discussion of fashion, see P. H. Nystrom, *Economics of Fashion*, especially Chs. I-VIII. The Ronald Press Co., New York, 1928.

phasis upon temporary than upon lasting values. Fashion assumes frequent change, early replacement, and a high rate of obsolescence. Fashion plays a large part in the field of conspicuous consumption, and is closely related to pecuniary emulation. Fashion accepts styles that are in favor among the well-to-do, styles which appear to be expensive. As a result, fashion is ordinarily considered to involve generous expenditure. Being in fashion is usually considered an evidence of generous means.

How to be fashionable at low cost. But fashion is not necessarily expensive. Fashion covers a wide range of commodities. To be fashionable in every respect does cost money. At the same time, there are many ways in which a family can observe the current fashion at little or no additional expense. The family with only a little extra money to spend may choose the inexpensive and avoid the expensive ways of being up-to-date.

A generation ago, only the well-to-do could afford to discard well-made clothing before it was worn out, simply to have the latest style. In recent years, mass production of fashionable clothes from inexpensive materials has enabled people with small incomes to dress fashionably.

A family that can get efficient service from an automobile for three or four years must pay much more for its transportation if it keeps up-to-date by replacing its car every year. A family that uses its automobile enough every year to justify annual replacement can observe the current fashion in motor cars at little or no additional expense.

A family that plans to keep in fashion in its shelter, by owning its own home, and selling and moving every time the fashion in neighborhoods or architectural styles changes will find that keeping in fashion involves heavy expense. If, however, a family is planning to build a new home, by paying a little more for a lot in a fashionable neighborhood and building in the current style, it can be in fashion for a number of years with but little additional outlay.

The principle involved seems to be this: The higher-priced and more durable the commodities bought on a fashion basis, the more expensive is the frequent change necessitated by fashion. Fashion is expensive in the case of high-priced goods, in the case of goods which are otherwise purchased only at considerable intervals, and in the case of goods in which obsolescence exceeds depreciation. Fashion is not expensive in the case of articles which sell at a low price, or which must be replaced at frequent intervals, or which wear out before they go out of style.

It is, then, one function of intelligent choice to decide upon the extent to which a family can afford to observe the dictates of fashion in its purchases and in its manner of life. The family should decide on a reasoned basis as to the fields in which it is worth while to observe the current fashion, and the fields in which it is better to emphasize the more permanent values of durability and comfort and taste.

The place of habit in choice. If fashion is a convenient device helping to satisfy variety in consumption, so habit is a device for economizing the energy required in making frequently repeated decisions or choices. The formation of buying habits is an important part of intelligent choice. There are many choices which once carefully thought through and decided can be safely repeated every time a similar decision must be made.

For example, the housewife may need to decide what brand of butter the family shall use. She canvasses the brands of butter available. She finds out all that she can about each one, and may even spend some time studying what makes butter good. Then she selects from the kinds of butter available in the market the brand that suits her family best. She may spend several hours, scattered through several weeks, studying and sampling, before she makes her decision. But once the decision is made, no further time need be spent deciding what brand of butter to buy. She forms the habit of asking for the chosen brand.

What is included in habits of choice? Habits of choice usually include what and how much to get, where and how to get it, and how much to pay for it. They should also include how long to allow the original decision to stand as a habit, and the type of circumstances which warrant bringing the matter up for reasoned reconsideration.

For example, a housewife, after a careful consideration of the dietetic needs of her family, decides that her family should use not less than three quarts of fresh milk a day. She investigates the ratings of the local dairymen and decides upon the creamery she will patronize. How long should she allow this habit to stand? What sort of circumstances should bring the matter up for reasoned re-consideration?

In the first place, she should watch the quality of the milk. Is it always uniform? Or is the cream line and the keeping quality dropping off a bit? What do the monthly reports show about the rating of the dairy? Is it keeping its bacteria count down? Is its record good in other respects? Does the service continue to be as dependable as when she was buying milk on trial? And what about the price? If there is a general advance in milk prices without a corresponding increase in her family's income, she may find it wise to make some changes in her milk supply, supplementing the whole milk for the children with less expensive evaporated milk or dried skim milk for use in cooking. Or, if there is announced some discovery which indicates that more or less milk is necessary in the diet, she should first consider the scientific accuracy of the new theory, and then make the necessary readjustments in her milk-buying habits.

It is the part of intelligent choice to make wise use of habit. This wise use involves the original intelligent choice, and the setting of reasonable limits within which choice will be allowed to continue on a habit basis. The proper use of habit in choice will save mental wear and tear by reducing the number of daily conscious choices. It will settle each recurring decision for some time. It will leave time for more careful consideration of current choices than would otherwise be possible.

Does it do any good to try to choose intelligently? Many people are inclined to ask whether it does any good for the consumer to try to choose intelligently. Is not the consumer still largely at the mercy of the producer? Is it not true today, even as it was true before the development of our modern facilities for pro-duction, that the great body of consumers with moderate means must buy whatever is to be found in the market, pay the price that the producer demands, and make the best they can of a situation of per-sonal scarcity? Is there, after all, any essential difference, as far as the consumer is concerned, between a situation of actual scarcity and a situation of personal scarcity in the face of potential surplus?

The new strategic advantage of the consumer. According to traditional economic theory, the price of any good determined under competitive market conditions is fixed by supply and demand at a point at which the price is at the same time equal, on the one hand, to the marginal utility of the good to the consumer, and, on the other, to the cost of production of the marginal producer.[2] This means that if the price were any higher, producers could not find buyers for all the goods they would be willing to make at the higher price. If prices were lower, consumers would not be able to get all the goods they would be willing to buy at the lower prices.

This theory holds in either a seller's or a buyer's market, in a situation either of scarcity or of abundance, but with these differences: In a scarcity situation, there is not the means available to supply all or nearly all that is wanted of any commodity. The producer makes what he is able. The consumer satisfies his wants as best he can with whatever the producer turns out. The producer finds it comparatively easy to dispose of all his product at a price equal to or greater than his cost of production, for there are large numbers of consumers with unsatisfied wants for all sorts of commodities. The consumers who are willing and able to pay the producer's price get the commodities, and the rest do without.

In a situation of abundance, on the other hand, there is plenty of productive capacity, either actual or potential, to supply all that is wanted of a commodity. The producer sells what he can, and the consumer buys what best satisfies his wants. The consumer finds the market well supplied with a wide variety of commodities and services which are offered for sale at prices within his means. There are many producers with unused productive capacity, operating under conditions of decreasing costs, who are able and eager to produce for him whatever he is willing to pay for. Those producers who are able to produce at a price the consumer is willing to pay get the business. The other producers must do without.

In an economy of abundance, then, instead of the consumer adjusting his consumption to what the producer is able to make, the producer must adjust his output to the amount and sort of commodities which he can produce at prices the consumer is willing to pay. In an economy of abundance, the forces of supply and demand, instead of directing the limited available supply of a commodity into

---

[2] By definition, marginal utility means the utility to the consumer of any one unit in his available stock of a given commodity. It is what he would lose in ability to satisfy his want for that good, if he had one less unit of it. Similarly, by definition, the marginal producer is the producer who can just afford to stay in business at present prices. He would be forced to go out of business should prices fall. For further discussion of the theory of prices, see any standard text on economic theory.

the hands of those consumers who are willing and able to pay the highest prices, direct the limited demand for a commodity into the hands of those producers who can provide that commodity in the most desirable qualities at the most favorable prices.

The increasing importance of intelligent choice. Consumer choice takes on new significance as we approach an economy of abundance. Consumer choice is no longer primarily concerned with making the best of the limited means at our disposal; rather, it is concerned with the attainment of what the individual or family feels represents for it the good life. Intelligent consumer choice, more than any other single factor, is the basis for improving the quality of family life, the means for increasing the satisfaction secured by each member of the family group. The degree to which each individual, each family, is able to attain wisdom in consumer choice will determine largely the degree to which that individual or that family can progress toward the ideal of the good life.

At the same time, the consumer by his choices is directing the development of our whole economic system. Every time he decides to buy one thing instead of another, every time he decides to buy something in the market instead of producing it for himself at home, the consumer is shaping the course of industry. By intelligent choice the consumer may guide the development of our productive organization along the lines which will facilitate maximum service to the consumer.

Costs and choices. In making his choices, the consumer must always keep in mind the fact that even in a situation of abundance, it is impossible to get something for nothing. The continued existence of a situation of abundance depends upon our continuing to produce. Unless each consumer adds to the stock of goods and services available for consumption as much as he withdraws for his own use, it will not be long before we will find ourselves once more in a situation not only of personal but of actual scarcity. We can increase the amount of goods available for us to use only if each one of us does his part in adding not only the equivalent of what he uses, but a little more than he uses.

Therefore, whenever and whatever the consumer chooses, he must be willing to pay all the costs that are incurred in its production. Someone must pay them. If the consumer does not pay them directly in the price he pays for the goods, he will pay them indirectly in the form of taxes for poor relief, in expenses for the maintenance of injured workers, or in expenditures for public health.

On the other hand, the producer must recognize that the consumer will and should scrutinize all the costs entering into the price of the article he buys. No cost is legitimate unless it increases by an equal amount the capacity of the good to satisfy the wants of the ultimate consumer. If bakers can provide fresh bread by one delivery a day at the grocer's, then the additional cost of two deliveries is unjustifiable. If, however, some consumers insist upon having their bread within four hours of the time it leaves the oven, they must be willing to pay the higher cost. But no baker has a right to expect the majority of consumers to pay for a service they do not want. Nor can he expect to get their business if he refuses a service they are willing to pay for. If collection and delivery add 20 per cent to the cost of dry cleaning, the family that uses delivery service should expect to pay for it. But, if dry cleaning can be done for 20 per cent less on a cash-and-carry basis, consumers who bring in and call for their own clothing cannot be expected to pay delivered prices.

The effect of income on choice. It sometimes seems to the individual or the family with a small income that there is for them very little opportunity for choice. They must purchase a minimum of necessities at the lowest possible price. They have little or nothing to spend for the sort of thing one buys just because he likes it.

They know that every time they make an expenditure they are choosing. It is not so clear that every time they refrain from spending they are also exercising choice. The person who spends makes a positive choice. By so doing he helps determine what is to be produced. The person who refrains from spending makes a negative choice. By his refusal to buy he helps set the limit to the price the producer can charge and to the quantity he can sell.

In an economy of scarcity, the producer is primarily concerned with the man who makes the positive choices. He is interested in making things for the man who is willing to pay the price. He is but little concerned with the man who decides not to buy, for he knows that if one man does not buy, another will.

In an economy of abundance, on the other hand, most producers have unused productive capacity on their hands. For this reason it is entirely possible for consumers to get along without any of the product of any one producer. Every producer must take care not to get too many of the consumer's negative votes. In our present situation, the man with low income is, because of his negative choices, fully as effective as is the man with more money who makes a larger number of positive choices.

The consumer's three alternatives. The strategic position of the consumer is still further strengthened by the fact that in an economy of abundance even the person of rather limited means is no longer dependent upon the preferences of any one producer, for he can satisfy his wants in a variety of ways. Usually he thinks first of the possibility of purchase in the market. If a commodity or a service is not available in the market in the qualities and quantities he desires, or if the price is too high, then there is the possibility of making or doing for himself at home. And, finally, if there are some things which no one provides in the market, and which he does not feel qualified to undertake by himself, these may be provided by collective action, by spending his bit with others.

For example, every family must have bread. It can buy freshly baked bread, it can buy day-old bread, or it can buy or raise the materials and bake the bread in the home. Similarly, every family must have clothing. The market provides clothing in a wide range of qualities and materials at a variety of prices. And if these market offerings are not satisfactory, there is the possibility of buying materials and making clothing. Likewise, a family wants adequate educational opportunities for its children. The cost of a qualified tutor is prohibitive. By combining with its neighbors to organize and support a public school it can get excellent educational opportunities at moderate cost.

The choices of the necessitous buyer. In many lines there are some people, and in a few lines there are many people, who cannot take advantage of these alternatives. They must buy some of the commodities that are offered them, and must pay whatever price is asked. Is there anything to prevent the producer in these cases from raising his price to exorbitant levels? If there is great scarcity, or if one producer has a monopoly of the entire supply of a commodity, it may be possible for him to exact excessive prices from necessitous buyers. But in a situation in which there is abundant productive capacity—in fact, in any situation in which there is more capacity than is required to supply the wants of the man who must buy—prices to the necessitous buyer are determined by what the non-necessitous or marginal buyer is willing to pay.

Most people, for example, will pay high prices for wheat and for wheat products rather than go without. In time of acute shortage, such as existed during the World War, wheat prices rise to alarming heights. But ordinarily, when there is plenty of food to go around, bread sells for a nominal price, in spite of the fact that there are many necessitous buyers to be served. The people who must pay benefit from the negative choices of the people who will buy only if they are provided with good quality and good service at a fair price.

Consumer choice in the American economy. Consumer choice, then, no longer involves only decisions as to how to make the most of the limited resources at our disposal. Rather, we may begin by deciding on the basis of our varied interests, of our individual tastes, of our personal and social background, which of a long list of possible wants it will be most worth while to try to satisfy. In making such a decision, it is important to give proper place to present comforts and luxuries and to future necessities and luxuries as well. When we have decided upon the relative importance of the wants to be satisfied, the next step is to select the best means of satisfying them. When we have decided upon the commodities and services we desire, we must still choose between the methods by which they can be provided for us.

The greater the abundance of goods and services offered for our consideration by producers, and the greater the variety of ways in which we can satisfy our wants, the more complicated become our problems as consumers, and at the same time, the more freedom we have in the matter of personal choices.

Our problem, then, is to make our choices as consumers, whether we are choosing wants to satisfy, or the ways and means by which to satisfy them, in the way which provides the largest total of the highest quality of satisfaction of the family's most important wants.

QUESTIONS

1. Give some examples from your own experience of personal scarcity in the face of potential surplus.
2. How do you account for the fact that there is a surplus of fluid milk on the farm and a personal scarcity of milk in many families in the city? Could this situation be corrected by the education of families as

to the importance of plenty of milk in the diet?   By opening milk stations to which families not now buying milk could come to get milk at lower costs?

3. Which of the following items do you choose primarily on the basis of fashion, of habit, of emotion, of reasoned choice: a new hat, an automobile, a home, a loaf of bread, a pair of shoes, a box of candy, a radio, gasoline for your car, an easy chair, a pound of coffee, a moving picture program, a kitchen stove, new tires for your automobile, meat for a Sunday dinner, a fountain pen, a magazine, table linen, soap, a radio program, an engagement ring, a picture for your room?

4. Bring to class a current advertisement designed to stimulate reasoned choice, and another designed to stimulate rationalization by the consumer.   Which was more difficult to find?   Why?

5. From the consumer's viewpoint, under what conditions, if any, is a merchant justified in using sales methods which stimulate rationalization on the part of the consumer?   Could he accomplish equally good results by an appeal to reasoned choice?   If the consumer finds that a merchant with whom he is dealing is placing undue emphasis upon rationalization, making it difficult for him to exercise intelligent and reasoned choice, what can the consumer do about it?

6. What advantages do you or your family secure from observing current fashions?   In what fields of choice do you pay special attention to fashion?   Name three or four specific items in which you can afford to sacrifice up-to-dateness to economy.   Give two or three examples of cases in which you can observe the current fashion at little or no additional expense.

7. Name three specific items which you choose largely as a matter of habit. How did you develop each of these habits?   Could you by breaking any of these habits increase the total of the wants you are able to satisfy? Why or why not?

8. Make a list of items which you have found it is good policy to choose on an habitual basis.   In each case, which of the following should be included in the habitual procedure: the article, the brand to purchase, the amount of the purchase, the place of purchase, the time of purchase, the price to pay?   How long should each of these habits be allowed to stand without reconsideration?   In each case, what specific circumstances would justify the reconsideration of the buying habit?

9. In 1934, in order to provide employment for unemployed garment workers, the cotton garment industry was requested to reduce workers' hours from 40 to 36 per week without reducing their weekly earnings. The commission investigating labor conditions and costs found that it would increase the cost of the garments not over 10 per cent.   From

the consumer's viewpoint, is this cost justifiable? Does it or does it not add anything to the utility of the garments to have them made by workers working only 36 hours a week? How would such a price increase affect your choices of clothing? Will you buy just as many garments, and pay 10 per cent more for them? Or will you buy 10 per cent fewer garments? Or will you make some reduction in other items of your expenditure? What factors must be taken into consideration if you choose intelligently in this matter?

10. Keeping in mind the fact that the cost of advertising is usually spread over a large volume of production, so that the cost per unit is very low, select two advertisements which you feel help the consumer enough in satisfying his wants to justify their cost. Bring in two others that from the consumer's viewpoint are an unnecessary expense.

11. Give some examples of items for which you are entirely dependent upon some one producer; of items which can be secured in the market from a number of sources; of items which you can produce for yourself; of items which are ordinarily secured by collective expenditure.

12. "The greater the variety of ways by which we can satisfy our wants the more complicated become our problems as consumers." Do you agree? Why or why not? Give some original examples to support your position.

REFERENCES

Hoyt, Elizabeth E., *The Consumption of Wealth*, Part IV, Chs. XV-XX, pp. 155-218. The Macmillan Co., New York, 1928.

A discussion of some ways by which the consumer can control his consumption in the interest of better living. Miss Hoyt's whole work is worth reading. Her discussion provides an excellent background for improved consumer choice.

Nystrom, P. H., *Economics of Fashion*, Chs. I-VIII, pp. 3-161. The Ronald Press Co., New York, 1928.

An excellent discussion of the theory of fashion.

Nystrom, P. H., *Economic Principles of Consumption*, Ch. IV, pp. 51-72. The Ronald Press Co., New York, 1929.

A concise discussion of a number of the factors which control or modify consumer choice.

Reid, Margaret G., *Economics of Household Production*, Ch. XIII, pp. 209-215. John Wiley and Sons, Inc., New York, 1934.

A brief but pointed analysis of the family's problems of choice. It suggests that most families in their pursuit of more commodities overlook the existence of a wider range of possible choices which may add to the richness of living.

CHAPTER V

SATISFYING WANTS BY WISE PURCHASE
IN THE MARKET

The problem of the consumer-buyer. As we approach a situation of abundance, the varied and ever-lengthening list of goods which the family must buy makes the problem of the modern buyer increasingly difficult. The increase in our productive capacity is putting on the market every year not only long lists of new commodities, but also a bewildering array of variations in the things families are accustomed to buy. We are all familiar with cotton that looks like linen, and cotton that looks like wool. There are rayon and bemberg and acetates that look like silk. There are new weaves in most of these materials which combine varying proportions of silk and rayon, of cotton and wool, until even the professional buyer trained by years of experience in his trade finds it almost impossible to keep pace with the developments in even a rather limited field. How much more complicated, then, is the problem of the consumer-buyer, who wishes to select intelligently the long and varied list of commodities which the modern family needs.

The consumer-buyer vs. the commercial buyer. The situation of the consumer-buyer is fundamentally different from that of the commercial buyer. The consumer-buyer is buying goods for his own use, while the commercial buyer is buying commodities for re-sale. Ordinarily the commercial buyer must buy only a rather narrowly specialized line of goods. He is paid to spend most of his time studying the market offerings in his special field. He buys on a scale large enough so that he can afford to spend time and money testing the commodities he buys. He buys at frequent intervals, and can therefore profit by his past experience.

The consumer-buyer, on the other hand, must buy a great variety of goods. Within the family only a limited degree of specialization in buying is possible. There are some things which the man of the house usually buys, but the greater part of the buying in most families is done by the housewife. For the consumer-buyer, buying is only one of many tasks. Most of the family's purchases are small in scale. Some items are bought at frequent intervals, others once or twice a year, others only once in a lifetime. It is seldom possible for the consumer-buyer to apply any scientific tests to determine the quality of the commodities he is purchasing. In many cases he buys an article so seldom that he has no chance to profit by past experience. Compared with the specialized commercial buyer, the consumer-buyer seems very limited in experience, in information, and in judgment of the qualities of the goods he must buy. There is just one point at which the consumer-buyer has an advantage. He has first-hand knowledge of the purpose the goods must serve, which is something that the commercial buyer, buying goods for resale, can never have.

The nature of the market. The consumer-buyer is at a further disadvantage because the present marketing system has grown up along lines determined mainly by producers who have something to sell. Even the retailer, who talks a great deal about the service he is rendering to the consumer, is inclined to consider himself primarily a salesman for the manufacturer or wholesaler, rather than a purchasing agent for the consumer.

From the viewpoint of the consumer-buyer, a good market should offer for sale at a fair price a wide variety of goods and services from which he can easily select the article or articles which exactly satisfy his needs. The market should be so organized as to save his time and energy, and to reduce to a minimum the chance for mistakes in choice. The present marketing system is reasonably adequate both in the range of goods offered and in marketing services for saving the buyer's time and energy. In fact, the service which some retailers offer is so generous that it is frequently almost impossible for the consumer-buyer to purchase the goods he wants without paying for expensive and often unnecessary services. But the present market is obviously and admittedly inadequate in devices which will eliminate mistakes in selection. While there are a few exceptions, most merchants still look upon it as their job to persuade consumers to want what they happen to have on their shelves, rather than to keep available for them what will best suit their needs.

Few reputable business men would admit that they resort to deliberate falsehood in order to make a sale, but many business men maintain that people do not want to know what they are buying.

They insist that girls who cannot afford to buy coats made from expensive furs will be better satisfied with a rabbit coat if they are told that it is Hudson seal. They insist that milady gets more enjoyment out of a ten-cent cake of perfumed soap if she pays half a dollar for it. The many instances of items no one would buy at a low price selling very well at a higher price would seem to prove their point.

But what most of these business men overlook is the fact that their examples are usually taken from the field of conspicuous consumption. In almost every case, the consumer wants to be told something is better than it actually is only when he is buying a luxury that he knows he cannot afford. However, when it comes to the purchase of the rank and file of staple commodities, most buyers prefer to know what they are buying. When they buy canned fruits and canned vegetables, they want to know both the quantity and the quality in the can. When they buy sheets and pillow cases, they want cotton and not sizing. Even the most enthusiastic advocates of glamorous advertising do not dare maintain that people who sleep under flimsy cotton blankets will somehow be kept warm if they can only be made to believe that the blankets are all wool.

The law of sales has grown up to safeguard the business man rather than the consumer-buyer. While there is no legal basis for deliberate deception of the buyer, the law assumes an equality of knowledge on the part of buyer and seller which may be justified in the case of the commercial buyer, but is contrary to fact as far as the consumer-buyer is concerned. This is only natural. For the law has developed through the decision of cases involving commercial rather than consumer-buyers. It is only occasionally that a case involving the purchases of the ultimate consumer gets into court. The losses from individual purchases are too small, and the expense of a trial is too great. Even the pure-food laws and the laws requiring truth in advertising are enforced, not in the interests of the ultimate consumer, but in the interests of competitors whose customers may have been lured away by unfounded claims, or poisoned by illegal foodstuffs.

In recent years, the consumer has found that by going direct to the business firm involved, he can get much more effective adjustments for faulty or unserviceable merchandise, much more adequate restitution for misrepresentation by an overenthusiastic salesman, than he can secure through the law courts. It takes decades to change the common law of sales, and years to change the attitude of political enforcement agencies, but in a few months the consumers can, by themselves, with little or no organization, make or break a business man. Consumers must inform themselves about the qualities of the merchandise they buy, the cost of the services they receive, and the prices they should be expected to pay, and they must put this information into practice in their buying. Only by so doing will they get, in the not far-distant future, a marketing system reorganized to serve rather than to sell the ultimate consumer.

How to improve consumer buying. In our present market situation, then, the consumer-buyer needs to acquire a wide range of information about the goods that are available in the market. In the second place, he needs to develop the ability to analyze available products with regard to the use to which they are to be put. In the third place, the consumer-buyer needs to understand the fundamental principles that are involved in good buying, and to work out, on the basis of these principles, a set of buying policies and practices which will work to his advantage in the present market set-up.

Wise buying takes time. Time spent in buying can be made to pay good dividends, either in savings in money outlay, or in the increased satisfaction the members of the family secure from purchases which exactly suit their needs. If, by better buying, the consumer-buyer can save 10 per cent on his usual purchases, he can add 10 per cent to the amount of goods he can buy. If by better buying he can secure goods which satisfy his wants 10 per cent better, he can add 10 per cent to the enjoyment he gets out of living. A woman expects to study changes in styles in order to be well dressed; the household buyer should expect to spend just as much time studying the factors involved in every important purchase.

The problem of diversity in buying. It is entirely possible for the consumer-buyer to solve the problem of diversity in his buying, if he considers each purchase, large or small, as a separate problem. Most consumers do spend time upon the selection of important items involving considerable expenditure, and purchased only at long intervals. A family planning to furnish a new home usually finds time to study what for it is a good buy in furniture. A family seldom buys a washing machine or a kitchen stove or a refrigerator without looking over most of the market offerings. Because the consumer-buyer takes time to study each of these important problems as it arises, he finds that these purchases present no insoluble problems, even though in the case of these occasional large purchases he can seldom profit from his own past experience.

But the consumer is usually appalled at the problem of learning enough to buy intelligently the great variety of small items he must purchase at frequent intervals. It is entirely possible to learn about these items, too, if the buyer studies them one at a time. And in the case of most of his smaller purchases he can profit by his recent buying experience.

Sometimes he wonders if the time spent in the analysis of these smaller items really pays. In order to decide, he must look, not at the saving on a single purchase, but at the total saving from repeated purchases during the course of a year. The same family that spends considerable time on the purchase of a washing machine often feels that it is a waste of time to give much attention to the selection of the family's milk. However, if the family buys 2 quarts of milk a day, in the course of the year it buys 730 quarts. At 10 cents a quart, the annual expenditure for milk amounts to $73. For this amount the family could buy a good washing machine. And, if the family uses 3 quarts of milk a day, in the course of the year it buys 1,095 quarts, making, at 10 cents a quart, an annual expenditure for milk of $109.50. This is as much as the advertised price of a number of standard makes of refrigerators.

A penny saved is a penny earned. It is, of course, only common sense to spend the most time improving the buying of the articles in which the possibilities of savings are greatest. It is fundamentally important, however, not to overlook the possibilities of the sum of many small savings. If the family can save 10 per cent on every purchase of food at the grocery, for a family with a grocery bill of $40 a month the total amounts to $4 a month, or $48 a year. The total is worth while, even though many of the savings amount in themselves to only a single cent on a 10-cent item. The consumer-buyer must never lose sight of the fact that in the purchase of low-priced articles, pennies count. A saving of 1 cent in 10 is a saving of 10 per cent. Of course, it is not good buying to spend more than 1 cent's worth of time saving a single penny. But, if 10 cents' worth of time will provide the needed information for saving a penny a week, at the end of 10 weeks the original time spent is fully paid for, and the additional pennies saved come as profits on the original investment.

What buying involves. Buying is a complex process. Good buying involves finding the answers to a number of questions. Every purchase involves decisions as to what to buy, when to buy, how much to buy, where to buy, and how much to pay. Every decision involves a weighing of advantages, a balancing of benefits against costs and of disadvantages in quality or service against savings in money outlay. This is not, however, as intricate a problem as at first sight it would seem. For as he gains in experience, each buyer gradually develops policies to guide him in his decisions, and habitual buying practices which answer automatically many of these questions as they arise.

If the buyer finds he gets uniformly good satisfaction from well-made but moderately high-priced shoes, while cheaper shoes always prove unsatisfactory, he adopts the policy of buying shoes on the basis of quality rather than price. If he finds that coal regularly sells for less in the spring and summer than during the fall and winter, he enlarges his coal bin and makes a practice of buying a year's supply of coal at lowest summer prices. If he finds that certain stores carry the quality of merchandise he prefers, and give the kind of service he wants, he makes a practice of going first to these stores for any articles he desires. If he finds that his income is only sufficient to provide him with a low-priced car, he adopts the policy of always buying a car he knows he can afford to own and run.

What to buy. In determining what to buy, the consumer-buyer is primarily concerned with the selection of the article which will best satisfy a particular want or group of wants. This selection can be made intelligently only if the consumer-buyer has a clear idea of the uses to which the purchase is to be put; only if he has adequate information about what is available on the local market or can be secured in larger markets; and only if he knows what generally constitutes good quality and sound values.

There is no one source to which the consumer-buyer can go to find out the qualities and varieties of goods now offered in the market or to which he can turn to get expert information even about standards of quality for the commodities he must buy. Nevertheless, the consumer-buyer needs up-to-date information. What no one else will provide for him he must provide for himself.

Sources of information for the consumer-buyer. There are three methods by which the consumer-buyer can find out for himself about market offerings: inspection, testing, and trial. *Inspection* is the careful looking over of the goods on the market to determine as accurately as possible by the appeal they make to the senses their suitability for the use the buyer has in mind. By inspection it is possible to learn about the color and the style of a dress, the color and design and texture of a rug, the taste of a cheese, the tone quality of a radio, or the melody of a new song. By inspection something can be learned about the more obvious elements in workmanship, though today the experienced buyer knows that he cannot judge hidden workmanship or materials by surface perfection. Inspection is valuable in the case of goods bought primarily for their appeal to the senses.

Testing, on the other hand, is designed primarily to measure the durability of a commodity. But testing necessitates destroying a sample of the commodity in order to find out how long it will last. It is possible to test a sample of a bolt of cloth at small cost, but it is impossible to apply similar tests to a finished dress. One can test a lump of coal or a sample of fuel oil, but one cannot test the durability of an oil burner without destroying the oil burner. Even in the case of goods which can be tested, testing often involves too great an outlay in equipment, and too much scientific knowledge, to make it a method available to many consumer-buyers.

Trial is valuable because it shows the adaptability of goods to the special needs of the consumer. By trial he can find out just how well or how poorly the commodity satisfies his immediate need. However, trial is possible only in the case of commodities which are bought at frequent intervals, and which cost comparatively little, so that the buyer can afford to make an occasional mistake in selection.

For the most part, trial is confined to such items as soap, razor blades, canned goods, crackers, cosmetics, and similar articles purchased frequently in small quantities. Although trial as the consumer-buyer ordinarily practices it tells little or nothing about the chemical content, and often but little about the relative durability of different types of goods, it is worth while as far as it goes. It does give the buyer a chance to find out for himself just how well or how poorly the commodity in question satisfies his personal needs.

A modified form of trial of durable goods is sometimes possible by purchasing on approval. A radio dealer may allow a customer to try an instrument in his own home. Usually, however, he charges a fee for the privilege. Some furniture dealers allow consumers to try rugs and other expensive articles in their own homes to see which article suits them best in the environment in which it must be used. In these cases, the trial is only temporary; at best, it eliminates only obvious mistakes in selection.

For information which he cannot obtain for himself from these three sources, the consumer-buyer must rely upon market agencies: upon advertising, labels, and sales people. Since much of this market information is inadequate, some inaccurate, and some deliberately mis-informing, he must learn how to judge the value of the information he can secure from each of these sources. He must even learn to secure information from what is left unsaid. Market agencies at present are defective devices for exact information for the consumer-buyer. But, even so, in deciding what to buy, intelligent use of the limited facilities the market does afford will yield good dividends to the consumer-buyer in increased want satisfaction and in money savings.

When to buy. In determining when to buy, the consumer must decide primarily between convenience and cost. He must decide whether to buy when it is most convenient for him to make the pur-chase, or at the time when he can buy at the greatest saving in money outlay. In recent years the development of conveniently located re-tail outlets and the increasing difficulty of providing adequate storage space in the modern home have led the consumer-buyer to delay buying until he is ready to use his purchases.

From the point of view of the consumer there are a number of advantages in buying for immediate use. The merchant instead of the consumer provides a place to store the goods, and takes the risk of spoilage, changes in style, and changes in consumer need.

There are two principal disadvantages in buying as needed: The buyer cannot always find exactly what he wants when he wants it. The buyer must pay more for goods bought in small amounts at the time of use, since the consumer cannot expect the merchant to carry an adequate stock and assume all the risks without a reasonable com-pensation for service rendered.

Ordinarily it is good policy to buy for immediate use under the following conditions: if future needs are not clear; if marketing facilities are adequate and convenient; if merchants' stocks can be depended upon to contain the wanted commodities; and if the cost of frequent purchase is not excessive. The additional cost of buying as needed is not excessive if the charge is no larger than the cost of storage and of the probable loss through spoilage or price changes. In many cases the consumer-buyer may feel justified in paying a little more than actual saving in cost for the convenience of buying a commodity when he needs it.

It is good policy to buy in advance of need under the following conditions: if future need is definitely determined; if goods can be bought more conveniently in advance of need; if the quality is now but not always available upon the market; if prices generally are rising, or for any other reason goods can be bought cheaper now than when they are to be used; and if more income is available now and more needs must be provided for later.

When to buy seasonal goods. The consumer-buyer must give special attention to the timing of his purchases in buying seasonal goods. There are two types of seasonal goods. First, there are goods for which there is a seasonal demand. In a temperate climate with hot summers and cold winters there is a demand for ice or some other form of refrigeration in the summer, and a demand for fuel in the winter. In the spring and summer, there is a demand for lightweight clothing which is suitable to wear in warm weather. In the fall there is a demand for warmer clothing and heavy outergarments which will provide more protection from cold and stormy weather. Even the demand for automobiles varies with the season, and usually reaches its peak in the spring and early summer.

Second, there are goods of which there is a seasonal supply. The seasonability of most of these commodities is determined by the conditions under which they are produced. In a temperate climate it is possible to raise fruits and vegetables only during the spring and summer and early fall months. During the cold weather, these goods can be had only if they are stored or imported from warmer regions. Goods for which there is a seasonal demand cost more in season and less out of season. Goods of which there is a seasonal supply cost less in season and more out of season.

Every family must work out its own policy in regard to the purchase of seasonal merchandise, and must decide what to buy in season and what to buy out of season. It must decide which articles of clothing it is to buy in season, paying higher prices for the latest styles, and which articles it can buy with just as much satisfaction to the members of the family at low prices at the end-of-the-season sales. Every family must decide how much food it can afford to buy out of season, and whether or not, in view of its members' food preferences, these out-of-season foods are worth the extra costs.

New commodities. Another case requiring special attention involves the policy to be followed in buying newly introduced commodities. The price of a commodity is always high when it is first introduced. The first few units are produced on a small scale and offered to people who can afford to pay high prices. If they find the product satisfactory, its production is gradually expanded and sales are increased by periodic reductions in price. But while the commodity is becoming established, depreciation is rapid, for improvements in later models soon make earlier models obsolete. As the quality of the new models improves, the defects in the early model become obvious and the family soon wants to replace the obsolete equipment with a later model. This, as well as the high initial price, must be considered in counting the cost of buying a newly invented commodity.

Each family must decide, then, how soon it can afford to adopt the new commodities which are coming on the market. The wealthy family that places special emphasis upon up-to-dateness, or the family that has some special need and has inadequate equipment, may decide upon early adoption. The family with a small income, placing no special emphasis on being up-to-date in all respects, or the family suitably equipped with older devices, may well delay the adoption of a new commodity until the price decline brings it within easy range of the family's money income.

How much to buy. In determining how much to buy, the questions to be answered are these: How much of the commodity does the family need? How much does it ordinarily use? How long will the commodity keep? How much can the family save by buying in quantity? What wastes or extravagances may come from having a large amount of the commodity available? Is it more convenient to purchase the article as needed, or to have a stock on hand in the home? Here again is a problem of weighing advantages and disadvantages, and of deciding upon the relative merits of convenience, service, and cost.

Ordinarily when the consumer-buyer thinks of quantity buying, he thinks of buying in bulk, of buying apples by the bushel instead of by the pound, potatoes by the bushel instead of by the peck, canned goods in restaurant size cans instead of family size cans, gasoline from the tank wagon instead of from the service station, coal by the carload instead of by the ton. He thinks of quantity buying as something beyond the reach of the ordinary consumer-buyer.

There are, however, surprising savings to be had from quantity buying, even if the increase in quantity amounts to no more than substituting the purchase of the larger for the smaller of two packages of the same commodity. The first of the tables on page 114 shows the savings to be had simply by buying the larger of two common household sizes of articles purchased at frequent intervals by almost every family. In a few cases there is no saving. In other cases savings by buying the larger package run as high as 35 or 40 per cent.

The second of these tables shows the prices at which a number of these articles can be purchased in still larger containers. Here the savings are even more marked. For example, a family that can use No. 10 or restaurant size cans of fruit ordinarily can save at least 20 per cent per pound of actual food purchased over the cost of fruit in the No. 2 cans. Goods the grocer sells in bulk come to him in unbroken packages, macaroni in 20-pound cartons, prunes in 25-pound boxes, noodles in 10-pound packages, sugar in 100-pound sacks, and oatmeal in 22½-pound sacks. A family using such a quantity in the course of a winter can frequently save by buying an unbroken 10-pound package of noodles, a 22½-pound sack of oatmeal, or a 25-pound box of prunes or raisins. And the family buying in these amounts loses none of the advantages of packaging.

The consumer has a right to expect a saving from purchase in large quantities, for in most cases it costs less per pound to handle goods in larger quantity than in small packages. Suppose we use a case of canned tomatoes as an example. It takes less time for the cannery to put up a given quantity of tomatoes in large cans than to put them up in small cans, and also less time to label the large cans and put them into cases. It takes no longer to count them in the cannery inventory and to list them on the shipping bills. The wholesaler can handle a case of large cans as easily as a case of small ones. The grocer can unpack a case of large cans and place them in his shelves in the same time it takes for a case of small cans. It takes no longer to sell a large can, to take it from the shelf, list it on the order slip, and prepare it for delivery. And if it takes no longer per can,

SAVING BY BUYING IN LARGE CONTAINERS—IDENTICAL BRANDS

Light Housekeeping vs. Family Sizes

FOOD	SMALL CONTAINER			LARGE CONTAINER			SAVING BY PURCHASE IN LARGE CONTAINER
	Size	Price per Container	Cost per Pound	Size	Price per Container	Cost per Pound	
							Per Cent
Cornflakes..............	8 oz.	$0.10	$0.200	13 oz.	$0.13	$0.160	20.0
Olives (lge.), Queen.....	9½ oz.	.41	.689	21 oz.	.79	.601	12.8
Spinach No. 2..........	10 oz.	.125	.200	18 oz.	.17	.150	24.8
No. 2½.............	18 oz.	.17	.150	27 oz.	.23	.136	9.3
Cut wax beans........	10 oz.	.125	.200	19 oz.	.15	.126	36.8
Golden Bantam corn....	10 oz.	.125	.200	20 oz.	.15	.120	40.0
Graham crackers.......	1 lb.	.20	.200	2 lb.	.35	.174	12.8
Salmon................	8 oz.	.25	.500	1 lb.	.45	.449	10.2
Sliced dried beef........	2½ oz.	.15	.960	5 oz.	.25	.800	16.6
Baking powder.........	6 oz.	.23	.612	12 oz.	.43	.574	8.8
Cocoa.................	8 oz.	.13	.259	16 oz.	.25	.249	3.7
Evaporated milk.......	6 oz.	.04	.107	13 oz.	.08	.099	7.4
Rolled oats (reg.).......	20 oz.	.11	.088	48 oz.	.23	.076	12.7
3-minute oats..........	20 oz.	.12	.096	55 oz.	.25	.072	25.0
Pancake flour..........	1 lb.	.13	.104	2½ lb.	.23	.092	10.8
Tea (green)............	1½ oz.	.08	.811	8 oz.	.38	.760	6.3
Tea (black-mixed)......	1⅜ oz.	.10	1.163	8 oz.	.40	.800	31.2
Potato chips...........	2 oz.	.10	1.800	8 oz.	.25	.499	37.6
Bread.................	16 oz.	.09	.089	20 oz.	.11	.088	1.8
Bread.................	20 oz.	.11	.088	24 oz.	.13	.186	1.8
Pumpkin..............	20 oz.	.13	.104	29 oz.	.17	.093	10.7
Flour.................	5 lb.	.33	.066	24½ lb.	1.25	.0512	21.9

SAVING BY BUYING IN LARGE CONTAINERS—IDENTICAL BRANDS

Family Size vs. Commercial Size

Spices	Small Size	Cost per Ounce	8 Oz. Size	Cost per Ounce	Per Cent Saved Buying 8 Oz. Size	16 Oz. Size	Cost per Ounce	Additional Per Cent Saved Buying 16 Oz. Size
Cinnamon (1½ oz.)	$0.10	$0.066	$0.35	$0.043	34.9	$0.65	$0.040	7.5
Cloves (1½ oz.)....	.10	.066	.35	.043	34.9	.65	.040	7.5
Ginger (2 oz.)	.10	.050	.32	.040	20.0	.60	.037	7.5
Black pepper (2 oz.)	.10	.050	.25	.031	38.0	.45	.028	9.7

Canned Goods	No. 2 Cans Net Contents	Price	Cost per Pound	No. 10 Cans Net Contents	Price	Cost per Pound	Per Cent Saved by Large Pkg.
Peaches (halves)....	20 ounces	$0.25	$0.2000	104 ounces	$1.00	$0.1536	23.2
Apricots............	20 ounces	.30	.2400	104 ounces	1.25	.1920	20.0
Sliced peaches......	20 ounces	.21	.1680	104 ounces	.95	.1456	13.3
Cut wax beans.....	18 ounces	.15	.1328	106 ounces	.78	.1168	12.0
Pumpkin...........	20 ounces	.15	.1200	106 ounces	.52	.1784	34.7
Spinach...........	18 ounces	.20	.1776	96 ounces	.65	.1088	38.7
Tomatoes..........	20 ounces	.18	.1440	106 ounces	.75	.1120	22.2

it takes less time per pound of edible contents. It actually takes less time to sell a customer an unbroken case of canned tomatoes than it does to sell him a single can. The grocer saves the work of opening the case, putting the cans on the shelf, taking them off the shelf, and giving them one by one to two dozen different customers. What is true of canned tomatoes is equally true of flour, cornflakes, oatmeal, soap flakes, and any other packaged goods. The less expensive the product in the package, the more important becomes the saving in package costs. The package represents a comparatively small part of the cost of a fifty-cent item, but a comparatively large part of the cost of a fifteen-cent item in the same size and type of container.

The consumer who buys in quantity is not unreasonable if he expects a price reduction which represents approximately the savings to the merchant and the manufacturer from his buying in large quantity. For to the extent that this type of buying becomes general, the retailer can do a larger volume of business in a given space with a given number of clerks. Since packaging and handling represent so large a part of the cost of getting goods into the hands of the consumer, buying in quantity is one practical method of reducing the spread between manufacturer and consumer—a spread which in no small measure is due to the insistence upon elaborate and attentive service on the part of consumer-buyers who have no idea of what the service costs.

The fundamental principles involved in deciding how much to buy are these: If savings in price justify the storage costs involved, pay a fair return on capital invested in the goods, and cover possible losses from spoilage, it is wise to buy as large quantities as a family can use. When prices are rising, it is wise to buy as much as the family can use and as its income will permit, for the saving in initial cost will offset in part or in full the cost of storage and other carrying charges. On a falling market, however, it is wise to buy in small quantities as needed, for the decline in price tends to offset the saving from buying larger quantities. If prices are neither rising nor falling, the family can save by watching for temporary dips in prices and then by buying in quantity on these special sales. In this case, it is well to buy enough to carry the family along until the next bargain offer.

Quantity buying of seasonal goods. Seasonal goods present a special problem of how much to buy, closely connected with the problem of when to buy. It is usually good policy to purchase seasonal goods in quantity only at the time of year when the price is low, when the product is at its best, and in the season in which it can be stored most safely. If storage facilities are available and there is little or no risk of loss in storage, it is usually good policy to buy enough to carry the family over until the next period of low prices.

Many families buy a year's supply of coal in the spring or early summer at "lowest summer prices." On the other hand, the saving on fuel oil is so small and storage tanks cost so much that families using fuel oil buy it as they need it through the winter.

Flour purchased in the fall usually keeps much longer than flour purchased at the beginning of warm weather. And flour usually sells at the year's low in November and December.

Old-fashioned quantity buying. To the old-fashioned family of the nineteenth century—the family accustomed to thinking in terms of sides of beef, halves of hogs, and barrels of apples, crackers, and flour—quantity buying as practiced by the modern family of four or five members would look like rather small-scale buying. The old-fashioned type of quantity buying is out of the question for most modern American families, since there are no storage facilities available in the modern home for such large quantities of food.

Old-fashioned quantity buying permitted savings due in part to the quantity purchased, but even more to the fact that many of the articles bought in large quantity were in less fully processed form. The family that purchases a quarter of beef must cut its own steaks and grind its own hamburger. The family that buys half a hog must cure its own hams and bacon, and render its own lard. To make it worth while to buy flour in large quantity a family must do most of its own baking, including bread.

Most families today prefer to buy highly processed goods at slightly higher prices rather than to do the processing themselves. And yet the savings of old-fashioned quantity buying are still there for the families that are large enough and that have incomes limited enough to make it worth while to practice it.

Where to buy. In recent years there has been a great increase in the number and variety of stores offering their wares to the consumer. It is difficult to describe in detail typical marketing facilities. Marketing organization varies for different commodities and in different communities. Traditional marketing channels no longer hold. It is no longer safe to predict how goods will flow from the producer to the consumer. It is possible to buy motor oil in a grocery store; cigarettes and candy at a gasoline filling station; drugs in a department store; and alarm clocks, collar buttons, roller skates, lunches, and lawn chairs at the corner drug store. But if it is impossible to describe exactly the marketing facilities which would be found in a typical American community, it is possible to point out some distinctions and classifications which will help the consumer-buyer to analyze for himself in terms of his own needs the facilities in his own community.

The goods. Suppose we begin with some distinctions between the various types of goods which the consumer must buy from time to time. Students of marketing classify the goods consumers purchase as convenience goods, shopping goods, and specialty goods. *Convenience goods* are goods which are purchased in small quantities at frequent intervals. Ordinarily they are bought at neighborhood stores or at other stores so conveniently located that the frequently repeated purchases may be made with a minimum of cost in time and effort. *Shopping goods* are goods which are purchased only after a comparison of qualities, styles, and prices. They are usually purchased either in department stores or in specialty stores located around a retail shopping center. Stores handling shopping goods ordinarily locate close together so as to facilitate comparisons by the consumer-buyer. *Specialty goods* are relatively expensive articles purchased only at long intervals. Furniture, washing machines, radios, vacuum cleaners, oil burners, and automobiles are good examples. Because the purchase of specialty goods involves larger sums of money, the consumer expects to spend time going from store to store studying the market offerings before he decides what to buy. Dealers handling specialty goods usually locate outside the retail shopping district, where rents are lower, because they know their customers will seek them out. They find that the employment of salesmen to call upon prospective customers brings them more returns than does the payment of high rent for a convenient and easily accessible location.

The stores. Stores themselves are classified in a number of ways. They are classified on the basis of the type of goods they handle as grocery stores, meat markets, drug stores, clothing stores, dry-goods stores, hardware stores, book stores, news stands, and the like. They are classified on the basis of their organization as general stores, specialty stores, and department stores; on the basis of ownership as independent or home-owned stores and chain stores; and on the basis of the functions they perform as regular or integrated. The manufacturer-wholesaler-retailer set-up is designated as "regular." Integrated types include firms which unite both wholesaling and retailing in a single organization. Manufacturer's stores, mail-order houses, and the larger chain organizations operating their own wholesaling divisions are "integrated."

But more helpful than any of these classifications to the consumer-buyer is a classification of stores on the basis of the services they render. On this basis, stores may be classified as full-service, middle-class, and low-service stores. *Full-service stores* provide telephone and delivery service, credit, approval privileges, and an adequate number of intelligent and well-trained clerks to wait upon their customers, and help them determine what will best serve their needs. Full-service stores usually stock a varied line of high-grade merchandise. Their appointments are attractive. Often their equipment is expensive. Frequently almost unnecessarily elaborate services are provided for the comfort of customers, and the prices full-service stores charge necessarily reflect the cost of the service as well as of the goods they sell.

Middle-class stores may or may not give telephone and delivery service. The amount of credit they extend is usually more limited. Approval and exchange services are kept to a minimum. The number of clerks is usually somewhat smaller than in the full-service stores. The customer may be required to wait a little longer to be served. The appointments of middle-class stores are usually plainer and more practical. The variety of merchandise offered is somewhat smaller. Middle-class stores usually carry little in the way of luxury goods. In the staple lines first-quality merchandise may or may not be included.

Low-service stores usually do business on a cash basis. They provide no telephone service. They make a special charge for delivery service. Their clerks are usually paid less and are less experienced than are the clerks in either the middle-class or full-service stores, and as a result they can tell their customers less about the goods they are selling. In low-service stores, the appointments are plain but efficient. They are designed to display the goods plainly marked so that the customer can make his own selections with a minimum amount of help from the sales person. The clerk's chief duty is to wrap up the goods and collect the money.   Low-service stores are designed to sell goods with a minimum of expense.   The consumer can usually buy in a low-service store at somewhat lower prices than at either a full-service or a middle-class store, and he should be able to do so, since he is paying very little for service.

In selecting the store in which to trade, each consumer must decide whether in his own case it is more important to save time, energy, or money.   Store selection involves the problem not simply of selecting a place in which to buy goods of the desired quality at a reasonable price, but of deciding upon the services which are to accompany the goods the consumer is buying.   The full-service store caters to the buyer who wants high-quality goods and elaborate service.   The middle-class store serves the buyer who wants good merchandise and efficient service at moderate cost.   The low-service store meets the needs of the buyer who wants the most he can get for his money in the way of merchandise.

The customers.   Many customers' difficulties in deciding where to buy are due to the fact that there are ordinarily only three classes of stores to serve four types of consumer-buyers: those who can afford service and are willing to pay for it; those who can afford service but do not want to pay for it; those who cannot afford service, but want it; and those who cannot afford service and do not want it.

The needs of the first and of the fourth group are met by the full-service store on the one hand, and by the low-service store on the other.   In the larger cities buyers in the second group can find middle-class stores handling high-grade merchandise with a minimum of service.

In the smaller communities, these buyers in the second group who want high-grade merchandise must buy in full-service stores, for middle-class stores can secure a volume of business sufficient to justify the handling only of middle-class merchandise.

The buyers in the third group, who want, and in many cases need, services they cannot afford to pay for, face a difficult problem. Mothers kept at home to care for small children, elderly people of modest means who find it hard even to get to the neighborhood grocery or the corner drug store, the employed homemaker who must do the family buying in addition to making her contribution to the family's not too generous money income, must work out their problems either by buying a little less in the full-service stores or by buying lower-grade merchandise than they really prefer in the middle-class stores, and doing with a little less in the way of service.

Shopping out of town vs. buying at home. In recent years the general adoption of the automobile has freed the consumer-buyer from purely local markets. There has been a tendency for stores handling shopping goods to concentrate in retail shopping centers serving the country for twenty-five or fifty or a hundred miles around. Just as families living in the suburbs of large cities as a matter of course shop in the metropolitan stores, so families living in smaller communities now do most of their shopping in these retail shopping centers. Trade in the smaller communities, even in the dry-goods stores, is coming more and more to be trade in middle-grade goods bought on a convenience basis. Since market offerings of high-grade merchandise are confined to the larger shopping centers, the consumer wanting such goods must go to the market where they are sold. He can do so at moderate expense if, when he visits the shopping center, he buys enough to justify the transportation costs which are involved. But while it may be necessary to go to the shopping center for many of the things he desires, the consumer should buy at home whenever he can find in the local market what suits his need, not simply to patronize home industry, but in order that the local dealer will have on hand what he needs at times when it may be inconvenient or impossible for him to go to a more distant market.

The chain store vs. the independent. The consumer-buyer is frequently under pressure to buy at some one type of store, particularly where the independent merchants have organized to build up sentiment to help them in meeting the competition of chain stores. They use the trade-at-home and other similar arguments to try to hold business by appealing to emotion rather than reason. As a consumer, the buyer is not interested in the question of the chain store versus the independent as such. His problem is: "Where can I get most nearly what I need for what I can afford to pay?" He is interested in the relative advantages of the chain and the independent stores from the point of view of quality of goods, quality of service, and the prices they charge.

The chain stores seem to have a little advantage over the independent merchant in the case of standardized goods, goods where service is a minor matter, and goods in which it is easy for the buyer to identify the quality of the product.   In communities where the consumer-buyer is not personally acquainted with the store proprietors—and this is true in most large cities—the chain stores have a greater advantage than they do in the smaller communities.

The advantage of the independent merchant on the other hand lies primarily in his ability to cater to some special class of trade.   This means that he must know his customers and their needs and keep on his shelves exactly what they want.   The independent merchant usually expects to give his customers more information about the goods he sells and more personal service.   The independent merchant has the advantage in dealing with consumers who want high-grade merchandise, and who appreciate excellent service.

However, there is more difference between the efficient chain store and the poorly-managed chain store, and between the well-managed independent store and the poorly-managed independent store, than there is between the average of chain and independent.   For, after all, efficient retailing is peculiarly dependent upon the personality and ability of the manager of the particular unit.   The well-managed chain unit is usually a better place to trade than the poorly-managed independent store, and the high-grade independent in its turn is a better place to trade than is the less efficient chain store unit.

Sales policies.   In deciding between two stores which provide about the same qualities of goods and about the same amount of service, it may be well to consider the merchandising policies of the two stores.   Does the merchant sell goods in packages of standard size, or does he make it difficult for the consumer to compare values by stocking goods put up in odd-sized packages and containers?   Do all of his goods contain plain quantity marks or is the net weight figure hidden away in very small type under a fold in the package?   Does he give credit wisely?   Can he be depended upon to send the same quality of goods when he fills a telephone order as he does when he sells for cash in the market?   Is he on the alert to help the consumer-buyer satisfy his wants better than the consumer-buyer knows how to satisfy them himself?   Does he consider himself primarily as a salesman for the manufacturer or as a buyer for the consumer?   In deciding where to buy, merchandising policy involving quality of service is fully as important to the consumer-buyer as are policies regarding the quality of merchandise the store handles.

After all, the problem of deciding where to buy is a question of deciding where the consumer-buyer can get most nearly what he wants for a given expenditure of time, energy, and money. How each family decides must depend largely upon the relative importance of time and money in the family's economy. The family should buy in the store that offers most nearly the quality of goods desired in combination with the services the family feels it can afford to pay for. The family must decide whether to buy goods and low service at a low price or goods plus the convenience of service at a higher price. And it must decide whether the savings in time and energy which come from purchasing at a full-service store are worth the additional money cost.

What price to pay.   In some ways the most difficult problem facing the consumer-buyer is that of deciding what price he should pay for each of the great variety of goods he buys. His problem is complicated by the fact that what is apparently the same article sells for different prices in different stores in the same community, for different prices in the same store at different times of year, and even for different prices on different days of the week.

The consumer can understand the reason for price variations which are due to differences in quality of merchandise. He can understand why prices are higher in full-service stores than in low-service stores. He can see the reason for seasonal fluctuations in prices. He can even see why a merchant may make certain items leaders to stimulate business on dull days. The consumer feels that the price he pays should depend definitely upon the quality of the merchandise, the quantity he buys, the time of year, and the type of service he receives. And yet he knows from experience that there is no dependable relationship between the price he is asked and any or all of these factors.

He has found from experience that a high price may be an indication of high-quality merchandise, of elaborate or efficient service, of fashion, or of a deliberate attempt to exploit a group who are willing to pay a high price for the prestige which goes with a trade name or a label.

He has also found from experience that a low price may be an indication of inferior quality, or of good quality with a minimum of service; it may be due to a fortunate purchase, or to an oversupply of last season's merchandise; or it may be an indication of a merchant's need for ready money, of a cheap type of advertising, or of efficient merchandising.

In deciding whether or not to buy a given article at a given price, the consumer-buyer is influenced by two factors: he wants to know what is a reasonable charge for the quality of goods and type of service involved, and he must decide whether he can afford to pay the price asked.

Ordinarily the consumer considers the price to be fair if it is in line with the cost of producing goods and rendering selling service. If it actually costs $40 to provide him with a suit of clothes of the desired quality, if it costs $10 to manufacture and market by efficient methods a pair of shoes of the kind he wants, he is willing to pay the price. He is unwilling to pay for quality he does not need or for services he does not desire. He is also unwilling to pay arbitrary charges not actually incurred in rendering him a service. If it actually costs $1 to call for, dry clean, press, and deliver a suit of clothes, he will pay $1 for the complete service. If 25 cents of this amount represents the cost of pick-up and delivery, he expects to pay only 75 cents if he takes in his suit and calls for it when it is ready. If he buys goods out of season, if he is content with what he can find in end-of-the-season remainders, if he buys in larger than usual quantity, he expects corresponding reductions in prices. If the general trend of prices is downward, he expects to pay for his purchases on the basis of present costs, not on the basis of the actual cost of the goods in the merchant's stock. And if the trend of prices is upward, while he may not like it very well, he cannot object to being charged a price which will enable the merchant to replace the goods now on his shelves with higher-priced merchandise.

The more the consumer-buyer knows about the prices which are being charged in various stores for similar goods and similar services, the better able he will be to judge the reasonableness of the prices he is asked. The more he is able to analyze costs, the more he breaks costs up into charges for goods and charges for selling-services, the better will he be able to judge whether or not he should buy a given article for a given price.

In the last analysis, the price the consumer-buyer should pay depends not so much upon the reasonableness of the price asked, as upon how much the article is worth to him. This depends first upon the inherent satisfactions he can obtain from the article in question;

second, upon the cost of acceptable substitutes; third, upon the satisfactions which could be secured by other use of the same amount of money; and fourth, upon the cost and desirability of buying materials and equipment and making the article at home for his own use.

The consumer-buyer alone can decide how much an article of a given quality is worth to him. He alone can decide how much more that article is worth if he can buy it in a store that gives delivery service, how much more it is worth if he can buy it on credit, how much more it is worth if he buys it in a store which can be depended upon to stand back of the merchandise it sells.

The whole problem of buying sometimes seems to resolve itself into a question of what price to pay. Ordinarily the consumer decides whether to buy one quality or another quality in part at least on the basis of comparative prices. He decides whether or not to buy goods when it is most convenient on the basis of comparative costs. He decides how much to buy at a time on the basis of the savings from quantity purchases. He decides what store to patronize on the basis of whether or not the difference in services is compensated for by differences in prices. He even decides whether or not he can afford to buy the things which will best satisfy his wants by comparing prices with the income he has available to spend.

It is highly important, then, that the consumer-buyer learn all he can about prices. The more intelligent he becomes about the prices he is charged, the more he knows about the reasons why certain goods and certain services cost certain amounts, the more he knows about the prices which are asked in different stores for different qualities of goods, and for different types of services, the more intelligently will he be able to answer the five questions that good buying involves—what to buy, when to buy, how much to buy, where to buy, and how much to pay.

Helps for the consumer-buyer. Good buying has been defined as the art of securing goods which as nearly as possible satisfy the consumer's needs, with a minimum outlay of time, energy, and money. If the consumer is to buy efficiently, he must have adequate information about the types and qualities of goods available in the market, about the stores in which they are on sale, about the marketing services which are available, and about the prices which are asked. For this information he must depend very largely upon the merchant from whom he buys and upon the manufacturer whose goods he is considering. There are three usual sources to which he can turn for this information: the advertising about the goods on sale, the labels upon the merchandise itself, and the salesmen with whom he deals.

Advertising. Advertising is perhaps the most widespread medium of communication between the producer and the consumer. It should be one of the most helpful to the consumer-buyer. Some advertising is, some is not. The advertising sections of the leading magazines and the metropolitan newspapers give a fair cross section of most of the merchandise which is available on the market. Most advertising tells who makes a product, who sells it, and when and where it can be had. Some advertisements give information about prices. Some include statements about quality. In many cases, the consumer can learn through advertising the uses of new products and new uses of old products.

The consumer cannot expect to find any one advertisement which will give him all the information he needs about a product. National magazine advertising can call his attention to the product, tell him who makes it, what it is good for, and occasionally something about what it ought to cost. Local newspaper advertising more often tells where commodities can be had, when they will be on sale, and the price at which they are offered. Radio advertising is for the most part reminder advertising of the repetitive type. In magazine, newspaper, and radio advertising, statements about quality are usually too general to be helpful, though some of this advertising gives interesting descriptions of materials used, types of construction, and processes of manufacture. Pamphlets, dealer aids, and direct-mail advertising may contain more detailed information about a product than it is possible to include in effective newspaper or magazine advertising. For example: Manufacturers of household appliances put out pamphlets which give specifications, diagrams showing mechanical construction and working parts, and detailed descriptions of the ways in which the equipment can be used to the best advantage. Automobile manufacturers provide their dealers with highly illustrated descriptive folders giving detailed specifications for their entire line of cars. Some canning companies put out booklets describing in detail the products they sell under their various labels.

The consumer will be better able to read advertising intelligently if he understands what the advertiser is trying to accomplish. He must keep constantly before him the fact that the advertiser is attempting to create an impression which will be sufficiently favorable to make his reader want to buy his product. The advertiser can do this in many ways—by the facts he gives, by the illustrations he uses, by the associations he builds up in the minds of his readers. Often he can create a favorable impression more easily by implication than by direct statement.

The consumer-buyer will find it easier to secure from advertising the information he desires if he persistently keeps in mind the specific facts he wishes to learn. Instead of looking for information about "quality," he should seek facts about style, color, weight, shape, and size. Rather than information about "economy" he should seek facts about fuel consumption, repair costs, depreciation, and probable obsolescence. Instead of information about uses in general, he should seek facts about the uses to which he as an individual is to put the article.

He should begin by deciding whether the advertisement as a whole is intended primarily to inform or to persuade. He must decide whether it creates a true picture of the product, whether it conceals essential facts, whether it deliberately creates a false impression. If the advertisement is illustrated, he must decide whether the pictures are designed primarily to attract his attention, to give him information about the product, to help in creating a favorable impression by building up favorable associations, or to persuade by implication. He must analyze each statement to decide how much dependence he can put upon it. He must discount superlatives. He must constantly be on his guard against "puffing." For "puffing" has legal standing. The courts have ruled that truth in advertising simply means that the advertising can contain no openly false statements. Exaggeration is not falsehood. Saying that an article is the best of its kind is not falsehood. Leaving out part of the story is not falsehood. "Puffing" may be in poor taste, but it is a legitimate device for persuading people to buy. The courts apparently have had confidence in the ability of the American people to see through the glittering generalities which are found in much modern advertising.

On the basis of the information he can get from advertising, the consumer decides whether or not he will give further consideration to a given product. And he must remember that much advertising is designed primarily to pique his curiosity about the commodity, to attract him to the store where it is on sale, to give a salesman a chance to work upon him as a prospect. If he decides to inspect an article, he can learn from the advertising what features to look for, what questions to ask the salesman, what sales arguments to be on guard against.

From the consumer's point of view advertising at the present time is far from perfect. By its very nature, advertising is limited in its ability to answer many definite questions about specific qualities or specific uses of a product. The consumer's problem is complicated by the fact that it is not safe to ignore every item which is poorly advertised. The consumer-buyer should do his best to get behind the advertising smoke-screen and find out what goods are actually like. And he should buy what best fits his needs regardless of the way it is advertised. He must not expect too much of advertising; he must use it for what it is worth as a buying aid, since, properly used, it can be made to yield much information.

Personal selling. For more specific information about commodities, the consumer-buyer must depend upon the salesman. From him he can get individualized answers to his personal problems. The salesman should know the product he sells, how it is made, what it is good for, how much it costs. He should be able to answer all kinds of questions about its suitability for various uses.

If the consumer is to get the most help from a salesman, he must remember that the salesman's primary object is to sell goods. In some cases he is interested in building up a permanent clientele which will come back to him again and again to get the selling service he renders. In other cases he is interested simply in making a single sale. He will use every device he knows to get the customer to buy his merchandise. While most salesmen do not deliberately make false statements about what they are selling, they have found they can sell more goods if they tell a customer what they think he wants to know. While they do not like to lie about a product, they can often promote sales by diverting attention from fundamental defects in the article. Ordinarily salesmen are not hired to volunteer information about the weaknesses of the goods they sell.

If the buyer is to get the largest amount of help from a salesman he must enlist his co-operation. He must tell him definitely what he wants. If the first thing the salesman shows him is not what he wants, he should not say simply: "I don't like that," but rather, "That will not suit my needs for this reason and for that reason.

What I want must have this and that specific characteristic." In buying a piece of dress goods, for instance, it doesn't help the salesman at all to say: "I don't like that," or "That won't do." Suppose instead the customer says: "For my purpose I must have a certain color, with a small figure, smaller than that figure and larger than this. The fabric must tub. It must iron well. It must not wrinkle easily. I want it to wear every day for the entire season." Then the clerk knows what sort of goods to show next. If the buyer does not know exactly the sort of commodity he needs, he may tell the salesman exactly what purpose he has in mind, and let him suggest an article to fill his needs.

If the consumer is to get the most help from a salesman, he must be able to ask intelligent questions about the product he is buying, and he must know enough about the article to be able to judge the accuracy of the salesman's information. He must be able to phrase his questions in such a way as to determine whether the salesman is telling him actual facts about the article he is selling, or merely what he thinks the customer wants to know. It frequently helps to ask interestedly about a few qualities which he definitely does not want, or points which he knows to be weaknesses, and do it in such a way that the salesman will think he wants the qualities he is trying to avoid.

If the consumer is to get the most help from salesmen, he must be able to detect the high-pressure salesman before he gets well under way. He must learn how to anticipate the run of the salesman's prepared argument, and to break in at inconvenient places with irrelevant or disconcerting questions. He should deliberately break up the salesman's carefully learned story. And if he finds the salesman cannot answer his questions about the article, if he finds he can give him little or no help in his buying problems, he must know as much about dismissing the salesman as the salesman knows about closing a sale.

The consumer will find that he can secure more help in his buying problem from a conscientious and intelligent salesman than he can secure in any other way. He should constantly be on the alert to find such a salesman. He should try to find a salesman with a point of view and set of values similar to his own. Once he has found such a person he should ask for the same salesman every time he is in the store. In this way, he will establish a more permanent and personal relationship. The salesman will come to value his business, and can learn from repeated contacts the sort of thing the customer wants. When he has once found such a salesman he can afford to go out of his way to give him his business, for such a salesman can save the buyer both time and money as well as insure satisfaction from the goods purchased.

Labels. Because of the nature of modern manufactured products and packaged goods, it is difficult for the salesman to know much more about many of the goods he is selling than does the consumer-buyer. When new, ready-made clothing of good quality and of poor quality may look very much alike. A winter coat made of an all-wool fabric looks almost the same as a coat of a similar model made of a cotton thread wrapped with shoddy woolen fiber. A part-wool blanket containing less than 5 per cent wool looks about the same in the store as a part-wool blanket containing 25 per cent wool. Walnut furniture may be solid walnut or walnut veneer. In some cases walnut furniture is not walnut at all, but gum-wood or birch stained to resemble walnut. It is very difficult for an amateur to detect these differences once an article of merchandise is carefully finished and ready for sale.

There is only one way by which reliable information about manufactured goods can be made available to the salesman and through him to the consumer. That is proper labeling by the manufacturer, who knows what went into the making of the article. For many years manufacturers have used labels chiefly to identify their product. Recently there has been a tendency to supplement information in advertising with information upon the label attached to each article sold.

There are a number of difficulties in the way of working out informative labels. Most of these involve the terminology to be used. If a label is to be of any value to the consumer-buyer it must use terms with which he is familiar. At the same time, this terminology must conform to the customs of the trade, and it must be exact enough to be enforceable in legal actions. Otherwise, it would be impossible for reputable manufacturers to protect their product from the competition of mis-branded merchandise offered by their less scrupulous competitors.

The labeling found on most merchandise still leaves much to be desired. It is often lacking in detail and vague in terminology. Like much advertising, many labels are impressionistic rather than informative. Even in their present state, however, labels contain information of value to the consumer.

The consumer-buyer can get help from labels only if he takes time to read them carefully. It is important that he consider not only what the label says, but what it leaves unsaid. A label reading "10 per cent pure Australian virgin wool" tells him nothing about the other 90 per cent of the material in the fabric.

He must know what the terms used in the label mean to the trade. Much percale is advertised as "80 square." Most consumers assume that such a fabric will have 80 threads to the inch each way. They do not know that the trade takes the thread count in the gray cloth, that ordinarily a piece of cloth 40 inches wide is required to give a piece of finished goods a yard wide, and that the thread count on a finished 80 square percale is probably 72 by 84 threads per square inch. And what is even more important, they do not realize that the thread count alone is not a complete indication of quality. The tensile strength of the thread used in weaving the cloth is as important as the number of threads to the inch.

The consumer-buyer must learn what statements can be depended upon, and what statements have no exact meaning. In ready-made garments there is no uniformity in the sizes used. The wise buyer does not rely on the size as marked, but measures the garment or tries it on. "Fast color" means little, but "fast to sunlight," "fast to washing," "fast to perspiration," have definite meaning. "Guaranteed not to shrink out of fit" means nothing, for there is no way to determine what "out of fit" means. "Guaranteed not to shrink more than 3 per cent" has definite meaning.[1]

Books and periodical literature. There is a great mass of printed material other than advertising dealing more or less directly with consumer buying problems. There are numbers of pamphlets available from impartial sources. The Department of Agriculture publishes from time to time Farmers' Bulletins dealing with consumer buying problems. The bulletins of the Bureau of Home Economics include much scientific and practical material. The American Home Economics Association issues some pamphlet material, as well as reprints of articles published in the *Journal of Home Economics* (Washington, D. C.).

---

[1] Clarice L. Scott, "Labels on Clothes We Buy," in *Journal of Home Economics*, Vol. 26, No. 9, p. 546. November, 1934.

Most of the leading magazines from time to time feature articles dealing with consumer problems. The household departments of the women's magazines publish material which is helpful in acquainting the consumer with new products on the market. There are a number of magazines devoted primarily to the home and its furnishings. Another type of magazine, of which *Parents' Magazine* (The Parents' Institute, Inc., Chicago) is a good example, is helpful in selecting play equipment, books, and educational materials for children. The American Medical Association's lay magazine, *Hygeia* (Chicago), often contains valuable information, especially concerning the purchase of food and drugs. And if the consumer-buyer has access to them, either through business connections or through a public library, he can learn a good deal about the market situation from trade journals dealing with retail trade or with specific industries.

Many magazines publish non-advertising pamphlet material designed to help the consumer solve his buying problems. A number of the women's magazines publish pamphlets giving detailed specifications and commercial standards for various types of commodities. Some personal finance companies put out pamphlets on consumer buying problems as an additional service to their clients. Much of this material is decidedly worth while. Some of it must be read with due regard for the source from which it comes.

There is also a considerable general literature about buying. Some of it, like Chase and Schlink's *Your Money's Worth* (The Macmillan Co., New York, 1926) and Schlink and Kallet's *100,000, 000 Guinea Pigs* (Vanguard Press, New York, 1932), is primarily intended to make the rank and file of consumers conscious that they have buying problems. Books like Baldwin's *Shopping Book* (The Macmillan Co., New York, 1929) and Brindze's *How to Spend Money* (Vanguard Press, New York, 1935) are designed to give definite help in buying. There is much helpful material in the standard works in home economics, both in general works and in books dealing with the detailed problems of food, clothing, home equipment, and home management.

There is, then, a great deal of information available for the literate consumer in books and periodical literature. As is the case with advertising, the value of this material varies. Some of it is helpful to one group of consumers, some to another. Some of it is highly reliable, and some is from sources which could hardly be called impartial. Some of the material is of permanent value; some soon goes out of date.

If the consumer is to find this mass of material helpful rather than confusing, he must select wisely, read carefully, and analyze thoroughly, and he must always keep in mind the sources from which the material comes, its probable authenticity, and what is most important of all, its applicability to his own personal buying problems.

Consumers' Research. Some time before the publication by Chase and Schlink of *Your Money's Worth*, a Consumers' Club had been organized in White Plains, New York. This organization was expanded in response to demand from readers of the book that the authors make available for them current information of the sort suggested in *Your Money's Worth*.[2] The Consumers' Club grew. In 1929 it was formally incorporated as a membership organization— not for profit—and its name was changed to Consumers' Research.

Consumers' Research is just what its name implies—a research organization engaged in securing information for its members about the goods they buy. In five years it had over 60,000 members subscribing to its service. It provides its members with information in the form of an annual *Handbook of Buying*, which is supplemented by five confidential bulletins available to ultimate consumer subscribers only, and four non-confidential or general bulletins which may be read by anyone. The annual *Handbook* provides a manual of information about consumers' goods. It gives definite information about a great variety of products. Usually there is a bit of material describing the strong and the weak points of the commodity in question. Then follows a list of specific brands, with the findings and recommendations of Consumers' Research concerning each one of them. Each brand is listed as recommended, not recommended, or intermediate. To the extent that space permits, brief statements of the reasons for each listing are given.

Consumers' Research faces a tremendous task in trying to prepare a comprehensive report upon the great variety of products on the American market. It makes no pretense of having a complete list. It selects commodities and brands on the basis of their general availability. It is expanding its service as rapidly as the growth of its membership will permit. In order to remain entirely free from

---

[2] Stuart Chase and F. J. Schlink, *Your Money's Worth*, p. 254. The Macmillan Co., New York, 1926.

any bias in its judgments, it makes use of no income other than that received from the subscriptions and occasional small contributions of its member consumers.

While it is impossible for Consumers' Research to conduct its own tests of all the articles it lists, it has access to many tests made by experts. Several hundred technicians and scientists in various fields contribute, either on a volunteer basis or for a fee, the findings of tests of products and materials which they have carried out. In certain classes of goods where test data are not available or applicable, Consumers' Research secures opinions from highly qualified and disinterested experts. It names the authorities upon which it is depending for its information, so that its members may judge for themselves the value of the information, except in cases where to give such reference to the authority might result in serious economic hazard, such as loss of a job, to the person concerned. Consumers' Research makes its recommendations upon the best information anywhere available for consumers. In case of differences of opinion, Consumers' Research resolves the differences in the direction which will best protect the consumer's interests.

The material which Consumers' Research publishes is available only to subscribers to the organization. Upon subscribing, they must agree to keep the information provided them confidential. They are allowed to use it only within the limits of their own immediate families. This requirement is necessary to protect the organization from suit for libel by manufacturers whose products they do not recommend. There are many circumstances under which it is not legal to broadcast opinions which may be detrimental to a business interest, but able counsel holds that it is entirely within the law for an organization to provide information about goods, whether favorable or detrimental, on a confidential basis for the use of its subscribers only.

There are, of course, definite limits to the service which Consumers' Research or any other similar organization can perform. In a country as large as the United States, no service can be devised which can tell each of its subscribers what in his case is the one best buy available in his local market. No service will be able to list all the brands of all the articles offered for sale in every market in the United States. No service can carry out all the tests which its members may ask for, nor can it fully satisfy their infinitely diverse judgments of what standards of efficiency or economy a given product should meet. But Consumers' Research does provide a clearly indexed and classified file of information about market offerings which can nowhere else be found.

Legal protection for the consumer-buyer. There are a number of laws which are intended to protect the consumer-buyer from the more obvious types of fraud. The federal government in 1906 passed the Pure Food and Drug Law, which prohibits the sale of food or drugs which are unfit for human consumption.[3] Every state has a Pure Food and Drug Law of its own, supplementing the federal law and regulating the sale of foods and drugs within the state. Every state has laws regulating weights and measures. Every large city has a department devoted to the enforcement of these laws.

The Department of Agriculture establishes grades for agricultural products. Potatoes and fruit are frequently sold by government grade. Government-graded meats are available in many of the better markets. Grades for the more common kinds of canned goods have been established. In most cases the use of these grades in the retail trade is voluntary. If products are labeled with government grades, they must come up to government specifications.

Through the Bureau of Standards, the Department of Commerce sponsors commercial agreements in which manufacturers agree upon standard specifications for their products and upon the terminology to be used in describing them. Production to these specifications and the use of these labels are voluntary. Recently blankets and a few other articles have been appearing on the market bearing "Department of Commerce" labels.

The Federal Trade Commission sponsors "trade practice agreements." When the terms of these agreements are accepted by a stated majority of a trade, any violations are prosecuted by the Federal Trade Commission as unfair competition. The definitions worked out for "pure dye silk" and "weighted silk" and the agreements for labeling part-wool knit underwear are typical of these agreements.

The Federal Trade Commission was not set up as a consumer

---

[3] See E. R. Groves and L. M. Brooks, *Readings in the Family*, pp. 367-369, J. B. Lippincott Co., Chicago, 1934, for a concise description of the administration of the Federal Pure Food and Drug Act, together with a list of proposed provisions to be included in a revision of the law.

agency. Its function is to enforce anti-trust laws and to maintain fair competition. Its activities are limited to cases in which unfair competition is involved. In spite of the fact that it is powerless to act in case of any practice which is universal in an industry, no matter how detrimental that practice may be to the ultimate consumer, the Federal Trade Commission has done more than any other single government agency to protect the interests of the consumer.

The American people are always more vocal when their interests as producers rather than their interests as consumers are at stake. Since this attitude is reflected both by Congress and the courts, the consumer can expect little direct aid from government enforcement agencies. Nevertheless, the National Recovery Program provided for at least nominal recognition of the interests of the consumer. In both the AAA and the NRA there was provision for consumer representation.

The Agricultural Adjustment Administration established a Consumers' Counsel to advise consumers of profiteering in food prices. The National Recovery Administration included a Consumers' Advisory Board to look out for the interests of the consumer. The activities of these two groups were co-ordinated in the Consumers' Division of the National Emergency Council, which sponsored County Consumer Councils in some two hundred counties throughout the United States.

This experiment with County Consumer Councils was an attempt to interest consumers personally in their own problems. These councils undertook various lines of work. In some communities they developed into code-enforcement agencies. In others they emphasized the fact-finding side of their work. They ran retail price studies, milk consumption surveys, and a variety of similar studies. In some communities they emphasized educational features. There was no appropriation for the support of the work of these councils. They had no funds even for office supplies. Under these conditions, their activities were necessarily restricted.

But the County Consumer Councils have resulted in gathering together groups of consumers who are definitely interested in their common problems. While the councils themselves in many cases have not been able to show the tangible results their members wished, they may yet prove to be the nucleus from which may grow effective local consumers' organizations.

The Consumers' Counsel of the Agricultural Adjustment Administration collected information on price changes and suggested ways for consumers to adjust to higher food prices. This material has been published in the *Consumers' Guide*.

The Consumers' Advisory Board in the NRA did the best it could with an inadequate staff and small funds to present the interests of the consumer at code hearings. None of the New Deal consumer agencies have been at all effective in protecting the interests of the consumer. The Consumers' Counsel never was expected to prevent sharp rises in the price of farm products to the consumer. The Consumers' Advisory Board was unable to prevent the inclusion in many codes of provisions for maintaining monopoly prices. It was unable to secure the adoption of code provisions guaranteeing minimum standards of service to the consumer. In spite of the efforts of the Consumers' Advisory Board, codes were used to reduce the service an aggressive and forward-looking business man might like to render, but with which his competitors did not want to bother.

Perhaps it is just as well for the consumer to realize that he can expect little or no direct help from the government in the solution of his problems. In the last analysis, good buying must be an individual matter. It is not possible by legislation to protect the fool from his folly. The most that the government can do at present is to outlaw deliberate deception and obvious falsehood.

The consumer-buyer himself is the only one who can know what is best for him to buy. The consumer-buyer can do a good job of buying only by constant attention to detail, only by constant study, observation, and thought about his buying problems. He must use the same care in his own buying that he would expect to use if he were employed as buyer for a large business concern. He must watch the details of every transaction. He must add every sales-slip as a matter of habit. He must insist upon an itemized list of his purchases, and check up to see that every purchase is delivered as originally specified. He must see to it that the price he is charged for what he buys corresponds to the price he was asked per piece or per pound or per yard for the article. He must follow up his purchases, to determine which prove to be good buys and which are unsatisfactory.

He must work out for himself a variety of devices for adding to his efficiency as a buyer. He can become familiar with easily accessible sources of market information. He can build up a small reference library of buying aids. He can even accumulate a few simple devices for testing the goods he is to buy.

He must keep constantly before him the fact that buying is one of the most important jobs to be done in the modern family. He must remember that in spite of Pure Food and Drug Laws, in spite of "Truth in Advertising" laws, in spite of "Better Business Bureaus," in spite of all our talk about "Service" and "Satisfied Customers," the old rule of *caveat emptor* (let the buyer beware) still holds. If the buyer does beware, if he devotes plenty of time to intelligent consideration of market offerings, he can greatly increase the satisfactions he makes available to his family.

QUESTIONS

1. There are those who maintain that the legal doctrine of *caveat emptor* (let the buyer beware) as now applied in cases involving commercial buyers should be changed to the doctrine of *caveat vendor* (let the seller beware), in all cases involving a consumer-buyer. Others believe that the doctrine of *caveat vendor* is impractical because it would render business men liable for mistakes of consumer-buyers, and for defects in the goods they sell, over which they have no control. They maintain that the only practical method is to apply the doctrine of *caveat emptor* impartially throughout the entire market structure.

   (a) Does the doctrine of *caveat emptor* justify misrepresentation, puffing, and the use of half-truths in selling?

   (b) Does the doctrine of *caveat emptor* imply any responsibility on the part of the manufacturer, the wholesaler, or the retailer for defective merchandise? For providing complete and accurate information about the goods he sells? About the relative value of his own and his competitor's offerings?

   (c) Does the doctrine of *caveat emptor* imply that the consumer-buyer can and must look out for his own interests in all market transactions? How can he do so?

2. Work out a table showing the comparative cost of the purchase in large and small units of identical brands of canned goods, cosmetics, paint, soap, and motor oil in the stores in your own community. How do the savings from quantity buying compare with those indicated in the table on page 114 in the text?

3. With which of the four types of buyer described in this chapter would you identify each of the families described in question 10, page 81? In what type of stores would you advise each of these families to do most of its buying? Why?

4. (a) Work out a set of recommendations to guide each of the families described in question 8, page 80, in adjusting their buying practices to the reduction in their money incomes. (b) Suppose that with the return of prosperity, their incomes return to their former levels. What changes in buying practices and policies would you then recommend? Give your reasons for each of your recommendations.

5. From the point of view of the consumer-buyer, evaluate the usual arguments for and against the chain store, the mail-order house, and any other form of integrated marketing.

6. A study of food prices in a middle-western city showed that on the same day identical brands of evaporated milk sold in different stores for the following prices: 6 cents, 7 cents, and 8 cents per tall can. The wholesale quotation on this item was 5¾ cents. How can you account for this wide variation in prices to consumers? Which of these prices was a fair price? How do you tell?

7. Collect all the different types of advertising material you can find for some well-advertised article which your family buys: for example, coffee, cigarettes, cold cream, shaving soap, tooth paste, mechanical refrigerators, radios, automobiles, towels, mattresses, furniture, plumbing, floor coverings, insulating materials, paint, roofing, and automobile tires. Include examples of national advertising, newspaper advertising, pamphlets, dealer aids, direct mail advertising, a transcription of radio advertising, a description of billboard and signboard advertising, and if you have access to them, examples of advertising in trade journals and of advertising programs directed to wholesalers or retailers urging them to handle the article in question. List all the facts which the consumer can learn about the article from each type of advertisement.

8. List the information you want to find on the label of a can of peas, a pair of shoes, a spring coat, a davenport, a spool of thread, a sheet, and a bath towel. How much of this information is now available on the articles offered for sale in your community?

9. How many people of your acquaintance are subscribers to Consumers' Research? How many of them are familiar with its service? What is their opinion of the value of its service to the consumer-buyer?

10. As a consumer-buyer what should be your attitude toward the following types of legislation: pure food and drug legislation, truth-in-advertising legislation, tariff on wheat, tariff on sugar, tariff on textiles, compulsory government grading of consumer goods, legislation authorizing or pro-

hibiting price agreements and production control, and minimum wage legislation?

11. List the ten most effective ways in which you can increase your efficiency as a buyer.

REFERENCES

Andrews, B. R., *Economics of the Household*, Revised Edition, Chs. XIV, XVI, pp. 337-367 and 403-434. The Macmillan Co., New York, 1935.

A clear and detailed description of the characteristics of the marketing organization for food and clothing.

Brindze, Ruth, *How to Spend Money: Everybody's Practical Guide to Buying*. The Vanguard Press, New York, 1935.

An entertaining and informative handbook of buying.

Chase, Stuart, and Schlink, F. J., *Your Money's Worth*. The Macmillan Co., New York, 1926.

A readable and now almost classic attack on modern methods of merchandising. Chiefly interesting because the authors get down to actual cases. More recent material of a similar nature is available in Schlink, F. J., and Kallet, Arthur, *100,000,000 Guinea Pigs*, Vanguard Press, New York, 1932, and in Phillips, M. C., *Skin Deep*, D. Appleton-Century Co., New York, 1934. These later books deal in similar vein with the pure food and drug and the cosmetic problem.

Handbook of Buying, and general bulletins. Consumers' Research, Inc., Washington, N. J.

Available only to members of Consumers' Research. Excellent and helpful material on consumer problems.

Annual Buying Guide and *Monthly Reports*. Consumers Union of the United States, Inc., New York, New York.

The *Annual Buying Guide* is for the confidential use of members only. Monthly reports are not confidential.

Hoyt, Elizabeth E., *The Consumption of Wealth*, Ch. X, pp. 97-110; Ch. XVII, pp. 176-185. The Macmillan Co., New York, 1928.

Ch. X contains an interesting evaluation of selling and advertising. Ch. XVII discusses the consumer's need for standards.

Kyrk, Hazel, *Economic Problems of the Family*, Chs. XXII and XXIII, pp. 434-494; Ch. XVII, pp. 311-329. Harper and Bros., New York, 1933.

An excellent analysis of consumer buying problems. Miss Kyrk's analysis of the effectiveness of the market as a medium for serving the consumer, and of the legal position of the consumer in the market, are especially worth while.

Reid, Margaret G., *Economics of Household Production*, Ch. XVII, pp. 273-305. John Wiley and Sons, Inc., New York, 1934.

An analysis of the problem of buying for the household, together with some specific suggestions of ways to increase buying efficiency.

Waite, W. C., and Cassidy, Ralph, Jr., *The Consumer and the Economic Order*. Chs. VI, VII, XI, XIV, XV, and XVII. McGraw-Hill Book Co., Inc., New York, 1939.

Chs. VI and VII give a comprehensive discussion of governmental and other devices for the protection of the consumer-buyer. Ch. XI describes and evaluates advertising from the consumer's viewpoint. Chs. XIV and XV describe the marketing system, and the effect of the consumer's purchasing habits upon marketing costs and retail prices. Ch. XVII discusses the problems involved in the purchase of consumer goods.

Weiss, E. B., ed., in collaboration with Mermey, Maurice, *The Shopping Guide*. Whittlesey House, McGraw-Hill Book Co., Inc., New York, 1937.

Eighteen buyers, merchandise managers, and research experts from a number of great American department stores pass their experience in buying for their departments on to the consumer to guide her in her buying. Covers most of the articles handled in department stores.

See also current magazines, pamphlets, dealer aids, and government publications for current discussion and illustrative materials.

For a thorough analysis of the marketing system from the point of view of the consumer, see two standard texts:

Coles, Jessie V., *The Consumer-buyer and the Market*. John Wiley and Sons, Inc., New York, 1938.

Reid, Margaret G., *Consumers and the Market*. F. S. Crofts and Co., New York, 1938.

CHAPTER VI

SATISFYING WANTS BY PRODUCTION FOR USE
IN THE HOME

Production for use in the American economy. It has
frequently been said that we are living in a market economy. This
means that families purchase the things they need with money earned
working for others. And yet if we had to use everything just as we
buy it we would see how far from complete much of our commercial
production really is. If we had to pay someone outside the family
to do everything that is done for us we would find it necessary to
get along without a great many things that most families now enjoy
as a matter of course. For in spite of the fact that we live in a
market economy, we still do many things for ourselves at home.

Most families spend more time producing goods and services for
the use of their members than they spend in earning and buying. If
the time spent by the housewife and the time spent by all the other
members of the family in making and doing for themselves at home
are added together, in most cases the result will be considerably more
than the time spent by the husband earning money outside the home.
Only families with two or more full-time wage earners spend more
time satisfying their wants by producing for market than they spend
producing for use at home.

The table on page 142 shows the amount of time spent upon
homemaking by a group of farm families, a group of town families,
and two groups of city families. The city families were from the
business and professional level, and apparently were able to afford
some paid household service. To these figures is added a rough estimate of the amount of time spent by the husband in earning the
family's money income. The estimate in the case of the farmer is a
mere guess. The estimate assumes a 9-hour day and a 6-day week
in small towns. It assumes a 44- or 50-hour week for the business
and professional man. In every case the hours of employment have
been generously estimated. The point is not so much to indicate
accurately the amount of time spent in earning the family income as

to give a conservative picture of the real importance of production for use in the modern American family.

What is production for use? If a family is to make wise use of home production in satisfying its wants, it must understand clearly just what production for use is. It must understand clearly all the varied activities it involves. It must see production for use in its

TIME SPENT IN PRODUCTION OF GOODS AND SERVICES TO SATISFY FAMILY
WANTS [1]

TYPE OF FAMILY	HOURS PER WEEK SPENT IN HOME-MAKING			HOURS PER WEEK SPENT IN EARNING			TOTAL HOURS PER WEEK SPENT PROVIDING FOR WANTS OF FAMILY
	House-wife	Others	Total	Hus-band	Wife	Total	
Farm families.........	51.6*	9.5*	61.1	60‡	12.3*	72.3	133.4
Town homemakers.....	51.5*	12.1*	63.6	54‡	3.3*	57.3	120.9
Business and professional families in cities 50,000 to 250,000...........	47.6†	30.5†	78.1	50‡	2.0†	52.0	130.1
Business and professional families in cities over 250,000..............	44.9†	36.6†	81.5	44‡	2.4†	46.4	127.9

* From Maud Wilson, *Use of Time by Oregon Farm Homemakers.* Station Bulletin 256, Agricultural Experiment Station, Oregon State Agricultural College, Corvallis, 1929, p. 29.
† From Committee on Household Management, President's Conference on Home Building and Home Ownership, *Household Management and Kitchens,* pp. 27 and 28. Washington, 1932.
‡ Author's estimate on basis of usual length of working day.

relation to the family's purchases in the market. It must understand how to select wisely the types of home production activity in which the family is to engage.

Production for use has been defined as "all unpaid productive activities carried on by individuals for themselves or for their families."[2] Production in this sense includes much more than the making of commodities, or even than the final processing of commodities.[3] Production has been defined as "any activity which is intended either to satisfy someone else's wants, or to build up potential want-satisfying power in something or somebody."[4] The preparation of the food,

---

[1] Hazel Kyrk, *Economic Problems of the Family,* Table XV, p. 93, and Table XVI, p. 96. Harper and Bros., New York, 1933.
[2] *Ibid.,* p. 43.
[3] Production involves the creation of utility. Utility has been defined as the power to satisfy wants. Utility can be added to commodities in a number of ways: by changing the form of an article, by moving it from a place where it is not wanted much to a place where it is wanted more, by keeping it from a time when it is not wanted much to a time when it is wanted more, or by transferring it from a person who does not want it much to a person who wants it more. Utility can be created by the rendering of personal services.
Miss Kyrk says, "Household production is more a process of creating time, place, and possession utilities, and less of creating form utilities than heretofore." (*Op. cit.,* p. 52.)
[4] John D. Black, *Production Economics,* p. 25. Henry Holt and Co., New York, 1926.

the planning of the meals, the setting of an attractive table, all are intended to satisfy the wants of others.   Washing the dishes and putting the home in order are intended to build up potential want-satisfying power in something.   Teaching the children how to perform some of the simpler household tasks is building up want-satisfying power in somebody.

Sometimes people get into interminable discussions as to just where production stops and consumption begins.   They argue at length whether gardening for fun, getting the car ready for a trip in the country, preparing the food for a picnic, and broiling a steak over a camp fire are production or consumption.

Most families are not concerned with these fine-drawn distinctions. What they want is to secure for the members of the family the largest amount of satisfaction possible.   Whether that satisfaction derives from activities which are considered purely consumptive or definitely productive is of no consequence.

Factors determining the amount and type of home production activities.   *The type of community*.   There are a number of factors which influence the amount and type of home production activities in which families engage.   Much depends upon the size and type of community in which a family lives.   It is generally assumed that there is more opportunity for production for use in rural communities than in metropolitan areas, and that farm families spend more time in producing for use the raw materials which the family uses in such activities as cutting wood for fuel, and growing and processing a large part of the food supply.

But it is not safe to generalize.   The table on page 144 shows the time spent on various homemaking activities by farm and city families.   This table indicates that town and city homemakers actually spend more time upon the usual homemaking routine than do farm families.   It may well be that many farm families appear to be producing more for themselves primarily because they are in a position to divert to their own use part of the goods they are producing for market.   The farm family engaged in producing a specialty usually produces less for its own use than does the family engaged in general farming.   The family making a business of farming usually spends less time in producing for its own use than does the family living upon a subsistence homestead.

The type of community in which a family lives affects the type of home production activities much more than it does the actual amount of time spent upon home production. There are many things which a small-town family does because it cannot buy what it wants in the local market. There are other things which the metropolitan family does not do because it can buy processed articles more cheaply than it can buy the raw materials and process them itself. Fresh fruits and

TIME SPENT ON VARIOUS HOMEMAKING ACTIVITIES [5]

(A) By 288 Farm and 154 Town and City Families in Oregon
(B) By 559 Farm and 155 Town and City Families in a Number of States

ACTIVITY	GROUP	AVERAGE TIME PER WEEK		PROPORTION OF TOTAL TIME	
		Farm Families	Town and City Families	Farm Families	Town and City Families
		Hours	Hours	Per Cent	Per Cent
Meal preparation and clearing away	A	27.0	23.9	44.3	37.6
	B	26.8	22.4	44.1	35.5
Care of house..................	A	12.3	12.8	20.1	20.2
	B	12.8	12.3	21.0	19.5
Laundering....................	A	6.3	6.8	10.3	10.7
	B	6.2	7.0	10.1	11.1
Sewing and mending............	A	4.8	5.0	7.9	7.9
	B	5.8	6.6	9.6	10.5
Care of members of family........	A	4.4	8.0	7.3	12.5
	B	4.6	8.0	7.5	12.6
Buying and management.........	A	1.8	3.2	3.0	5.0
	B	2.4	3.9	4.0	6.2
All other......................	A	4.3	3.9	7.1	6.2
	B	2.3	3.0	3.8	4.7
Total.........................	A	61.0	63.4	100.0	100.0
	B	60.9	63.2	100.0	100.0

vegetables actually cost more than canned foods even in the height of the season. This is due to the greater cost of handling perishable fruits and vegetables. There is little to be gained from home canning by the family that must pay as much for raw materials as it pays for the processed product.

The family income. Among both farm and city families there is a definite relation between the amount of production for use and the adequacy of the family's money income. The family with a small income of necessity spends most of its time processing food,

[5] Hazel Kyrk, *op. cit.*, Table 13, p. 51. (A) Maud Wilson, Oregon State Agricultural College, unpublished data. (B) U. S. Bureau of Home Economics, unpublished data.

making clothing, and keeping up the minimum essentials of house-keeping routine.   Families with more generous incomes are able to buy most of the essentials, leaving time for the refinement and elaboration of the family's manner of living.

Opportunities for employment.   In most urban families the adequacy of the family's money income depends to a very considerable extent upon opportunities for employment outside the home.   When it is easy for several members of a family to find employment at good wages, they pay others to do for them many things they otherwise would do for themselves.   When it is difficult to find employment, the members of the family return to making and doing for themselves many of the things which they bought from others when they were employed.

Hours of employment.   The extent and types of home production activity in which a family engages depend also upon the usual hours of employment in occupations open to members of the family outside the home.   It has always been assumed that the housewife is to be the full-time worker in the home.   For many years the twelve-hour day in industry, and later the ten-hour day and the six-day week, made it impossible for the husband to do much work about the home.   During the World War came the general adoption of the eight-hour day and the Saturday half-holiday.   Since 1930 there has been a definite trend toward the six-hour day, or the eight-hour day with a five-day week.   This shortening of the hours of employment outside the home has made it possible for the wife as well as the husband to find employment.   At the same time the short day has made it possible for the husband as well as the wife to spend more time upon home production activities.

The size of the family.   The size of the family has a definite bearing upon the amount of production a family can afford to carry on in the home.   Ordinarily, the larger the family, the more it does for itself at home.   There are more people to work in the large family.   Since any given income must be spread over a larger number of individuals, there is less money to spend per individual.   If a large family is to maintain anywhere near the same sort of a standard as that maintained by smaller families with the same amount of income it must supplement its money income with home production activities.

The savings from production for use are much greater in the case of the large family than in the case of the small family. For a family of two or three, there are many items which can be purchased for a small amount in the market. These items can perhaps be produced for less at home, but the total saving is so small that it hardly seems worth while to go to the trouble to do at home what is being well done for the family at low cost in the market. The large family, however, finds that even small expenditures repeated for four or five members amount to enough so that the savings from home production assume real importance.

The work involved in home production activities does not ordinarily increase in proportion to the increase in the number of individuals served. It takes almost as long to bake a small cake as to bake a large one. It takes just as long to get out the equipment and to clean up when baking one pie as when baking two. The amount of equipment needed to work effectively is just as great if sewing is done for one person as for two or three.

The make-up of the family. The make-up of the family and the stage of the family in the family life cycle have a bearing upon the amount and type of production carried on in the home. This is particularly important in connection with the activities inevitably connected with rearing the children. The table on page 147 shows clearly the relationship of the age of the children to the time spent upon homemaking. The families with small children spend much more time on essential household tasks, many of them directly connected with the physical care of the children. The family with children of high school age may find it well to provide supervised recreational activities in the home. The family with pre-school children must spend considerable time upon their physical care. An elderly couple usually do enough to keep themselves occupied, but they avoid as far as possible the heavier household tasks.

The abilities of the members of the family. The type of home production activity in which a family engages depends upon the special abilities of its members. The housewife who is a good cook spends more time upon the preparation of food. The housewife with a talent for clothing design makes her own clothing. The husband with mechanical ability repairs the family car and makes minor repairs around the house. The husband with athletic ability organizes and supervises the children's outdoor play activities.

EFFECT OF CHILDREN IN HOUSEHOLD UPON LENGTH OF HOMEMAKER'S
WORKING WEEK AND AMOUNT OF HELP RECEIVED [6]

CHILDREN IN THE HOUSEHOLD	NUMBER OF HOME-MAKERS	AVERAGE PERSONS IN HOUSE-HOLD	TIME PER WEEK			
			Homemakers Only		Help Received in Home-making	Total Time Spent in Home-making
			All Work	All Home-making		
Farm Homemaker			*Hours*	*Hours*	*Hours*	*Hours*
No children..............	89	2.7	60.5	44.9	4.3	49.2
No children under 6........	105	4.6	62.3	51.0	12.5	63.7
Youngest child between 1 and 6	78	5.0	66.5	56.0	10.7	66.8
Youngest child under 1......	16	5.7	77.3	69.4	11.9	81.3
Total.................	288	4.2	63.9	51.6	9.5	61.1
Town Homemaker						
No children..............	23	2.6	49.5	44.2	5.6	49.9
No children under 6........	53	4.5	52.5	47.9	11.0	59.0
Youngest child between 1 and 6	69	4.7	56.8	54.9	12.9	67.8
Youngest child under 1......	9	5.3	67.3	65.5	28.2	94.2
Total.................	154	4.4	54.8	51.5	12.1	63.6

The family's equipment and other resources.   Finally, the type of home production activity in which a family engages depends upon the equipment and materials and other resources which the family has at its disposal.   A family living in a large house can engage in more and different types of production for use than can a family living in a small city apartment.   A family with an electric sewing machine may find that it pays to spend time making clothing at home. A well-equipped laundry may make it profitable for a family to do its own washing.   If a family has a supply of fruit jars and kettles and canning equipment, it may find it pays to do home canning.   A family without any of this equipment may decide that the savings in its case will not be large enough to justify the investment in the necessary equipment.   Every family, then, produces for its own use at home whatever will enable it to make the best use of all its varied resources.

Trends in production for use.   Because of the constantly increasing variety of goods and services offered for sale on the market, we have come to assume that the Industrial Revolution and the development of the factory system started a trend which would eventu-

[6] Hazel Kyrk, *op. cit.*, Table XVI, p. 96.   From Maud Wilson, *Use of Time by Oregon Farm Homemakers*, Station Bull. 256, Agricultural Experiment Station, Oregon State Agricultural College, Corvallis, 1929, p. 29.

ally take production entirely out of the home, leaving only consumption behind. We have been finding in recent years, however, that many trends can be reversed. What we had supposed to be a trend in home production now appears rather to be a cyclical change. Both the amount and the types of home production activity vary as the changes in the business cycle increase or decrease the opportunities for gainful employment. They vary with the changing needs of the family as it passes through successive stages of the family life cycle. The division of productive activity between industry and the home is being constantly adjusted to take advantage of invention and scientific development, which from time to time offers first new sorts of goods in the market and then new types of equipment for facilitating production for use at home.

It has been said that the invention of the spinning mule and the power loom, the power sewing machine, and the steam laundry, took many activities out of the home. Now electricity, which makes inexpensive power available in small units, in electric sewing machines and electric washers, is bringing these same activities back into the home.

The importance of production for use. Production for use is an important element in the family economy for a number of reasons. By producing for itself at home a family can secure many goods and services it cannot afford to buy in the market. Few family incomes are sufficient to purchase everything the family wants. There are many things which the family can do for itself with little or no money outlay. There are many things which can be secured for not over half the money outlay if the family buys materials and does the final processing at home.

By production for use, a family is able to make for itself articles which are not available in the market in suitable form. This is particularly important for families that want commodities that are a little out of the ordinary in size, style, color, or quality. By producing for their own use they can get exactly what they need; they are not forced to get along with something almost as good or to pay for nonessentials in order to get the things they want. A family with members larger or smaller than the average finds considerable advantage in making clothing at home, because each garment can be made to fit. A family wanting to buy an article of better quality than those offered ready-made on the market can buy high-grade materials and make exactly what it wants for itself.

By production for use the unsalable time of the members of the family can be put to good use in the home. There are families with older men or women who cannot work the long hours or work at the high speed which many industrial processes require. But these same individuals can spend some time every day at their own convenience doing or making things for the family at home. Physically handicapped individuals who are not able to do the sort of work required outside the home can make substantial contributions to the things the family has to use. Housewives mistakenly barred from employment simply because they are married can make good use of their time in ways which add a great deal to the well-being of their families. And boys and girls below the legal age for gainful employment can begin to contribute definitely to the family support by taking over activities in the home which are entirely within their capabilities. The outstanding advantage of home production activities lies in the fact that by careful planning the family can make use of unsalable labor under conditions so well adapted to the abilities of the individual workers that they are beneficial rather than detrimental to the workers involved.

Production for use eliminates or greatly reduces distribution costs. Distribution costs are a very large element in the cost of the goods a family buys in the market. The greater the variety of goods from which the consumer makes his selection, the more important the style factor, the greater the care required in handling, and the more perishable the product, the greater is the cost of distribution of a product.

The family that raises fruit and vegetables in its own garden eliminates entirely the cost of marketing these perishable foodstuffs, and the family that makes its own clothing eliminates the distribution cost involved in merchandising style goods. It must pay only the lower costs of distributing the standardized materials it uses.

There are many types of home production activity which in themselves provide satisfying leisure-time activity. There is a definite satisfaction to be had from seeing a tangible product take shape in a worker's hands. There is the same sort of satisfaction whether the product be an evening gown or a house dress, cake or bread, lampshades or slip covers. Flower gardening is definitely recognized as a hobby. Vegetable gardening has similar qualities, with edible by-products as well. Knitting and embroidery have a standing as leisure-time activities. There can be the same sort of satisfaction from any of the handicraft activities carried on in the home.

An equal amount of satisfaction of a slightly different type can be secured from the managerial activities which must be carried on in the home. The same satisfaction that many housewives go out of the home to secure in club work and committee work and various sorts of public service activities may be found in planning and co-ordinating the varied activities of a family. Whether home production is looked upon as a task or as fun depends largely upon the point of view of the person who engages in it.

Many types of home production activity have definite educational value for the younger members of the family. In their own home, boys and girls can learn by experience many of the common techniques of homemaking. And if a little attention is given to tying up home production activities with production outside the home, they can learn a good deal about the handling of materials, the fundamentals of industrial processes, and the nature and use of machinery.

For example, by working in the family garden, they can learn about soils and fertilizers, about seeds and plant varieties, and about all the processes of growth. By helping with home sewing they can learn a good deal about textiles, and the processes in the garment industry. They can learn about various mechanical trades by watching and working at minor repairs of various sorts at home.

By engaging in first one and then another type of activity they can discover for themselves their special interests and special aptitudes. As they grow older this will help them to determine their vocations. And what is even more valuable, by actual participation in the conduct of family affairs, young people can formulate for themselves the principles of family management and of the philosophy underlying happy home life.

Production for use makes a family independent of the market in a way which would otherwise be impossible. Through production for use a family can get along when employment is irregular or hard to find. Production for use aids the family when the offerings in the market are too high in price or are not to its liking. If a family can do for itself at home, it is not compelled to pay high prices for commodities which suit its needs only indifferently. Production for use is a factor which greatly strengthens the bargaining power of the family as a consumer-buyer. Even though the family ordinarily produces little for itself at home, the more it knows about the processes involved in production, the greater the variety of skills it has at its disposal, the greater is its knowledge of the goods which are offered for its consideration, and the stronger is its strategic position as a buyer when it goes to market.

Planning the home production program. *Selecting activities.* Ordinarily no two families engage in exactly the same combination of home production activities. Each family adjusts its home production program to its own family situation. In deciding what to produce for its own use, each family takes account of both the personal and financial aspects of the problem.

It is usually worth while to make an article at home if the family prefers the homemade to the factory-made article, even though very little cash saving is involved. It is worth while to make an article at home if the desired article cannot otherwise be had, either because it is not available in the market or because its price is prohibitive. It is worth while to produce for use in the home in order to make use of resources, either material or personal, which would otherwise be wasted. Often it may be worth while to engage in some home production activities for the fun of doing them, or because of the educational values they involve.

Of course, the time and energy as well as the financial resources of the members of a family are limited. In working out its home production program, the family must in the last analysis select a group of activities which will pay best both from the pecuniary and the personal viewpoint.

Estimating costs. What pays best can be determined only by a study of comparative costs. The problem of determining the cost of carrying on a home production activity is not exactly the same as the problem of estimating the cost of goods produced for sale on the market. It is more like the problem of figuring the cost of by-products. In estimating the cost of the principal product of an industrial plant it is important to include every element of cost, not only the direct costs like the labor and materials used but also a proper share of the overhead costs such as managerial expenses, the expense of maintaining machinery and equipment, and adequate allowances for depreciation. Unless an industrial concern includes all these costs and prices its product accordingly, it may soon find itself in the hands of a receiver.

On the other hand, when an industrial concern estimates the cost of by-products, it must count only the additional cost of putting the secondary product on the market. Assuming that the concern is able to get enough for its principal product to take care of all its fixed charges and overhead expenses, it can count as profits everything it secures from the sale of the by-product above the additional outlay the production involves.

Similarly, there are two ways to estimate the costs of home-production activities. In some cases a family is interested in computing the total cost of producing an article at home. In this case the family assigns a cash value to all the labor and materials it uses, puts in a definite allowance for overhead cost, estimates depreciation on all the equipment it uses, and includes every item that could possibly be charged to the carrying on of the activity in question.

This method is valuable if the family wants to compare the cost of home products with the cost of similar products purchased in the market. It is valuable also for the family that is making up its mind as to whether it is better for the members of the family to work and earn outside the home or to work for themselves within the family group. This method gives an interesting comparison of the relative efficiency of production in the home and production in the market, and is worth while if a family wants to know the amount it can afford to invest in labor-saving machinery and the amount it can afford to pay for labor to carry on activities in the home.

In other cases families may estimate costs of home production activities as business men estimate the cost of by-products. Most families consider the production activities which they carry on in the home as incidental to everyday family life. They assume that they must maintain a house equipped and run in the customary fashion. In deciding whether or not to carry on a given activity in the home they ignore such items as return on their investment in their home, the cost of fuel and light, and other operating items. They do not include depreciation on equipment on the basis that depreciation will go on whether they use their equipment or not. Unless cash is actually paid out for the work done, they make no charge for labor because they assume that otherwise there would be no cash return for the time spent on these home production activities.   They count only their current money expenditures.

Most families find that there are many situations in which neither of these two methods is entirely satisfactory.   While they need not include every item as in the first method, neither can they ignore all overhead charges as in the second.   A family should count overhead costs whenever it is necessary to purchase new equipment in order to engage in a given activity, and whenever the additional use of the present equipment will necessitate replacement sooner than would otherwise be necessary.   It should count overhead costs if an activity adds materially to the family's fuel, light, or other general operating expenses.

For example: If a family must buy a washing machine it should count the cost of the equipment as part of the cost of doing the family laundry.   If heating the water adds materially to the family's fuel bill, it should count the additional cost of fuel.   If a paid helper does the work it should count the outlay for labor.   But if the family already has a washing machine paid for and standing idle in the basement, it may decide to ignore that element of overhead in computing the cost of laundering the household linens.   If the work is to be done by some member or members of the family in otherwise unsalable time, it is reasonable to leave out any charge for labor.   Instead of assigning a definite cost to use of the equipment and a definite cost in the form of an assumed value assigned to the workers' time, it is just as logical to consider the savings in cash outlay for laundering as return on the family's investment in laundry equipment, and as wages earned by the family members.

In working out the family's home production program, time and energy costs are just as important to consider as are money costs.   If much time and effort are required to find exactly what the family wants among current market offerings, it may actually be easier to buy materials and produce for use at home.   If, on the other hand, heavy or long-continued or distasteful physical labor is required to produce an article at home, the family may decide that regardless of the additional money expense it will be worth while to purchase that commodity in the market.

Ordinarily families find that they can secure greater savings from production for use in the case of goods and services involving a high proportion of labor cost and a small proportion of material or equipment cost, and also in those involving special adjustments to consumer needs. They will find greater savings in items which must be produced on a small scale near the point of consumption, and in items which involve a high marketing cost for finished goods but a low marketing cost for the standardized materials used.

In deciding upon what to buy in the market and what to produce for use at home there is no one right answer. Every family must decide upon its home production program only after carefully balancing the money values and the human values that are involved. If time is plentiful and money is scarce, the family will find a different answer to its problem than it will if money is plentiful and time is scarce. If educational values are important it may find yet another answer. The important thing in deciding upon each item in the home production program is to determine whether or not the addition it will make to the goods or services available to the family is worth what it costs in money, time, and effort.

Increasing efficiency in home production. It is ordinarily assumed that home production is less efficient than industrial production. This is not necessarily true. It is possible, of course, to find many examples of inefficiency in home production, but it is equally possible to find examples of efficient production for use.

Inefficiency in home production may be due to a variety of causes. It may result from the use of incorrect methods, unskilled performances, inadequate or idle equipment, or inconvenient working space. It may be, and frequently is, due to poor planning.

There are a number of ways by which a family can increase its efficiency in home production. A family will ordinarily find it easier to produce efficiently if it concentrates upon a few types of production. Today this is entirely possible. Market offerings are so varied that it is no longer necessary for a family to engage in a great variety of home production activities.

A family will be able to increase its productive efficiency if it studies various methods of carrying on each household task. It can then select the method which best fits its individual situation. There are various sources from which information about methods is available. Government bulletins, extension classes, study groups, library facilities, and even commercial demonstrations are valuable aids in keeping up to date in methods and techniques of home production.

Productive efficiency can be increased by increasing the efficiency of the individual members of the family. In planning its home production program it should select activities which take advantage of the experience and aptitudes of members of the family. It should, as far as possible, practice division of labor among the members of the family group, assigning each task to the member of the family best fitted to perform it, and seeing that that member is properly instructed in the techniques involved. It should allow him to develop his skill by repetition in performance.

A family can increase its productive efficiency by providing adequate equipment for the tasks it is carrying on at home. By investing in modern household equipment, it can secure the same advantages from machinery as does the well-equipped industrial plant. Modern electrical devices such as the vacuum sweeper, the electric sewing machine, the electric washing machine, and the electric ironing machine all provide the power needed to do what otherwise would be rather heavy tasks. Modern attachments and automatic controls eliminate the need of manual skill; the skill is transferred to the machinery. Electric sewing machines come equipped with a number of attachments for doing difficult bits of sewing. Modern electric and gas stoves are equipped with automatic oven heat controls. Candy thermometers, deep-fat frying thermometers, and meat thermometers take the guesswork out of cooking. Pressure cookers are equipped with accurate gauges. Modern recipes are written in terms of exact temperature control. Heating plants can be equipped with oil burners and automatic stokers, and with thermostatically controlled humidifiers. And recently there have come on the market a number of types of power wood-working and metal-working machinery, which will enable the family to set up at moderate expense a power shop in which a mechanically-minded man can produce a great many of the items of furniture and equipment which the family needs.

A family can increase its productive efficiency if it provides adequate and well-organized working space for carrying on each activity in which it engages. There is plenty of material available suggesting layouts for an efficient kitchen, an efficient basement laundry, or an efficient home workshop. Each family has as its problem the adaptation of these ideal plans to its present available housing facilities.

A family can greatly increase its productive efficiency by careful management. The use of proper methods, the possession of adequate skills, the ownership of adequate equipment and convenient working space, by themselves are no guarantee of efficiency. Skillful management is also essential. By careful management it is possible to save time by having everything at hand before starting work. It is possible to do enough work at a time to make preparation pay. By doing a considerable amount of ironing at one time it is possible to save the current it takes to heat the iron. By timing various tasks and dovetailing the jobs to be done, it is possible to keep workers effectively employed all the time they are on the job. It increases efficiency to do work requiring concentration when the worker will be most likely to be free from interruption. The mother of small children finds it is more efficient to plan and cut out clothing when the children are asleep. She does bits of hand sewing when she must be in the living room watching the children. She can use fuel more efficiently by co-ordinating baking and oven meals. She can use her time in the kitchen to better advantage if she co-ordinates baking and meal preparation. She can save much effort if she plans to do work in the proper order, so that no one task will make it necessary to do over work she has already done. She will change a bed before she sweeps and dusts a room. She will see that the woodwork is washed before she mops the floor.

In working out the home production program, it is possible to avoid waste by beginning new activities on a small scale, and by experimenting first with each new type of activity in which the family is to engage. If a family is planning to raise a garden, the first year it can do what can be done with simple tools, concentrating on a few familiar products that it uses most frequently, and that can be grown most easily. The second year it can add a few new crops, and gradually work from the easy to the more difficult varieties. It can invest in more equipment, such as a wheel hoe. In the third or fourth year it may have expanded its activities to the extent that a mechanical planter may be desirable. And after two or three years of experimentation with annuals it will be in a position to plant berries and fruits—the things which require more knowledge, skill, and care, and which represent a larger original investment.

Or in taking care of the automobile, the family can begin by washing the car. Then it can take over the greasing of the car. Finally, if the members have some skill, they may begin making minor adjustments and gradually work up to the point where they can make some of the more ordinary repairs. Only when they are sure that they can carry on an extensive repair program should they invest in special tools and equipment for the purpose.

Adjusting the home production program to changing family needs. In working out the home production program it is important always to keep in mind the importance of adjusting the program from time to time to changes in the family's available resources and to changes in family needs.   Ordinarily a family will expand its home production program during a business depression to offset losses in income from reductions in wages and salaries, from irregular employment, or from investment losses.   During prosperity, on the other hand, when it is easy for the members of the family to obtain congenial and remunerative employment outside the home, it will decrease its production for use.

Similarly it will adjust its home production program to the changes in family needs and family resources as it passes from one stage to another of the family life cycle.   If the young married couple find it to their advantage for both husband and wife to find gainful employment outside the home, they will keep their home production activities to a minimum.   They will live in a small apartment, buy much of their food ready to go on the table, buy their clothing ready-made, send their washing to the laundry, perhaps even hire occasional help to do the weekly cleaning.   They will concentrate upon the accumulation of funds sufficient to buy a well-equipped home, or to set up financial reserves which can later be depended upon to add to the family's money income.

A family with small children, on the other hand, will find that it will be wise to carry on a considerable number of home production activities.   The types of activity selected will be those which can be combined effectively with the care of the small children, which the housewife can carry on without too much additional effort, and which can be carried on entirely within the home.   This is a period in which the hours of housework are so long, and the continuous care of small children so confining, that household help is especially desirable. Sometimes it is possible for a family to have this extra service only if the family's income can be stretched by using part of the paid helper's time to carry on money-saving home production activities.

During the elementary school period the mother is still confined to the home, but the personal care of the children is less wearing. She can often undertake other types of production for use.   It is well for the family to begin early to train the children in simple tasks about the home. The family may even during the elementary school stage begin to select some household tasks with regard to their educational value.

During the high school period the children are old enough to make a significant contribution to home production. If the family finds its money income is hardly adequate to meet the growing demands of the family, it can expand its home production program, using the labor of the children for the actual performance of many household tasks, and allowing the mother to concentrate more and more upon the management and co-ordination of the growing variety of family activities. During the high school period, the family should give the boys and girls a chance to familiarize themselves with most of the work done in the home. There should be definite attention to training in planning and management as well as in the details of performance. Many families find that even though their money income is adequate to purchase most of the things they need in the market, there are definite educational values from participation in household activities which in themselves justify a home production program.

As the children grow up and leave home, there is ordinarily a tendency to cut down gradually the family's home production program. During the college period, the changes in the program will depend mostly upon whether the boys and girls of college age are away at college or are living at home. If they are living at home, the family may continue a rather extensive production program, shaping it to meet the changing needs of the family. If the boys and girls are away at college and the family finds it is difficult to secure the money it needs to keep them in school, the housewife may continue on a somewhat smaller scale most of the production activities which she practiced during the high school period. But these activities will be selected now with an eye to the greatest money savings, and they will be continued only as long as it is necessary to supplement the family's money income.

In the years after the children have left home, most families find that their money income is fairly adequate. If one or two of the children are living at home and contributing their share toward defraying the family expenses, the family will be able to reduce home production to a minimum and to select the activities it does carry on solely on the basis of preference.

In the retirement period, home production assumes a new significance. Though it may be important to make the family's money income go as far as possible, it is even more important to provide some sort of work around the house which will keep the husband occupied at tasks that seem reasonably worth doing. In old age, the members of the family should plan to spend their time as far as possible upon what they like to do. They will prefer to continue without interruption their accustomed routine. They will continue for the most part only tasks requiring low energy output. They may be interested in some hobby. The type of activity in which they will engage will depend largely upon past habits and interests. In old age, home production activities are most important as worth while leisure-time activities.

The family should develop its home production program as an integral part of the family's life. When it seems desirable to expand the family's home production program, it will be possible to accumulate equipment in advance of need. Equipment should be purchased with regard to the length of time it is to be used, and should last as long as needed. If the family is to get its money out of the equipment it should be worn out about the time it is to be discarded.

By taking thought in advance it will be possible to develop the abilities which the various members of the family will need to use at various times during the life of the family. The young couple can thoroughly master the techniques of routine housework before child-care becomes an important problem. The young mother can concentrate upon acquiring the skills needed for care of small children. As the children grow older, she can be looking a little ahead and learning about problems and how to solve them before they arrive. The parents can keep constantly in mind the things they did not know how to do when they were married, which they want their boys and girls to be prepared to do. They can work out as part of the home production program a well-integrated educational program which will prepare their boys and girls for worthy membership, both in the present family, and later on in homes of their own.

Clearly, production for use is of vital importance in every family's affairs. The problem is much broader than that of working out ways and means by which under-employed families can eke out an existence on subsistence homesteads. The aim in our present social economy is not to try to make a family as nearly as possible self-sufficient and independent of its neighbors. Rather it is to devise ways and means by which families can produce for their own use at home goods and services which they would not be able to have were they to depend entirely upon purchase in the market. Although it may differ in character and extent, production for use is just as important in the city apartment as on the subsistence homestead. Its aim is to enable families everywhere to make available for their members the richest and most satisfying life it is possible for them to secure by wise use of all the means at their disposal.

QUESTIONS

1. List all the activities you know which can, if necessary, be carried on in the home to supplement the family's money income. Classify these in three ways, as follows:

   (a) According to who may engage in them, as: (1) women's activities; (2) men's activities; (3) activities suited to either men or women; and (4) activities requiring family co-operation.

   (b) Activities suited to families living: (1) on farms; (2) in small towns or villages; (3) in single houses in cities; and (4) in city apartments.

   (c) According to skill and equipment as: (1) activities which require special equipment; (2) activities which requre special skill; and (3) activities which require neither special equipment nor special skill.

2. It is frequently said that home production nowadays is a luxury rather than a necessity, undertaken primarily to perform those extra services that make life more worth living. Do you agree that this is true during periods of prosperity? During depression? For families with adequate money income? For families with low money income?

3. In what types of economic activity is there the greatest advantage in mass production? In what types of economic activity is there greater advantage in home production? For what types of commodities and services is there greatest saving in distribution costs by production for use at home?

4. What do you consider to be the relative importance of the following values which may be secured from production for use: (a) satisfying wants better; (b) satisfying more wants; (c) satisfying wants not otherwise possible; and (d) engaging in activity which is satisfying in itself?

Are there any other values to be secured from home production which you feel should be listed with these?   What are they?

5. (a) List the elements which should be included in determining the cost of commodities and services secured from household production.   (b) Under what circumstances should the family count as part of the cost of home production the time spent by members of the family?   (c) What difference would it make if: (1) the work is done by the housewife who is devoting her entire time to housekeeping; (2) the work is done in spare time by a member of the family who is earning; (3) the work is done by a member of the family who otherwise would be gainfully employed?

6. The husband of a family consisting of the man, his wife, and 2 children, 10 and 8 years old, is employed 6 hours a day, 5 days a week, on a job in which hours are limited by law.   He earns 50 cents an hour. He formerly was employed 50 hours a week, for 60 cents an hour.   In order that it may be possible for the family to live on his present earning, his wife is working 9 hours a day, 7 days a week, doing at home many things the family formerly paid for with their larger money income.

(a) How much time should the husband be expected to spend after hours helping his wife with the housework?   Why?

(b) Should he plan to use his time to supplement still further the family's meager money income, or to relieve his wife of part of her present burden?   State your reasons.

7. In estimating the cost of feeding a family at home and comparing this with the cost of feeding it in a restaurant or a boarding house, ordinarily only the actual cost of the food purchased and in a few cases the cost of ice and fuel are included in the costs of the home-planned meals.

(a) Is this a sound basis for deciding upon the relative advantage of boarding and of providing meals at home?

(b) Should the housewife count a share of rent for the space used in the kitchen and dining room, a return on the family's investment in kitchen equipment, table service, and the like, along with a definite charge for her own labor as part of the cost of feeding the family at home?

8. Which of the following statements is correct?

(a) The baker: "I can sell you baked goods of all kinds cheaper than you can bake them for yourself.   For I buy all my materials at wholesale, use the most efficient types of equipment, and have all the advantages of the efficient use of labor that come from large-scale production."

(b) The housewife: "I can cut my bill for baked goods in half by doing all my own baking."

9. A family owns its own home. It has an adequate set-up of furniture, a piano, radio, and home equipment of all the more usual kinds. In deciding whether or not to engage in various home production activities, should it count its original investment in this equipment as part of its cost? Why or why not?

10. (a) Estimate the possibilities of stretching a $20-a-week income by home production activities. Will this affect the earning power of other individuals outside the family? Why or why not? (b) Can a family with a $20-a-week income from the family head, now working a 6-hour day and a 6-day week, add more to its income by having him work 12 hours more for others, or by having him spend 12 hours outside of working hours doing things at home for his family? How do you decide? Explain fully.

11. (a) At how early an age should boys and girls be expected to perform some tasks around the home: (1) occasionally, (2) regularly, (3) during vacations, (4) during the school year?

(b) List some activities suitable: (1) for children of pre-school age; (2) for elementary school children; (3) for junior high school boys and girls; and (4) for senior high school students. Which of these activities have definite educational value?

(c) Should children's activities be selected on the basis of (1) economic advantage, (2) educational advantage, or (3) suitable leisure-time activity?

12. (a) On the basis of the estimates of time spent in various homemaking activities by farm and city families (see table, page 144), how much time should be spent in home economics courses in teaching the various skills involved? (b) This table indicates that only about 5 per cent of the time of the housewife is spent in buying and management. Does this mean that 5 per cent of the time in instruction is enough to devote to these topics? Why or why not? (c) Should the time spent in training be proportioned to the time spent by housewives in these various activities, should it be proportioned to the difficulties in the learning processes involved, or should it be determined on some other basis?

13. (a) Do you look for an immediate increase in home production? Why or why not? A permanent increase or decrease in home production? (b) What types of activities do you think will increasingly be put upon a home production basis? What types of activities will probably continue their trend away from home?

REFERENCES

Borsodi, Ralph, *Flight from the City*. Harper and Bros., New York, 1933. A description of one family's experiences during more than a decade upon a subsistence homestead. The book contains an unbiased presentation of the theory and practice of the homestead movement by a man who believes whole-heartedly in its underlying philosophy. It includes many cautions to warn the unwary of the difficulties adjustment to such a mode of life involves. Chs. II through VII discuss in detail the economic and engineering problems involved in the conduct of specific home production activities.

Hambidge, Gove, *The Enchanted Acre*. Whittlesey House, McGraw-Hill Book Co., Inc., New York, 1935.

Another account of a subsistence household, with carefully substantiated data.

Kyrk, Hazel, *Economic Problems of the Family*, pp. 41-76. Harper and Bros., New York, 1933.

Chs. III and IV contain a concise but thorough discussion of the amount and nature of modern household production, together with an analysis of the economic problems such production involves. Chs. V and VI consider the problem from the point of view of its effect upon the homemaker. A solid and carefully thought out discussion.

Reid, Margaret G., *Economics of Household Production*. John Wiley and Sons, Inc., New York, 1934.

One of the few books devoted entirely to a discussion of problems of household production. A comprehensive and detailed analysis of the problem, approaching it from many angles. The student should use the table of contents and the index.

CHAPTER VII

SATISFYING WANTS BY SPENDING TOGETHER

Spending together. The family is a fundamental economic unit, primarily because by spending together its members are able to enjoy a great many things which they could not afford if they spent as individuals their personal share of the family's income. Spending together in the family is but the first step in co-operative expenditure. Most families share in the support of a number of organizations in their community. When members of a family join a country club, they recognize that they are spending with the other members of the club to provide a golf course and a club house such as no one of them alone could hope to maintain. When they join a lodge, they are paying their share for certain satisfactions which come from membership in a fraternal organization. When they join a church, they are paying their share of the cost of maintaining the services of the church and of providing a proper place in which to worship. And when they contribute to the support of a hospital, which they may never use, when they contribute to the support of the various charitable organizations in the community, from which they personally may never receive a cent of benefit, and when they pay their taxes, they are spending together for common wants, just as truly as when they pay their membership fees at the country club.

There are three types of expenditures which people can well make together. First, we spend together for protection from common perils, defense from invasion from without, and what is today even more important, protection against dangers from within. These dangers include not only the dangers of physical violence, but danger of loss from fire, from unsanitary conditions, from physical hazards of unregulated traffic, from poorly maintained or poorly lighted streets, from poorly constructed buildings, from contaminated milk supply, and from contagious disease epidemics.

Second, we spend together to satisfy our common obligations to our less fortunate fellow men. We provide food and clothing and shelter for the unemployed, hospitalization and medical care for the sick, homes for dependent children, the necessities of life for the aged, and recreational and educational opportunities for the underprivileged. In these enterprises for the common good, we all bear our share of the expense.

Third, we spend together for the satisfaction of our common wants. We gather together a group interested in golf, and organize a country club, or we find a group interested in the drama and organize a Little Theater. Because we want good roads upon which to drive, we organize highway commissions, provide them with funds, and authorize them to build and maintain roads. Because we want schools for our boys and girls, we organize school districts, select school boards, levy taxes, and provide for ourselves the sort of schools we desire.

Private vs. public expenditures. There are two types of organization through which we can spend together. We may ally ourselves with private organizations, like a church, the Y.M.C.A. or the Y.W.C.A., the Boy or Girl Scouts, a club, a fraternity, a college, a hospital, or a private charitable organization. Or we may spend together through governmental units. If we spend together through private organizations of one sort or another, our participation is voluntary. Our expenditures, even for social obligations such as contributions to charity, are clearly a matter of choice. If we spend together through governmental units, our contributions are made in the form of taxes, fees, and special assessments. These payments are compulsory. Since this is so, participation is not so clearly a matter of choice. And yet, with a democratic government, we can have some voice in the determination of public expenditures. We are represented by elected representatives in the city council, on the school board, in the legislature, and in Congress, just as truly as we are represented by the governing board of the country club, or the officers of the lodge, or the trustees of the church, or the board of control of the charitable organization. In either case, we delegate our authority to determine the details of the expenditures which must be made for the common purposes to which we as members of a social or civic or political group are all committed.

Apportioning the cost of common expenditures. There are three ways of determining the amount of our share in a common enterprise. In some cases, we each contribute a pro rata share of the cost of the facilities and services which we enjoy. In other cases, we contribute in proportion to our ability to bear a share in the common expense. In still other cases we pay in proportion to the benefit we receive or the use we make of the common services.

If we join a country club or a lodge, we must pay the regular yearly membership fees. If we attend a state-supported college or university, we must pay the regular tuition fees. If we join a church we may pay in proportion to our ability to bear a share of the common expense. If we own property in a community we must pay a share of the expenses of carrying on the governmental activities in that community in proportion to the value of our property. If the city paves the street in front of our property, we pay a share of the cost of the improvement which is based upon the frontage of the property benefited. If we drive a motor car upon the highway, we pay a tax every time we buy a gallon of gasoline, which makes our contribution to highway support definitely proportioned to the use we make of the highways.

The economy of spending together. We contribute willingly to most of these common expenditures because we get so much more for our money when we spend it together than when we spend it as individual families. Even though we pay more than do some others associated with us in the common enterprise, we still are getting a service for less than it would cost if we had to meet the entire expense out of our own pockets.

Frequently there are a few well-to-do members in a church who contribute heavily to its support. The contributions of the majority seem very small by comparison. And yet even to these heavy contributors the cost of the services of the church is much less than would be the cost of maintaining a private chapel, a private organist, a private choir, and a privately supported spiritual adviser.

Most motorists are convinced that it is good business to pay a tax on the gasoline they use. A motorist who can drive fifteen miles on a gallon of gasoline finds that a three-cent tax costs him one-fifth of one cent per mile for his share of the construction and maintenance of the highway system. By driving on a paved highway, any motorist can save one-fifth of one cent a mile on maintenance and operating costs alone, and have the convenience and comfort of riding upon a widespread network of improved highways as clear gain from his expenditure.

Milk inspection service costs very little per person, if the city health department sets up a division to make regular inspections and tests. It would cost each family a great deal more than its share of the common charge personally to check up on its own milk supply.

One of the best examples of the economy of spending together is the public school. It is possible to provide for the education of the children in the public schools at a much lower cost per child than would be necessary if each family provided individual training for its own children at home. Suppose a family hired a tutor for each of its children for two hours a day. Suppose it employed special teachers from time to time to give instruction in music and art and physical education. And suppose it employed a nursemaid or a companion to supervise the activities of the children for the rest of the hours they spend in the public schools. The cost of the tutor alone, for two hours a day for the two hundred days of the school year would amount to $400, if the private tutor were paid only $1 an hour. This is about half the usual rate of pay for private lessons in music and art. A conservative estimate for providing anywhere near the same amount of mere book-learning that boys and girls get in the public schools would be $400, and it would include no provision for books and pictures and materials of all sorts which the public schools provide. A family can well afford to pay its share for the support of good public schools, in which the cost per pupil is around $100 per year, rather than to allow the schools to be closed and pay for the education of its own children at home. And even the families who find their share for the support of the schools is as much as $300 or $400 a year can better spend their money for public education than for private education, since by spending with other families in the community they can get not only a good education for their own children, but also the benefit that comes from living in a community which provides a good education for all the children of all the people.

Families of moderate means get an additional advantage from spending together for public schools. They are able to secure an education for their children when the children need it, but they are not compelled to pile up excessively heavy expenses during the stage of the family life cycle in which expenses are already at a peak. Instead, by paying taxes at a moderate rate for many years, they spread their payment for the support of schools over years when they have more income available. In effect they pay for their children's education on the instalment plan.

There are, then, advantages to spending together. By so doing, a family can secure many things that it could not afford to provide for its members if it were limited to what it could buy with its own resources. The family can by spending with others secure many services at lower cost than would otherwise be possible. And by spending with others, by sharing the expense on the basis of ability to pay, the family can make its contributions to the common expenditures at such times as it has the funds available. By spending together, it is possible for families to make their payments for common service in convenient ways.

The control of collective expenditure. We look upon our membership fees in club or lodge as part of our family expenditures. We consider contributions to charitable organizations as part of our family expenditures. We should look upon taxes similarly as part of our family expenditures. We should not look upon them as something taken away from us, for which we get nothing in return, but as our share of the expense of carrying on a common enterprise.

If we regard taxes and contributions as part of our family expenditures, we should scrutinize these common expenditures as carefully as we do our individual expenditures, to be sure that we get a dollar's worth for every dollar we spend with others. In order to do this, we must learn how to participate in the control of collective spending. This is a problem in citizenship. The means employed are political rather than economic. The chief problem in the control of collective spending is to determine what the majority of a group wants. This involves discussion, persuasion, and finally the casting of some sort of a ballot.

Majorities vs. minorities. It is easy enough to reach a decision in regard to expenditures which clearly satisfy the common wants of all the members in the group. It is not so easy to reach a decision in regard to the wants of minorities within the group. And yet there are the same economies to be had by spending together for the common wants of minorities as for the wants of majorities.

The result is that a group usually works out a spending program providing for the wants of both majorities and minorities. It spends as much as is necessary to satisfy the common wants of a large majority of the group. It decides upon a group of expenditures for the wants of minorities, apportioning these expenditures so that all of the members of the group share equitably in the benefits of these special expenditures from the common fund.   It makes certain expenditures from the common funds for special services for special groups, devising ways by which the members of these minority groups pay into the common fund the amount of the expenditures made by the group on their behalf.

Suppose we use the public school system as an example.   We all agree that it is to our common interest to provide from common funds a common school education for all the children of all the people. On the high school level we do not insist that every boy and every girl take a standardized high school course.   Instead we provide at little or no additional expense a variety of types of special training for groups of boys and girls with special interests and special abilities. We make the gymnasium and auditorium available for the use of still other groups by charging them rental to cover the additional cost incurred by their use of these facilities.

The need for proportional voting.   The greatest difficulty in getting our money's worth from spending together comes in determining a satisfactory program of spending for the wants of minority groups.   This difficulty is accentuated by the fact that it has proved almost impossible for a large group to work out any system of proportional voting.   When an individual votes with his dollar in the market to indicate his preferences for the commodities offered for his consideration, he can split his vote into a hundred separate parts. He can indicate that he considers this worth $\frac{1}{100}$ of a dollar, that worth $1\frac{0}{100}$ of a dollar, and the other offering worth perhaps a dollar and a half.   When an individual casts his ballot he casts just one vote.

As long as this is so, it is necessary for the members of the group to discuss a variety of ways of working out the details of their common expenditures, and by mutual give and take to arrive at a program which will serve equitably both the majority and minority interests of all the members of the group.   In taking part in this process we should recognize our responsibility to pay our full share of the cost of the various activities from which we benefit.   We should remember that we have a definite obligation to pay every year, according to our means, for services from which we may benefit only at longer intervals.   And we should recognize that there are a number of indirect benefits which come to every family living in a community with an efficient and complete set of government services.

Spreading overhead costs. In working out a program of collective spending which will give us the most for our money, we should be constantly on the alert to discover situations in which a slight additional expenditure will greatly increase the services we can secure from activities we are already maintaining. By spending only a small additional sum for heat and light and janitor service, and occasionally a little for equipment, a school gymnasium can be turned into a recreation center for an entire neighborhood. By providing a little in the way of equipment, and a little supervision, a school auditorium may be made the center of a Little Theater organization, which will provide worth while leisure-time activity for its members and pleasant entertainment for a large group in the community. By spending just a little more on a fire department, it may be possible to secure substantial reductions in insurance rates. One city found that by spending $25,000 a year more for fire protection it could secure reductions in rates which would save property owners a little more than $50,000 a year in insurance premiums. Such an additional expenditure is clearly worth while.

We must be constantly on the alert to eliminate from our spending program services which are no longer wanted by any considerable number in the group. As consumers, we should apply to our collective expenditures the test we apply to our individual expenditures: "Is the service worth what it costs?"

Cashing in on collective expenditure. And finally, if we are to get the maximum benefit from our common expenditures, we must be constantly on the alert to devise ways by which as individuals we can increase our use of the services for which we are spending together. If we are supporting a public library, we can get more for our tax money by using the services it provides. If we are paying for a park and playground program, we can get more for our money if we use freely these recreational facilities.

Every family must approach the problems involved in spending together as an integral part of its individual spending program. It must not only decide for itself what it can best buy in the market and what it can best make for itself at home, but it must go a step further and decide what it can do better for itself as an individual family, and what it can do better and at lower cost by spending with others. It must recognize that conscious and considered participation in group spending is an essential part of family management. It must recognize that the effectiveness of its members in group affairs will have a good deal to do with the way in which it is able to work out its peculiarly personal problems of family finance.

QUESTIONS

1. What proportion of their incomes do families of your acquaintance "spend together" for community activities? What proportion goes for voluntary and private organizations, and what part in the payment of taxes to various branches of government? Be sure to include both direct and indirect tax payments in your estimates.

2. List the institutions and activities in your own community which are financed by voluntary contributions or membership fees; by compulsory payments from tax funds.

3. As a tax-paying consumer who is interested in getting the most for his money, how would you evaluate local, state, and federal government activities with which you are familiar?

4. In what cases would the tax-paying families of your community get more satisfaction for their money from increasing government expenditures? From reducing or eliminating specific expenditures with a corresponding reduction in tax burden? How can the individual family go about securing these changes in government expenditures?

5. In what specific ways can individual families of your acquaintance increase the satisfaction they secure from their collective expenditures by more frequent use of the services the government or private agencies supply?

PART III

SOME PROBLEMS OF FAMILY FINANCE

CHAPTER VIII

FOOD

The place of food in family expenditures. Food is the first of the three fundamental necessities with which every family must be provided. Food is absolutely essential to existence. The want for food, however, is the easiest want to satisfy, since it is limited by the capacity of the human stomach. Yet for most families food is the largest single item of expenditure. In a study of national consumption in 1926, Elizabeth E. Hoyt estimated that 27 per cent of the national income was spent for food. This is more than twice the amount spent for any other item. Her estimates follow:

PERCENTAGE OF TOTAL NATIONAL CONSUMPTION ATTRIBUTED TO EACH MAIN CLASS OF GOODS AND SERVICES IN THE UNITED STATES, 1926[1]

Articles		*Percentage*
Food		27
Clothing		13
Shelter		12
Fuel and light		4
Sundries		
Furniture and furnishings	2	
Tobacco, candy, soft drinks, and gum	5	
Education and reading	1	
Health	2	
Automobile	5	
Other recreations (Theaters, ball games, club dues, etc.)	3	
Miscellaneous (Cosmetics, writing materials, street-car fares, contributions, etc.)	4	
Savings and insurance	12	
Taxes	10	
Total sundries		44
Total of all		100

[1] From Elizabeth E. Hoyt, *The Consumption of Wealth*, Table IX, p. 275. By permission of The Macmillan Company, publishers.

But any study of national consumption tells us very little about the proportion food represents in the consumption of individual families. Ordinarily the percentage of income spent for food by families in the upper income groups is considerably less than the national average. The percentage of income spent for food by families in the lower income groups is considerably more than the national average.

There are a number of factors which help to determine what proportion of its income a family spends for food: the amount of the family income, the size of the family, current food prices, the nearness of the family to the source of food supply, opportunity for home production and processing of food, and the relative interest of the family in good food and in other commodities.

The effect of income on expenditures for food. Families with larger incomes usually spend more money for food than do families with smaller incomes. The difference is not so much in the physical volume of food consumed as in quality and variety. In the lower income groups, most of the calories needed are derived from the lower-priced foodstuffs—cereals, potatoes, turnips, cabbage, and the cheaper cuts of meat. In the upper income groups, a larger proportion of the calories are derived from the higher-priced foodstuffs—the better cuts of meat, eggs, milk, butter, and the more expensive types of fruit and vegetables.

But although families with larger incomes spend more dollars for food than do families with smaller incomes, their food expenditures represent a smaller proportion of their income. In 1857 Ernst Engel formulated as the first of his laws of consumption the principle that the larger the income, the smaller is the proportion of the income which the family spends for food. And the truth of this principle has been borne out by every study of family expenditures from that day to this.

The effect of the size of the family upon expenditures for food. The amount a family spends for food depends upon the make-up of the family, the number of its members, their ages, their sex, their size, and the type of activity in which they are engaged. The scientific determination of exact food needs involves an elaborate calculation which takes account of all these factors. There have been a number of attempts to reduce these complicated calculations to simple terms, but so far none of them has been more than moderately successful.

However, although it is impossible to determine by rule of thumb the exact nutritional needs of a family, it is possible to draw some general conclusions as to the effect of the size of the family upon its expenditures for food. P. H. Nystrom, in his *Economic Principles of Consumption*, has added to Engel's law the following principles: [2] As the size of the family increases, the amount spent for food increases, but the per capita expense for food declines. As the size of the family increases, the proportion of the family's income spent for food increases, but it increases less rapidly than does the size of the family.

The effect of food prices upon expenditures for food. The amount of income a family spends for food depends upon food prices. When food prices are high, the family must of necessity spend a larger amount of its income for food. When food prices are low, the family is able to provide the food it needs with a smaller amount of its money income, and have more left over for other expenditures.

The effect of the location of the family upon food expenditures. The amount of the family's income that is spent for food depends upon the nearness of the family to the source of food supply. Families living in large cities must pay prices which include not simply the cost to the grower, but the cost of marketing as well. The difference is particularly important in the case of fresh fruits and vegetables and fluid milk. The difference is less marked in the case of canned goods which must be shipped from the farm to the cannery and then to the communities in which they are finally sold.

While the prices of specific articles of food vary a great deal from one section of the country to another—in many cases without any particular regard to the nearness of the source of supply—on the whole, food costs are higher in the East and North and lower in the South and West. There are some indications that when the cost of all types of food is taken into account, families living in the South Central and Central states are most favorably located in regard to the source of the majority of their food supplies.

The effect of home production of food upon food expenditures. Families living in the country and in small towns find there is further advantage in living in the region where food is produced. In many cases they are able to produce for themselves much

---

[2] P. H. Nystrom, *Economic Principles of Consumption*, pp. 318 ff.   The Ronald Press Co., New York, 1929.

of the food that they need. A farm family ordinarily buys a comparatively small part—one-third as an average—of the food that it uses. Many families in villages and small towns raise the larger part of their garden stuff and many provide their own milk supply.

The present trend toward subsistence homesteads has as its aim to make families as nearly self-sufficient as possible in regard to their food supply. The six-hour day and the five-day week leave industrial employees with considerable time which they can spend working for themselves. The subsistence homestead idea is particularly appealing to workers in industries in which there is seasonal unemployment, especially if this unemployment comes during the growing season. The general adoption of the subsistence homestead idea may reduce the demand for many types of food in the market. But families upon subsistence homesteads will benefit not so much by reducing their expenditures for food as by adding to the quantity of food they consume.

Nystrom formulates the following principles: [3] As the opportunity for home production of food increases, the amount of food consumed increases, the actual expenditure for food is somewhat less but the retail cash value of the food the family consumes is more.

The relation of the family's interests to food expenditures. The amount of the family income which is spent for food depends upon the relative interest of the family in good food and in other commodities. Some families take a very great deal of interest in the elaboration of their food supply. They are intrigued by new and unusual food. They enjoy elaborate and expensive dishes. They derive great pleasure from serving fresh food out of season. They are constantly on the lookout for some new eating place where they can buy a meal which will provide something just a little bit different.

Other families get very little enjoyment out of food as an experience. They want plenty of nutritious and palatable food. They like to be able to select their food with regard to their personal preferences. They recognize the fundamental importance of food expenditures, but they are not particularly interested in mere gustatory delights. They are concerned with securing an adequate supply of good food at a moderate cost in order that they may have as much of their income as possible to spend on other more interesting experiences.

---

[3] P. H. Nystrom, *op. cit.*, p. 321.

The science of food consumption: nutrition.   Although there have been many attempts to apply science to the solution of problems of consumption, it is in connection with food that we have been most successful in working out a sound scientific basis for consumption. Nutrition is a well-developed science. The fundamentals of proper feeding are clearly defined. According to the science of nutrition, proper feeding involves the provision of a sufficient amount of food to provide the caloric energy used in bodily activity, and the chemical elements necessary to provide for growth and for the repair of the daily wear and tear upon the human machinery. But quantity is not the only factor to be considered. Not only must the food supply be adequate, but it must be made up of the proper proportion of proteins, carbohydrates, and fats. It must include an adequate supply of certain minerals, especially calcium, phosphorus, and iron, and it must provide in addition an adequate amount of certain invisible substances, the vitamins, which act as catalytic agents and make it possible for the human body to make the maximum use of the food consumed.

In spite of the development of the science of nutrition, statistics of food consumption for the country as a whole indicate that in certain respects our diet is faulty. Since foods high in energy have been easy to obtain, our list has been adequate as far as quantity is concerned. But it has included too little milk, fruit, and vegetables. As a result, we still lack the minerals and vitamins that are essential to proper balance in the diet. Recent statistics show that the national diet is improving.[4]   In the twenty years covered by the survey reported in *Recent Economic Changes,* there has been a noticeable decline in the per capita consumption of meats and of cereals, and an increase in the consumption of fruits and vegetables and dairy products. These statistics indicate that an increasing number of families are becoming familiar with the fundamentals of good nutrition, and are enjoying more scientifically balanced diets.[5]

At the same time, however, we must remember that certain vital elements are still lacking in our diet, notably milk. A recent survey made in connection with the government's 1933-34 crop reduction program indicated that in spite of the low prices farmers are receiving for their dairy products, as a nation we still need several million more

[4] *Recent Economic Changes in the United States.* McGraw-Hill Book Co., Inc., New York, 1929.
[5] *Ibid.,* Ch. I, pp. 24-51.

RESTRICTED DIET FOR EMERGENCY USE: APPROXIMATE YEARLY QUANTITIES OF FOOD FOR INDIVIDUALS OF DIFFERENT AGE, SEX, AND ACTIVITY [6]

ITEM	Child under 4 Years	Boy 4 to 6 Years; Girl 4 to 7 Years	Boy 7 to 8 Years; Girl 8 to 10 Years	Boy 9 to 10 Years; Girl 11 to 13 Years	Boy 11 to 12 Years; Girl Over 13 Years; Moderately Active Woman	Active Boy 13 to 15 Years; Very Active Woman	Active Boy over 15 Years	Moderately Active Man	Very Active Man
Flour, cereals..........pounds	85	140	175	195	195	280	370	280	455
Or—									
Bread...............pounds	40	65	80	90	90	130	170	130	210
Flour, cereals........pounds	60	95	120	135	135	195	255	195	315
Milk, or its equivalent* ..quarts	182	182	182	182	†182	†182	182	91	91
Potatoes, sweetpotatoes . pounds	100	110	125	140	140	160	225	160	300
Dried beans, peas, nuts...pounds	...	8	18	20	25	30	30	40	50
Tomatoes, citrus fruits...pounds	50	50	50	50	50	50	50	50	50
Leafy, green, and yellow vegetables...........pounds	30	30	45	50	50	40	25	40	25
Dried fruits............pounds	3	3	6	8	10	15	10	15	10
Other vegetables, fruits...pounds	12	20	30	40	45	50	50	50	50
Fats‡.................pounds	10	20	30	30	35	55	65	55	75
Sugars§...............pounds	8	20	30	40	45	65	70	70	80
Lean meat, fish, poultry..pounds	...	5	15	22	28	35	35	40	50
Eggs..................dozen	10	10	10	8½	8½	7½	6	6	6

* Approximately equivalent to the food value of 1 quart of fluid whole milk: 17 ounces of evaporated milk; 1 quart of fluid skim milk and 1½ ounces of butter; 5 ounces of American Cheddar cheese; 4½ ounces of dried whole milk; 3½ ounces of dried skim milk and 1½ ounces of butter.
† For the adult woman this may be reduced to 91 quarts. For pregnant or nursing mother it should be increased to 273 quarts.
‡ Including butter, oils, bacon, and salt pork.
§ 1 pint (1½ pounds) of molasses or heavy cane or sorgo sirup is approximately equivalent in fuel value to 1 pound of granulated sugar. The unrefined molasses and sirups are also valuable for their calcium and iron content.

cows if we are to provide every individual in the country with even the minimum requirement of a pint of milk a day.

Slow application of the principles of nutrition. Why have we been so slow in putting our knowledge of nutrition into practice? There are a number of reasons. In the first place, during prosperity most families have had no difficulty in securing a food supply that was more than adequate in caloric content. As a result, the majority of families have felt well fed, and have not been concerned about the nutritional adequacy of their diet. The comparatively few families with incomes too low to enable them to provide an adequate diet are, for the most part, the families who have never heard of the science of nutrition.

In the second place, the scientific determination of the diet for a family is not a simple process. It requires lengthy mathematical

[6] Hazel K. Stiebeling and Medora M. Ward, *Diets at Four Levels of Nutritive Content and Cost*, p. 34. U. S. Dept. of Agriculture, Circular No. 296, Washington, D. C., 1933.

ADEQUATE DIET AT MINIMUM COST: APPROXIMATE YEARLY QUANTITIES OF
FOOD FOR INDIVIDUALS OF DIFFERENT AGE, SEX, AND ACTIVITY [7]

ITEM	Child under 4 Years	Boy 4 to 6 Years; Girl 4 to 7 Years	Boy 7 to 8 Years; Girl 8 to 10 Years	Boy 9 to 10 Years; Girl 11 to 13 Years	Boy 11 to 12 Years; Girl over 13 Years; Moderately Active Woman	Active Boy 13 to 15 Years; Very Active Woman	Active Boy over 15 Years	Moderately Active Man	Very Active Man
Flour, cereals.........pounds	70	100	150	170	175	260	350	260	435
Or—									
Bread.............pounds	30	50	70	80	80	120	160	120	200
Flour, cereals.......pounds	50	70	105	115	120	180	240	180	300
Milk, or its equivalent*.quarts	365	365	273–365	273–365	†273–365	†273–365	273–365	182	182
Potatoes, sweet potatoes.pounds	100	110	125	140	140	160	225	160	300
Dried beans, peas, nuts.pounds	...	8	18	20	25	30	30	40	50
Tomatoes, citrus fruit..pounds	50	50	50	50	50	50	50	50	50
Leafy, green, and yellow vegetables..........pounds	60	60	90	100	100	75	50	75	50
Dried fruits...........pounds	3	5	12	17	20	30	20	30	20
Other vegetables, fruits.pounds	25	40	60	80	90	100	100	100	100
Fats‡.................pounds	8	12	25	32	40	65	75	65	85
Sugars§..............pounds	5	12	25	35	40	50	55	60	65
Lean meat, fish, poultry.pounds	...	10	30	45	55	70	75	75	100
Eggs.................dozen	20	20	20	17	17	15	12	12	12

* Approximately equivalent to the food value of 1 quart of fluid whole milk: 17 ounces of evaporated milk; 1 quart of fluid skim milk and 1½ ounces of butter; 5 ounces of American Cheddar cheese; 4½ ounces of dried whole milk; 3½ ounces of dried skim milk and 1½ ounces of butter.
† For the adult woman this may be reduced to 182 quarts. For pregnant or nursing mother it should be increased to 365 quarts.
‡ Including butter, oils, bacon, and salt pork.
§ 1 pint (1½ pounds) of molasses or heavy cane or sorgo sirup is approximately equivalent in fuel value to 1 pound of granulated sugar. The unrefined molasses and sirups are also valuable for their calcium and iron content.

calculations to determine the exact caloric requirements of each member of the family, the exact nutritional value of each type of food served, and the exact weight which should be allowed for each portion. Families with inadequate incomes have usually lacked the necessary mathematical background to make these calculations, even if they had known their value; and families with adequate incomes and the necessary educational background cannot be bothered with weighing out food in milligrams. What they want is first and second helpings in generous portions.

In the third place, the scientifically trained nutritionists have of necessity been concerned with working out and perfecting the details of their science. It takes many years of scientific experimentation to reduce a science to simple enough terms to make it generally applicable.

[7] *Ibid.*

ADEQUATE DIET AT MODERATE COST: APPROXIMATE YEARLY QUANTITIES
OF FOOD FOR INDIVIDUALS OF DIFFERENT AGE, SEX, AND ACTIVITY [8]

ITEM	Child under 4 Years	Boy 4 to 6 Years; Girl 4 to 7 Years	Boy 7 to 8 Years; Girl 8 to 10 Years	Boy 9 to 10 Years; Girl 11 to 13 Years	Boy 11 to 12 Years; Girl over 13 Years; Moderately Active Woman	Active Boy 13 to 15 Years; Very Active Woman	Active Boy over 15 Years	Moderately Active Man	Very Active Man
Flour, cereals..........pounds	60	80	110	120	120	170	230	220	290
Or—									
Bread...............pounds	50	75	100	120	120	190	240	240	350
Flour, cereals........pounds	30	30	40	40	40	40	70	60	60
Milk, or its equivalent*...quarts	365	365	365	365	†365	†365	240	182	182
Potatoes, sweetpotatoes..pounds	100	100	100	110	125	160	300	160	350
Dried beans, peas, nuts...pounds	...	7	10	15	15	30	30	30	35
Tomatoes, citrus fruits...pounds	75	75	75	90	90	100	100	100	100
Leafy, green, and yellow vegetables...........pounds	60	75	90	90	110	110	100	100	100
Dried fruits.............pounds	7	10	15	20	25	30	45	35	40
Other vegetables, fruits...pounds	90	100	125	150	175	270	300	270	270
Fats‡.................pounds	10	15	28	35	42	65	80	65	95
Sugars§...............pounds	7	15	30	40	45	75	115	75	115
Lean meat, fish, poultry..pounds	...	25	60	75	90	110	150	125	150
Eggs...................dozen	20	20	20	20	15	15	15	15	15

* Approximately equivalent to the food value of 1 quart of fluid whole milk: 17 ounces of evaporated milk; 1 quart of fluid skim milk and 1½ ounces of butter; 5 ounces of American Cheddar cheese; 4½ ounces of dried whole milk; 3½ ounces of dried skim milk and 1½ ounces of butter.
† For the adult woman this may be reduced to 182 quarts. For pregnant or nursing mother it should be increased to 365 quarts.
‡ Including butter, oils, bacon, and salt pork.
§ 1 pint (1½ pounds) of molasses or heavy cane or sorgo sirup is approximately equivalent in fuel value to 1 pound of granulated sugar. The unrefined molasses and sirups are also valuable for their calcium and iron content.

Circular No. 296. Under the stress of the depression, however, there was considerable progress in making scientific principles of nutrition available in simple terms for the use of families living on relief or on restricted incomes. All through the depression, home economists were engaged in working out usable information concerning economical diets which at the same time would be nutritionally sound. Perhaps the outstanding contribution was the bulletin by Stiebeling and Ward entitled *Diets at Four Levels of Nutritive Content and Cost,* published by the Bureau of Home Economics of the Department of Agriculture.[9] This bulletin contains no particularly new scientific information concerning nutrition, but it puts principles heretofore available only to nutrition experts into a form which can be easily used by the ordinary housewife. The material in this bulletin makes it possible to check up on the nutritional adequacy of the family's diet, not in terms of proteins, carbohydrates, and fats, and **not**

[8] Hazel K. Stiebeling and Medora M. Ward, *op. cit.,* p. 35.
[9] *Ibid.*

LIBERAL DIET: APPROXIMATE YEARLY QUANTITIES OF FOOD FOR INDIVIDUALS
OF DIFFERENT AGE, SEX, AND ACTIVITY [10]

ITEM	Child under 4 Years	Boy 4 to 6 Years; Girl 4 to 7 Years	Boy 7 to 8 Years; Girl 8 to 10 Years	Boy 9 to 10 Years; Girl 11 to 13 Years	Boy 11 to 12 Years; Girl over 13 Years; Moderately Active Woman	Active Boy 13 to 15 Years; Very Active Woman	Active Boy over 15 Years	Moderately Active Man	Very Active Man
Flour, cereals..........pounds	45	55	65	65	65	105	125	125	200
Or—									
Bread................pounds	30	45	60	60	60	120	150	150	240
Flour, cereals.........pounds	25	25	25	25	25	25	25	25	40
Milk, or its equivalent*...quarts	365	365	365	365	†365	†365	240	182	182
Potatoes, sweet potatoes..pounds	100	100	100	100	110	150	300	150	350
Dried beans, peas, nuts...pounds	...	2	3	5	5	10	10	10	10
Tomatoes, citrus fruits...pounds	75	75	80	90	110	120	120	120	120
Leafy, green, and yellow									
vegetables...........pounds	60	75	90	90	120	150	180	180	180
Dried fruits............pounds	5	5	8	10	15	25	30	25	30
Other vegetables, fruits...pounds	140	200	300	300	300	350	400	400	400
Fats†.................pounds	10	15	27	35	40	65	80	65	100
Sugars§...............pounds	7	15	30	35	40	75	115	75	115
Lean meat, poultry, fish..pounds	10	40	90	120	150	200	250	220	250
Eggs...................dozen	25	30	30	30	30	30	30	30	30

* Approximately equivalent to the food value of 1 quart of fluid whole milk: 17 ounces of evaporated milk; 1 quart of fluid skim milk and 1½ ounces of butter; 5 ounces of American Cheddar cheese; 4½ ounces of dried whole milk; 3½ ounces of dried skim milk and 1½ ounces of butter.
† For the adult woman this may be reduced to 182 quarts. For pregnant or nursing mother it should be increased to 365 quarts.
‡ Including butter, oils, bacon, and salt pork.
§ 1 pint (1½ pounds) of molasses or heavy cane or sorgo sirup is approximately equivalent in fuel value to 1 pound of granulated sugar. The unrefined molasses and sirups are also valuable for their calcium and iron content.

in terms of calories and vitamins, but in terms of the amount of meat and potatoes, milk and bread, butter and eggs, tomatoes and canned peas that should be included in the family's diet. These food requirements are stated in terms of what a family needs for a year. Once the yearly requirements are known, it is easy to work out what a family needs for a week, or a month, or for any other period.

To quote from the bulletin: [11] "The restricted diet for emergency use provides approximately the minimum requirements of the body for the various nutrients, but allows little margin for safety. It represents good food selection when a fully adequate diet is beyond reach, but is not recommended for use over indefinite periods. It represents quantities of 'protective' and other foods below which it is not safe to reduce the food supply. Continuous effort should be made to increase the quantities of milk, vegetables, fruits, lean meat, and eggs in accordance with the allowances suggested in the adequate

---

[10] Ibid.
[11] Ibid., p. 4.

diets. The minimum- and moderate-cost adequate diets provide, it is believed, enough of the different nutrients to cover average requirements for maintenance and growth and to furnish a margin of safety as well. The liberal diet is fully adequate. It includes items from different food groups in such quantities and proportions as will promote better-than-average nutrition. It permits a greater variety in food than may be provided by the other diets."

The tables on pages 180-183 were taken from this bulletin. They show the approximate amount of each of the principal groups of foodstuffs which are needed for individuals of different ages and occupations at four typical cost levels.

It is interesting to compare in detail the requirements as outlined for the restricted or emergency diet and the liberal diet. The restricted diet is low in physical volume of food intake. Its aim is to provide the minimum amount of food at the lowest possible cost. Consequently, the diet is very heavy in cereals, and has a minimum amount of milk, butter, and meat. The liberal diet, on the other hand, keeps the amount of cereals used to a minimum, provides a generous amount of fruit and vegetables, a liberal amount of milk and butter, and a great deal more lean meat, poultry, and fish than does the restricted diet.

It is interesting to compare the cost of these four types of diet. The authors computed the cost for a family of five, consisting of two moderately active adults and three children, three, five, and thirteen years old. They used specific articles of food in each of the major groups in the proportions shown in the table on page 185.

They priced these diets using the Department of Labor retail food prices for April, 1933. They found that a month's food supply for the family of five cost $18.96 for the restricted diet, $26.33 for the adequate diet at minimum cost, $42.50 for the adequate diet at moderate cost, and $48.99 for the liberal diet. These figures indicate the great variation in cost between different types of nutritionally adequate diets.[12]

How to use the tables. How can a family use this material in planning its food expenditures? The steps in the procedure are as follows: First, the family selects the diet which most nearly meets personal preferences and available income. Second, it works out the

---

[12] Hazel K. Stiebeling and Medora M. Ward, *op. cit.*, pp. 55 and 56.

GROUPS OF FOOD IN DIETS AND THE PROPORTION OF SPECIFIED ARTICLES COMPRISING EACH GROUP (PER CENT) [13]

ITEM	Proportion of Total Pounds in Diets Suggested for—		ITEM	Proportion of Total Pounds in Diets Suggested for—	
	Liberal and Moderate Cost Level	Minimum Adequate, and Emergency Cost Level		Liberal and Moderate Cost Level	Minimum Adequate, and Emergency Cost Level
Flour, cereals:			Other vegetables and fruits:		
Wheat flour........	76	70	Apples...........	34	
Corn meal........	10		Bananas.........	11	
Prepared flour.....	3		Grapes..........	11	
Oat breakfast foods.	3		Peaches.........	9	
Rice.............	2		Corn............	8	
Macaroni, noodles..	2	30	Onions, turnips, beets, etc.......	6	
Wheat breakfast foods...........	1		Watermelons......	5	100
Rye flour.........	1		Cantaloup.......	4	
Corn breakfast foods.	1		Pears............	4	
Cornstarch........	1		Cucumbers.......	2	
Total...........	100	100	Celery..........	2	
Milk:			Strawberries......	2	
Fresh whole milk...	97	50	Pineapples........	2	
Condensed and evaporated milk......	3	50	Total..........	100	100
Total...........	100	100	Dried fruits:		
Potatoes, sweetpotatoes:			Raisins..........	40	
Potatoes..........	83	100	Prunes..........	40	100
Sweetpotatoes	17		Other............	20	
Total...........	100	100	Total..........	100	100
Dried beans, peas, nuts:			Butter.............	100	100
Dried beans.......	45		Other fats:		
Peanuts..........	33	100	Lard.............	40	
Dried peas........	5		Vegetable oils and shortenings......	40	100
Nuts (in shell)......	17		Bacon, salt pork...	14	
Total...........	100	100	Margarine........	6	
Tomatoes, citrus fruits:			Total..........	100	100
Tomatoes, fresh....	15		Sugar, molasses, other sweets:		
Tomatoes, canned...	35		Sugar...........	75	
Oranges..........	32	100	Molasses.........	16	100
Grapefruit........	10		Other...........	9	
Lemons...........	8		Total..........	100	100
Total...........	100	100	Lean meat, poultry, fish:		
Leafy, green, or yellow vegetables:			Beef.............	34	30
Cabbage..........	50	50	Pork............	39	50
Lettuce..........	18		Veal............	5	
Peas............	11		Lamb and mutton..	3	20
Snap beans........	6		Poultry..........	11	
Carrots..........	5		Fish.............	8	
Spinach, kale, collards, etc........	5	50	Total..........	100	100
Asparagus........	3		Eggs........... ..	100	100
Peppers...........	2				
Total...........	100	100			

[13] Hazel K. Stiebeling and Medora M. Ward, *op. cit.*, p. 11.

family's food requirements in each of the major food groups for a year. Third, it works out a detailed list of the amounts of each of the articles of food to be included within each of the major food groups. Fourth, it reduces its yearly requirements to a monthly or weekly basis. This is easy to do for items like bread and flour and milk: simply divide the yearly total by 12 or by 52, as the case may be. In working out the monthly or weekly requirements for fruit and vegetables, however, it is necessary to take into account the part of the year in which fresh fruits and vegetables are in season, and to plan to fill in the other months with supplies of canned goods. Fifth, the housewife can provide herself with a market list if she reduces the round numbers of pounds and quarts to terms in which the articles are usually purchased. Pounds of flour should be reduced to 24½-pound or 5-pound sacks, macaroni and noodles to 8-ounce or 6-ounce packages, pounds of potatoes to bushels or pecks, and pounds of bread to loaves of the size usually purchased. Sixth, by estimating the cost of each of these items on the basis of the prices usually charged in the community, taking account of seasonal price changes of articles like eggs, and fruit and vegetables, and making adequate allowance for possible price increases, she can determine the amount of weekly or monthly income which must be spent for food if the family is to have an adequate diet of the type which it has chosen.

Each family must select for itself the type of diet which is suited to the family's preferences and to the family's income. It is entirely possible to make a great many variations from the specific selection of foods suggested in these tables. These changes can be made safely so long as the relative proportions between the different groups remain the same, so long as there is provision of the minimum amount suggested in each of these main divisions.

Stretching the food budget. Whenever it is necessary to cut down current expenditures, whenever more money is needed for some new commodity, even the families most clearly aware of the importance of proper feeding are inclined to consider first all the possible economies in food expenditures. It is important, therefore, to consider the various ways of cutting food costs and at the same time of maintaining or increasing the nutritional adequacy of the family's food supply.

Food economy through substitution. It is possible to substitute less expensive for more expensive foodstuffs. The four diets set up in the Stiebeling bulletin assume this sort of substitution. The cost of providing a family with any one of these types of food supply can be further reduced if the family buys more of the lower cost foods and less of the higher cost foods in each group.

Just what are the lower cost foods depends in part upon the amount of labor and the amount of risk involved in their production, in part upon the care required in handling, the perishability, the season of the year, and the accessibility of the consumer to the areas in which each type of food is produced. Apples cost less, are less perishable, and can be marketed more economically than can pears or peaches or cherries. Cabbage costs less to grow and to market than does cauliflower or broccoli or Brussels sprouts. Winter carrots purchased by the peck sell for less than new carrots by the bunch because it actually costs less to grow and market them. Pasteurized milk costs less than raw milk because it may be produced under less stringent regulations. Evaporated milk costs less than either, in spite of the cost of processing it, because it may be produced from surplus milk, and may be distributed at a much lower cost than can fluid milk.[14]

Food economy through better buying. *Buying in season.* Most families by taking thought can buy to better advantage. It is not necessary for a family to limit itself entirely to the cheapest types of foodstuffs. At the height of the season, many of the more expensive foods are low enough in price so that many families can afford them. By buying food only when it is in season, paying attention to changing prices, and buying what will give the most value for the least money each week in the year, they can enjoy a wide variety in the food they use, and at the same time keep food costs at a minimum.[15]

Buying the most economical quality. Every family can save substantially on its food expenditures by paying attention to the quality of the merchandise it buys, by buying a quality good enough but no better than is needed for the purpose for which it is intended, and paying no higher a price than the grade in question is worth. This does not mean that a family should always buy either the lowest grade or the lowest priced article on the market. Rather it means

[14] For substitutes equivalent to one quart of fresh whole milk, see footnote to the table, "Restricted Diet for Emergency Use," p. 180.
[15] See Hazel K. Stiebeling and Medora M. Ward, *op. cit.*, pp. 49 and 50, for charts showing both the relative cost and the season of greatest abundance of a number of common fruits and vegetables. The more perishable foods—fresh fruits, vegetables, eggs, and meats—show the largest seasonal variations in price.

that the buyer must keep always in mind the importance of buying the quality which gives the best value for the price and for the use intended.

The following table shows the relative prices of different grades of canned goods, as indicated by the distributor.

PRICE * OF FOODS OF DIFFERENT COMMERCIAL GRADES AS INDICATED BY THE DISTRIBUTOR, WHEN SOLD IN CANS OF SAME SIZE [16]

FOOD	SIZE OF CAN	PRICE PER CAN OF GRADES		
		Fancy	Choice or Extra Standard	Standard
Fruits:	*No.*	*Cents*	*Cents*	*Cents*
Apricots.................	2½	25.00	22.50	....
Fruits for salad...........	2½	....	25.00	21.00
Peaches..................	2½	16.33	14.50	12.50
Pears....................	2½	23.00	19.50	13.50–17.00
Plums...................	2½	....	19.00	12.50
Vegetables:				
Corn....................	1	7.50	......	5.60
	2	11.50–14.50	9.50	6.25
Peas....................	1	14.00	10.00	6.30
	2	19.00	15.00	9.50–11.50
Spinach.................	2½	15.00	12.50	....
Snap beans..............	2	19.00	......	6.25– 8.30
Tomatoes...............	2	....	12.00	6.25– 7.50
	3	....	17.00	12.00

* Based on retail prices of 1932, Washington, D. C.

This table shows the considerable savings that can be made by purchasing a lower grade wherever that grade will do as well as the better one. For example, it shows that in No. 2 cans, the choice grade of canned corn costs 50 per cent more and the fancy grade costs more than twice as much as the standard grade put out by the same distributor. And there is even a larger difference in the case of snap beans.

Intelligent and economical purchase of food products would be much easier if goods were sold under standard grades, and carried more informative labels. While canned goods and meats and some fruits and vegetables are very often sold under standard grades in the wholesale market, usually these grade markings are lost before the goods are offered to the consumer. As a result, it is not uncommon to find a standard grade selling for more than a choice grade, and occasionally a fancy grade selling for less than either.

Until such time as standard grades are adopted and enforced in

[16] Hazel K. Stiebeling and Medora M. Ward, *op. cit.*, p. 42.

the retail as well as in the wholesale markets, the consumer must constantly scrutinize the quality of every article he buys. He can judge for himself something of the quality of the fresh fruits and vegetables offered for his inspection. But as far as canned and packaged goods are concerned, there is no way for him to find out very much about the quality or the quantity of the product he buys until he opens the container. Too often the price and the pretty picture on the label fail to give any reliable indication of the food values to be found inside.

In the last few years, an increasing number of the meat markets selling the better qualities of meats have begun to carry graded meats. Not many of these markets tell their customers the grades of meat they carry. Very few advertise the grades of meat they offer on special sales. But in an increasing number of markets it is possible by asking for it to secure government graded meat.

Few consumers have access to information showing the relative prices of meats of different grades. Prices both of grades and of cuts change from time to time, depending upon consumer demand and upon the amount of the various qualities of meat animals coming upon the market. It is possible for the consumer to judge to some degree the difference in the prices he should pay for meat of different grades, from the prices packers are paying for the various grades of meat animals. This information can be found on the market page of most daily newspapers. The names given to the lower grades of animals in these market quotations are a little too suggestive to the ordinary consumer.

It frequently is better economy in buying meat to buy the cheaper cuts of high-quality meat than to buy the more expensive cuts from less well-finished or from older animals. It is usually better economy to pay a few cents more a pound for hamburger made of good quality chopped beef than it is to buy cheap hamburger made of artificially colored beef-hearts and suet, or to pay meat prices for hamburger which has been adulterated with cereal and weighted with water.

If consumers will give thought to the question of quality, if they will ask for exactly what they want, and if, when they find goods of the quality they want marked in a way that makes them easy to identify, they will give the retailers who carry such goods their patronage, it will not be long before adequately labeled and properly graded food will be on sale in the majority of reputable groceries and meat markets.

Buying the most economical quantity. A family can save on its food expenditures if it buys each kind of food in the quantity which in its case is most economical. It is possible to buy too much or too little. In deciding what is the correct quantity to buy, there are a number of factors which must be taken into account—how much of each kind of food the family needs, how much can be used without spoiling, and what size of purchase will provide the needed quantity at the lowest cost per pound of edible food.

Ordinarily there is a considerable saving from buying food in quantity. Potatoes and apples sell for a lower price by the bushel or peck than they do by the pound. Oranges frequently sell for less in ten-pound lots than they do by the dozen. Canned and packaged foods usually sell for less per pound of edible contents in the larger than in the smaller containers.

The following table shows the price per pound of foods of identical quality when sold in cans of different sizes.

PRICE PER POUND * OF FOODS OF IDENTICAL QUALITY WHEN SOLD IN CANS OF DIFFERENT SIZES [17]

FOOD	COMMERCIAL GRADE AS INDICATED BY THE DISTRIBUTOR	PRICE PER POUND WHEN IN				
		8 or 9 Ounce Can	No. 1 Can	No. 2 Can	No. 2½ Can	No. 3 Can
		Cents	Cents	Cents	Cents	Cents
Vegetables:						
Beans, cut..........	Extra standard..............	....	9.1	6.6	....	....
	Standard...................	....	8.7	5.0	....	....
Beans, lima.........	Extra standard..............	....	14.0	10.0	....	....
Corn..............	Fancy.....................	....	10.9	9.2	....	....
	Extra standard..............	....	9.1	6.6	....	....
	Standard...................	....	8.2	5.0	....	....
Peas..............	Extra standard..............	....	14.0	10.0	....	....
Tomatoes..........	Fancy.....................	....	....	10.1	....	8.2
	Extra standard..............	....	10.0	7.0	....	....
Fruits:						
Apricots...........	Choice....................	16.0	12.5	....	12.3	....
Cherries...........	Choice....................	....	12.5	....	12.3	....
Fruit salad........	Choice....................	....	17.0	....	14.4	....
Grapefruit.........	Fancy.....................	12.5	....	10.0	....	....
Peaches...........	Fancy.....................	14.0	12.5	....	9.1	....
Pears.............	Fancy.....................	....	15.0	....	11.2	....
Pineapple, sliced....	Fancy.....................	22.2	....	....	8.9	....
	Fancy.....................	....	13.0	....	9.6	....

* Based on retail prices of 1932, Washington, D. C.

[17] Hazel K. Stiebeling and Medora M. Ward, *op. cit.*, p. 40.

The table on page 114 gives similar figures for a number of packaged foods. A study of these tables shows that there is appreciable difference in the proportion of saving from quantity buying for various commodities. Every family must decide for itself in the case of each commodity it buys whether or not the savings to be had justify the practice of large-quantity buying for that commodity.[18]

In large-quantity buying the large family has a decided advantage. In buying for its everyday needs, it uses the larger packages, and is therefore able to secure much of its food at a decidedly lower cost per pound than can the smaller family. But if the small family has adequate refrigeration and other storage facilities, if it plans carefully to use up all leftovers, if it re-cans or re-packages part of the contents of the larger containers, even the small family can effect substantial economies in food outlay from quantity buying.

Each family must decide for itself, then, how much work it can afford to do, how much thought it can afford to take, how much it can afford to spend on storage facilities, in order to avail itself of the advantages of quantity buying.

The short-weight problem. The family can effect further savings if it is constantly on the alert to see that it gets the quantity for which it pays. Many consumers buy a package of cheese, a can of peas, a carton of butter, or a loaf of bread, without paying attention to the quantity of food the package contains.

It is important to watch the net weights on packages of foods. Much food is put up in packages which are just a little below standard size. There has been some progress in recent years in the adoption of standard sized containers for canned goods. The table on page 192 shows the average net weight and contents of standard cans for fruits and vegetables. This table shows only one style of can, the No. 1 tall, between the No. 1 can and the No. 2 can. There are actually in use three sizes of cans between the No. 1 and the No. 2.

It is also important to watch net weights because of the tendency of stores selling on price to use under-sized, short-weighted, or slack-filled containers. A few years ago, many stores offered butter in 14-ounce cartons instead of in pounds. They sold No. 1 talls, containing 16 ounces of vegetables, for No. 2 cans, which ordinarily hold 20 ounces. They handled cans containing 6 slices of pineapple instead of 8. They sold No. 2 cans of peas containing 12 ounces of peas and

---

[18] See also Hazel K. Stiebeling and Medora M. Ward, *op. cit.*, Table 25, p. 39.

8 ounces of liquid instead of 13 ounces of peas and 7 ounces of liquid. In many cases the prices they charged for these under-sized or slack-filled containers were slightly under the prices their competitors were charging for goods of similar grade in standard sized containers. Actually they were charging more per pound of contents for their apparently lower-priced food.

COMMON SIZES OF STANDARD CANS FOR FRUITS AND VEGETABLES [19]

Can Size	Average Net Weight	Contents	Approximate Number of Servings	Can Size	Average Net Weight	Contents	Approximate Number of Servings
		Cups				*Cups*	
Buffet or picnic..	8 ounces........	1	*2	No. 2½..	28 ounces........	3½	5–7
No. 1....	11 ounces........	1⅓	2	No. 3....	33 ounces........	4	6–8
No. 1 tall.	16 ounces........	2	3–4	No. 5....	3 pounds, 8 ounces	7	10–14
No. 2....	20 ounces........	2½	4–5	No. 10...	6 pounds, 10 ounces	13	20–26

* Small.

Many people feel that the matter of net weights is too small to bother with. And yet, if butter is selling for 30 cents a pound, a 14-ounce carton selling for 28 cents actually costs the customer 32 cents a pound. A 16-ounce can of beans selling for 9 cents costs the customer more per pound of beans than does a 20-ounce can selling for 10 cents. The peas in a No. 2 can containing 12 ounces of peas and 8 ounces of liquor cost 8⅓ per cent more than do the peas in a No. 2 can containing 13 ounces of peas and 7 ounces of liquor.

Most stores have found that it does not pay to be caught deliberately misrepresenting the quantities of edible food in the packages they sell. But there are still profits to be made by selling a 16-ounce can of beans to the careless buyer who asks for a can of beans, and a 14-ounce carton of butter to the customer who asks for some butter. Especially on a rising market, when there is active consumer resistance to price increases, merchants frequently reimburse themselves for rising costs by scanting weight rather than by openly raising their prices.

For example, in the late summer and autumn of 1934, increasing prices of flour and other materials led a number of bakers to increase the prices they asked for their bread. In one community, before the

---

[19] Hazel K. Stiebeling and Medora M. Ward, *op. cit.*, p. 39.

price increase, a 22-ounce loaf of bread had been selling for 11 cents, and a 24-ounce loaf for 12 cents. The bakeries raised the price of the 24-ounce loaf to 13 cents. Instead of raising the price of the 22-ounce loaf, they brought out a new "split-top loaf" weighing 20 ounces, which they featured with full-page newspaper advertising. This "split-top loaf" was wrapped in the same size wrappers as was the old 22-ounce loaf. The wrapped bread looked the same size to the customer, although the net weight on the package, in very small figures, was changed to 20 ounces. The bakeries actually added more to the price of the 22-ounce loaf by cutting off two ounces from its net weight than they would if they had raised the price of the loaf from 11 to 12 cents. But because few customers pay any attention to the net weight of the bread they buy, the bakers encountered less resistance to the 10 per cent increase in the price of the smaller loaf than they did to the 8⅓ per cent increase in the price of the larger loaf.

After a few experiences like this, merchants try to justify the practice of raising prices by scanting quantities, on the basis that consumers prefer to pay the accustomed price for a smaller quantity rather than a higher price for the quantity they usually buy. Nevertheless, these same merchants do all in their power to divert the attention of the consumer from the change in quantity. For, though they do not like to admit it, even to themselves, they know that consumers ordinarily pay the same price for a smaller quantity only because they do not know that the quantity has been reduced. Obviously, then, if the consumer is to get the most for his food dollar, he must constantly watch the quantities he buys.

Buying in the most economical form. If a family must effect the maximum economy in its food expenditures, there are further savings which can be had from buying each type of food in its most economical form. Many foods sell for less in bulk than they do in packages. They sell for less when they are put up in inexpensive packages than when they are sold in expensive containers. Unadvertised articles usually sell for less than do the more highly advertised brands.

It is never wise for a family to decide always to buy goods in either their lowest or their highest priced form. Unless they are sure of the way bulk goods are handled, most buyers prefer to pay a small premium for packaged goods. If food deteriorates rapidly in inexpensive packages, the consumer can afford to pay something for the more expensive containers. For example, the family that buys from a grocery with a high turnover in coffee may find it satisfactory to save money by buying its coffee in parchment paper bags or cardboard containers. But if the coffee must stay for some time on the grocer's shelf, it may be much better to pay a little more for the same grade of coffee sealed in a tin.

If the buyer finds that an advertised brand of canned goods is always uniform in quality and is well suited to his needs, he can afford to pay a little more for the advertised merchandise. The buyer must decide in each case whether or not the trade name of the advertised article is a dependable guarantee of quality, and if it is, how much he as an individual consumer can afford to pay for the assurance of uniform quality.

In the case of fruit and vegetables which are sold in various sizes for various prices, the consumer must decide which size gives him most nearly what he wants for the price he can afford to pay. The following table shows the diameter, approximate weight, and approxi-

ORANGES: NUMBER IN CRATE, APPROXIMATE DIAMETER PER ORANGE, APPROXIMATE WEIGHT PER DOZEN, AND VOLUME OF JUICE PER DOZEN OF SPECIFIED SIZE [20]

SIZE AND NUMBER IN CRATE	APPROXIMATE DIAMETER OF FRUIT*		APPROXIMATE WEIGHT PER DOZEN†		APPROXIMATE VOLUME OF JUICE PER DOZEN‡		
	Florida Oranges	California Oranges	Florida Oranges	California Oranges	Florida Oranges	California Navel Oranges	California Valencia Oranges
	Inches	Inches	Pounds	Pounds	Cups	Cups	Cups
Large:							
80	...	3¾	...	10.4	...	8.5	...
96	3⅝	3⅝	10.0	8.8	...	...	...
100	...	3½	...	8.4	...	7.1	...
126	3¼	3⅛	7.6	6.7	9.9	...	7.1
Medium:							
150	3⅛	3	6.4	5.6	7.1	5.7	...
176	3	2⅞	5.4	4.8	5.9	4.2	...
200	2⅞	2¾	4.8	4.2	...	...	...
216	2¾	2⅝	4.4	3.9	4.8	3.4	4.0
Small:							
250	2⅝	...	3.8	...	4.2	...	...
252	...	2½	...	3.3	...	2.9	3.5
288	2½	2⅜	3.3	2.9	3.5	...	...
324	2⅜	2¼	3.0	2.6	2.8	...	...

* Data for Florida oranges from Bureau of Agricultural Economics, U. S. Department of Agriculture; for California oranges, from California Fruit Growers Exchange.
† The approximate net weight of 1 crate of Florida oranges is 80 pounds; of California oranges, 70 pounds.
‡ Data from Food Utilization Section, Bureau of Home Economics.

[20] Hazel K. Stiebeling and Medora M. Ward, *op. cit.*, p. 44. See p. 42 of the bulletin for similar information on prunes, and p. 44 for information on grapefruit.

mate volume of juice per dozen for each of the more common sizes of oranges.

Using the information this table contains, the consumer can determine for himself the relative value of each of the sizes of oranges offered in his local market.

For example, on the basis of the juice they contain, if California navels, size 216, sell for 34 cents, size 80's are worth 85 cents a dozen. If Florida 250's are selling for 42 cents a dozen, 288's, one-eighth of an inch smaller, are worth only 35 cents; and 324's, a quarter of an inch smaller, are worth only 28 cents. Because of the slight differences in diameters, it is easy for stores under heavy price competition to mix two sizes, and offer them at a price a little below the going price for the larger size. It is almost impossible to judge such small differences in the size of oranges accurately. Consumers should, therefore, always ask for oranges by size, and check up on their purchases occasionally by weighing a dozen of the fruit to see if it comes up to standard weight for the size ordered.

A case of Florida oranges weighs 80 pounds. A case of California oranges weighs 70 pounds. Using the following formulæ, it is easy to check the size or weight of the fruit.[21]

$$\frac{70}{\text{size}} \times 12 = \text{weight of a dozen California oranges.}$$

$$\frac{80}{\text{size}} \times 12 = \text{weight of a dozen Florida oranges.}$$

$$\frac{70}{\text{weight}} \times 12 = \text{size of Florida oranges.}$$

$$\frac{80}{\text{weight}} \times 12 = \text{size of California oranges.}$$

The importance of small economies in buying food. All food economies look small, and to many people they seem too small to bother with. However, they are repeated at frequent intervals throughout the year. The consumer must never overlook the importance of frequent small savings. The saving of a cent or two on a single item hardly seems worth while; but if, without decreasing either the quantity or the quality of the family's food supply, it is possible to save one cent in ten on every food purchase, in the course of a year this saving amounts to more than a whole month's expenditure

---

[21] Hazel K. Stiebeling and Medora M. Ward, *op. cit.*, p. 44.

for food. If a family spends $500 a year on food, a saving of 10 per cent frees $50 each year for other more interesting expenditures. If the consumer wants to get his money's worth for every dollar he spends for food, he must never relax his attention to all the details of quantity, quality, and price.

Food economy through home production and processing. Most families can secure their food at lower money cost if they are willing to buy foods in less completely processed form and do more of the work of food preparation in the home. Most families do at least the final preparation and serving.[22]

There are two ways by which the family can increase its savings from these home production activities. One is to increase the time spent on the activities. The other is to spend that time so far as possible upon those activities which yield the largest savings over the cost of fully processed food. Ordinarily there is more to be saved from home production of those articles in which labor represents a very large part of the cost of production. In most cases there is a larger saving in the home preparation of fussy salads, in the baking of layer cakes, of fancy cookies, and of fancy rolls than there is in the baking of beans or of bread. Ordinarily there is more advantage to home production of articles which are adapted to small-scale production and which can be processed with the equipment found in the ordinary kitchen than in the production of types of food which are well adapted to large-scale production or which require experience and equipment. There is more to be gained from the making of jelly, which must be made in small batches and put up in glass containers, than in the processing of non-acid vegetables which can be handled by machinery, put up in tin, and which require processing at high temperatures. Ordinarily there is more advantage to home processing of articles which are expensive to distribute. There is more saving in the growing of fruits and vegetables which are difficult to ship, or which must be picked green in order to get them to their destination in salable condition, than in growing foods which can be picked when fully ripe and handled without special equipment.

How much can be saved by home production and processing of food depends upon how far back the family can go toward the production of the raw materials. A family that raises its own garden stuff can save much more by canning its own fruit and vegetables than can

---

[22] See table, "Time Spent on Various Homemaking Activities," p. 144.

the family that buys the raw materials in the market and puts them in the cans. The family living in a small community where it can buy direct from the producer can save more on home canning than can the family living in a large city where it must buy the fresh fruit and vegetables in small quantities from the grocer.

It is impossible to lay down any general rules about the desirability of any types of home production. Every family must decide for itself, in the light of its individual situation, how far and along what lines it is wise to carry on home production and home processing activities. In making its decision it must consider the personal preferences of its members and the time, skill, equipment, and materials available.

Financing food purchases. The problems that are involved in financing the family's purchases of food depend upon the way it buys its food supply, and upon the amount and source of its income. Most families buy their food as they need it throughout the year. There is only a little variation in the amount of their monthly food expenditures. Such families must set aside each month an amount sufficient to cover their ordinary food expenditures.

On the other hand, there are a large number of families, especially in the small towns and open country, that stock up on food when it is cheap in the summer and early fall. Studies of the monthly sales of chain grocery stores indicate that many families spend more for food in the fall than they do the rest of the year. This is especially true of farm families who get the largest part of their year's income when they market their crops in the fall, and immediately invest a considerable portion of it in stocks of food to carry them through the winter. The financing problem of such families is twofold. In the first place, they must have a substantial sum of money to invest in food in the late summer and early fall when food is cheap. In the second place, they must provide a small but highly essential allowance for current purchases which must be made from week to week throughout the year.

Both of these problems are easily met by the family with generous income. Such a family spends only a small proportion of its income for food. Its problem is largely one of providing variety, of catering to the tastes of the individual members of the family, of deciding how far the family can afford to go in the purchase of exotic fruits and vegetables, and new and different types of food so as to get the most personal enjoyment out of the necessary business of eating.

The family with a small but regular income finds it easy to set aside a fixed amount for food each week or month. This always represents a large portion of the family income. And it is highly important that the family stay within the budget limits it has set. This family is interested in making all possible economies in its food expenditures in order to raise its scale of living elsewhere. The problem for this family is to secure an adequate diet at a minimum cost, and to plan its food purchases so as to keep its food expenditures within the budget limit even in the months when foods are high in price. If the family with a regular income desires to buy in quantity, if it wants to stock up when prices are at their year's low, it must make special provision for the funds with which to finance such purchases.

The family with an irregular income received occasionally in large increments is not much bothered by the problem of financing occasional large expenditures for food. It must be sure to keep enough out of each occasional instalment of income to care for its recurring purchases until the next instalment of its income arrives. The farm family has funds available for stocking its food supplies in the fall when prices are low. Its chief problem is to have money for coffee, prepared breakfast food, bread, fresh fruits and vegetables, and other groceries that must be purchased from week to week throughout the year. The same thing is true of the factory worker who is employed nine months of the year at good wages. He must save enough while he is working to buy his necessities—milk, butter, eggs, coffee, bread, fresh fruits and vegetables—during the months when he is unemployed. Similarly, the salesman working on a commission basis in a highly seasonal industry must set aside enough of his income to finance his expenditures for food the rest of the year. When his money is coming in it looks like a generous income. He has to be constantly on guard lest he spend too much for non-essentials, leaving him nothing for fundamental necessities later on in the year.

It is these families with irregular incomes that can benefit most by stocking up on staples when they are in funds. In this way they can take advantage of quantity buying and assure themselves of a major part of their food supply. But they must be sure to provide sufficient funds for food that cannot be bought in advance. Their most difficult problem is to provide for the regular expenditures that come every month in the year.

Feeding a family—an individualized problem. There is
no one best way to feed a family. There are a number of typical
diets which a family can follow, and each one of these types of diet
is capable of wide variation. There is no one best way to secure
the family's food supply. Some families find that they can get food
which better suits their needs if they produce and process a great deal
of it themselves. Others prefer to buy almost everything they need
in the market. There is no one best way to make food money go
farther. Each family has its own pet food economies. Each family
must decide for itself the extent to which in its case it is wise to use
each of the available methods of providing the family with its food
supply. In making its decision, it must keep in mind the amount of
money, the amount of time, the personal skills, and the equipment
available, the market offerings both of processed foods and of raw
materials, and the personal preferences of the members of the family.
Each family must work out for itself the combination of materials
and methods which will best provide its members with an adequate
and attractive food supply.

QUESTIONS

1. How does the proportion of money income spent for food by families
   of your acquaintance compare with the proportions suggested in this
   text?

2. Compare the national food habits of various European peoples. How
   many of these European food customs can well be adopted by Americans?
   Which, if any, of these food customs are not suited to American
   conditions?

3. (a) Compile from the figures in the tables giving food requirements for
   individuals of various sexes and ages the amount of milk needed by each
   of the families described in question 10, page 81. (b) If these families
   lived in your community, how much would they need to spend to satisfy
   the milk requirement with fresh fluid milk? With 50 per cent milk
   substitutes?

4. In working out a food budget for each of these families, how much
   emphasis should be placed upon economy, how much upon nutritional
   adequacy, how much upon personal preference, and how much upon
   the desire for social prestige?

5. Using these tables, work out the dietary requirements of your own
   family. How does your family's present food consumption compare
   with these tables? At which of the four levels of nutritive content and
   cost is your family living?

6. In which items can a family in your community make the largest savings: (a) by quantity buying, (b) by buying no better quality than is needed, (c) by buying in season only, (d) by substituting less expensive foods of equal nutritive value for more expensive foods, (e) by watching weights and measures, (f) by producing or processing foods at home?

7. Suppose a family with a regular monthly income decides that it can save on its food expenditures by buying in quantity when prices are at their year's low. How can it finance the first of these quantity purchases?

8. A factory worker 40 years old can count upon regular employment 8 months of the year. His family consists of a wife, age 38; a boy, age 15; and a girl, age 11. How much should he plan to save when he is working to use for food during the months he is unemployed? How do you tell?

9. When are the following foods available in your community in highest quality and at lowest price: eggs, strawberries, asparagus, oranges, cabbage, carrots, lard, dressed chickens?

10. How do the families of your acquaintance change their food purchases to adjust to high prices of meat, cereals, fruit, dairy products? How do they adjust their expenditures to a general rise in food prices?

11. Compare the food economies which should be practiced by a family consisting of a man and his wife and four children, with those which are feasible for a family consisting of a young couple both of whom are employed.

REFERENCES

Andrews, B. R., *Economics of the Household*, Revised Edition, Chs. XIII and XIV, pp. 297-367. The Macmillan Co., New York, 1935.

An interesting and thorough analysis of the personal, social, and economic aspects of the problem of feeding a family.

Blinks, Ruetta Day, and Moore, Willetta, *Food Purchasing for the Home.* J. B. Lippincott Co., Chicago, 1932.

A detailed study of the problems involved in buying wisely each of the more common types of foods used by the American family.

Hambidge, Gove, *Your Meals and Your Money.* Whittlesey House, McGraw-Hill Book Co., Inc., New York, 1934.

An entertainingly written presentation of the material contained in the bulletin by Stiebeling and Ward.

Hawley, Edith, *Economics of Food Consumption.* McGraw-Hill Book Co., Inc., New York, 1932.

A description of food resources and market organization.

Monroe, D., and Stratton, S. M., *Food Buying and Our Markets*. Barrows Co., Boston, 1925.

A description of foodstuffs and markets. A concrete and usable handbook on food buying.

Nystrom, P. H., *Economic Principles of Consumption*, Ch. XIII, pp. 313-326. The Ronald Press Co., New York, 1929.

An analysis of the facts of food consumption by families of various sizes in various income groups, living in different sections of the country.

Recent Economic Changes in the United States, pp. 24-51. McGraw-Hill Book Co., Inc., New York, 1929.

A discussion of changes in the food consumption and food habits of the American people from 1909 to 1929.

Stiebeling, Hazel K., and Ward, Medora M., *Diets at Four Levels of Nutritive Content and Cost*. U. S. Dept. of Agriculture, Circular No. 296. Washington, D. C., November, 1933.

A detailed analysis of four typical nutritionally adequate diets, together with many interesting suggestions as to how to secure adequate and satisfying food at reasonable cost.

See also standard works on nutrition, such as:

Bogert, L. Jean, *Nutrition and Physical Fitness*. W. B. Saunders Co., Philadelphia, 1931.

Rose, Mary S., *Feeding the Family*. The Macmillan Co., New York, 1929.

Rose, Mary S., *Foundations of Nutrition*. The Macmillan Co., New York, 1933.

Sherman, Henry C., *Food and Health*. The Macmillan Co., New York, 1934.

CHAPTER IX

CLOTHING

Clothing is second in the triumvirate of fundamental necessities. Ordinarily, clothing expenditures are thought of as being smaller than expenditures for either food or shelter. However, Miss Hoyt's estimates (see page 175) show that for 1926 the American people as a whole spent a little more for clothing than for shelter. She estimates that the current outlay of the American people for clothing was 13 per cent of their total consumption, while current outlay for shelter was 12 per cent. These are figures for the country as a whole, but for most urban families, particularly in the lower and middle income groups, the amount of money that can be spent for clothing is less than the necessary current outlay for food or for shelter.

Many families find that the problem of clothing the family adequately and economically presents difficulties out of proportion to the amount of income that is involved. Clothing expenditures, unlike the more regular expenditures for food and shelter, come in varying amounts at irregular and often unexpected intervals. In no two years in the life of a family are there exactly the same individual needs or personal preferences, exactly the same social demands, or exactly the same wear and tear on the family's wardrobe. Then, too, according to the Bureau of Labor Statistics Cost of Living Index, clothing prices vary more widely and more rapidly than do prices of almost any other group of commodities the family buys. And the qualities of goods offered for sale vary even more than do clothing prices. Since, then, both the items a family needs and the prices it must pay for clothing vary from year to year with no particular reference to the changes in the family income, suggesting the proportion of its income which a family should spend for clothing is of little help.

The problem of clothing the family of generous means presents a decided contrast to the problem of clothing the family with a moderate or a low income. For families with generous incomes, the provision of funds for the purchase of a complete outfit of clothing each year for each member of the family is not a difficult problem. These families are chiefly concerned with elaborating their standard, or with providing the extra articles which some unusual social event may demand. The lack of pressure for more money for clothing is clearly indicated by the fact that, in the upper income groups, as the income increases clothing takes a smaller and smaller proportion of the family's income.

For the family with a low income, providing the family with adequate clothing is a different sort of problem. It has been said that the workingman's clothing problem is that of trying to look no different from the member of the white-collar class. And many white-collar families with only moderate incomes find that they are continually faced with the problem of how to be fashionable at a minimum expense. In the lower income groups, the presence of a steady and insistent pressure for more adequate clothing is clearly evidenced by the fact that in these groups, as the income increases, families spend a larger proportion of their incomes for clothing.

Families in the lower income groups with small regular incomes from wages or salaries find that the problem of financing their clothing purchases is complicated by the fact that clothing expenditures do not come regularly in small amounts throughout the year, but call for heavy seasonal expenditures. The family must buy its spring clothing in March or April, its summer clothing in June, and its fall and winter clothing in September and October. Even if the family plans to buy all that it can between seasons, it is impossible entirely to eliminate seasonal peaks in clothing expenditures.

In order to keep to a minimum the current outlay for clothing, many families in the lower income groups put off the purchase of clothing as long as possible. In these families the unexpected failure of a garment may call for an unplanned expenditure which though not large in itself is sufficient to upset seriously the family's spending program.

Whiting Williams [1] in one of his books describes vividly the situation of the colored laborer in the steel mill who had to walk five miles to and from his work for a week in order to use the carfare for a pair of new half soles for his boy's shoes. Many families in much less straitened circumstances find it necessary to make similar ad-

[1] Whiting Williams, *Mainsprings of Men*, p. 17. Charles Scribner's Sons, New York, 1925.

justments in their expenditures to replace a cap lost at school, or a pair of trousers torn climbing the back fence, or a dress that shrank when it was washed, or an overcoat made of inferior material that wore out a year too soon.

The family's clothing standards. We must recognize at the outset that the importance of clothing to the individual family varies from occupation to occupation, from community to community, and from social group to social group. Some families find that it is of the utmost importance for their members to be well dressed. Other families regard more than a minimum amount of comfortable clothing with indifference. Families that must be well dressed at low cost find it essential to give a great deal of thought to their clothing expenditures. And even the families that are comparatively indifferent to clothing itself are interested in planning to keep clothing expenditures down so that they may have their money to use for other purposes. It is safe to say that probably not over 5 per cent, and certainly not over 10 per cent, of the families in this country have reached the income levels in which increasing income brings a smaller proportion spent for clothes. At least 90 per cent of the families in the United States, for one reason or another, are concerned about making the most of their clothing money.

Since clothing is obviously of different import to different people, each family must work out for itself a clear conception of the place clothing is to have in the family's living standards. The clothing standard as it is finally determined will reflect definitely the family's underlying philosophy of life. In working out this standard, the family must determine as definitely as it can to what extent it is to emphasize fashion, to what extent good taste, to what extent durability and suitability, and to what extent quality of materials and workmanship.

The problem can be simplified greatly if the family works out a separate standard for each of the types of clothing it must provide. For example, for everyday wear, the family may decide to emphasize suitability, durability, and taste. For social events, it may place more emphasis upon suitability and fashion, and get a quality of materials and workmanship which is sufficient to make a garment last only as long as it is needed. If quality of materials or workmanship adds to the satisfaction the individual gets from the garment, the family may decide to get the best quality it can afford. The family trying to work out for itself a high standard of living on a moderate income must remember that extremes are always expensive, and that they are not always in good taste. A family with a high standard of living insists upon good taste always, and upon fashion to the extent that the family's income will allow.

In addition to working out standards to guide the selection of clothing on the basis of the use to which it is to be put, each family must decide upon the relative importance of clothing for various members of the family, and here, too, work out some principles to guide in clothing selection. The following table shows the relative importance given to clothing expenditures for various members of the family in the income groups covered by the Bureau of Labor Statistics in its 1918-1919 Cost of Living Survey.[2]

SCALE OF CLOTHING EXPENDITURE FOR VARIOUS MEMBERS OF THE FAMILY USING EXPENDITURE FOR HUSBAND AS A BASE [3]

MEMBER OF FAMILY	INCOME LEVEL					
	Under $900	$900 under $1,200	$1,200 under $1,500	$1,500 under $1,800	$1,800 under $2,100	$2,100 and over
Husband......................	1.0	1.0	1.0	1.0	1.0	1.0
Wife..........................	.8	.8	.9	.9	.9	.9
Son, 15 years and over..........	1.0*	.9	.9	.9	.9	1.1
Daughter, 15 years and over......	.9*	1.0	1.1	1.1	1.1	1.3
Son, 12 and under 15 years.......	.7*	.7	.6	.6	.6	.6
Daughter, 12 and under 15 years..	.9*	.7	.6	.6	.6	.7
Son, 8 and under 12 years........	.6	.6	.6	.5	.5	.5
Daughter, 8 and under 12 years...	.6	.6	.6	.5	.5	.5
Son, 4 and under 8 years.........	.5	.5	.5	.4	.4	.4
Daughter, 4 and under 8 years....	.5	.5	.5	.4	.4	.4
Son, under 4 years...............	.3	.3	.3	.3	.3	.3
Daughter, under 4 years.........	.4	.4	.3	.3	.3	.3

* Based on a small number of cases.

This suggested scale applies only to families in the lower income groups. In these groups the husband uniformly spends more for clothing than does the wife. In the upper income groups, on the other hand, especially among professional men and business executives, the wife in many cases spends more upon her clothing than does the husband. In both the upper and the lower income groups there seems to be a tendency for the children under fifteen years of age to spend considerably less for their clothing than do their parents.

[2] U. S. Bureau of Labor Statistics Bulletin No. 357.
[3] Hazel Kyrk, *Economic Problems of the Family*, Table LXXV, p. 351. Harper and Bros., New York, 1933. Calculated by M. L. Cowles from data in U. S. Bureau of Labor Statistics, Bulletin No. 357; unpublished thesis, University of Chicago, 1929.

But sons over fifteen years old uniformly spend more for their clothing than do their fathers, and daughters spend more than do their mothers. The unmarried daughter over fifteen uniformly spends more for her clothing than does any other member of the family.

These figures suggest that for men and for boys under fifteen, there is ordinarily more emphasis placed upon durability than upon fashion, while for women and girls there is more emphasis upon the latest style. For boys and girls over fifteen there is, and probably should be, more emphasis upon fashion than for the adults. And boys and girls should, if the family's finances will permit, be given a sufficient allowance for clothing to enable them to carry on the experimentation that is necessary if they are to work out for themselves a satisfactory philosophy of clothing.

Buying ready-made clothing. As soon as a family has worked out satisfactory clothing standards for the different types of clothing it must buy for each member of the family, the next problem is to find in the market at a price the family can afford to pay the garments which most nearly satisfy the family's clothing standards. Wise selection of ready-made clothing is a difficult task. In the retail stores, and to some extent in the wholesale market as well, there is but little relation between quality and price. Some stores charge a moderate price for garments carefully made from good materials. Other more fashionable stores charge a much larger price, not so much for superior materials and workmanship as for the styling of the garment and for the prestige of the label bearing their name. And occasionally, even the stores making a practice of handling only excellent merchandise, produced by supposedly reliable firms, unknowingly offer for sale at first-quality prices carefully tailored clothing made of decidedly inferior materials.

This is not surprising, for ready-made clothing is made by hundreds of manufacturers. A few of them sell goods under the manufacturer's label. More sell their output unbranded in the wholesale market, or carrying the label of the retail store in which it is to be sold. All of these garments are made of fabrics purchased by the clothing manufacturer from the textile industry. Here again there are a large number of mills turning out a wide variety of products. Every year in the unending quest for variety there is a tendency for the mills to develop new fabrics. Many of these are new weaves which can be manufactured more economically, which will have the appearance of more expensive fabrics, or which will provide the wearer with an element of novelty. The buyer for the ready-to-wear department ordinarily sees these new weaves only after they are made up into garments. The continual variation in fabrics makes it difficult for the professional buyer, and almost impossible for the consumer-buyer, to judge the value of current market offerings. Only a store that selects and tests its own fabrics and has them manufactured to its own specifications can be sure of what it is offering to the retail trade. Only the very large store doing a volume of business much greater than the average can afford to tear down even one garment out of a hundred, examine it for quality of workmanship, and test the materials used in order to be sure it is getting the quality specified. And even the very large store, testing one out of a hundred garments, can do no more than make a random sampling of a few of the many models it displays.

For the most part then, as far as quality of materials and workmanship are concerned, the clothing buyer must make the best use he can of his own knowledge. He must learn how to judge the suitability and durability of materials. He must develop the ability to judge from external evidences the probability of good workmanship. And after he has gone as far as he can in mastering all the knowledge available to the amateur, he must fall back for the rest upon the willingness and the ability of the store from which he buys to stand back of its merchandise.

Furthermore, buying ready-made clothing involves more than simply the selection of a well-made and durable garment. There are a number of rather intangible factors which help a family to dress well on a moderate income. It is important for the clothing buyer to have a feeling for fashion trends, to sense the direction fashions are taking almost before they start, and to plan the purchase of clothing so as to ride along on the crest of a style wave. And it is even more important for the individual to have a flair for selecting what for him is most suitable and attractive in the current fashion. If, as sometimes happens, the current style in its more extreme forms is personally impossible, the individual must learn how to adapt the current style to personal needs, keeping enough of the current style to indicate recognition of fashion trends, but for the most part adhering to styles which are personally more suitable.

Help for the consumer-buyer. The consumer with his limited knowledge must depend for help in buying upon the store in which he buys, upon the clerks who serve him, and upon the information given in the labels on the articles he buys. In the case of ready-made clothing there is no adequate help from any of these sources. The consumer should select his store with care. But, with few exceptions, he can expect the store itself to know very little about the ready-made goods it handles. The buyer for the retail store purchases on the wholesale market, often selecting the merchandise on the basis of the manufacturer's reputation rather than on the basis of standards of quality. All the consumer can hope for is a prompt and reasonable adjustment in case he buys an obviously defective garment.

And if the professional buyers for the retailer know little about the goods they are selling, they can give the clerks very little information which can be of definite help to the consumer-buyer. About all the clerks can do at present is to add their judgment to the opinion of the consumer. The salesman's judgment is based, of course, upon the handling of a great deal more merchandise than is the consumer's, but nevertheless it is often faulty.

There is clearly a definite need for better labeling of ready-to-wear garments. From the consumer's standpoint, every garment should bear an informative label. This label should contain not only the maker's name, but also an accurate statement of the size of the garment, the quality of the fabric, the type of workmanship, the material in the lining, the tendency to shrinkage, directions for cleaning, and any other information which may be of help to the ultimate consumer. Manufacturers of part-wool underwear and of other inexpensive garments are making a beginning in better labeling. But it is fully as important that informative labeling be extended to include high-grade and expensive merchandise. For one mistake in the purchase of an expensive garment is more costly than many mistakes in buying relatively inexpensive articles like underwear or hose.

The consumer can give the necessary impetus to the development of better labeling by always asking for adequately labeled merchandise, and by buying such merchandise wherever it is available. If their customers begin to ask for informative labels, retailers whose whole volume of business is so small that they cannot economically test for themselves the merchandise they sell, in their turn will begin to insist that the manufacturers label their garments. The retailers can then turn their attention to the development of an intelligent sales force, trained in fashion trends, personality types, and all the rest, well versed in helping the customer to select from adequately labeled merchandise the particular articles which best suit his needs.

Stretching the clothing budget by better buying. There are a number of ways by which it is possible for a family to increase the amount of clothing it is able to secure. These fall under two heads. One is to find ways of buying to better advantage in the market. The other is to buy materials and make some of the garments at home.

In buying garments in which fashion is the most important factor, a family can make its money go farther if it buys no better quality than is needed to make the garment last out the season. On the other hand, in buying goods in which fashion is not important, it can frequently save money in the long run by paying a little more for better-than-average quality and using the garments for more than one season. And if the members of the family can use the sizes usually found in the season's remainders, clothing can usually be bought at a considerable reduction at the end-of-the-season sales. If a garment is to be worn for more than one season, it is important to avoid extremes of style, or to buy a garment which is easy to adapt to changing fashion trends.

In buying clothing for rapidly growing children, it is important to buy garments which will wear reasonably well, but unless there are younger children to whom the garments can be passed on, it is usually economy to buy garments which will wear out about the time they are outgrown. Similarly, for the younger members who want to keep strictly in fashion it may be better to buy less expensive and less durable garments which will be worn out by the time they are outmoded.

Stretching the clothing budget by making clothing at home. The family can provide itself with many articles of clothing at a saving in money outlay by buying materials and making the garments at home. It would be very difficult nowadays to find a family that makes all its own clothing. But it would be almost as hard to find a family that makes none of it. The table on page 211 shows the very considerable proportion of women who do home-sewing of one sort or another.

There are a number of factors to be taken into consideration in deciding which garments to buy and which garments to make at home. In some families one type of garment is more important and in other families another. If the family must make its money go as far as possible, it will make at home those articles of clothing on which there is the largest total saving in money outlay. If, on the other hand, the housewife's time is more limited than the money at her disposal, she will make the articles on which there is the largest saving per hour of labor.

Occasionally, a family decides to make some garments for itself, not because it lacks the money with which to buy them but because the desired size or quality of garment is not available in the market. This is especially important in the case of a family with some members who are "outsize," either too tall or too short, or too stout or too thin, to be fitted easily in ready-made garments.

And sometimes a family makes articles it could buy because with the savings on garments which are easy to make at home it can buy some more elaborate garment which otherwise could not be had. The saving from making house dresses and underwear can be used to buy a new dinner gown or a new street dress. The saving from adapting last year's winter coat to the current style helps to pay for a new evening wrap. Each family should do what in its own case will give it most nearly what it wants in the way of clothing.

Does it pay to make clothing at home? It is hard to tell exactly how much can be saved by making clothing at home. It is not easy to compare the homemade and the ready-made garments, either as to quality of materials, workmanship, or style. Only the grades of materials used in the better grades of garments are usually on sale in the stores. Both the workmanship and styling of the homemade garments may be either superior or inferior to ready-made clothing, depending upon the taste, the artistic ability, and the skill of the home dressmaker.

Usually the materials for a homemade garment cost from one-third to one-half of the cost of a ready-made garment of comparable quality. Ready-made trimmings may run the cost a little higher. Usually the more handwork involved in finishing, the larger is the saving in money outlay, but also, the larger is the amount of work which must be done upon the garment.

If the family must spend considerable money for a sewing machine, dress forms, patterns, and other equipment to be used in clothing making, a part of this expenditure should be counted in comparing costs. After the equipment is paid for, however, making more clothing adds nothing to the family's current outlay. The saving from every additional garment made represents more dividends upon the family's investment in capital equipment.

PROPORTION OF WOMEN MAKING CERTAIN GARMENTS AT HOME [4]

	TUCKER	HASTIE AND GORTON		BUREAU OF HOME ECONOMICS		
	Rural and Village	Rural	City	All Communities*	Rural and Village	Cities over 5,000
Total number of answers........	4,138	1,450	2,989	1,981	1,095	748
Garments for women and for girls over 14 years of age:	Per Cent	Per Cent	Per Cent	Per Cent	Per Cent	Per Cent
House dresses..................	90.0	84	14	80.0	87.1	73.9
Summer wash dresses..........	84.0	78	18	82.1	86.3	79.0
Silk dresses...................	46.8	50	57	60.9	61.5	62.4
Wool dresses..................	42.3	61	56	59.2	63.6	54.3
Skirts........................	25.5	48	11	44.1	48.2	39.7
Blouses.......................	42.6	65	51	41.2	45.3	36.9
Aprons........................	77.5	91	22	80.4	88.9	72.9
Coats.........................	11.1	8	8	24.4	27.3	21.5
Hats..........................	33.8	15	12	31.9	33.6	29.9
Slips.........................	....	84	21	76.6	81.2	73.4
Petticoats....................	....	67	19	58.6	64.7	52.5
Chemises.....................	†‡83.8	58	12	46.6	46.8	48.2
Bloomers.....................	....	84	20	61.9	70.3	51.1
Nightgowns	....	77	21	79.9	86.3	74.2
Garments for children:						
Cotton dresses................	64.9	63	16	34.2	40.0	27.9
Wool dresses.................	30.7	52	12	27.2	33.2	20.1
Cotton suits..................	32.5	23	4	17.1	20.4	13.5
Wool suits....................	26.2	15	3	11.9	14.9	8.6
Shirts or blouses	....	23	7	17.1	22.2	11.1
Coats.........................	46.0	21	6	23.2	27.5	18.4
Hats..........................	17.6	13	13	14.8	17.2	12.3
Sleeping garments.............	....	55	15	38.6	45.6	31.2
Drawers or bloomers..........	‡61.9	..	..	34.7	41.0	27.4
Petticoats....................	†49	†9		31.2	36.3	25.8
Slips.........................	....	..	..	31.0	36.4	25.4

* 138 did not give size of community.
† Grouped as "Undergarments."
‡ Undergarments and sleeping garments.

If the housewife has time available for sewing without incurring extra expense for other services, and if she cannot sell her services elsewhere, there is no item for labor to be added in computing the money cost of a homemade garment. It is only fair to recognize that there is a labor cost involved, but since the labor in the garment involves no money outlay, it is more logical to count the saving on the

[4] O'Brien and Campbell, "Present Trends in Home Sewing," U. S. Dept. of Agriculture, Miscel. Pub. No. 4, 1927.

finished garment as wages for the housewife's labor than to say that her otherwise unsalable labor represents an item of money cost in the homemade garment.

Even when the money outlay for homemade clothing is the same as for ready-made garments it may be more economical in the long run to make them at home. Suppose instead of buying a ready-made house dress of flimsy material which will wear six months, the housewife spends an equal amount of money upon good material and makes herself a dress which will wear for a year. There is no immediate saving in current outlay but in the course of a year there is an actual saving of 50 per cent. Suppose again the clothing allowance calls for boy's pajamas at a dollar a pair. If the family makes pajamas at home of a better grade of materials than is found in ready-made pajamas selling for a dollar, there will be little or no immediate saving in money outlay. But the homemade pajamas will wear twice as long, and next year there will be no item for pajamas in the clothing budget. If the family has the necessary equipment and the housewife has the necessary time for making clothing at home, the family can save nearly half of the cost of ready-made garments of comparable quality.

Financing clothing expenditures. Because clothing expenditures come in varying amounts at irregular and often unexpected intervals, they present difficulties in financing which are out of proportion to the amount of income they involve. There are three points at which the financing of these expenditures requires special consideration: (1) in planning for the occasional purchase of expensive garments; (2) in providing adequate funds for seasonal peaks of expenditure; and (3) in setting up reserves for unexpected clothing demands.

There are two usual ways to finance these expenditures. One is to accumulate the necessary money in advance, and the other is to buy on credit. Either method works fairly well for the family with generous income. Neither is practical for the family with definitely limited resources.

The family with a generous income usually has a balance in the bank on which to draw for any unexpected or occasional expenditure. The seasonal peaks in its clothing budget can, if necessary, be spread over two or three months by using the thirty- or sixty-day credit offered as a matter of course by the full-service stores in which it usually buys.

The family of small or moderate means receiving its income in a few large increments at irregular intervals can take care of large occasional expenditures when it receives its income. Its special problem is to have adequate reserves for emergencies.

The family with a small regular income needs every cent of its money for something every month in the year. The pressure of immediate necessities is too strong and the margin of income above necessary expenses is too narrow to make it advisable to set aside much in any one month for future expenses. Even if it has a small savings account to fall back upon, it is not safe to draw upon this reserve for anything but major emergencies.

Neither is it expedient for families with small incomes to use credit for clothing expenditures. These families ordinarily can buy on credit only in stores selling on the instalment plan. Instalment clothing houses sell for the most part to families with meager and often uncertain incomes. The result is that their credit losses are large and their collection costs are high. Because consumers object to paying what low-grade instalment credit costs, these concerns conceal a considerable part of their financing charges in a high mark-up. And since their customers buy on a price rather than on a quality basis, the instalment houses keep their prices in line with those of competitors selling on a cash basis. They can do this only by selling a decidedly inferior grade of merchandise. As a result, although the prices they charge are not much higher than are prices in the cash stores, if quality is considered, the merchandise they sell is very expensive. In fact, in some cases the garment purchased on the instalment plan is worn out by the time the last instalment is paid.

But if it is impracticable for the family of small means either to set aside money in advance, or to pay the excessive cost of instalment buying, they must find some other way to provide the occasional expensive items of clothing that every family needs, to care for the usual seasonal peaks of clothing expenditure, and to take care of any unexpected emergency outlay. They can do a good deal in solving this problem if they will plan their clothing expenditures in considerable detail for some time in advance of actual purchase. Whenever possible, non-seasonal items of clothing should be taken care of in months in which there is ordinarily very little clothing expenditure. Whenever possible, seasonal expenditures should be spread over at least two months. And articles of clothing calling for large expenditure should be dovetailed so that no two of these items come in the same month, and in so far as possible, no two of them come in the same year.

Suppose we consider the case of a family consisting of husband, wife and two children—a boy fourteen years old and a girl twelve. The family's clothing standard calls for a fall topcoat and winter overcoat for the husband once in three years, a winter coat and a spring coat for the wife once in three years, and an overcoat once in two years for each of the children. It will be much easier for a family on a small regular income to finance these purchases if they buy the boy a coat one year and his sister a coat the next year. Since the children are still growing rapidly, they decide to buy overcoats for them at the beginning of the season. In order to spread the clothing expenditures along through the year, the wife buys her winter coat at the January sales. The next year her husband buys his winter overcoat at the January sales. The third year both husband and wife buy new light-weight coats. The wife buys hers at Easter, and the husband buys his early in the fall before it is time to get a coat for one of the children.

By planning clothing expenditures over a period of years, the family with regular income is able to provide adequately for these large occasional items. By similar planning it is possible to spread many seasonal expenditures through the year. The remaining seasonal peaks in clothing expenditures can be dovetailed into expenditures for some other items in the budget.

Suppose a family finds that both mother and daughter need a complete new spring outfit. And father wants to buy a new winter overcoat at the January sales. If the family can buy enough coal in the fall to carry them through until February, and then buy enough more in February to last until spring, there will be no call for fuel in either January or March, and the money usually spent for coal can be added to the usual allowance for clothing expenditures.

The importance of planning clothing expenditures. Providing the family with clothing is not a simple problem. Neither is it a problem which it is impossible to work out. Making the most of the clothing allowance is largely a matter of planning. Planning is required wherever it is necessary to co-ordinate the expenditures of a number of people for a varied list of articles. But planning takes time. How much time the family can afford to spend in planning its clothing expenditures depends upon how important clothing is to members of a family and upon how hard clothing demands are pressing upon the money available for clothing.

In making a clothing plan it is necessary to take into account seasonal and non-seasonal, occasional and regular, predictable and emergency expenditures. In working out a clothing plan it is important to know not only the family's yearly money income, but also the amounts and the intervals at which it is received. In working out a clothing plan it is wise to keep in mind the individuals who much prefer to handle their own clothing money and the individuals who prefer to have their clothing planned for and provided by the homemaker. Because no two families have exactly the same needs nor exactly the same personal, material, and pecuniary resources, each family must work out its own plan in the way which will make the best use of its available ability, equipment, and money income.

QUESTIONS

1. Give some examples from your own experience of variations in family clothing standards.

2. What elements are most influential in determining the clothing standards of families of your acquaintance?

3. How much do families of your acquaintance spend for clothing? What garments do they buy ready-made? What garments do they make at home? To what extent do they "make over" clothing? To what extent, if at all, do they pass clothing on from one member of the family to the next?

4. You are shopping for ready-made clothing in the stores in your community. Make a definite list of specifications for the garment desired. How much can you find out about clothing offerings from inspection, from labels, from the sales person? In what type of stores do you find the best selection of merchandise? The most intelligent and helpful sales force? In what ways could the selling service be improved? From your observation of other customers, what could shoppers do to improve the service which stores can render?

5. Compare the cost of buying materials and making the following articles at home with the cost of buying articles of similar quality in the stores of your community: little girls' dresses, boys' or men's shirts, women's house dresses, summer wash dresses, silk dresses, underwear.

6. Compare the problems of clothing the families described in question 10,

page 81. Describe in some detail what seem to you to be desirable clothing standards for these families. How many and what sort of garments should each family buy? To what extent will it be feasible to economize by making clothing at home? In what stores should they purchase their clothing?

REFERENCES

Andrews, B. R., *Economics of the Household*, Revised Edition, Chs. XV and XVI, pp. 368-434. The Macmillan Co., New York, 1935.

An interesting discussion of the great variety of problems involved in clothing the family, together with a consideration of the broader social implications of many of these problems. These chapters include specific suggestions in regard to budgeting, buying, and clothing economies.

Dooley, W. H., *Economics of Clothing and Textiles*. D. C. Heath and Co., Boston, 1934.

A high school text in economics, taking its examples wherever possible from the clothing and textile industry. As a result, it contains much excellent and informative material about clothing. Use index and table of contents.

Hess, Katharine Paddock, *Textile Fibers and Their Use*, Revised Edition. J. B. Lippincott Co., Chicago, 1936.

A detailed description of the methods of manufacturing of textiles, with a discussion of their qualities and uses. Excellent background for the clothing buyer.

Latzke, Alpha, and Quinlan, Beth, *Clothing*. J. B. Lippincott Co., Chicago, 1935.

See especially Units Four, Five, and Six for typical clothing budgets, suggestions for planning and financing clothing expenditures, and definite information which will help in wise buying of the clothing the family needs.

Nystrom, P. H., *Economic Principles of Consumption*, Ch. XIV, pp. 327-347. The Ronald Press Co., New York, 1929.

An estimate of trends in clothing consumption, together with an analysis of individual clothing requirements in families at various living levels.

Nystrom, P. H., *Economics of Fashion*. The Ronald Press Co., New York, 1928.

A fascinating and detailed description of the psychology and economics of fashion, together with a brief history of fashion and an analysis of the origin of styles, especially in clothing.

CHAPTER X

HOUSING

The house itself. Shelter is the third of the triumvirate of fundamental necessities with which every family must be provided. The house in which the family lives must provide the physical qualities needed in shelter. It must be dry and airy, warm in winter and cool in summer, and must provide thorough protection from the elements. In addition it must be conveniently arranged, and must provide privacy and comfort, and adequate space and facilities for carrying on all the various activities in which the family wishes to engage. At the same time the house must be available at a price the family can afford to pay, economical to run, easy to care for, and not too expensive to keep in repair.

Location. The house should be conveniently located with regard to transportation facilities, employment, school, neighborhood stores, retail shopping center, church, and places of amusement. Each family must decide for itself the relative importance of each of these elements in determining the location of the home.

Neighborhood. The neighborhood determines the social contacts which the family has with its immediate neighborhood group. These contacts may not be very important to a family of adults living in a large city, since they pick their friends from a wider area. They may see very little of the families living in adjacent apartments. In small communities, however, immediate neighbors are an important element in the social scheme. The neighborhood in which a family lives has a definite bearing upon its social standing in the community. Whether or not there should be such social distinctions, in both large and small communities there is a "right side of the tracks." Unless a family's social position is unusually secure, it cannot ignore entirely the effect of the neighborhood upon its social position in the community.

A family with children finds that regardless of the size of the community in which it lives, the neighborhood pretty largely determines the children's playmates. The neighborhood determines also the public school the children attend. There are inevitable differences in the physical plant, the staff, and, most of all, in the children themselves in the different schools of a city. A progressive school system adapts its instruction as far as possible to the immediate needs of the children in each school. It is important, therefore, for the family with children to select the neighborhood in which it lives, not only with regard to the children's playmates, but also with regard to the school which they will attend.

And finally, the neighborhood determines to a considerable extent the community facilities which the family may have available. In selecting the neighborhood it is important to consider not only the school, but also the parks and playgrounds, the supervised recreational opportunities, the library facilities, and all the other social use income that may be available.

The effect of shelter upon other expenditures. The importance of proper shelter cannot be judged adequately by the direct expenditure it involves. Although expenditure for the house or apartment itself is a major item, when the family selects its home it fixes definitely the amount of many other family expenditures. The cost of fuel and light, the cost of keeping the house in good repair, the burden of cleaning, the housekeeping tasks, even the chance to stretch the income by gardening or sewing or cooking or other home production activities is determined by the type of house in which the family lives.

The long-time nature of shelter choice. Ordinarily a family buys a home with the idea of securing adequate shelter for the entire life of the family. Even families renting their homes find it inadvisable to move at frequent intervals, since moving is upsetting to family routine, and involves much hard work and expense both in direct moving costs and in incidental expenses for replacement of furniture that will not fit the new apartment. Families who are renting find it much better, once they have secured suitable housing, to live in the same home until major changes in the family situation make it imperative to secure a different type of shelter.

Adapting shelter to changing family needs. The problem of selecting suitable shelter is complicated by the fact that the family's need for shelter varies from time to time, just as do its other needs. At various stages in the family life cycle the family can use to good advantage different types of shelter. When a young couple are first married, especially if both are employed, they may secure shelter economically by renting a small apartment. When the children begin to come they need to move to larger quarters. When the size of the family is definitely established, they can move to a home which will provide them with adequate space in which to rear their family. They will need the usual living quarters with a bedroom for the parents and, if possible, a bedroom for each of the children. At this stage of the family life cycle perhaps more than at any other the needs and preferences of families vary. Some families need a library or study, some a music room which can be shut off from the rest of the house, or a recreation room where the children can engage in strenuous activities that are upsetting to the rest of the household. Some families need an extra room for grandfather or grandmother, or for resident help. When the children go away to school, the parents may still want the large house to care for the whole family during vacations. But after the children are settled in homes of their own, the parents may find the large house too expensive and burdensome. They may prefer to move to a heated and lighted apartment where someone else assumes responsibility for most of the management a home involves.

Many families find that it becomes advisable to move from one community or one neighborhood to another, because of changes in employment, or because they are not content to live permanently in the same neighborhood, even though they stay in the same community. As their income increases, they may want to move from a declining neighborhood to a newly built-up section. Or again, a family may start out in an inexpensive location with no yard. When the children begin to play about, the family moves to provide them with more space and proper playmates. When the children finish elementary school, it may be wise for the family to move nearer to high school to save the time and expense involved in going a long distance to and from school every day.

Selecting a suitable home for a family is not an easy task. Since the selection is made only at long intervals, and since the needs of the family change markedly from time to time, the selection should be made only after a careful balancing of advantages. Most families find it impossible to secure a perfect home. They have not the means, for one thing, and it is almost impossible to find a home which will serve equally well all the diverse demands of the family upon its shelter.

It is important, therefore, to weigh advantage against advantage and disadvantage against disadvantage—the social advantage of one neighborhood against the easy accessibility to the neighborhood store and shopping center in another; the advantage of the low rent and high operating cost of a commodious old house against the higher rent but lower operating cost of a new one; small expenditures of time and money on transportation against land enough for a garden; suitability to immediate needs against suitability to future needs for shelter. All of these considerations and many more must be balanced against the amount of income the family has available to spend on its shelter.

The following table gives a detailed list of points to consider in choosing a home. Probably in no case will all of these points enter into the decision. The list is designed rather to suggest the variety of factors which must be weighed in the selection of a home for the family.

POINTS TO CONSIDER IN CHOOSING A HOME

I. Renting.

    A. Price.

    B. Location.

        1. Nearness to:

            a. Transportation facilities.

            b. Place of employment.

            c. School.

            d. Church.

            e. Business district.

            f. Neighborhood stores.

            g. Places of amusement.

        2. Neighborhood.

            a. Social restrictions.

                (1) Color line.

                (2) Foreign element.

                (3) Class of people.

            b. Zoning restrictions.

            c. Voluntary restrictions in contracts issued by original owners of plat.

            d. Type and size of houses.

e. Paving and other street improvements.

f. Public utilities available (gas, electricity, water, sewer).

g. Topographical considerations.

h. Parks and playgrounds.

i. Size of lots.

j. Type of streets.

    (1) Through streets.

    (2) Major residential.

    (3) Minor residential.

    (4) Dead end and cul de sac.

    (5) Courts and alleys.

C. The home itself.

  1. Qualities of a good lot.

    a. Size—width and depth.

    b. Shape.

    c. Low or high ground.

    d. Type of soil.

    e. Filled or natural.

    f. Condition of adjoining lots.

    g. Corner vs. inside lot.

    h. Trees, shrubbery, condition of lawn.

    i. Fruit and vegetable garden.

  2. Qualities of a good house.

    a. Number of rooms.

    b. Size of rooms.

    c. Arrangement of rooms.

    d. Cross ventilation.

    e. Number of halls and stairways.

    f. External appearance.

    g. Type of construction.

    h. Quality of materials.

    i. Structural defects.

    j. Style.

    k. Basement.

    l. Heating system.

        (1) Type.

        (2) Size.

        (3) Estimated fuel consumption.

        (4) Location of radiation.

    m. Storm windows, insulation, weather-stripping.

II. Buying.

  A. Business considerations.

    1. Cash or appraisal value of house.

    2. Acquisition cost.

      a. Down payment required.

      b. Salesman's commission.

      c. Cost of searching title.

    3. Cost of financing purchase.

      a. Interest rate.

      b. Cost of first mortgage.

        (1) Rate of interest.

        (2) Premium to secure loan.

        (3) Tax on mortgage.

      c. Terms of second mortgage or instalment contract agreement.

        (1) Interest rate.

        (2) Premium charged.

        (3) Inflated value of property to cover usual discount rate on second mortgages and instalment contracts.

    4. Probable resale value.

      a. Rising or falling market for real estate.

      b. Rising or falling price level.

      c. Rising or falling interest rate.

      d. Probability of appreciation of value of land.

      e. Probability of depreciation of buildings.

      f. Probability of obsolescence due to:

        (1) Changes in styles of houses.

        (2) Changes in character of neighborhood.

        (3) Changes in use of land in neighborhood.

    5. Cost of owning the home.

      a. Imputed interest on investment.

      b. Taxes.

        (1) Assessed valuation (effect of sale on valuation, etc.).

        (2) Tax rate.

      c. Reserve for depreciation.

      d. Repairs and replacements.

III. Building.

  A. Architect.

    1. Cost.

    2. Services rendered.

B. Method of building.
  1. Contract basis.
  2. Contractor on labor and materials basis.
  3. Personal management without contractor.
C. Financing cost of building.
  1. Payments under contract.
  2. Money necessary from time to time to meet bills for labor and materials.
  3. Money necessary to carry on building operations.

The place of shelter in the family's standard of living.

The family will find it easier to select its home intelligently if it has thought through carefully the place which shelter is to have in the family's standard of living.   Each family must consider whether in its case physical or social or economic considerations are more important.   It must decide whether it prefers quantity or quality of housing.   Will its need for shelter be better suited by a large, rambling, old-fashioned house without hardwood floors, with well-worn woodwork and outmoded plumbing, a house that children cannot hurt and that can be secured at low cost; or by a small compact modern home, completely equipped and carefully planned in every detail, an expensive gem of a house of which the family can always be proud but which must be treated with respect?   Does the family want a house in which its members can carry on a variety of activities, without interference with one another, or does it prefer a small home in which activities are limited to what can be done by one person in a kitchenette, or to common activities of the family in the one common living room?   Should the family live in a fashionable neighborhood, in a substantial neighborhood, or in an ordinary neighborhood?   Are the needs of the children or of the adults to receive primary consideration?   To what extent are considerations of economy to rule in securing shelter?   Does the family's standard call for renting or owning its home?   The relative importance of all the varied elements which shelter involves must be thought through in their relation to the family's standard of living.

How much should a family spend for shelter?

For many years there has been a feeling that there ought to be some one percentage of its income which a family should spend for shelter.   This belief probably originated from Engel's studies.   He formulated as one of his laws of consumption, the principle that regardless of the amount of the family's income, the proportion of its expenditure for shelter remains the same. His principle, drawn for workers' incomes, has been assumed to hold for incomes generally.

Recent studies have clearly indicated that there is no basis for such an assumption. There are a number of factors which help to determine both the amount and the proportion of the family's income which goes for shelter.

The effect of income on shelter expenditures. Studies of family expenditures for a number of occupational and social groups at different income levels indicate that the proportion of the income which is spent for shelter does vary with the amount of the family's income. For a given occupational or social group, living in a given community, there is convincing evidence that the families with the smaller incomes spend a larger proportion of their income for shelter than do the families with the larger incomes. This tendency for the proportion spent for shelter to decrease as the income increases seems to hold good for groups with incomes of $5,000 or less. One study of a group of families with incomes ranging upward from $10,000 indicated that in the upper income groups, as family income increased, a larger proportion of it was spent for shelter.

The effect of the size of the family upon expenditures for shelter. Studies of family expenditures seem to show that in a given income group, the larger families spend a smaller proportion of their income for shelter and a larger proportion for food and clothing than do the smaller families living on the same income. It is easy to see why this must be so. Personal needs for food and clothing vary directly with the size of the family. Expenditures for shelter are in the nature of family overhead. An obvious form of economy is to keep this overhead expense as low as is consistent with minimum shelter needs.

The effect of the community in which the family lives upon its expenditures for shelter. More important than either the income or the size of the family in determining the proportion of the family income which must be spent for shelter is the community in which a family lives. Ordinarily, the larger the community, the larger is the proportion of the family income which must be spent for shelter, and at the same time, the less adequate and desirable is the type of shelter which a given expenditure will secure.

In the open country and the small town, almost every family lives in a single dwelling surrounded by a generous plot of ground. In moderate sized cities, the size of the lot is somewhat smaller. The double house, the flat, and occasionally the apartment appear. They provide shelter for only a comparatively small proportion of the families in the community.[1]

In large metropolitan centers a very large proportion of the population live in multi-family dwellings. Families in the lower income groups, who must live close to their work, live crowded into apartments and tenements. The larger the city, then, the smaller is the space available for the family, the larger is the number of families housed on an acre of ground, and the more expensive is the shelter they occupy.

In many cases the rate of growth of a community is fully as important as the size of the community in determining the cost of shelter. In a rapidly growing community, adequate housing is usually hard to find. No one builds rental property until he is sure of an adequate return on his investment. A shortage of decent dwellings develops. A family that wants a good place to live must pay a premium for suitable housing. If the housing shortage is acute, it must pay a premium for any housing and put up as best it can with what is available. When building gets under way, there will usually be a larger proportion of new housing than in the ordinary community, but it will be held for a premium. The family may be forced to buy a home on the instalment plan in order to be sure of a place to live. As a result of these conditions, in a rapidly growing community, shelter usually takes a larger proportion of the family income than in a community which is growing at a less rapid rate.

On the other hand, in a declining community, shelter costs are low. Since no one wants to buy a home in such a town, there is plenty of desirable property for rent at a reasonable figure. In such a community a family can secure adequate shelter with a smaller proportion of its income. It can choose from a variety of houses. However, if the town has long been on the decline, not much "strictly modern" housing will be available.

The effect of building costs and restrictions upon expenditures for shelter. There is a very definite relationship between building costs in a community and the family's expenditures

[1] See table, "Dwellings and Families by Class of Dwelling," p. 21.

for shelter. In a growing community, if building costs are low, building proceeds at a rapid rate. If building costs are high, no building is begun until an obvious shortage exists, which will force rents to a point at which they will pay a fair return upon the builder's investment.[2]

In communities in which rents are not high enough to justify new building, high building costs affect the quality of shelter which is available. Since repairs and improvements involve a large proportion of labor cost, high wage rates in the building trades tend to delay improvements, and to keep repairs and redecoration at a minimum. In all communities, then, high building costs lead to the accumulation of dingy and out-of-date dwellings. At the present time one of the things which would do more than anything else to solve the problem of providing American families with adequate shelter at low cost is to discover some way of reducing labor costs in the building trades.

It is important also to understand the relation of building restrictions to shelter costs. An adequately enforced building code can do a great deal to eliminate overcrowding and jerry-building. Properly enforced zoning ordinances help to eliminate undesirable areas and to stabilize property values. They also increase the desirability of residential areas. It is always important, however, to be on the alert for unnecessary building regulations which add nothing to the desirability of housing but add greatly to its cost.

The effect of price levels upon expenditures for shelter. In periods of changing prices, shelter costs do not change as rapidly as do many other prices. Rents are usually fixed for several months in advance. When prices are rising, rents tend to lag behind food and clothing prices. Building costs frequently advance faster than rents. When rents once start up, there usually has accumulated a sufficient housing shortage so that they continue to increase for some time after other prices have reached their peak and begun to decline. In 1918 and 1919, for example, prices of food and clothing shot up

---

[2] In the years just following the World War in a number of the larger cities of the country, unreasonable restrictions imposed by building trades unions, by combinations of contractors, and by monopolistic practices of materials men, forced prices of building materials and wages in the building trades out of line with prices and wages in other industries. This helped to maintain rents at an excessively high level for several years. In 1934, one of the biggest difficulties encountered by the Federal Housing Administration in its attempt to stimulate business in the building trades was the insistence by the building trades unions upon higher wages and shorter hours than were in effect in other industries. It is impossible for a family with an income earned at the rate of 40 or 50 or 60 cents an hour to meet the cost of building a new home or modernizing an old one at the rate of $1.20 to $2.00 an hour for building trades labor.

rapidly. These prices broke in 1920, recovered a little in 1923, but never reached anything like their war-time peak. Shelter costs, however, continued upward until 1924.

As a result of this tendency for rents to lag behind other prices, when prices are rising rapidly the proportion of the family income spent for rent tends to be low compared to the proportion spent for items more immediately affected by price increases. On the other hand, when prices are declining, the proportion spent for rent will tend to be somewhat larger than the proportion of the income spent for items for which prices are decreasing more rapidly. Studies made during the World War probably underestimate the proportion of income families in the larger cities spend for rent. Studies made in 1924 probably somewhat overestimate the percentage of income a family should spend for shelter.

The effect of home ownership upon expenditures for shelter. The family's current outlay for shelter depends in part at least upon whether a family owns, rents, or is buying its home. The family that owns its own home free and clear in most years spends a smaller proportion of its current income for shelter than does the family that is renting. The family pays itself no interest on its investment. It counts taxes, insurance, and repairs as its entire shelter cost. The family that is renting, on the other hand, must ordinarily pay enough to cover the landlord's expenses for taxes, management, and upkeep, and also give the landlord a reasonable return upon his investment. The family that owns a mortgaged home may spend nearly as much for shelter as does the family that is renting. For in recent years mortgages have commanded a considerably higher rate of interest than landlords have been able to secure from rental property.

The family that is buying a home and paying monthly instalments of interest and principal must make the largest current outlay. A family buying a home on the instalment plan must pay taxes, repairs, and insurance like any other home owner, and make its monthly payments of interest and principal as well. Perhaps it should count its payments on the principal as savings. But ordinarily families look upon these payments as prepaid shelter costs.

How much should a family spend for shelter? Clearly there is no one answer to the question: "How much should a family spend for shelter?" In this as in so many other problems of family management and finance, a variety of factors must be considered. In some communities, real estate men set as a maximum one week's pay for a month's rent. There are authorities who advocate spending for shelter one-ninth, one-sixth, one-fifth, and one-fourth of the family income. In a few of the larger cities, it has been suggested that families with larger incomes living in apartments in which everything, including maid service, is furnished can afford to pay as high as half their income for rent for such an apartment. For "rent" here includes not only payment for shelter but also for most of the operating expenses for which a family would pay in addition to shelter were it living in its own home.[3]

The family must decide not only upon the amount it can afford to pay for shelter, but also upon whether it is better to rent or to own its home. In recent years the importance of home ownership has been emphasized until to many families it has come to overshadow all other considerations in securing shelter for the family. As a matter of fact, it should be only incidental. Both owning and renting are only means. The end the family has in view is the securing of the most suitable and satisfactory shelter possible with the means at its disposal.

Arguments in favor of home ownership. The usual arguments in favor of home ownership run somewhat as follows: It costs less to own than to rent. Home ownership reduces shelter costs to a definitely known figure. The family that owns its home is not subject to rent increases. A family can reduce shelter costs by making its own repairs.

Home ownership induces thrift, especially if the home is purchased on the instalment plan. A home is a safe investment for a family. The family may profit from increases in property values. A family that owns its own home finds it easier to establish its credit. Home ownership is a means of establishing financial independence.

Home ownership makes the family independent of control by a landlord. There are no restrictions upon children. There are no limits to the size of the family. There are no restrictions upon pets. The family is free to make such alterations and improvements in its home as it pleases. The family can secure healthful exercise from work around the home. A neighborhood of owned homes is usually

---

[3] See table, "Tenure of Homes of the United States," p. 20.

better kept up than is a neighborhood made up largely of rental property.

Home ownership provides security for the family. It assures the members of the family of a home in their old age. It guarantees them a place to live during periods of unemployment. It provides them with a permanent environment. Home ownership makes it unnecessary for the family to be adjusting continually to new conditions.

Home ownership in many cases increases the family's social prestige and strengthens its position in the community. Home owners are considered to be permanently identified with the community. They are expected to assume more civic responsibility. Their voice has more weight in community affairs.

Arguments in favor of renting. There are a number of less familiar but equally plausible arguments in favor of renting a home. They run as follows: It costs less to rent than to own. For the same expenditure, a family can maintain a higher shelter standard by renting than by owning. The family renting its home pays for shelter as it goes. By investing in sound securities the amount it would spend if it bought a home, it can frequently secure a larger return upon its investment. The renting family is in no danger from loss of capital through decline in property values. If rents decline, the renter can benefit from reductions in shelter costs. The renter's chief obligation is the payment of a periodic sum. The renting family has no responsibility for the management of the property in which it lives. If it rents an apartment, it may have no responsibility for providing heat, utilities, or many other operating expenses.

The renter is free to move at any time when conditions become unsatisfactory, or when better housing is available elsewhere. The renter can therefore adjust more easily to changing shelter needs. If his income is radically reduced, he can move to less expensive quarters to bring his shelter expense into line with his income. He is not faced with fixed charges for maintaining his home. If his income increases he can move to a better neighborhood.

The renter can bargain better than can the home owner in selling his services to his employer. He can move to another town if necessary in order to take advantage of promotions. In case he loses his job, he is not tied to the community in which he lives by his investment in his home.

**Some common misconceptions in regard to home owner-
ship and renting.** Obviously, these arguments cannot all be valid
as they are stated. It cannot cost more both to own and to rent.
It hardly seems reasonable to have more freedom both as a home
owner and as a renter, and yet these conflicting arguments are commonly and sincerely advanced. The difficulty lies in the fact that
some of these arguments involve failure to distinguish between two
meanings of the same term, some are based upon facts that are no
longer true, some involve the failure to distinguish between cause
and effect or between means and end, and some are valid in one
situation but not in another. If these arguments are properly
qualified, there is an element of truth in all of them. As they stand,
they include a number of common misconceptions.

Misconceptions: It is cheaper to own than to rent. One of the
most widespread of these misconceptions is the belief that it is cheaper
to own than to rent. This belief involves the failure to distinguish
between cost and current outlay. The advantage in current outlay
is usually with the family that owns its own home free and clear.
The home-owning family makes no monthly payments for rent.
Instead, once or twice a year it must pay the taxes upon its home.
Once in three or four years it must spend something for repairs and
improvements.

The family renting a home, on the other hand, makes a regular
monthly payment to the owner of the property. This payment must
be large enough to cover taxes, insurance, and repairs, and in addition, to give the owner of the property a fair return on his investment
and allow him to set up adequate reserves for depreciation, so that he
can maintain his capital investment intact. The current outlay of
the renter must be larger than that of the home owner if he is to
pay the landlord a fair return upon his investment in rental property.

In comparing costs, however, the home owner cannot ignore either
interest or depreciation. While the home owner ordinarily does not
pay himself interest upon his investment in his home, he must recognize as a part of the cost of the home the interest his money could
have earned had he invested it in income-producing securities instead
of in a home. While the typical home owner does not set up cash
reserves against depreciation, he must take account of the decrease
in the value of his property in counting the cost of home ownership
over a period of years. If the home owner adds allowances for

interest on his investment and for depreciation he will find that the total cost of owning a home is not very different from the total cost of renting the same sort of a home.

Misconceptions: Landlords enjoy large profits. Most tenants have an exaggerated idea of the profit the landlord is able to make from rental property. As a matter of fact, the landlord must rent his property at going rentals. He can count as interest on his investment what is left out of current rentals after he has made all necessary expenditures for taxes and for maintenance, and has set up adequate allowances for depreciation. Some years current rents will give him a good return from his investment in rental property. In other years vacancies and low rents may bring down his income from his property to a point where he may receive but little over the actual cost of taxes and repairs. Over a period of years, a landlord is doing well if he averages a net income of from 5 to 6 per cent upon his investment. If he makes more it is in most cases because of increases in property values rather than because of income from rents.

Misconceptions: Real estate always increases in value. There is a widespread belief that over a period of years, real estate will inevitably increase in value. This belief grew out of experiences during the latter part of the nineteenth and the early part of the twentieth century.

The facts are these: In a growing community, land tends to increase in value. Buildings, on the other hand, inevitably decline in value with the passage of time. Part of this loss of value is due to depreciation, part to obsolescence. The depreciation and obsolescence are ordinarily figured as a percentage, not of the original cost, but of the reproduction or replacement cost of the building. Any increase in building costs tends to check the decrease in building values. Any decrease in building costs tends to accelerate such loss of value.

During the nineteenth century the population of the whole country increased rapidly. As a result, land increased steadily in value, even during periods of declining commodity prices. During the first two decades of the twentieth century the drift to the cities caused a rapid increase in land values in the principal urban centers, and prices increased, slowly at first and then rapidly during the World War. Building costs increased with other prices. The housing shortage which developed during the war period was sufficient to hold up rents and building costs so that property values in many communities increased for four years or more after other prices had begun to decline.

During this period, a man could buy a home, live in it for ten or fifteen or twenty years, and sell it for more than he paid for it. The increase in land values and the increase in building costs were more than sufficient to offset depreciation in buildings. While property owners expected occasional temporary declines in property values during a business depression, it was assumed that over a period of years their property would continue to increase in value.

But such increase in property values can never be counted upon to continue indefinitely. If at any time land values fail to increase as rapidly as buildings depreciate, if at any time building costs decline or old buildings become obsolete, home owners can expect their property to decline in value.

Since 1920 there have been a number of forces at work making for declining property values. Large cities are no longer growing rapidly. Population is no longer increasing rapidly. The declining rate of population growth is removing the constant pressure for more land which existed during the entire history of the country up to the close of the World War.

The development of the automobile has placed economical transportation within the reach of the majority of the people of the country. It is no longer necessary for families to pay a premium for a home within easy access of work or school or shopping district. It is now possible for families to spread out away from business centers in a way which was not possible before 1920. Now that economical transportation is available, new building takes place on cheap new land in the environs. As houses pass out of style, there is little tendency to replace them with modern property. Instead, people who want up-to-date homes move out to new suburbs. As a result, whole neighborhoods become obsolete, and land and buildings alike decline in value.

Since 1920 the long-time trend of prices has been downward. Eventually this should make itself felt in lower building costs. Prices of materials and equipment cannot indefinitely go against prevailing price trends. Builders will be forced to reduce their charges if they are to market homes in competition with low-priced commodities. There are various ways in which building costs may be reduced. In recent years there have been a number of developments which make winter building possible. This allows more regular employment in the building trades, and more regular employment usually results in lower wage rates and higher worker income. A number of new types of material which can be applied at lower labor cost have been developed, as well as a number of units of home equipment which are completely assembled at the factory ready to be installed in the home. There is under way at present considerable experimentation in large-scale and even in factory production of houses. All of these developments sooner or later will bring lower building costs. As building costs decline, new houses will cost less, and it will be necessary to increase the rate of depreciation upon older properties.

In the years following the World War there have been a number of developments which have added materially to the rate of obsolescence of houses. The introduction of the electric light, the bathtub, and central heating has made it necessary either to improve old property or accept heavy losses in values. The development of the built-in tub and the shower, of more efficient laundry tubs and kitchen sinks, of new types of electric light fixtures, of improved hot-water heaters, and of air-conditioning plants have continued to accelerate the rate of obsolescence.

The new emphasis upon style in architecture, with fads in styling and with rapid changes in fashionable design, have helped to render old housing obsolete, and have placed in use many extreme types that will in turn soon be outmoded. The new types of houses such as were shown at the Century of Progress exhibits at Chicago in 1933 and 1934 indicate the possibility of further radical changes both in design, in equipment, and in building costs. The family must face the probability that in the future both owner and renter will be required to pay for depreciation at a higher rate than in the early years of the century.

If it is not possible to count upon steadily increasing property values, neither is it possible to count upon steady declines in the value of real property. It is important to distinguish clearly between long-time and short-time trends in property values. Property values change with changes in the business cycle. During every business depression real property tends to decline in value. It ordinarily regains at least part of its depression losses during the next period of prosperity. During a depression the market is flooded with property which must be sold. Few families have ready money with which to buy. As a result, homes sell for a time well below the cost of new building. As long as this is true, few new homes are built. Because of deferred maintenance, houses wear out even faster than usual. As a result, each period of recovery brings a housing shortage, and each period of prosperity sees rising property values.

Even when the long-time trend of prices is downward, families that are able to buy at depression lows may be able to secure excellent bargains in housing. They will be protected against serious loss from depreciation by increasing values during the next period of prosperity. But families buying during prosperous times must be on their guard. It is no longer clear that they can count upon each succeeding period of prosperity to carry their property to new high values. If they are forced to dispose of their property during a period of depression, they can expect to take heavy losses. Even if they sell at the same stage in the business cycle in which they bought they must expect losses from depreciation and obsolescence.

Misconceptions: Home ownership always provides security for the family. A common misconception of another sort is the belief that somehow or other the ownership of a home always gives a family security. This is a typical example of our tendency to confuse cause and effect. Because many people who own homes are in an enviable position of security it is commonly believed that any family can obtain this security by buying a home for itself. This is not true. It is not home ownership that gives security; instead, it is security that makes home ownership possible. To the family that has already attained security in employment, in savings, in social position, and family status, home ownership can add many other advantages. But the family whose situation is in any way insecure may find that owning a home is a handicap rather than a help in its quest for security.

In any discussion of security we must distinguish clearly between the security to be gained from home ownership in an agrarian situation and in an urban situation. Ownership of a farm home provides opportunity for employment. In an urban situation ownership of a home is simply one way of making an inevitable expenditure for shelter. Security lies in finding and keeping a job, not in owning a home.

Experiments are now under way to determine whether subsistence homesteads will provide urban workers with security during periods of irregular employment. The subsistence homestead differs from the ordinary urban home in that it does provide opportunity for self-employment. It does provide an opportunity for a family to produce for its own use some of the things it needs. But even the subsistence homestead is not sufficient to provide a family with its entire living. The ownership of such a homestead can provide security for a family only if in the course of a year its members can earn enough money to finance necessary purchases in the market, including the tools and equipment they need for efficient home production.

Misconceptions: Home ownership insures the stability of the family. Another current misconception involving failure to distinguish between cause and effect is the belief that stability of the family itself can be secured by the ownership of a home. This argument assumes that a stable family must have one place to which its members can come as a permanent home. It is probable that there is a larger proportion of stable families among home owners than among renters. But this is not because home ownership causes stability. Rather, it is due to the fact that a certain amount of stability in the family situation is absolutely essential if a family is to get together the funds necessary to purchase and maintain its own home.

Stable family life depends upon permanence of personal relations, not permanence of residence. The fact that approximately half of the families of the country live in rented homes is not an indication that the stability of the family is declining, but that under modern conditions family stability is attained through personal rather than locational factors.

Misconceptions: Every family should live in a new house. Another misconception which is often implied rather than stated is the assumption that every family should be able to live in a new house. This desire to provide families with new houses confuses new houses with adequate housing. Without question, much of our present housing is obsolete. Without question, also, much of our new housing has been so poorly built as to be entirely inadequate. Adequate housing must be well built of good materials. Well-built housing lasts a long time. Really well-built housing should provide adequate shelter for a family for not less than fifty years. But under modern conditions, with present rapid changes in design and styling, a house can be called a *new* house for not more than five years of its fifty-year life. Under present conditions, if all our new housing is built as well as it should be, not over 20 per cent of the population can expect to live in new houses.

Provided that an old house is adequate to its needs, it is no more necessary that a family should live in a new house than it is that every family should drive a new car. Just as there are many families that prefer a second-hand automobile in a higher price class to a new car in a lower price class, so there are many families that prefer adequate and well-built older housing to the smaller new houses that are available for the same expenditure.

Misconceptions: A family buying a house on the instalment plan owns its own home. Finally, there is the common misconception that a family buying its home on the instalment plan owns its home. A family buying its home on the instalment plan can be said to own its home only if it has available in some form easily convertible into cash, investments which are equivalent in value to the unpaid balance upon its property. A family with no other resources than its current income owns only an equity in its home. Such a family is in a position very similar to the individual who has put his entire savings into the stock market and is trading on a narrow margin. Only too often under these circumstances buying a home on the instalment plan turns out to be a marginal speculation in real estate. If the value of the property increases it may be possible to sell out and double the money the family has invested. But if the property declines in value, a part or all of the home owner's equity will be wiped out. It is absolutely fundamental that every family understand this essential difference between buying upon the instalment plan and actually owning a home.[4]

The decision to own or to rent. Each family must decide on the basis of the comparative advantage in its own situation whether to own or to rent the home in which it lives. If the family's shelter needs can be definitely determined, if the family's income is clearly assured, if the family's position in the community shows every indication of being permanent, and if real estate values can be depended upon, then the advantage may lie with home ownership. But if the family's shelter needs are not definitely determined, if its income is uncertain, if the family is not sure of remaining permanently in the

---

[4] The chart, "Buying a Home," page 248, illustrates the fundamental difference in the position of families buying a home outright, buying a home subject to a single mortgage, and buying a home on an instalment contract.

community, or if real estate values are likely to decline, it may be better for the family to rent. It is important to decide between owning and renting in the way which will give the family most nearly the sort of shelter it needs for the price it is able to pay. For after all, it is the quality of the family's shelter which is fundamental, and not the ownership of it.

Financing shelter expenses. The problems which a family must face in financing its expenditures for shelter depend upon whether it rents or owns its home or is buying it on the instalment plan. Each method of providing the family with shelter brings with it a set of characteristic financing problems.

Renting. The family that rents its home must make payments for shelter at regular intervals. The amount of the rental payments is ordinarily determined for some time in advance. Rent must be counted as one of the family's regularly recurring fixed charges.

And yet, while rent is a fixed charge, it can be adjusted to changes in the family's income. If its income increases, the family can move to more expensive and more desirable quarters. If its income decreases, it can move to less expensive quarters.

If rents increase, the family can decide whether to pay the increased rent for its present house or to move to less desirable quarters. If rents decrease, the family can secure the advantage of lower shelter costs.

The family with a regular income finds it comparatively easy to make provision for its regular rental payments. It simply sets aside the necessary amount out of each regular increment of income. It must be careful only to see that the payment for shelter does not take too large a portion of the family's income. When this proves to be the case, the family can remedy the situation by moving to less expensive quarters.

The family with an irregular income must be sure to set aside out of each increment of income enough to take care of these regular rental payments until the next instalment of income is available.

Owning. The family which owns its home is freed from the necessity of making regular weekly or monthly payments for shelter. Instead it must make provision for taxes, insurance, repairs, and improvements, and reserves for depreciation. If the home is owned subject to a mortgage, the family must pay the interest on the loan at regular intervals. It must either make regular payments to amortize the principal of the mortgage, or it must make provision for refinancing the loan when it becomes due.

Any mortgage payments, taxes and insurance premiums, and expenditures for necessary repairs are minimum charges which must be met every year. The rest of the expenditures for shelter can be made whenever it is most convenient. The larger repairs and improvements can be made when income is available. If the family faces unusually heavy demands upon its income for other purposes, the property can be allowed to depreciate for some time, and then be brought back into condition when the family's financial situation improves.

If the family considers the purchase of a home as an integral part of its investment program, and if it intends to keep intact the capital it has invested in its home, it must make adequate provision for depreciation and obsolescence. It can reduce depreciation by keeping the property in good repair. It can reduce losses from obsolescence by carefully planned improvements designed to modernize the property. And it must in addition set up adequate reserves in some other form to offset inevitable losses in value which come to all property with passing time.

On the other hand, if the family regards its purchase of a home as the payment for shelter for some time in advance of immediate need, it may decide not to set up any reserves against depreciation and obsolescence. It may decide not to make any extensive repairs or improvements. It may find that it is better policy to wear out its home in much the same way it wears out its furniture or its automobile. This does not mean that it will deliberately abuse its property. It will from time to time make such repairs as will keep the property attractive and liveable. But it will plan to use up its investment in shelter during the life of the family. It will not count upon the value of its home as an important item in the family's estate. And if, after some years, it finds a home better suited to its present needs, it will trade in the old home for the new one, just as it trades in the old car for the newer model.

The family that owns its own home can adjust its shelter expenditures to changes in income in a number of ways. It can adjust to temporary reductions in income by making only the minimum expenditures necessary to maintain a clear title to its home, postponing all provision for repairs or depreciation until more income is available.

If the family income is temporarily reduced to a point where there is no money available with which to meet even the minimum of fixed charges, the family whose home is unencumbered by any loans may be able to mortgage its home for a considerable fraction of its value, and use the proceeds of the loan to pay the fixed charges until adequate current income is again available. This expedient can be used only once. It should be used only if the decline in income is temporary, and only if the proceeds of the loan will be adequate to take care of minimum charges until current income is again available. In estimating the charges which must be met, the family must remember that the mortgage will add interest payments to present fixed charges, and that eventually the principal of the loan must be repaid.

If a family's income is permanently reduced to a point which makes it unwise to try to maintain its present home, the family can trade for a home which will be less expensive to own and operate. If the family's income has been so far reduced that it is unable to pay its taxes and make the minimum of emergency repairs upon an inexpensive home, it will find it almost impossible to pay rent for any adequate quarters. In this case, it may sell its home and pay rent for some time out of the proceeds.

While the family that owns its home can adjust its shelter expenditures to temporary changes in the family income more easily than can the family that is renting, it can adjust to permanent changes in the family situation only by disposing of its property. Whether it can dispose of its property without loss depends largely upon the market for real estate at the time when the family is forced to sell.

The family with a regular income finds it necessary to plan in advance to meet the recurring charges for taxes and repairs and insurance. If it has a generous income, it can plan its other expenditures so as to have money available for shelter in the months when taxes and other large payments are due. If its income is small, it may find it wise to set aside some funds each month just as it would if it were paying rent. The amount it sets aside for shelter expense should be adequate to pay taxes and insurance, and to take care of all emergency repairs. If the family has sufficient income available, it should include enough to provide from time to time for more extensive repairs and improvements, and to set up an adequate depreciation reserve.

The family with an irregular but adequate income ordinarily finds it easy to take care of its occasional payments for shelter when income is available. It is not faced with the necessity of setting aside reserves for regular payments of rent at frequent intervals. It must, however, be sure to provide adequately for the minimum of fixed charges which home ownership involves; for a family can continue to own its home only so long as it keeps its taxes paid. If the property is mortgaged, even for a small part of its actual value, the family can retain title to its home only so long as it keeps up its regular interest payments, and makes such payments upon principal as the terms of the mortgage demand.

Buying. Buying a home on the instalment plan involves a series of payments. Like the home owner, a family buying on the instalment plan must take care of taxes and insurance, it must pay for any necessary repairs or desired improvements, and it must set up its own allowances for depreciation. Like the renter, this family must make regular payments upon the reducing-mortgage or instalment contract. These regular payments include the interest on the unpaid balance and instalments upon the principal.

A very large proportion of these payments are fixed charges. If this family is to retain its equity in the property, it must make every payment upon the instalment contract when due. It must keep the taxes on the property paid in full, and the insurance in force. Frequently the mortgage or instalment contract contains some stipulations concerning repairs which must be made in order to maintain the value of the property. The purchaser must meet every one of these expenditures, or he may forfeit his entire equity in the property.

A family will find it easier to meet these heavy fixed charges if the terms of the purchase agreement can be arranged so that payments will come due when income is available. The family with a regular monthly income usually finds it convenient to pay for its home in monthly instalments. The family receiving its income in larger increments at irregular intervals may prefer to make quarterly or semi-annual payments of interest and principal.

Because of the large proportion of fixed charges in its current expenditures for shelter, the family buying a home on the instalment plan finds it difficult to adjust its shelter expenditures to changes in income. If its income increases the problem is not serious. It can either accumulate reserves out of which to make payments in the future, or it can make additional payments upon the balance due upon the home.

If, on the other hand, the family's income is materially reduced, it faces a more difficult problem. If the family has been paying for some time upon its home so that it has a substantial equity in its property, it may be able to refinance the balance due over a longer period, and in this way reduce the monthly payments it must make. Suppose, for example, the original agreement involved the payment of a principal of $5,000, and called for monthly payments of $50. The family has been paying on this contract for six and a half years, and has reduced the principal of the contract to $2,500. If it refinances its loan, giving a mortgage for $2,500 against the property, it may be able to reduce its payments to $25 a month. It will take another eleven years to complete payments on the property, but the family will be able to meet the required payments out of its current income.

Or, if the family can find someone with money to lend on a straight mortgage, it can pay off the reducing mortgage in full, and substitute a mortgage upon which it must make only the semi-annual interest payments. In this way it can reduce its payments from $600 to $150 per year. If it can accumulate something to pay upon the principal of the loan, it can invest this so as to have it available to use in paying the principal of the mortgage when it comes due.

And finally, if the family's income is reduced to such an extent that it is obviously impossible for it to finish paying for its home, the family may sell its equity or trade it for less expensive property which is within its means.

There are three ways in which a family can protect its equity in its home. One is to insure the chief wage earner for an amount equal to the balance due upon the home. In case of his death, the insurance policy would yield an amount of money sufficient to provide the family with a home free and clear which can either be lived in at minimum expense or be turned into cash as seems best at the time.

The second is to protect the equity in the home with other savings, which can be drawn upon from time to time to meet payments. It is not wise to enter into a contract calling for payments so large that they take all the family's margin above current expenses.

The third way to protect the family's equity in the home is to set aside savings equal to the entire amount due upon the home, or at least enough to make it possible to refinance with a first mortgage. If it seems advisable to purchase the home on the instalment plan, the family may deem it wise to hold these savings in reserve against a variety of contingencies. These savings should be so invested that they can readily be converted into cash if at any time it seems advisable to complete the payments due upon the home.

There are a number of situations in which it may be necessary for a family to undertake the purchase of a home on the instalment plan. In case of a severe housing shortage, many families are forced to buy a home in order to secure adequate shelter. They can choose between buying a permanent home, upon which they will plan to complete the payments, and buying a home upon which they will pay as little as possible, in which they can live until they can find suitable housing. If they intend to complete the payments upon their home, they should make as large a down payment as possible, financing the balance with a first mortgage, and insisting upon the lowest current cash price.

If they are planning to pay instalments only until they can find more suitable property, they may decide to make as small a down payment as possible, and make only the minimum payments the contract calls for, counting these minimum payments upon the contract as rent, and considering the down payment as a premium necessary to secure suitable shelter. In this case, if the property increases in value, they may eventually be able to sell out their equity at a profit. If it declines in value, they can turn the property back to the former owner, and consider that they will simply have paid a rather high rent for the time they lived in the house. In this latter case, however, they must recognize exactly what they are doing. And they must recognize the possibility that if they are financially responsible, they may be held for the balance of the payments due, even though the property may decline in value to such a point that they do not wish to complete their payments upon it.

The table on pages 243 to 245 shows a typical method of paying for a home on the instalment plan. In this case it is assumed that a family buys a $6,000 home, making a down payment of $1,000, and paying $50 a month on the balance of $5,000. The family pays 6 per cent interest on the unpaid balance of the reducing mortgage. Interest for the preceding month is taken out of each monthly payment, and the balance credited upon the principal of the loan. The

Buying a Home on the Instalment Plan

Purchase Price: $6,000
Down Payment: $1,000

Payments on Balance: $50 a month
Interest on Unpaid Balance: 6 per cent

Monthly Payment		Interest	Principal	Balance Due on Home
1.	$50.00	$25.00	$25.00	$4,975.00
2.	50.00	24.88	25.12	4,949.88
3.	50.00	24.75	25.25	4,924.63
4.	50.00	24.62	25.38	4,899.25
5.	50.00	24.50	25.50	4,873.75
6.	50.00	24.37	25.63	4,848.12
7.	50.00	24.24	25.76	4,822.36
8.	50.00	24.11	25.89	4,796.47
9.	50.00	23.98	26.02	4,770.45
10.	50.00	23.85	26.15	4,744.30
11.	50.00	23.72	26.28	4,718.02
12.	50.00	23.59	26.41	4,691.61
13.	50.00	23.46	26.54	4,665.07
14.	50.00	23.33	26.67	4,638.40
15.	50.00	23.19	26.81	4,611.59
16.	50.00	23.06	26.94	4,584.65
17.	50.00	22.92	27.08	4,557.57
18.	50.00	22.79	27.21	4,530.36
19.	50.00	22.65	27.35	4,503.01
20.	50.00	22.52	27.48	4,475.53
21.	50.00	22.38	27.62	4,447.91
22.	50.00	22.24	27.76	4,420.15
23.	50.00	22.10	27.90	4,392.25
24.	50.00	21.96	28.04	4,364.21
25.	50.00	21.82	28.18	4,336.03
26.	50.00	21.68	28.32	4,307.71
27.	50.00	21.54	28.46	4,279.25
28.	50.00	21.40	28.60	4,250.65
29.	50.00	21.25	28.75	4,221.90
30.	50.00	21.11	28.89	4,193.01
31.	50.00	20.97	29.03	4,163.98
32.	50.00	20.82	29.18	4,134.80
33.	50.00	20.67	29.33	4,105.47
34.	50.00	20.53	29.47	4,076.00
35.	50.00	20.38	29.62	4,046.38
36.	50.00	20.23	29.77	4,016.61
37.	50.00	20.08	29.92	3,986.69
38.	50.00	19.93	30.07	3,956.62
39.	50.00	19.78	30.22	3,926.40
40.	50.00	19.63	30.37	3,896.03
41.	50.00	19.48	30.52	3,865.51
42.	50.00	19.33	30.67	3,834.84
43.	50.00	19.17	30.83	3,804.01
44.	50.00	19.02	30.98	3,773.03
45.	50.00	18.87	31.13	3,741.90
46.	50.00	18.71	31.29	3,710.61

Monthly Payment		Interest	Principal	Balance Due on Home
47.	$50.00	$18.55	$31.45	$3,679.16
48.	50.00	18.40	31.60	3,647.56
49.	50.00	18.24	31.76	3,615.80
50.	50.00	18.08	31.92	3,583.88
51.	50.00	17.92	32.08	3,551.80
52.	50.00	17.76	32.24	3,519.56
53.	50.00	17.60	32.40	3,487.16
54.	50.00	17.44	32.56	3,454.60
55.	50.00	17.27	32.73	3,421.87
56.	50.00	17.11	32.89	3,388.98
57.	50.00	16.94	33.06	3,355.92
58.	50.00	16.78	33.22	3,322.70
59.	50.00	16.61	33.39	3,289.31
60.	50.00	16.45	33.55	3,255.76
61.	50.00	16.28	33.72	3,222.04
62.	50.00	16.11	33.89	3,188.15
63.	50.00	15.94	34.06	3,154.09
64.	50.00	15.77	34.23	3,119.86
65.	50.00	15.60	34.40	3,085.46
66.	50.00	15.43	34.57	3,050.89
67.	50.00	15.25	34.75	3,016.14
68.	50.00	15.08	34.92	2,981.22
69.	50.00	14.91	35.09	2,946.13
70.	50.00	14.73	35.27	2,910.86
71.	50.00	14.55	35.45	2,875.41
72.	50.00	14.38	35.62	2,839.79
73.	50.00	14.20	35.80	2,803.99
74.	50.00	14.02	35.98	2,768.01
75.	50.00	13.84	36.16	2,731.85
76.	50.00	13.66	36.34	2,695.51
77.	50.00	13.48	36.52	2,658.99
78.	50.00	13.29	36.71	2,622.28
79.	50.00	13.11	36.89	2,585.39
80.	50.00	12.93	37.07	2,548.32
81.	50.00	12.74	37.26	2,511.06
82.	50.00	12.56	37.44	2,473.62
83.	50.00	12.37	37.63	2,435.99
84.	50.00	12.18	37.82	2,398.17
85.	50.00	11.99	38.01	2,360.16
86.	50.00	11.80	38.20	2,321.96
87.	50.00	11.61	38.39	2,283.57
88.	50.00	11.42	38.58	2,244.99
89.	50.00	11.22	38.78	2,206.21
90.	50.00	11.03	38.97	2,167.24
91.	50.00	10.84	39.16	2,128.08
92.	50.00	10.64	39.36	2,088.72
93.	50.00	10.44	39.56	2,049.16
94.	50.00	10.25	39.75	2,009.41
95.	50.00	10.05	39.95	1,969.46
96.	50.00	9.85	40.15	1,929.31

Monthly Payment		Interest	Principal	Balance Due on Home
97.	$50.00	$9.65	$40.35	$1,888.96
98.	50.00	9.44	40.56	1,848.40
99.	50.00	9.24	40.76	1,807.64
100.	50.00	9.04	40.96	1,766.68
101.	50.00	8.83	41.17	1,725.51
102.	50.00	8.63	41.37	1,684.14
103.	50.00	8.42	41.58	1,642.56
104.	50.00	8.21	41.79	1,600.77
105.	50.00	8.00	42.00	1,558.77
106.	50.00	7.79	42.21	1,516.56
107.	50.00	7.58	42.42	1,474.14
108.	50.00	7.37	42.63	1,431.51
109.	50.00	7.16	42.84	1,388.67
110.	50.00	6.94	43.06	1,345.61
111.	50.00	6.73	43.27	1,302.34
112.	50.00	6.51	43.49	1,258.85
113.	50.00	6.29	43.71	1,215.14
114.	50.00	6.08	43.92	1,171.22
115.	50.00	5.86	44.14	1,127.08
116.	50.00	5.64	44.36	1,082.72
117.	50.00	5.41	44.59	1,038.13
118.	50.00	5.19	44.81	993.32
119.	50.00	4.97	45.03	948.29
120.	50.00	4.74	45.26	903.03
121.	50.00	4.52	45.48	857.55
122.	50.00	4.29	45.71	811.84
123.	50.00	4.06	45.94	765.90
124.	50.00	3.83	46.17	719.73
125.	50.00	3.60	46.40	673.33
126.	50.00	3.37	46.63	626.70
127.	50.00	3.13	46.87	579.83
128.	50.00	2.90	47.10	532.73
129.	50.00	2.66	47.34	485.39
130.	50.00	2.43	47.57	437.82
131.	50.00	2.19	47.81	390.01
132.	50.00	1.95	48.05	341.96
133.	50.00	1.71	48.29	293.67
134.	50.00	1.47	48.53	245.14
135.	50.00	1.23	48.77	196.37
136.	50.00	.98	49.02	147.35
137.	50.00	.74	49.26	98.09
138.	50.00	.49	49.51	48.58
139.	48.82	.24	48.58	. . . . .
Total $6,948.82		$1,948.82	$5,000.00	

Payment on principal $5,000.00
Interest payment 1,948.82
Total monthly payments $6,948.82
Down payment 1,000.00
Total outlay for home $7,948.82

totals at the end of the table show the total amount paid in monthly payments, the amount paid in interest, and the amount paid upon the principal of the loan.

Cash value vs. credit price. In buying a home on the instalment plan, it is important for the family to understand clearly the difference between the asked price and the actual cash value of the property it is buying. Most states limit by law the maximum rate of interest which can be charged either on first or second mortgages. In order to cover the high risk which lending on second mortgages always involves, there is a tendency to mark up the property when it is sold on the instalment plan to a point where the price charged will include a profit large enough to pay for the risk the seller assumes.

Suppose, for example, a contractor builds a row of houses for sale on the instalment plan. He is interested in securing his builder's profit from the houses. He wants to get his money out of the property and build another block of homes. So he proceeds as follows:

He first buys the lots on which he builds. These cost him $1,000 each. On each lot he builds a house costing him something less than $4,000. If he can sell these homes for $5,000 each he will make a fair builder's profit from the enterprise. The fair cash value of these homes then would be $5,000.

But he must sell these houses on the instalment plan. He knows that he must discount the securities which he receives at the going rate for first and second mortgages. The discount he must take for the sale of the first and second mortgages on the property is $1,000. Therefore he advertises these properties for sale at $6,000; terms, $1,000 down; balance of $5,000 financed by first and second mortgages to be repaid in monthly instalments of $50, like rent. As he sells the properties, he takes the $5,000 in mortgages which he secures in part payment, and discounts them for $4,000 at a mortgage company. The $4,000 he receives, together with the $1,000 down payment, gives him his fair cash price for the property.

The family buying one of these homes pays $1,000 for the privilege of buying a home on the instalment plan. The down payment is simply the payment for financing charges. Its first payment upon the principal of the mortgages represents its first real payment upon the home itself. If it is forced to sell the property for cash, it can get only the $5,000 cash price for the property. If it sells to someone who will assume the outstanding obligations against the property, it may be able to recover some of the original $1,000 it paid for financing charges.

The charts on pages 248 to 250 show in graphic form the relative situation of three families, one buying for cash, another buying on a mortgage, and a third paying $1,000 down and making the balance of its payments on the instalment plan.

When property is being sold rather generally on the instalment plan, it is customary to quote all customers the long price. It is often difficult to find out what actually is a fair cash price for property. If the family really wants to know how much it should pay for its home, it can get a fair idea by inquiring as to discount rates for mortgages and instalment contracts. By subtracting these discounts from the asked price, it can arrive at a rather close estimate of a fair cash value for a home. If it is possible to do so, the family should insist upon buying on a cash price basis, and do its own financing on first mortgage terms.

Sources of mortgage money. There are a number of sources to which a family can turn for mortgage money. Among them are the building and loan associations which lend money on reducing mortgages. In recent years life insurance companies have been lending to families that want to buy their own homes. They offer terms which include the insurance policy that will protect the family's equity in its home in case of the death of the chief wage earner. Their terms usually call for slightly higher payments, for their contract covers the insurance premium as well as the payment upon the loan. In most communities families owning desirable property can borrow moderate sums on first mortgage terms from individual lenders, lawyers handling estates, and trust companies. Some individual lenders insist upon regular payments upon principal as well as interest. Other lenders insist that no payments other than the interest be made during the period for which the mortgage is to run.

In 1933 the Home Owners Loan Corporation was organized to refinance homes upon which foreclosures were imminent. In 1934 the Federal Housing Administration was organized to guarantee mortgages which banks might wish to make in order to encourage new building and extensive home repair programs. For some years there have been a number of federal agencies specializing in farm loans, which almost always involve the farm home as well as the productive farm plant.

BUYING A HOME

1. THREE WAYS OF FINANCING THE PURCHASE

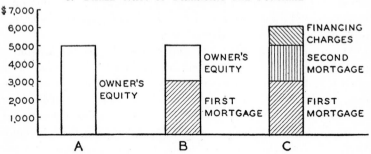

Family A. Buys home with savings.
Pays the lowest cash price, $5,000.
No financing charges.
Owns home free and clear.

Family B. Buys home with savings of $2,000, supplemented by first mortgage of $3,000 bearing interest at 6 per cent.
Purchases home at lowest cash price, $5,000.
Does own financing.
Financing charges are the annual interest payments.
Owns home subject to first mortgage of $3,000.

Family C. Buys home with savings of $1,000, used as down payment and supplemented by first mortgage of $3,000 and second mortgage of $2,000.
Purchases home on instalment plan for $6,000.
Financing charges include $1,000 mark-up in the price to cover discounts upon mortgages used in financing sale, and annual interest payments.
At the time of purchase the buyer has no equity in the home.
He has used his down payment to cover financing charges.

2. SITUATION IF PROPERTY VALUES INCREASE 20 PER CENT

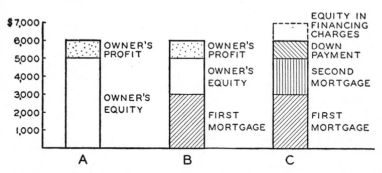

Suppose each of these families is able to sell its home for $6,000, the new cash price.

Family A. Makes a profit of $1,000. This is a profit of 20 per cent on its investment of $5,000.

Family B. Makes a profit of $1,000. This is a profit of 50 per cent on its investment of $2,000.

Family C. Gets back its down payment on the property. The only way Family C can realize a profit on its investment is to find a family that wants to buy on a time-payment basis, that will pay a "credit price" and assume the obligations outstanding against the property. In this way it may be able to realize something on its investment in financing charges.

Family C can realize a profit from a general increase in property values only if this general increase is great enough to cause the value of its property to increase by more than the original $1,000 mark-up for financing charges.

3. Situation if Property Values Decrease 20 Per Cent

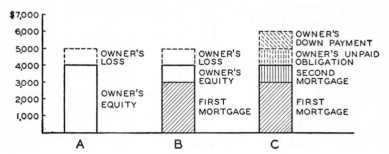

Family A.   Loses $1,000 of its investment in the home. This is a loss of 20 per cent of the original investment of $5,000.

Family B.   Loses $1,000 of its investment in the home. This is a loss of 50 per cent of its original investment of $2,000.

Family C.   Equity in financing charges wiped out.

                Second mortgage holder's equity cut down $1,000 which is just offset by original down payment.

                Family C can get out its investment of $1,000 only if it can sell the property on the instalment plan to another family who will pay the time-payment price in order to buy a home which is already financed. If it cannot find an instalment buyer, it has the alternative of completing its payments on the property, or of allowing the mortgage holders to foreclose.

            This example shows why individuals and mortgage companies lending money on second mortgages insist upon a substantial premium, either for finding mortgage money or as a mark-up in the price of the home, to offset the risks they run.

In financing the purchase of a home, therefore, the family should canvass all the possibilities for securing a loan. It should select the source which will provide the most convenient terms for repayment at the most reasonable cost. In planning to finance its purchase, the family must remember that the larger the down payment it can make, the better are the terms it should secure in financing the balance. The family must remember also that the smaller the down payment, the greater is the risk of loss to the lender in case he is unable to complete payments upon the property, and consequently the higher is the interest rate. The family must realize clearly that the smaller its equity, the greater is its risk of loss in case of a decline in property values. It should buy on a small equity only after carefully counting all the costs, including the heavy risks which it may run.

Conclusion. Clearly, providing the family with shelter is not an easy task. The family must expect to spend plenty of time and thought upon the problem. Shelter is one of the major items of family expenditure. It is one upon which many other phases of the life of the family depend. If the family cannot find property which it would like to buy at a price it can afford to pay, it should rent for a time until suitable property is available. It should not be in too much of a hurry to set the family up in a permanent home. But even in renting, it should give careful consideration to the proper selection of shelter. For after all, whether the family owns or rents, adequate shelter is of fundamental importance to satisfactory family life.

QUESTIONS

1. What proportion of the families of your acquaintance own their own homes? Rent? Live in single houses, double houses, apartments?

2. From the latest census of families (*Population*, Vol. VI, 1930) find out all you can about housing in your community in 1930. In just what ways has the situation changed since the census was taken?

3. Collect a set of photographs of homes which will illustrate a number of typical housing conditions in your community. Supplement these photographs with floor plans, giving size of rooms, arrangement, wiring, heating, ventilation, etc. Show interior views if possible. Get the actual cost of housing per family, per individual, and per room in each of these typical situations. Find out about the types of families living in these different housing situations, their incomes, jobs, social standards, etc.

4. To what extent is the neighborhood a factor in each of the above housing situations? Visualize your conclusions by means of photographs and dia-

grams showing the lot size, layout, street improvement, and public utilities. Add a description of each neighborhood which will include existing zoning regulations or voluntary restrictions on the use of the property. On a map show the neighborhood in its relation to business centers, schools, churches, transportation facilities, etc.

5. Make a list of specific points to inspect in selecting a ready-built home. Where may defects in design, faulty workmanship, inferior materials, or carefully hidden weaknesses most often be discovered?

6. It is important for most families who buy a home to own readily marketable property. What elements affect most definitely the marketability of residence property?

7. What is the smallest down payment it is safe to make on a new home? The smallest monthly payment which will assure the family that it will be able to pay for its home before it is worn out? How do you determine this?

8. Suppose that a family buys a home for $6,000, paying $1,000 down, and financing the balance with a reducing mortgage bearing interest at 6 per cent. Its monthly payments are $50 a month. The value of lots in the neighborhood is $1,200. The house (but not the lot) depreciates 5 per cent a year for two years, 3 per cent for three years, and 2½ per cent for the next fifteen years. The property is assessed at $4,500. The tax rate is $20 per $1,000 of assessed valuation. The insurance rate is 50 cents per $100 of the face of the policy. Repairs average 2 per cent a year over a five year period. This family bought its home with the understanding that it was to be paid for "like rent." Rents for similar properties are $50 a month.

(a) Compare the shelter cost of this family at the end of five years with the cost of renting a similar home during this period.

(b) According to the table on pages 243 to 245, what is the balance due on the mortgage?

(c) After making necessary allowance for depreciation, what is its equity in its home worth (assuming land values are unchanged)?

(d) Suppose that the family had saved each year and invested, at 3 per cent compound interest, the difference between rent and its total outlay for its home; how much, more or less, than its equity would its savings be worth?

(e) Suppose that rents and property values had increased 20 per cent. How would this have affected the relative advantage of owning and renting? Suppose rents and property values had declined 20 per cent?

(f) What conclusions can you draw from this example as to the relative cost of saving and buying, and the cost of buying and paying for a home on the instalment plan? Remember that a family must pay for shelter while it is saving the purchase price of its home.

REFERENCES

Andrews, B. R., *Economics of the Household*, Revised Edition, Chs. XI and XII, pp. 232-296. The Macmillan Co., New York, 1935.

An excellent discussion of the problems involved in housing the American family. In addition to the discussion of the problems faced by the individual family, there is a detailed discussion of minimum housing standards, of housing legislation, 1935, and a description and evaluation of a number of movements designed to raise the standards for American housing.

Halbert, Blanche, *Better Homes Manual*. University of Chicago Press, Chicago, 1931.

A handbook giving the contemporary viewpoint on home ownership and financing, the methods of keeping the cost of the house down, points to be considered in building or buying, selection of the site, fitting of the house to its site, determination of architectural style, choice of materials, selection of equipment, furniture, and furnishings, and planning the home grounds.

Gray, Greta, *House and Home*, Third Edition. J. B. Lippincott Co., Chicago, 1935.

A thorough and practical treatment of house planning, covering the architectural, sanitary, esthetic, social, and economic phases of the subject. The revised edition discusses recent governmental housing projects and describes new developments in lighting, heating, and air conditioning. See Ch. XXII for a discussion of owning *vs.* renting.

Kyrk, Hazel, *Economic Problems of the Family*, pp. 416-424. Harper and Bros., New York, 1933.

A brief discussion of the advantages and present obstacles in the way of more widespread home ownership by American families.

Nystrom, P. H., *Economic Principles of Consumption*, Ch. XV, pp. 348-384. The Ronald Press Co., New York, 1929.

A description of American housing. An excellent discussion of the relative advantages of home ownership and home renting, and an analysis of the various elements determining the cost of housing American families.

Peters, F. F., *Houses of Stone*. Published by the author, Westport, Conn., 1933.

A description of the principles involved in the design and construction of the Flagg masonry type of field stone houses. Especially interesting for the author's analysis of the importance of planning a house for the functions it is to perform. Contains floor plans and devices which are equally applicable to many types of construction.

President's Conference on Home Building and Home Ownership.

A shelf of publications dealing in much detail with the great variety of problems involved in housing the American people.

Tucker, Milton, *Buying an Honest House.* Little, Brown and Co., Boston, 1930.

This book describes in terms the ordinary householder can understand what the home owner has a right to expect when he buys a home. The author confines himself to structural details, materials, workmanship, and how to detect any scrimping on quality or defective workmanship.

CHAPTER XI

HOUSEHOLD OPERATION

Everyone recognizes that food, clothing, and shelter are fundamental to individual existence. In the same way there is a long list of items which are fundamental to the maintenance of a home for a family. The house itself is important. But the house is only the shell. It must be provided with furniture, furnishings, and equipment, and with water, fuel, light, storage facilities, and refrigeration or other facilities for the preservation of food. Adequate provision must be made for removal of sewage, garbage, and the litter which inevitably accumulates around the home. Every home must be provided with the supplies and facilities necessary for the cleaning, ordering, laundering, and repairing which go on in the home. And many families find that the efficient maintenance and operation of a home demand not only adequate and efficient equipment but also some personal service to supplement the work of the individual members of the family.

There are a great variety of these items. Some of them involve substantial expenditures. Others require only nominal outlays, but the total of these small expenditures is a substantial sum. The chief thing they have in common is that they all involve overhead expenditures incidental to the smooth functioning of the home.

Each item in the list requires study. Here, as in all items of family expenditure, there is the problem of balancing quality against cost, of balancing cost of equipment or of service against the effort as well as against the money to be saved. In a discussion of this sort it is possible to point out only a few of the more important characteristics of each type of activity. Each family must work out the details for itself with due regard to the local situation. And if a family moves from one community to another, the whole problem of the best way to maintain and operate a home must again be worked out in the new situation.

PUBLIC UTILITIES

The water supply. Every family must be provided with an adequate water supply. Urban families are chiefly concerned with the quality of the water they use. They want an abundant and effortless supply of pure, pleasant-tasting water, not too hard, and under sufficient pressure to make possible the use of modern plumbing and sewage disposal.

In the city, the water supply is usually a municipal monopoly. The charges for water are nominal. In some suburban districts and in the open country, water usually comes from private wells. If electric current is available, a family can easily supply itself with water under pressure by use of an electric pump. In the open country, a family must consider the relative cost and dependability of the windmill, the gas engine, and the hydraulic ram as sources of power. If it is to be provided with water under pressure, it can choose between a gravity and a pressure system.

Water is a necessity so fundamental and so generally available that most families take it for granted. It is only families with meager cash income, who must drive their own wells and pump their water by hand, and occasionally urban families, during a period of severe shortage, that are conscious of the part which an adequate and effortless water supply plays in the smooth operation of the variety of activities going on in the home.

Lighting. When the urban family thinks of light, it thinks of electric light as a matter of course. But it is only since the World War that electric lights have come into general use even in the larger metropolitan areas. In the rural districts as late as 1930, only 13.5 per cent of all farms had electric power.[1] Their lighting problems must be solved by the use of kerosene or gasoline lamps. There are many sections of the country in which the kerosene wick lamp is still standard lighting equipment. An increasing number of families now supplement the wick lamp with the more expensive kerosene or gasoline mantle lamps.

For families on a kerosene-lighting basis, the problem is still largely one of providing an adequate amount of light, although recently there has been a tendency to give some thought to the designing of attrac-

---

[1] See table on page 23, "Number of Sanitary Bathtubs, Telephones, and Wired Homes Compared with Total Non-farm Population, 1913-1928." See also B. R. Andrews, *Economics of the Household*, pp. 471 ff. The Macmillan Co., New York, 1935.

tive as well as efficient lighting fixtures. For most families, electric lighting is a decorative device as well as a means of providing adequate light. Unless they must effect the utmost economy, they usually choose the more attractive rather than the more efficient lighting equipment.

Electric rate systems. If a family is to use electricity to good advantage, it must understand the nature of the rate structure under which local charges for electric current are determined. Here, again, it is impossible to generalize. There are hundreds of different rates charged for electric current in different communities. In general, however, these rates can be classified roughly as follows:

The flat rate. Under the flat rate system the customer is charged a flat rate per month, per quarter, or per year, regardless of the current consumed. No meter is necessary. No complicated billing service is involved.

The fixture rate. In order to bring charges more nearly into line with the quantity of current consumed, the fixture rate is sometimes substituted for the flat rate. In this case a flat rate per opening, or per fixture, is charged. The more openings for the use of current, the more electricity the family will probably consume. Therefore the more it should be expected to pay for service.

Meter rates: Uniform or straight-line meter rate. In order to relate the charge for service directly to the amount of current used, it has become common practice to install a meter which measures the customer's consumption of electricity, and base the charges on the amount of current consumed. There are a number of ways to compute the charges where a meter is used. The simplest way is to charge a certain number of cents per kilowatt of electricity used. This is known as the uniform or straight-line meter rate. The rate charged per kilowatt is the same regardless of the amount of electricity consumed. This rate has the advantage of being simple and easily understandable.

Suppose, for example, that the rate in a certain community is five cents per kilowatt. A family pays five cents for each kilowatt it consumes. If it uses more electricity it will pay five cents for each additional kilowatt. If it uses less electricity, it will save five cents for each kilowatt it reduces its consumption.

Meter rates: Step rates. In order to encourage customers to increase the use of electricity, sliding-scale rates are sometimes introduced which give lower rates to larger consumers of current. These rates are of two main types, step rates and block rates. Under the step rate, the cost per kilowatt depends upon the quantity of current consumed. All electricity used is paid for at this rate.

Suppose, for example, that the step rate for domestic consumers of electricity is as follows:

Step 1.	0–100 kilowatts	8 cents per kilowatt hour
Step 2.	101–200 kilowatts	7 cents per kilowatt hour
Step 3.	201–500 kilowatts	6 cents per kilowatt hour
Step 4.	501–1,000 kilowatts	5 cents per kilowatt hour
Step 5.	1,000 kilowatts and over	4 cents per kilowatt hour

Under this system a family using 80 kilowatts of electric current would pay the 8-cent rate. This would make the current cost $6.40 for the month. If the family used 110 kilowatts, however, the charge would be at a rate of 7 cents per kilowatt hour, or $7.70. If the family used 250 kilowatts in a month, the charge would be at the rate of 6 cents, or $15.00.

The chief difficulty with this rate comes from the fact that it is unfair to the customer who uses just a little less than the amount which would put him over into the next step, in which he would buy his current at a lower rate. For example, a family using 95 kilowatts of current at 8 cents a kilowatt would be billed for $7.60, while a family using 101 kilowatts, which is just enough to secure the 7-cent rate, would pay only $7.07. The regressive element in these rates leads to extravagant use of current by families whose consumption is near the point which will entitle them to the lower rate.

Meter rates: Block rates. In order to eliminate the obvious unfairness of the step meter rate, and to encourage the use of electricity, many companies use the block meter rate. Under this rate the schedule is similar to that under the step rate, but with this difference: Whereas under the step rate the customer pays for all of his current at the rate to which his use entitles him, under the block rate he pays for the first block of current he consumes at a high rate. He pays for the second block of current at a lower rate, and for a third block at still lower rates.

Suppose the block meter rate for domestic consumers is as follows:

First 100 kilowatts .... 8 cents per kilowatt hour
Next 100 kilowatts .... 7 cents per kilowatt hour
Next 300 kilowatts .... 6 cents per kilowatt hour
Next 500 kilowatts .... 5 cents per kilowatt hour
Additional kilowatts .... 4 cents per kilowatt hour

Under the block meter rate the family using 80 kilowatts of current would pay the 8-cent rate. Its current would cost $6.40. But if the family used 110 kilowatts, it would pay for 100 kilowatts at 8 cents, or $8.00, plus 10 kilowatts at 7 cents, or 70 cents. Its total bill in this case would be $8.70.

Because under the block system every customer pays for some electricity at the high rates, it is not necessary to charge as high a rate in each block as would be necessary under the step rate system. Under the block rate, the rate in each succeeding block is dropped as much as possible to stimulate the use of more current.

From the point of view of the domestic consumer, the chief disadvantage of the block meter rate lies in the fact that small users must pay for the same amount of electricity at high rates as do the large users. This rate definitely discriminates against the small user. If the number of kilowatts in the initial step is large, the small user may not be able to get the benefit of the lower rate.[2] Nevertheless, many small users prefer this rate because it is easy to understand.

Meter rates: Demand or readiness-to-serve rates. In order to avoid this apparent discrimination against the small user, many companies use a demand or readiness-to-serve rate. There are a number of types of demand rate. The fixture rate already described is a rough sort of demand rate. For commercial and industrial users, the Hopkinson rate is frequently used. In this rate there are two charges, a demand charge based on the maximum demand or the maximum amount used at any one time during the month, and an energy charge, based upon the total amount of energy consumed. Both demand and energy charges may be block rates. Because the use of the Hopkinson rate involves the use of a rather expensive maximum demand indicator as well as a meter, the Hopkinson rate is usually available only to large users of electricity.

For domestic consumers it is more usual to use a Wright demand

---

[2] Some companies maintain that this apparent discrimination is justified because there is a certain amount of expense, billing, meter reading, and the like, which is incurred by the company for each customer served. They claim the small customer's account is just as expensive as is the account of the large user, and that the heavier charge to the small user is simply a customer charge.

rate. The Wright rate is in effect a block rate in which the size of each block of current is determined by the consumer's demand for electricity. This demand is measured in terms of the "connected load." Connected load is simply the amount of total wattage of current-using equipment connected to the customer's meter. Because domestic users seldom turn on all their lights, and almost never use all their lights and all their equipment at the same time, the rate is usually based not on the total but on the "active" connected load. This is usually determined on an arbitrary basis, somewhat as follows: In the case of residence lighting consumers the first 500 watts of rated capacity may be considered 60 per cent active. The rated capacity in excess of 500 watts may be considered $33\frac{1}{3}$ per cent active. The company can, if it desires, compute equipment load, radio, refrigerator, vacuum cleaner, toaster, stove. and the like on a similar basis.

The theory underlying the use of the connected load as the basis for determining the size of the block of current to be charged at each step in the rate is this: A very large part of the cost of providing electricity is overhead cost. A small part is due to the direct cost of generating the current used. The overhead cost depends upon the size of the plant which the power company must maintain. The size of the plant, in turn, is determined by the connected load. Each customer is charged for part of his current at a high rate to cover his share of the overhead expense. His share of the overhead cost is determined by his share of the connected load.

Once the overhead expense has been cared for, the direct cost of producing electricity is comparatively low. If the power company can stimulate the use of electricity "off the peak," that is, at a time when part of the generating capacity of the plant would otherwise be idle, it can provide this additional electricity at very low cost.

Under the demand rate, each customer is given a rating which determines the amount of electricity he must buy at each step of the rate schedule. For example, a power company charges for each block of electricity as follows:

First block	9 cents per kilowatt
Second block	6 cents per kilowatt
Next two blocks	3 cents per kilowatt
Balance	2 cents per kilowatt

Suppose a family has a connected load which gives it a rating of 10 kilowatts. If it uses 80 kilowatts in a month, its bill would be computed as follows:

First 10 kilowatts @ 9¢	$0.90
Second 10 kilowatts @ 6¢	.60
Next 20 kilowatts @ 3¢	.60
Balance, 40 kilowatts @ 2¢.......................	.80
	$2.90

The average cost per kilowatt in this case would be 3.625 cents.

Ordinarily the amount of current consumed varies with the connected load. Suppose for purposes of comparison, however, that we assume that another family with a rating of 20 kilowatts per step also uses 80 kilowatts in a month. Its bill would be:

First 20 kilowatts @ 9¢	$1.80
Second 20 kilowatts @ 6¢	1.20
Next 40 kilowatts @ 3¢	1.20
	$4.20

The average cost per kilowatt in this case would be 5.25 cents.

This type of rate is designed to stimulate the use of electricity by making it possible for every family to get into the lower brackets of the rate where it can secure cheap electricity. If a family has a low connected load and uses enough electricity to get into the lower steps of the rate, it can operate additional equipment very economically. But it will find it difficult to cut down its electric power bills by economizing on the use of electricity. Under the demand rate, a family always saves the low-priced, not the high-priced, electricity. A reduction of 10 per cent in current consumed does not bring a 10 per cent reduction in the bill. On the other hand, any increase in use is an increase in the use of low cost current. An increase of 10 per cent in current consumed adds much less than 10 per cent to the total charge for electricity.

Suppose the family above with the 20 kilowatt connected load, without increasing its connected load, increases its consumption 25 per cent, from 80 to 100 kilowatts. Its new bill would be as follows:

First 20 kilowatts @ 9¢	$1.80
Second 20 kilowatts @ 6¢	1.20
Next 40 kilowatts @ 3¢	1.20
Balance, 20 kilowatts @ 2¢	.40
	$4.60

It would pay 2 cents per kilowatt for the additional current consumed. It would use 25 per cent more electricity, but it would increase its monthly bill 40 cents, or less than 10 per cent.

On the other hand, if this family reduced its consumption of electricity 25 per cent, from 80 to 60 kilowatts, its new bill would be as follows:

First 20 kilowatts @ 9¢ $1.80
Second 20 kilowatts @ 6¢ 1.20
Next 20 kilowatts @ 3¢ 60
                                                  ————
                                                   $3.60

In this case the current saved would be 3-cent electricity. A reduction of 25 per cent in the use of current would save 60 cents, or 13⅓ per cent of the monthly bill.

Economizing in the use of electricity. Suppose a family finds it necessary to reduce its expenditures for electric current. If it is operating under a flat rate, it can secure economies in direct proportion to its reduction in the use of current. If, on the other hand, it is operating under a demand rate, it can secure more economies by reducing its connected load. Reducing the connected load cuts expenses in two ways. It cuts down the amount which must be paid for at each of the higher steps in the rate schedule, and at the same time it helps to reduce the amount of current which the family actually consumes. If the wattage of lamps in a fixture is cut from 125 to 100 watts, every hour the light burns there is a saving of 20 per cent. If it is cut to 75 watts, the saving in consumption would be 40 per cent. Under the demand rate, reducing the wattage reduces the connected load. If the connected load is reduced 20 per cent, there will be not only the reduction in current consumed but a 20 per cent reduction in the amount of current paid for at the 9-cent, 6-cent, and 3-cent rates as well as a saving in 2-cent electricity.

The table on page 263 illustrates the effect of reduction in use, reduction in connected load, and reduction in both use and connected load. In this table it is assumed that the family in question has a connected load of 20 kilowatts and a monthly consumption of 100 kilowatts.

Section A gives the family's original bill. Section B shows the result of reducing its consumption 20 per cent, from 100 to 80 kilowatts. The family saves 20 kilowatts of 2-cent electricity, a saving of 40 cents on a bill of $4.60. In this case a reduction of 20 per cent in the amount of current consumed saves 8.7 per cent in the monthly bill. Suppose, however, that instead of reducing its consumption of current, it reduces its connected load 20 per cent, from 20 to 16 kilowatts. Section C of the table shows that under its new rating the bill for 100 kilowatts is $4.08. The monthly saving is 52 cents, or 11.3 per cent of the original bill.

CUTTING THE COST OF ELECTRIC CURRENT: REDUCTION IN USE
vs. REDUCTION IN CONNECTED LOAD

A. Connected load........... 20 kilowatts Consumption.............100 kilowatts	B. Connected load........... 20 kilowatts Consumption reduced 20%.. 80 kilowatts
Bill: First 20 kilowatts @ 9¢...........$1.80 Second 20 kilowatts @ 6¢.......... 1.20 Next 40 kilowatts @ 3¢........... 1.20 Balance, 20 kilowatts @ 2¢........ .40 Total, 100 kilowatts..............$4.60	*Bill:* First 20 kilowatts @ 9¢...........$1.80 Second 20 kilowatts @ 6¢.......... 1.20 Next 40 kilowatts @ 3¢........... 1.20 No kilowatts @ 2¢................ Total, 80 kilowatts...............$4.20 *Saving on bill, 40 cents, or 8.7%.*

C. Decreasing connected load
    rating 20% from 20 to... 16 kilowatts
Consumption remains....;...100 kilowatts
	D. Decreasing connected load
	    rating 20% from 20 to... 16 kilowatts
	Consumption reduced 20%.. 80 kilowatts

Bill: First 16 kilowatts @ 9¢...........$1.44 Second 16 kilowatts @ 6¢.......... .96 Next 32 kilowatts @ 3¢........... .96 Balance, 36 kilowatts @ 2¢........ .72 Total, 100 kilowatts..............$4.08 *Saving on bill, 52 cents, or 11.3%.*	*Bill:* First 16 kilowatts @ 9¢...........$1.44 Second 16 kilowatts @ 6¢.......... .96 Next 32 kilowatts @ 3¢........... .96 Balance, 16 kilowatts @ 2¢........ .32 Total, 80 kilowatts...............$3.68 *Saving on bill, 92 cents, or 20%.*

Suppose that the family reduces by 20 per cent both its consumption of current and its connected load. According to section D, the new bill is $3.68. The saving from reducing both connected load and current consumption is 92 cents or 20 per cent of the original bill.

This is an excellent example of the importance of analyzing a situation and acting as the situation demands. The family must first learn how economies can be made. It must make its economies that way. If the connected load is the significant factor in its electric rate, it must keep down its connected load, but it can use electricity freely at slight additional cost. If it is paying for current on a straight-line meter rate, it can ignore the connected load, except as the use of large bulbs inevitably increases consumption of current. In computing the cost of electric equipment, it should estimate the cost of current at the rate which the family will pay for current actually used by that additional piece of equipment.

Other public utility rates.   What applies to electric power rates applies also to gas and to telephone service—in fact, to all public utilities.   The family should, in each case where it is within its power, select the rate classification which will give it most nearly the service desired for a reasonable price.   In the case of the telephone, a family making only a few calls may find it wise to use the less expensive metered service.   The family making many calls may find unlimited service more economical.   If a family uses the telephone only occasionally, a two- or a four-party line may be satisfactory; but if, for business or professional or social reasons, it is imperative to be able to use a telephone on a moment's notice, the family should pay the higher charge for a single-party line.   In any case, the family should compute the cost of the service it needs in each of the ways in which it may be obtained.   It should select the type of service to use only after comparing both cost and quality of service.

FUEL

The family's fuel needs.   Every family must be provided with heat for cooking.   In most sections of the United States, families need some provision for heat in their homes.   Most families consider a generous supply of hot water a definite aid to efficiency and comfort. But the amount of heat which a family needs, the type of fuel and of heating equipment it will use, and the amount the family must spend for fuel depends to a large extent upon local conditions.   In the North, fuel for heating the home is a major item of expense.   In the South, it is a relatively minor expenditure.   Fuel is not very expensive in localities near the source of a fuel supply, but is high in price in isolated communities which must import their fuel from a distance. Because of these local differences, it is difficult to discuss heating problems in general terms.   Because of the differences both in needs and in available fuel, a family must work out its heating problems in terms of the facilities and needs of its own immediate situation.

Estimating fuel costs.   The first step in working out the family's heating problems is to find out about the types of fuel available in the community, their relative heat values, and their local cost.   The family should consider any special local advantages in the supply of each of the available fuels. It must adjust its heating habits to local advantages.

For example, anthracite coal is slightly higher in heat value than is bituminous coal. It is much cleaner to handle. It costs considerably more at the mine. In New England higher freight charges on bituminous coal nearly offset the higher price of anthracite at the mine. The difference in the price of the two coals is so small that for heating residences in New England anthracite is used almost exclusively. In the Middle West, on the other hand, the lower freight charges on bituminous coal make the difference in price of the two coals so great that anthracite is regarded as distinctly a luxury fuel.

In general, the problem of providing heat, whether it be for cooking, for heating the home, or for heating water, involves considerations of economy, convenience, and cleanliness. There are two factors which are important in determining the most economical way to provide the heat the family needs. One is the heat value of the fuel. The other is the efficiency of the equipment in which the fuel is to be used.

The heat value of fuel is usually measured in terms of the cost per million British thermal units. Or it can be computed on the basis of the number of B.T.U.'s secured in one cent's worth of each of the common types of fuels. The cost per B.T.U. depends, of course, upon local prices for various types of fuel.

But the cost per B.T.U. in the fuel is only part of the story. How much of the heat value is available for actual use depends upon the efficiency of the equipment in which the fuel is burned. Low-priced coal in an inefficient stove may cost more than higher-priced gas, or still higher-priced electricity, provided the more expensive fuels are used in more efficient equipment.[3]

---

[3] There are a number of sources of figures giving estimates of the relative efficiency of heating and cooking devices.

For heating equipment, Consumers' Research suggests the use of the following formula for computing comparative fuel costs. Heat obtained for $1 \cance = \dfrac{\text{Heating value} \times \text{efficiency}}{\text{Cost of fuel}}$. Heating value must be expressed in B.T.U.'s per lb., gal., or cu. ft., depending on the fuel used. Cost of fuel must be expressed in cents per lb., gal., or cu. ft. For efficiencies use the following, which are average values:

Per Cent Efficiency

Semi-bituminous	47
Bituminous	45
Anthracite (hand-fired)	50
Coke	47
Oil	60–65
Gas, with gas-designed furnace	75 (See p. 266.)

Most of the information about the relative efficiency of heating devices is given in terms of averages, or includes a wide range between maximum and minimum efficiency. The actual efficiency attained in using various types of fuel in various types of equipment depends in part, of course, upon the condition of the individual unit in which fuel is consumed, and in part upon the way in which it is handled by the operator. A furnace may be fired efficiently or wastefully. A gas stove may be used with care, the gas flame reduced as soon as the water starts to boil, the oven lowered to maintain just the desired temperature, or the flame may be left turned on full regardless of the amount of heat actually needed. An electric stove may be operated efficiently or inefficiently. The efficient operation of the electric stove involves, chiefly, turning off the heat long enough before the food is cooked so that the heat in the element is used in cooking instead of being dissipated into the room after the stove is no longer in use.

The efficiency of equipment depends also upon the amount and kind of use. A coal range used for intermittent cooking is decidedly less efficient than a gas or an electric range. A number of estimates indicate that if the electric range has an efficiency of 100 per cent, gas stoves have an efficiency of perhaps 80 per cent, and coal ranges of not much over 10 per cent. On the other hand, if the coal range is run continuously, if at the same time that it is providing heat for cooking meals it is being used to heat two or three rooms at the back of the house, if in addition it is connected with the range boiler to supply hot water for the family, it can be made into a highly efficient heating unit.

In deciding what fuel is most economical, each family must determine for itself as closely as it can the cost of providing heat for cooking, heating the home, and heating water by each of the alternative methods which are available. There are no rules which can be laid down to guide it, for so much depends upon the situation in the individual home.

	Per Cent Efficiency
Gas, unvented direct heater	90
Gas, with conversion burners	70
Electricity	100

NOTE: This material is reprinted, by special permission, from Consumers' Research *Handbook* of July, 1932, page 5, column 6.

Consumers' Research also gives information about the relative efficiency of various types of cooking equipment using different types of fuel. For up-to-date information, consult the latest *Handbook of Buying*. (Available to members only.) Books on household equipment often have worth while discussions. See especially, Louise J. Peet and Lenore E. Sater, *Household Equipment*, Chs. IV–VIII, and XVI. John Wiley and Sons, Inc., New York, 1934.

Unless fuel consumption is a very considerable item, the family may find that convenience is more important than cost in determining the fuel to use. For many families the convenience of the gas range or the electric range is sufficient to justify the extra cost for fuel consumed. One of the greatest advantages of the oil burner or gas furnace lies in the convenience of having the furnace tended automatically. With the oil burner the householder has nothing to do except to make sure that the oil tanks are kept full; and he need not even do this in the case of the gas furnace. There is no coal to be shoveled, there are no ashes to be removed. There is no furnace man to supervise.

A large element in convenience is the adaptability of heating equipment to the use of automatic controls. Thermostatically controlled oil heat gives more uniform room temperature with less attention than does a hand-fired and hand-controlled furnace. A thermostatically controlled hot water heater provides a constant supply of hot water of just the temperature which is desired. A thermostatically controlled oven will cook at exactly the rate desired, without thought on the part of the housewife. Some electric ranges are even equipped with clocks which will turn off the heat when the food is done. All these controls are convenient. Many of them add to economy of operation as well.

Cleanliness is another element to be considered. Indirectly, cleanliness is a factor in the cost of house operation, even though it may not appear in the actual calculations of fuel economy. Dusty coal, a smudgy oil burner, a smoky coal range, a sooty kerosene stove, can add materially to the cost of housecleaning, and to the depreciation in household equipment. If there is only a little difference in the cost of a clean fuel and a dirty fuel, cleanliness is certainly worth paying for. One of the most attractive features of the oil burner and the gas furnace is the cleanliness which is involved. There is no coal dust about the house. There are no ashes to make dirt. On the other hand, if the oil burner fails to burn properly, if the flues become plugged and the burner smokes, a lot of damage can be done in a short time.

Coal dealers have been trying various devices to make their coal more attractive. They suggest coke for the particular housewife. They are now offering oil-treated coal, which is dust-free. The home owner can keep down the dirt hazard by building a dust-tight coal bin, or by installing a convenient sprinkling system for keeping down the dust in the coal and ashes.

The problem the family faces in regard to fuel can be summarized as follows: It should select its heating equipment with regard to use. It should select its fuel with regard to local supply and price. Wise provision for heating will use the combination of equipment and fuel which in the local situation will give the most convenience, comfort, and cleanliness at the lowest possible cost.

FURNITURE, FURNISHINGS, AND EQUIPMENT

The problem of furnishing a home. Every family must be provided with furniture, furnishings, and equipment of various sorts for carrying on the ordinary routine activities of the home. Furniture, furnishings, and equipment are all essential to the smooth operation of the household. But each of these groups presents somewhat different problems of selection, maintenance, and finance.

Furniture consists for the most part of large units, usually comparatively expensive, and ordinarily intended to last for many years. Furniture is definitely in the class of articles which the economist calls *durable goods*. It is an outstanding peculiarity of durable goods that they cannot be bought in small quantities as needed. A whole bundle of utilities comes wrapped up together. Years of use must be purchased at one time, and that long in advance of need. As a result, if a family is to purchase these goods, it must make a considerable investment of capital.

For example, if a family is to have a good rug upon the floor, it must invest in a rug which will give five or ten or fifteen or even more years of service. When it buys a well-made chair, it must pay for from ten to twenty-five years of service. It must buy perhaps fifty or one hundred years of use if it selects a really high-grade dining room or bedroom suite.

And yet, while furniture will last for many years, even the best of it eventually wears out. The poorer grades go to pieces all too soon. Even the best passes through a period of uncertain age, when it is neither modern nor antique. As a result, the family must plan to add to its stock of furniture from time to time, or else set up savings with which to refurnish whole rooms when their present furniture wears out or goes too badly out of style.

Problems of selection. There are a number of points to be considered in selecting furniture. In the first place, it is important to know how long the furniture is to last. It is possible to buy furniture well enough made to last the entire life of the family. On the other hand, there is much shoddy furniture on the market which will begin to look worn out within a couple of years. The family should decide how long it wants furniture to last, and select quality accordingly. If the family expects to live in rented quarters for a few years, if it may be moving about a good deal, it may decide to buy comparatively inexpensive furniture, planning to discard it after a few years or trade it in when the family is ready to settle down in a home of its own. On the other hand, if the family knows definitely what sort of furniture and furnishings it wants for its permanent home, it can begin to accumulate lifetime furniture from the very outset.

But durability is only one factor to consider. Style in furniture is equally important. Especially if the family is selecting furniture which will last the entire life of the family, it is important to select pieces which are so styled that they will "grow old gracefully." If the family plans to buy a few pieces of furniture, and to add others from time to time as new needs arise and as funds become available, it is highly important that the first few pieces set a standard for future purchases. These first few pieces must reflect the personality of the family. They must create the kind of atmosphere in which the family will like to live for years to come.

If, on the other hand, the family is buying furniture with the idea of discarding it entirely in a few years, if it is planning from time to time completely to refurnish whole rooms, replacing the old furniture with the latest style, it can indulge its fancy for extremes of style which would be entirely out of place for the family which is planning to accumulate its furniture a piece or two at a time.

In the selection of furniture, whether it be for a lifetime or only for a few years, it is important always to keep in mind not only whether a piece of furniture will wear, whether it is comfortable, whether it will perform the task it is intended to perform, but also whether it is suitable for the situation in which it is to be placed, whether it blends with the other pieces already in the room, whether it is well designed, whether it has in itself real artistic merit. This is a matter of taste. In the selection of furniture good taste is just as important as knowledge of styles and workmanship.

Financing the purchase of furniture. Most families find that they are not able to go into the furniture market and select exactly the pieces of furniture they would like to own. Very few families have money enough at the outset to buy a complete outfit of lifetime furniture. Most families must compromise by buying a few pieces of furniture which they really like, and a sufficient number of less desirable pieces to let them get started in housekeeping.

They have a number of alternatives before them. They can decide between buying for each room a few excellent pieces or a larger number of less expensive ones. Or they can furnish one room, perhaps the living room, just as they would like it, and use inexpensive things for the rest of the house, planning to replace these with better ones as soon as money is available. If their funds are very limited, they can decide between buying some cheap new furniture, and buying used furniture of somewhat higher quality.

There are a number of ways in which the family may pay for the furniture it needs. It can save enough money to buy a complete outfit of new furniture, and pay cash for it. Or it can work out a comprehensive plan for the articles it will eventually accumulate, and then buy a few pieces at a time as funds become available. If the family is able to do so, of course, paying cash for a complete outfit is more desirable. But for a family just starting out in housekeeping, the plan of buying a little at a time has some very definite advantages. The members of the new family can experiment a bit, to see if their first ideas about furniture are really as good as they think them to be. They can invest from time to time in pieces which they find they actually need. In this way they will be less likely to have a lot of standardized but, to them, useless pieces of furniture cluttering up their apartment. Of course, as styles change, they may find at times that it is necessary to wait several years before they can find just what they want to fit their growing ensemble. But if they use good taste and considerable care in selection, their furniture will grow as an entity in a way that a standardized five-room newly-wed's outfit never does.

If a family has no money saved with which to buy, it may find it necessary to pay for its furniture on the instalment plan. This method is convenient, because it allows the family to have its furniture immediately and take care of the payments out of future income. Especially the family of moderate income finds that the instalment payment plan simplifies the problem of large purchases of furniture. It allows them to refurnish a room or a number of rooms with only a moderate down payment.

But in buying on the instalment plan, it is important to be on guard at a number of points. Instalment financing always costs money. Ordinarily it adds from 10 to 20 per cent to the cost of the purchase. In stores specializing in instalment business, even though they advertise "no financing charges," the extra percentage is added in marking the price on the article. If in shopping for furniture in cash and credit stores prices seem the same, the family must remember that furniture can be cheapened in many unseen ways so as to make the credit furniture look "just as good" as the furniture sold in cash stores.

Instalment houses usually do most of their business with families of small means who must buy the cheaper lines of furniture. Usually the styling of their furniture is not as authentic or as up-to-the-minute as the styling of furniture in the high-grade cash stores. In some cases their furniture is poorly built in order that it may wear out about the time the last payments are made.

It is especially important to distinguish between low-grade and high-grade instalment houses. The low-grade stores resort to any tactics which they find will make a sale. They will tell customers that the inferior qualities of furniture which they handle will wear better than the high-grade pieces sold in reputable stores. They sometimes go so far as to show one grade on the floor and make deliveries of an apparently identical but decidedly inferior piece of merchandise from the warehouse. If the customer suspects the store of this practice, it is well to identify the article purchased in some way so that it will be possible to tell if a substitution is made.

If the family is interested in buying good furniture, it is better to buy in cash stores and pay the financing charges for time payments. In this way the family can know what it is paying for furniture and what it is paying for financing. And it is wise to buy in as high-grade a store as can be found in the community, for, at best, it is difficult for an amateur to judge good furniture. It is worth paying a little extra for furniture from a reputable house which can be depended upon to help its customers select what best suits their purpose, and which will stand back of its merchandise.

For most families furniture is an important purchase. They must live with their furniture a long time. Few families can afford to discard furniture even if it proves to be unsatisfactory. They cannot afford to make any mistakes in selection. A family must expect, therefore, to spend considerable time analyzing its own needs. It must spend enough time shopping to learn about the various market offerings. It can well afford to work out a long-time plan for furnishing the home. It must learn how to tell good furniture from poorly made furniture. It must spend considerable time studying construction, materials, design, styles, and the current fashion. It must learn as best it can the reputation of the various furniture houses in the community. It should buy when, and only when, it is sure it has found in the market just the pieces of furniture which it needs.

Furniture for the nomadic family. The problem of providing furniture for the home is peculiarly difficult for the family which is not permanently settled in a community. It costs money to move furniture from place to place. Moving damages furniture more than years of use.

Families that must move frequently have three alternatives. They may buy good furniture, and spend what is necessary for moving and repairs. They may buy inexpensive furniture and abandon it when they must move, or sell it for what it will bring. Or they may rent a furnished apartment, paying for the use of the furniture.

None of these plans is entirely satisfactory. The ownership and care of good furniture is expensive. It costs almost as much to move good furniture as to buy cheap new furniture. The family's furniture may not all fit the new house or apartment. But the family does have the advantage of living with its own things. There is a certain element of permanence in the immediate environment, even though the family moves from place to place at frequent intervals.

Under the second plan the family is provided with new furniture from time to time. But in order to keep costs down it must buy inexpensive and cheaply made furniture. Sometimes this furniture looks good enough when it is new, but if the family appreciates quality in furniture, cheaply made furniture is never entirely satisfactory. Materials and finish are inevitably inferior. Even though the family gets the benefit of variety by replacing its furniture at frequent intervals, it loses the sense of permanent environment which only its own long-lived-with possessions can bring.

If the family depends upon furnished apartments, it has no investment of its own in furniture, but it must pay much higher rent for an attractively furnished apartment than for an unfurnished apartment.

Nevertheless, families—especially those without children—that are not permanently settled in a community find it well to keep their inventory of furniture as low as possible. They put most of their money into easily portable furnishings, which they can take with them wherever they go.

Furnishings. Every family, whether it is on the move or is permanently settled in the community, must have a stock of household furnishings. These furnishings usually require smaller outlays for individual items than does furniture.

Usually furnishings are somewhat less durable than furniture of comparable quality, though this is not necessarily true. Most furnishings must be replaced from time to time. Silver and china may be heirlooms. Solid silver may last for several generations. Fine china, with proper care, can be passed on from generation to generation. Table linen does in time wear out, though fine linens, carefully used, will last for many years. Curtains and other hangings ordinarily last for several years, though some families prefer more frequent change to too great durability. Bed linen and towels, now usually made of cotton instead of linen, must be replaced after only a few years of steady wear. Blankets may last somewhat longer, but they, too, wear out in the course of time.

In selecting furnishings, it is not quite so important to consider durability and quality of workmanship as it is with the more expensive items of furniture. A mistake can be discarded a little sooner. But taste is highly significant, for furnishings fully as much as the somewhat more standardized articles of furniture determine the character of the home. The combination of silver and china, the table linen, the books on the living room table, the music on the piano, the pictures on the walls, all reflect the character of the family. In some furnishings style is an important factor. In others it is relatively unimportant. A few carefully selected items in the latest style show that the family is not unmindful of current fashion. At the same time, well-worn and familiar articles give evidence of family permanence which is lacking in articles of passing fancy.

For the family that must move at frequent intervals, furnishings are especially important. It is surprisingly easy to create a home for a family even in a standardized furnished apartment by the use of a few carefully selected bits of furnishings the family brings with it. Its own table linen, silver, and china, and its own tall candlesticks, add a bit of the family's personality to the meal served on a rented dining table. In the living room a few favorite books, a table cover or two, a few small but excellent etchings or paintings on the wall, and a little music on the rented piano, are enough to make over a very ordinary rented apartment into a home.

In buying furnishings, a family must decide between buying a few articles of excellent quality, and a larger number of items of lower quality. If it buys high-quality articles, it will not find it necessary to replace them as often. It will get some additional satisfaction from the use of nicer things. At the same time, expensive linens, china, and silver usually require more care. They are too good to be used and discarded. If they are to retain their attractiveness they must never be misused. On the other hand, high-quality bed sheets and heavy towels will stand more concentrated abuse in laundering than will lighter fabrics. They represent a larger initial investment, but they often prove much more economical in the long run.

The advantages of a large inventory of furnishings. There are a number of advantages to be had from maintaining a generous inventory of furnishings. A generous inventory makes possible a degree of flexibility in routine housework which is impossible for the family which has just enough dishes for a single meal, just enough clothing to last from one wash-day to the next, just one change of linen for the beds, and just one tablecloth in reserve. A family with a well-stocked china closet can serve guests in larger numbers or provide the family with several meals without having to stop to wash dishes. A family with a generous supply of linens and clothing can use commercial laundry service. If it has a three weeks' instead of a two weeks' supply, it can often secure lower rates by sending a large bundle every two weeks instead of a small bundle every week. And if the family does its own washing, a generous inventory will free it from the necessity of washing on the same day every week. In case of rain the washing can be postponed for a day or two, until the weather is again suitable for drying the laundered articles out of doors.

A generous inventory makes possible greater variety in the conduct of household affairs. The family with two sets of china can serve on one set part of the time, and on the other part of the time. The family with a number of tablecloths can use color part of the time, and part of the time enjoy the simple coolness of conventional white.

A generous inventory of furnishings provides a flexible element in the family's financial structure. If the family runs into a number of years of heavy expenses, or of reduced income, when it is difficult to find money for replacement of furnishings, it can use up its investment in furnishings in the same way that it uses any other item of invested savings. Then when the period of financial strain is past, it can gradually rebuild its inventory along with the rest of its savings program.

If, as frequently happens, a family finds it necessary for a year or two to cut its current outlay to a minimum, a generous inventory of furnishings will make it possible for life within the home to go on with much the same comfort as before, even though the family may be forced to change very materially the way it spends its money outside the home. It is only if the period of financial stringency is very long continued that the well-stocked family will be forced to reduce its manner of living below that which it enjoyed in more prosperous times.

Each family must decide for itself how large an inventory of furnishings it can afford to maintain. The larger the inventory, the larger is the investment of capital the family has tied up in household goods. Each family must decide for itself what proportion of its invested capital should be thus tied up.

Financing furnishings. Most families find that the easiest way to maintain an adequate stock of furnishings is to buy a few articles every year. Unless the family is unusually pressed financially, it is not wise to go for more than a year or two at most without making substantial additions to the family's inventory of furnishings. For while the majority of items in the family's inventory are relatively inexpensive, the total is rather larger than most families realize.

It is not hard to find money for four pairs of sheets and a dozen pillow cases one year, for a pair of blankets next, and for a new bedspread the year after. But if the family lets its inventory of bedding run too low, it will find that it costs a considerable sum to replace two dozen sheets, three dozen pillow cases, six high-grade wool blankets, and the comforters that are needed for three bedrooms.

The essential point in financing the purchase of furnishings is to plan for these purchases long enough in advance so that they can be made when the expenditure will cause the least strain upon the family budget. In making plans for these purchases it is important not to underestimate the amount that will be involved.

The family starting out at housekeeping frequently is overwhelmed by the total of these apparently incidental expenditures. It can handle its problem more easily if it will first purchase the minimum essentials necessary for starting housekeeping, and then plan to make some definite additions to its inventory each year for several years. In these first years it can get along with a smaller number of each kind of article than can the older family, both because the family is smaller and because all of its furnishings are new. By the time the first furnishings are beginning to wear out, it can have its inventory built up to a place where yearly replacement will be all that is necessary.

Equipment. Equipment consists of articles which are used to perform various tasks about the house. Equipment is valued for the work which it can do, for the savings it can effect either in time, effort, or money, or for the fun it can provide.

Equipment falls roughly into two classes: the larger items, such as the stove, the refrigerator, the sewing machine, the washing machine, the vacuum cleaner, the piano, and the radio, which, like furniture, involve a considerable investment; and the small items, such as pans, can openers, orange squeezers, apple corers, paring knives, cake tins, ramekins, rolling pins, bottle openers, knife sharpeners, thimbles, scissors, needles, thread, stepladder, hammer, saw, clothesbars, clothespins, and many more. As in the case of furnishings, the cost of each of the small items seems negligible, but the total cost of an adequate supply of these small articles requires a considerable sum of money.

Families buy equipment with regard to the activities they carry on in the home. Since families specialize in various forms of home production activity, not all families will buy the same items, or even the same types of equipment. Ordinarily it is better to provide equipment enough for the efficient conduct of one or two activities in which the family engages regularly than to spend the same amount of money for a little equipment for each of a great variety of occasional activities. Every family should secure as rapidly as possible equipment which will reduce the time and effort required for each necessary and frequently repeated task. A family can afford to make a much larger investment in equipment which it uses often than in equipment it uses only occasionally. The more frequently it uses a piece of equipment, the greater will be the savings in money, time, or effort it will receive as dividends upon its investment.

Selecting small equipment. A family usually selects small and inexpensive equipment on the basis of convenience. It is desirable to provide the family with as many items of small equipment as funds will allow. In selecting this equipment, as in buying the larger pieces, the family should buy the minimum essentials for everyday activities first. It should plan to add other items from time to time as funds become available, buying these with regard to frequency of use and to the convenience added in proportion to their cost. As in the case of furnishings, the expenditure for any single item of equipment is so small that it is easy to acquire many small tools and devices if they are bought one or two at a time as funds become available, or as some particular need for a specific tool arises.

Selecting expensive equipment. A family usually selects larger and more expensive pieces of equipment primarily on the basis of efficiency and comparative cost. It estimates the comparative cost of carrying on home production activities with and without a given piece of equipment, and takes account of how much it will use the article in question. It buys expensive equipment only after careful analysis of the needs and resources of the family to determine whether or not the investment is actually justified. It buys only after a thorough survey of market offerings.

In selecting these larger items of equipment, it considers performance, ease of operation, the skill required in operation, mechanical perfection, availability of service, and finally—if all these details are satisfactory—style and design. Its problem is to secure the best combination of these qualities which is available at the price the family is able to pay.

A family ordinarily will get more equipment for its money if it works out for each major item of equipment detailed specifications which will assure adequate performance and economical operation, and at the same time call for no more expensive qualities than are needed for the work the equipment must do.

For example, if a family has a small apartment, with three heavy rugs which must be swept once a week with a vacuum cleaner, it may find that a low-priced, rebuilt machine will be good enough to do the work required. On the other hand, a family living in a large house, with half a dozen heavy rugs to be swept twice or three times a week, may find it will get more for its money in the long run if it buys a new and unusually well-built cleaner.

Engineering principles in equipment design. Especially in selecting power equipment is it important to consider the relative mechanical perfection of the competing units available in the market. Mechanical perfection involves not only quality of workmanship and quality of materials used, but soundness of design, the reduction to a minimum of wearing parts, ease of servicing, ease of making adjustments necessary for efficient operation, provision for taking up any play which may develop in wearing parts, freedom from noise and vibration in operation, positive and if possible automatic controls, adequate safety devices, and the like. In deciding upon the machine to purchase, the family must consider mechanical perfection in its relation to availability of service and ease of repair. If a family must make its own adjustments and repairs, simplicity of design is important. If a machine has been brought to a high state of perfection, and if adequate efficient service is easily available in case the machine does get out of order, a more complicated piece of equipment may be highly desirable. A family must consider mechanical perfection in relation to its own immediate situation.

Esthetic values in equipment design. For many years we have assumed that in obviously utilitarian devices, esthetic values were of minor importance. In recent years, however, we are learning that just because an article is useful, it does not need to be ugly. We are learning that it is just as worth while to give a little thought to attractive design in a stove which is to be used three times a day in preparing meals, as to the styling of a chair which is to be sat upon three times a day in consuming the meals. And we are finding that attractive equipment is not necessarily more expensive.

But attractive equipment differs from attractive furniture in one respect: Attractive equipment must be easy to care for. It must be easy to keep clean. It must be simple, even austere in design, rather than ornamented or ornamental. There is no place for scrollwork to catch the dust, for sharp corners to tear the hands, or for purely decorative gadgets. Equipment is attractive when it is simple in line, well proportioned, and, above all, obviously suited to its use.

The decisive character of comparative costs and current outlay. In deciding whether or not to buy a given piece of equipment, a family must compare both the cost and the current outlay involved in the purchase and use of the equipment with the cost and current outlay involved in the performance of similar services by other means. In comparing costs it is important to distinguish between total costs and yearly costs, between average yearly costs and actual yearly costs, and between actual yearly costs and current outlay.

Total costs. Total costs include all costs incurred during the entire life of the equipment. In computing total costs, the family must include the amount of the original investment, interest upon the investment, repairs, operating costs, taxes, and any other items which may be involved. To make it easy to compare the cost of various methods of performing the same service, it is usually convenient to state total costs as average yearly costs. Average yearly costs are usually determined by dividing the total cost by the number of years of effective service the equipment is expected to render.

Actual yearly costs. It is important to understand clearly the difference between these yearly averages of total costs and the actual cost of operating a given piece of equipment for a given year. The actual costs of ownership and operation of a piece of equipment vary from year to year. To determine these actual costs it is necessary to estimate overhead or ownership costs: depreciation and obsolescence, or actual loss in resale value during the year, interest on the family's present investment in the equipment, and any taxes or other expenses incidental to owning the equipment; and operating costs: fuel or power used, service charges, repairs, and any other items involved in operating the equipment during the year.

Depreciation and obsolescence. In determining the actual yearly cost of a piece of equipment for a given year, it is necessary to understand the difference between losses in value from depreciation and losses in value from obsolescence. Depreciation is loss in value from physical deterioration. Obsolescence is loss in value from changes in style or improvements in new equipment which render old equipment less valuable than new equipment.

Usually the loss in resale value of a piece of equipment is greatest the first year the equipment is in use. The new equipment often has suffered very little from physical deterioration from the first year's use. Most of the loss in value the first year of the life of a piece of equipment comes from obsolescence. A new machine becomes second-hand as soon as it is installed in a customer's home. It can be offered for resale only on the second-hand market. Usually by the end of the first year new and improved models are available, which have some features not available in the older equipment. Almost always the newer models are styled somewhat differently from the older models. Obsolescence from the improvement of new models is especially important in the case of comparatively new types of equipment. Until a device is perfected, improvement in design and performance in the new models is sufficiently marked to cause rapid decrease in the value of the older equipment.

New equipment, then, decreases rapidly in value largely because of the comparatively rapid rate of obsolescence. Older equipment, having lost a large part of its original value from obsolescence in the first few years of service, declines in value more slowly. Over a period of years wear and tear gradually reduces its value, until depreciation catches up with obsolescence. In the last few years of the life of a piece of equipment, unless there are some radical changes in design which render it entirely obsolete, losses in value are due for the most part to depreciation.

Current outlay. Current outlay includes all items of expense actually incurred during a given period. If the machine was purchased and paid for during the year, the entire purchase price must be included as part of the current outlay. If the family is setting up cash reserves against depreciation and obsolescence in order to be able to replace the machine when it wears out, these amounts must be counted as part of the current outlay the equipment involves. In computing current outlay, the family includes only the expenditures actually made during the period in question. If there are no payments on the original purchase price, if the family pays itself no interest on its investment, if it sets up no depreciation reserves, ownership in itself may involve no current outlay.

In deciding whether to buy equipment or use some other means of securing similar service, the total cost of the various methods is usually the determining factor. In deciding when to replace existing equipment, comparison of actual yearly costs of old and of new equipment is essential. In deciding when to buy and how to finance, comparison of the current outlays involved is equally essential.

Buying used equipment. Because of the high rate of obsolescence of new equipment, many families find they can reduce costs by buying used equipment. In buying used equipment, they must be sure that the loss of value is due to changes in style or minor improvements rather than major changes in design. They must be sure the equipment is well built, made of durable materials, and in good condition, so that there will be no excessive outlay for repair bills. They must be sure that the older model is adequate to their needs.

Replacing obsolete equipment. From time to time every family must decide whether or not to replace existing equipment with more up-to-date devices. New equipment may do better work. It can usually be operated at lower cost. But the use of new equipment involves higher interest charges and higher charges for depreciation and obsolescence. In deciding whether to replace a given piece of equipment or to use it for another year, a family must compare the actual cost of using the old equipment for another year with the actual cost of using the new equipment for the same period. In a few cases the new equipment is so much more economical to operate that it actually costs less to use the new machine than to continue to operate the old machine for another year. In most cases, however, the new equipment is somewhat more expensive. If this is true, the family must balance the increased cost from the use of new equipment against its greater efficiency, convenience, ease of operation, dependability, and generally superior performance.

Financing purchases of expensive equipment. The family can finance the purchase of expensive equipment by accumulating the funds needed and paying cash, or by buying on the instalment plan. It is always better to pay cash for equipment if the cash is available. If the family does not have the ready money, it must decide whether the immediate purchase of the equipment is important enough to justify the rather heavy interest and financing charges which instalment buying necessarily involves.

Instalment buying is clearly legitimate if the use of the equipment will cut down enough on current outlay to provide funds for meeting the instalment payments. It may be legitimate if the family has sufficient income in sight to make the instalment payments, and if the use of the equipment over a period of years will more than save its cost, including the cost of financing the instalment purchase.

For example, if the family is spending $10 a month on laundry service, and finds that it can buy a washing machine and do the laundry at home for $1 a week for hot water, soap, and other expenses, the saving on laundry bills will be enough to more than cover a $5 a month payment on the laundry equipment. Or again, if the family has $5 a month available for payments on a sewing machine, and in the course of five years the family can save more than the cost of the machine in reduced clothing expenditures, it may be well to begin to get the benefits from the use of the sewing machine immediately, and make it help pay for itself.

Buying on the instalment plan is not desirable if the family is not sure of the income necessary to complete the payments. Instalment buying is not desirable if the instalment charges add so much to the cost of the equipment that the family can secure the services the equipment would render more cheaply in some other way. This, again, is a matter which each family must decide for itself. And it must decide in the case of each piece of equipment which it is planning to purchase.[4]

To buy or not to buy: some examples. A few examples will illustrate the relative significance of cost and current outlay in deciding upon the purchase of expensive household equipment. In deciding upon the purchase of a mechanical floor-waxing device, the family should consider how often the floors must be waxed, how much of the floors must be waxed, and how much time and effort the machine will save. It must compare the cost of waxing the floor without a machine, with a rented machine, and with an owned machine. On the basis of comparative costs, the family will decide whether it will pay to invest in this particular piece of equipment. Then it must consider whether it has available for current expenditure the funds the investment in the equipment involves. If funds are available the family may decide to buy floor-polishing equipment to get the benefit of lower total costs. If it has other uses for its money, it may decide to rent floor-polishing equipment because of the lower current outlay renting requires.

In deciding whether or not to buy an electric refrigerator, the family must compare the cost of electric and of ice refrigeration; it must consider the convenience of electric refrigeration, the freedom from daily purchase of ice, the possibility of making frozen desserts, the convenience of an adequate supply of ice cubes, the savings

---

[4] For a discussion of the cost of instalment credit, see Ch. XVIII, especially pp. 424-426.

through better preservation of foods. Then it must decide whether the superior service is worth what it costs. It must decide whether it can afford to throw away its present investment in an ice refrigerator. It must balance the probability of increases in the charges for ice against the possibility of higher charges for electric current and the probability of mechanical failures and repairs. Even though in the long run the electric refrigeration might prove to be more economical, it must decide whether or not it can now spare the funds for the investment in equipment.

The purchase of the family's equipment, then, is largely a problem of comparative costs. The family must decide what is the best way to get done the things it wants done. It must decide what is the cheapest way. It must then balance quality of service against additional expense. It must balance savings in cost against savings in time and effort. It must finally decide on what will give it the most of what it wants at a price, in money, time, and effort, which it can afford to pay.

THE PAID HELPER IN THE HOME

The need for relief from housework. There are certain minimum essentials in the keeping of any home. Meals must be prepared and served, the table set and cleared, and the dishes washed. Each day the house must be put in order. There is the weekly cleaning and mending. There is washing to be done at home or sent out to the laundry. And if the family includes small children, there is the necessity for frequent attention to their needs, for constant supervision of their activities, and for considerable physical care.

Most of these essentials offer possibilities for almost infinite elaboration. Much of this elaboration adds to the family's comfort. More adds elegance to the family's manner of living. Almost all of it adds to the family's enjoyment of life, provided only that the elaboration can be secured without too much physical strain upon any one member of the family. In most families, the degree of elaboration which is possible depends upon the time, the facilities, and the help which is available to do the work which the desired elaboration requires.

In the majority of American families, the burden of the minimum essentials as well as of desirable elaboration falls directly upon the homemaker. No homemaker is much concerned about how to use the leisure which would be hers if housework could be cared for in thirty, or even in forty, hours a week. It is only if her family is small, or if her income is generous enough to provide her with paid helpers, or if she is unusually skillful in organizing the activities of all the members of the family group, that she is able to enjoy the luxury of a few eight-hour work-days each week.[5]

Usual sources of relief. There are a number of ways to relieve a homemaker of an undue burden of household routine. The family can patronize a variety of commercial services. It can send soiled linens to the laundry; it can send clothing to be mended and cleaned at the tailor's or dry cleaner's. It can have the windows washed by the window-washing service. It can buy much of its food ready to serve at the bakery and delicatessen. Or it can provide power machinery with which to perform these tasks easily at home. Or it can divide much of the routine housework among various members of the family group. This is especially effective in larger families, with older children or relatives living in the home. Or it can employ paid helpers.

Recent tendencies. The tendency in recent years has been toward the use of commercial services and mechanical equipment. There is, of course, still considerable division of tasks among the various members of the family. Shorter hours in industry have made it possible to increase the number of tasks to be done by men about the home. But families are smaller than they were even a generation ago. In these smaller families there are fewer members to share in household tasks. There are fewer families with older children to help care for the younger children. There are fewer families with relatives living in the family group. And at the same time that there has been this decline in the number of family members who can share in the housework, there has been a very definite decline in the proportion of families who are employing full-time paid helpers.

And yet, the use of commercial services and mechanical equipment is only partly satisfactory. There are many types of housework which cannot be done by machinery. There are many types of work which cannot be done outside the home. In families without resident relatives or older children any considerable reduction in the homemaker's burden must come from the employment of paid helpers.

Types of household helpers. A family may exercise a considerable degree of choice in the type of household helpers it employs.

---

[5] For estimates of time spent in homemaking, see tables on pp. 142 and 144.

It may employ part-time or full-time workers. It may employ help living outside the home, paid by the hour, or resident help provided with a living and paid by the week or month. It may hire highly skilled or semi-skilled or unskilled workers.

It may pay various rates of wages, which depend usually upon the services it receives. It may pay $150 or $200 a month and living for the services of a butler or chauffeur or graduate nurse or formally trained professional housekeeper. It may pay from $25 to $50 a month and living for an experienced general houseworker. It may pay 50 or 60 cents an hour for a skilled laundress. It may pay 20 or 25 cents an hour for a semi-skilled worker. Or it may pay a few dollars a week and board and room for a young and inexperienced apprentice helper.

Why families employ paid helpers. There are a number of reasons why families find it worth while to employ either part-time or full-time helpers. Paid helpers relieve the homemaker, and her husband, too, in many cases, of a considerable part of the physical burden of long-continued or heavy work which must be done about the home. They can provide part of the energy, and in many cases actual physical strength, which the members of the family may lack. Properly selected, they place at the disposal of the family many skills which the members of the family do not possess. This is obviously true in the case of the carpenter, the plumber, the mechanic, and the electrician. It is generally recognized in the case of the special skills required in nursing and medical care. It is equally true of the skills involved in cooking, sewing, cleaning, and child care.

Many families with small children find it essential to employ paid helpers at least occasionally in order that the mother may from time to time get some relief from the long hours and confining activity which the care of small children inevitably involves. It is now a commonly accepted principle of child care that small children should be left quietly at home rather than being taken about with their parents. It is also generally recognized that adequate provision for relief from responsibility and for wholesome recreation is essential to both the physical and mental health of the mother.

Many families find it worth while to employ a paid helper in order to free the homemaker and other members of the family for earning, for participation in worth while community activities, or for purely social and recreational engagements. Many families with generous incomes find it worth while to employ paid helpers that they may enjoy the comfort and satisfaction of a more elaborate standard of living. Some families employ paid helpers in part at least for the prestige values involved. Families with more limited means frequently find that it pays to employ paid helpers at least part of the time, in order to make it possible for the members of the family to carry on more production for use in the home.

Why many families do not employ household help. In spite of all the advantages to be had from the employment of household helpers, comparatively few families employ paid helpers in their homes. There are a number of reasons why this is so. In many communities, it is very difficult to find properly qualified household employees. Sometimes this is due to lack of organization in the labor market. There is no single recognized agency to which a family may turn with the assurance that it can secure qualified helpers of the type it desires. More often the difficulty in securing suitable helpers is due to an actual shortage of experienced household employees. In most communities there is never a surplus of experienced houseworkers, even though the market may be flooded with inexperienced help. The cheap help often have so many disabilities that most families find these low-grade helpers are not even worth their keep.[6]

Another and an equally important reason why so few families employ paid helpers is that helpers cost money. Experienced houseworkers are in a position to demand relatively high wages. Only a few families have incomes adequate to enable them to employ full-time experienced help by the hour. While it takes less money to pay the wages of equally qualified resident helpers, only a few families have houses large enough to provide the extra room a resident helper requires.

A family can use for paid helpers only that part of its income which is left over after it has paid for the living of the members of the family. The question is not whether a paid helper is or is not worthy of his hire. Rather a family faces the practical situation of how much

---

[6] There are a number of reasons which have been advanced for this shortage of qualified household employees. Long hours, the isolation of household employment, and the imagined or actual lack of social esteem in which household employment has sometimes been held, all are significant. Perhaps even more important is the fact that ordinarily it has been possible for a person with capacity and training to find more pleasant, more remunerative, and more socially desirable employment. It is certain that the fear of social disapproval makes some houseworkers refuse to do certain types of work which need to be done. This limits their effectiveness enough to make them useless in many situations.

surplus it can find to pay for household help. A family with a moderate income can employ paid helpers only if the helpers will work for considerably less than the head of the family is able to earn. The lower the family income, the lower, inevitably, is the grade of help the family can command. It must content itself with helpers who are either very young or superannuated or inexperienced or definitely lacking in some of the qualities of a high-grade household employee. Low-grade helpers require much more supervision than do trained or experienced workers. The homemaker finds that as she seeks employees in the lower paid groups, the ratio of help received to effort expended in training and supervision drops lower and lower until it often reaches a point where actually it is easier for her to do the work herself than it is to get her low-grade helper to do the work satisfactorily.

Many families do not employ paid helpers because they feel that the help they receive is not sufficient to offset the adjustments which the presence of a helper in the home inevitably involves. The employment of paid helpers always necessitates some changes in the family's mode of living. A paid helper never does things just as the family has been accustomed to having them done.

Many homemakers regard the presence of a paid helper in the home as a definite invasion of family privacy. They prefer privacy to the relief or the freedom a paid helper might bring. Probably some people are oversensitive about the presence of an outsider in the home. Nevertheless, in a small modern house or a compact city apartment, even an unobtrusive helper finds it difficult to keep always in the background.[7]

In families with children the presence of a helper in the home makes some social adjustments necessary. In the interests of the worker's efficiency it is often necessary to curtail somewhat the activities of the children. In the case of small children, there are some problems which come from the quality of English spoken and the kind of conversation the paid helper carries on with the children. The presence of a helper with tastes and social standards different

---

[7] Many housewives are not entirely consistent in their attitude toward outsiders in the home. They complain about the isolation housework imposes. At the same time they do not want the relief and companionship a paid helper in the home might bring. In many cases, of course, the type of helper they can afford to employ is uncongenial. Then, too, some housewives feel that it is socially demeaning for them to work in the kitchen with their help. For them, the presence of a paid helper merely means that they exchange the isolation of the kitchen for the isolation of the living room.

from those of the family often creates problems in the years in which the children are developing fundamental attitudes. Still other types of problems arise in families with adolescent boys and girls.

Finally, many homemakers do not employ paid helpers because they do not know how to use paid helpers to good advantage. Some housewives seem to suffer from a feeling of inferiority in the presence of household helpers. Some know so little about the way housework ought to be done that they fear domination by the trained and superior professional domestic. As a result, either they are overinsistent upon some minor details of the work, in order to prove to themselves that they are in complete command of the situation, or they are unable to make the suggestions necessary if the work is to be done as they want it.[8]

The need for paid helpers in various stages of the family life cycle. While it is true that it is often difficult to obtain properly qualified helpers, that few families have incomes generous enough to enable them continuously to employ full-time, or even part-time, helpers in their homes, that the use of paid helpers involves personal adjustments, and that many homemakers find it difficult to use helpers to good advantage, there are times in the life of every family when the family needs the help which only the paid household employee can give.

There is a positive need for some paid help in the home when the children are small. The public schools take the older children off their mother's hands for a few hours every day. But in most communities nursery schools are available only for a few of the younger children. A mother can secure relief from the constant burden of child care only by the use of a paid helper.

There are times in the life of every family when the physical burden of housework is too great for the homemaker to carry alone, and when the only source of relief seems to be the paid houseworker. There are other times when for a shorter or longer period health considerations make relief from heavy household tasks imperative. There are times when illness of some members of the family necessitates extra care of a sort which places an impossibly heavy burden upon the members of the family. In many families, in old age, there

---

[8] See Lydia R. Balderston, *Housewifery*, Fifth Edition, pp. 333 ff., J. B. Lippincott Co., Chicago, 1936, for description of training courses which have been organized in many cities for both the homemaker employer and household employee.

comes a time when it is no longer wise for the members of the family to try to carry on the heavier tasks about the home.

While it may often seem that the family cannot afford to pay for the help it needs, in the long run the employment of a reasonable amount of help is a sound investment in the health and happiness of the members of the family. In the United States, in recent years at least, too many families have been taking pride in being able to do all their own work. Only too frequently they find when it is too late that they have done all their own work for a few years at the expense of permanent injury to their health, or at the expense of some essential personal elements in child care or other phases of family life which would have been much more valuable than the small amount of money saved by doing without paid helpers.

The wise use of paid helpers. If, then, there are these periods in the life of almost every family when paid helpers are essential to the long time well-being of the family, it is important for the family to give some thought to methods of management which will enable it to get the most that is possible to get in return for the money it is able to pay for personal service.

The first problem is for the family to decide when it needs help and what type of help it needs. It must spend some time analyzing its own immediate problems. It must consider carefully the types of work it needs to have done. It must decide upon the types of work which the members of the family can easily do for themselves. It must decide upon the type of services which will give the greatest relief to all the members of the family.

The family is limited, of course, in the selection of helpers to the types of help which are available in the community. It must choose partly on the basis of the amount it can afford to pay, and partly on the basis of the type of work it wants done. The ideal method is to hire a worker who just fits the job. Most families find, however, that unless they have unlimited funds at their disposal, they usually must hire a reasonably satisfactory worker at a price they can afford to pay, and then make such adjustments as are necessary to fit the job to the worker.

Once a worker is employed, the problem of directing his activities is similar to the problem of co-ordinating the activities of all the members of the household. This planning, directing, and co-ordinating is an essential part of household operation, whether or not the family employs paid helpers.[9] If the family is well organized as an efficient unit, the introduction of a paid helper offers no essentially new problems. It largely involves the analysis of the kind of work the family needs to have done, and the selection of the individual who will have the combination of experience and skills and personal characteristics the family can use to best advantage.

The employment agreement. It is of utmost importance that before a worker is hired, the employer and the worker come to a definite understanding as to all the details of the employment contract. Such an understanding must include arrangements as to wages, hours, living conditions, duties required, time off, time on call, and the length of notice to be given by either party for the termination of the employment relationship.

In working out such an agreement it is important to go into sufficient detail in talking over the terms and conditions of employment so that both employer and employee understand thoroughly just what each can expect of the other. It is not safe to take anything for granted. In household employment there are no hard-and-fast working rules which are binding on both parties to the employment contract. Except in the case of the professional domestic servants, there are but few customs which are generally recognized by both employer and employee, or even by all employers or all workers. The relationship between homemaker and paid helper is personal. The needs of each family are highly individualized. In the family there is usually only one paid helper—or at most two or three. In such a small group it is entirely possible to consult the personal preferences of both employer and worker in regard to many matters. It is highly important that such preferences should be given mutual consideration.

Every household employment agreement should include a definite understanding in advance as to some fundamental principles to be followed in adjusting to the emergencies which inevitably

---

[9] In the case of the small family, most of this direction is informal. Most of the planning is done at odd moments while working at some other task. Most of the co-ordination comes from the give and take of the members of the family.

However, as the children begin to assume their share of the work to be done about the house, planning becomes more complex, and direction a little more formal. The work to be done must be broken up into specific tasks. These tasks must be analyzed to determine the skills and the capacities required. Then they must be assigned to the various members of the family with due regard to their individual interests and abilities. In order to develop the abilities of younger members, training is necessary. Direction must be specific. There must be a certain amount of check-up to be sure that everyone is doing his or her share in carrying on the family's routine activities. It becomes necessary to set up a more definite time schedule so that each task will be done at the appointed time, so that someone else will be able to do the task which is to follow.

arise. Here, again, there must be mutual consideration on the part of both employer and employee. There must be definite provision for both give and take. There must be a definite understanding as to the sort of situation in which the employer's needs are to take precedence over the employee's preferences, and the sort of situation in which the worker's desires are to be given primary consideration.

For example, it may be agreed that in case of sickness, the arrival of unexpected guests from out of town, or some similar unforeseeable emergency, the helper may be expected to forego her afternoon off, or to work longer hours. There must be definite understanding as to what her compensation for such extra duties shall be. If, on the other hand, the helper occasionally is visited by family or friends from out of town, it is only fair to adjust her afternoon off to allow her to spend a few hours with them.

It should also be recognized that the household helper may have some demands upon her outside of her job. It is important to have a definite understanding at the outset as to the conditions in which the worker's outside duties are to take precedence over the convenience or preference of the employer. If it becomes evident that the employment relationship may involve frequent adjustments which will be inconvenient or unpleasant for either employer or worker, it should not be entered into.

In some ways, the most important part of the employment agreement is provision for adequate flexibility in employment relations. Both employer and employee must regard each other as human beings. They must be willing to make occasional concessions. And they must always be careful to be reasonable in their demands. The essential element in household employment relationships is the development of a spirit of co-operation which will carry over into the employment relationship the same mutual consideration which marks all family life at its best.

QUESTIONS

A. PUBLIC UTILITIES

1. What are the characteristics of a good water supply? How does your local water supply measure up to these standards?
2. Evaluate each of the types of electric rates described in the text from the point of view of the domestic consumer.
3. What type of electric rate is used in your community? Under this rate, how much will the installation of an electric refrigerator using 60 kilo-

watt hours of electricity a month increase a family's electric light bill? Explain.

4. What types of telephone service are available in your community? Compare the quality and the cost of these types of telephone service.

5. What factors should a family consider in deciding whether or not to install a telephone? In selecting the type of service it is to use?

B. Fuels

1. What types of fuel are available for domestic use in your community? How much does each kind of fuel cost? Which types are most commonly used in your immediate neighborhood? Why?

2. Find out from a coal dealer in your community how much each of the types of coal he sells costs at the mine, how much he paid for freight, and how much he gets for his services in handling the coal. When you consider the nature of the work, the hazards of mining coal, the distance the coal is shipped, and the cost of operating a local coal yard, is anyone along the line getting too much for handling coal? What do you need to know in order to decide intelligently?

3. A housewife who is used to cooking on a gas stove installs an electric range. Explain in detail how she must change her habits if she is to operate an electric range efficiently.

4. Compare the cost and the convenience of cooking with gas, kerosene, gasoline, coal, and wood. Which type of fuel would you recommend to families in your community? Why?

C. Furniture, Furnishings, Equipment

1. Shop in your community for some one or more rather expensive articles of furniture. Select, for example, a dining room suite, or a bedroom suite, a davenport or a room size rug for the living room. What did you find out from your shopping trip about quality, style, design, fashion, price, and financing charges? Using all this information and any other material which you have available, indicate what you consider to be the best buy you found on your shopping trip.

2. (a) A couple of your friends are planning to be married next June. They want a detailed list of the furniture, furnishings, and equipment necessary to completely furnish a modern six-room home. Make them such a list. (b) They have saved $1,000 to invest in furniture, furnishings, and equipment. This must cover everything they will need to start housekeeping. Make a list of the articles they should buy with this $1,000. Describe in some detail the qualities as well as the quantities of each item they should buy. Keep in mind the way they will want to live, and the types of activity they will want to carry on in their new home. Do not

overlook any items. They must be able to keep house with the items you list.

3. (a) Shop in your own community for some relatively expensive piece of equipment, such as an electric refrigerator, a vacuum cleaner, a washing machine, a radio, a sewing machine, or an oil burner. What can you find out from the salesman about each of the makes on sale? Compare them as to mechanical efficiency, attractiveness in design, suitability to the desired use. (b) Having in mind the needs of an actual family, and using all the information at your disposal, which of the available makes of the article you are studying do you consider to be the best buy? Explain in detail how you arrived at your decision.

4. The head of a family works for a company with a nation-wide organization. He has worked up through the company to the position of branch manager. In this capacity he can expect to be transferred at least once in five years, and perhaps oftener. These changes make it necessary to move from 500 to 1,000 miles. The family has two children, a boy and a girl, now in junior high school. The family furniture, purchased when they were married, is now in Wilmington, Delaware. The head of the family has recently been transferred to Milwaukee, Wisconsin. (a) How much of their furniture, furnishings, and equipment should the family move to Milwaukee? How much should they abandon? (b) What arrangements should they make for securing furniture and equipment in their new location?

D. THE PAID HELPER IN THE HOME

1. What types of paid helpers are available in your community? What is the usual rate of pay for each type of worker?

2. In what proportion of your friends' homes are paid helpers employed? Find out why helpers are employed in some and not in others.

3. What type of helper should each of the following families employ?
    (a) Family with two children, one three years and one six months old.
    (b) Family with three children of high school age, mother recovering from severe injuries received in an automobile accident.
    (c) An elderly couple.
    (d) A family with three children in elementary school, one six, one eight, and one eleven years of age.

4. Having in mind an actual family situation, draw up a sample employment agreement, covering every point which a carefully drawn employment contract should include. Be sure to make the agreement flexible, and adapted to the specific situation. How does your agreement compare with the employment standards suggested by such organizations as the Women's Bureau of the U. S. Department of Labor, or the Y.W.C.A.?

REFERENCES

A. Public Utilities

Glaeser, Martin G., *Outlines of Public Utility Economics*, Chs. XXVII-XXX, pp. 600-675. The Macmillan Co., New York, 1927.

These chapters will be of interest to the student who wants a thorough understanding of the public utility rate and service problem. This is a standard text in public utility economics. Read especially Ch. XXVII, in which the author discusses standards of service for various utilities, and Ch. XXX, in which he describes the more common types of utility rate systems. Ch. XXVIII explains the theory of monopoly price which underlies utility rate regulation. Ch. XXIX analyzes in considerable detail the cost factors which underlie scientific rate determination.

Jones, Eliot, and Bigham, Truman C., *Principles of Public Utilities*, Chs. VII and VIII, pp. 288-442. The Macmillan Co., New York, 1933.

A description of the various types of rate structures and service standards in use by various public utilities.

B. Fuels

Beery, Pauline G., *Chemistry Applied to Home and Community*, Ch. I, pp. 1-58. J. B. Lippincott Co., Chicago, 1926.

Included in a discussion of the chemistry of fuels are a number of tables showing relative desirability of domestic fuels.

Consumers' Research, Inc., *Handbook of Buying*, Vol. 7, part 2, p. 5, column 6. July, 1932. (See also latest *Handbook of Buying*.)

Consumers' Research gives information about the relative heat value of various types of fuel and the relative efficiency of various types of heating and cooking equipment. For the latest information consult the latest *Handbook of Buying*. (Available only to members.)

Peet, Louise J., and Sater, Lenore E., *Household Equipment*, Chs. IV-VIII, pp. 52-119; and Ch. XVI, pp. 288-309. John Wiley and Sons, Inc., New York, 1934.

A description of the more common types of domestic fuels, and cooking and heating equipment, with an analysis of thermal efficiency of the various fuels in relation to the types of equipment in which they are used.

C. Furniture, Furnishings, and Equipment

Balderston, Lydia R., *Housewifery*, Fifth Edition, Chs. IV-VII, pp. 84-203. J. B. Lippincott Co., Chicago, 1936.

Excellent and full discussion of the following: selection and placing of working equipment; equipment for the laundry and for cleaning; household supplies used with equipment in household work; household furnishings.

Baldwin, William H., *The Shopping Book*, Chs. II-V, pp. 34-123. The Macmillan Co., New York, 1929.

A discussion of the points to consider in buying floor coverings, furniture, house furnishings, china, and glassware. *The Shopping Book* gives information concerning qualities, types of products, construction, materials, and trade terminology. While some of the material in the book eventually will become out of date as new processes are developed, the discussion of the points to consider in shopping for each product described shows the method of analysis which the consumer-buyer should follow. This is the kind of book to read just before a shopping trip.

Brindze, Ruth, *How to Spend Money*. The Vanguard Press, New York, 1935.

Use index for detailed information about many types of furnishings and equipment.

Nystrom, P. H., *Economic Principles of Consumption*, Ch. XVI, pp. 385-418. The Ronald Press Co., New York, 1929.

A discussion of available types of home furnishings and equipment, their cost and their use at various levels of living.

Peet, Louise J., and Sater, Lenore E., *Household Equipment*. John Wiley and Sons, Inc., New York, 1934.

A detailed analysis of the more common types of household equipment now on the market.

Rutt, Anna H., *Home Furnishing*. J. Wiley and Sons, Inc., New York, 1935.
A discussion of the art of furnishing an attractive home.

D. The Paid Helper in the Home

Andrews, B. R., *Economics of the Household*, Revised Edition, Chs. XVII-XIX, pp. 435-516. The Macmillan Co., New York, 1935.

An excellent discussion of the problems housework involves, and the ways in which the work of the home can be lightened by the use of proper equipment and of paid helpers. The author analyzes in considerable detail the social as well as the purely personal aspects of the problem of housework and household employment.

Balderston, Lydia R., *Housewifery*, Fifth Edition, Ch. I, pp. 16-19; and Ch. XIII, pp. 333-336. J. B. Lippincott Co., Chicago, 1936.

A discussion of household employment problems from the housekeeper's point of view. See Ch. XIII for a discussion of new courses which are being developed in many sections of the country for the study of employer and employee relationships.

Reid, Margaret G., *Economics of Household Production*, Ch. XVI.   John Wiley and Sons, Inc., New York, 1934.

A brief analysis of the problems involved in the employment of paid labor in the home. Has a carefully selected bibliography. Includes some suggestions concerning attempts to improve conditions of household employment.

Watson, Amey E., "The Re-organization of Housework," *Annals of the American Academy of Political and Social Science*, Vol. 160, pp. 165-177.   March, 1932.

A discussion of the possibility of reorganizing housework so as to make it a more attractive type of employment. The article discusses the types of work which must be done in the home, the sources of relief now open to homemakers, and suggested standards for household employment. The author is a recognized authority on household employment.

Women's Bureau, U. S. Department of Labor, Bulletin 93, "Household Employment in Philadelphia" (1932); Bulletin 106, "Household Employment in Chicago" (1933); Bulletin 112, "Standards of Placement Agencies for Household Employees" (1934); Bulletin 138, "Reading List of References on Household Employment" (1936).   Government Printing Office, Washington, D. C.

Bulletins issued from time to time dealing with various phases of household employment.

CHAPTER XII

THE AUTOMOBILE

The place of the automobile in American family life.
For the majority of American families, the maintenance of the family automobile is a major item of expenditure. For many families, the family car represents the largest single investment in family equipment. Many husbands and wives each own a car when they are married. If they do not, they often buy a car before they buy their furniture. A family will usually buy a car before it buys a home.

And yet it is only since the World War that the automobile has become a significant factor in American family life. A study of registration figures shows that, like the bathtub and the electric light, the family automobile came into its present general use in the years after 1918.[1] In 1930, in a country with less than 30 million families, more than 23 million passenger cars were registered. Even if some allowance is made for cars used primarily for business, and for families owning more than one car, in all probability in 1930 not far from two-thirds of the families in the United States owned automobiles.

Further, the ownership of automobiles is not confined to any one economic level, nor to any one section of the country. Analysis of sales indicates that automobiles are purchased and maintained by families in all walks of life. In fact, contrary to experience in the adoption of bathtubs and electric power, there are more cars per thousand population registered in rural than in urban areas. Registration figures indicate that the percentage of families owning cars is usually larger in the small towns and moderate sized cities than it is in the densely populated metropolitan areas.

The original automobile was a horseless carriage, a new and local means of transportation. Most families still think of the cost of the family car simply as a major item of local transportation expense. But the automobile is no longer significant merely as a means of local transportation. The development of a nation-wide network

---

[1] See page 23.

of hard-surfaced roads has made the automobile a widely used means of long distance travel. And today, as in the early stages of its development when it was still a rich man's toy, the automobile is an important recreational facility.

REGISTRATION OF MOTOR VEHICLES, 1900-1937 [2]

Year	Total	Passenger Cars, Busses, and Taxis	Trucks and Road Tractors
1900	8,000	. . . .	. . . .
1903	33,000	. . . .	. . . .
1904	55,000	. . . .	. . . .
1905	78,000	77,000	1,000
1906	107,000	106,000	1,000
1907	142,000	140,000	2,000
1908	198,000	194,000	3,000
1909	312,000	306,000	6,000
1910	468,000	458,000	10,000
1911	640,000	620,000	20,000
1912	944,000	903,000	41,000
1913	1,258,000	1,194,000	64,000
1914	1,711,000	1,626,000	86,000
1915	2,446,000	2,310,000	136,000
1916	3,513,000	3,298,000	215,000
1917	4,983,000	4,657,000	326,000
1918	6,147,000	5,622,000	525,000
1919	7,565,000	6,771,000	794,000
1920	9,232,000	8,226,000	1,006,000
1921	10,463,000	9,483,000	980,000
1922	12,238,000	10,960,000	1,279,000
1923	15,091,000	13,538,000	1,553,000
1924	17,594,000	15,461,000	2,133,000
1925	19,937,000	17,496,000	2,441,000
1926	22,001,000	19,237,000	2,764,000
1927	23,133,000	20,219,000	2,914,000
1928	24,493,000	21,379,000	3,114,000
1929	26,501,000	23,122,000	3,380,000
1930	26,545,000	23,059,000	3,486,000
1931	25,814,000	22,348,000	3,466,000
1932	24,115,000	20,884,000	3,231,000
1933	23,874,000	20,644,000	3,231,000
1934	24,952,000	21,532,000	3,419,000
1935	26,231,000	22,583,000	3,647,000
1936	28,166,000	24,178,000	3,987,000
1937	29,705,000	25,450,000	4,255,000

The automobile nowadays is used for so great a variety of purposes that the family organizes many phases of its life around its car. The location of its home, the church to which it belongs, the school which its children attend, the stores in which it buys, the types of recreation it enjoys, and even the friendships it is able to maintain are determined in large measure by the availability of an automobile.

Within a single decade, in fact within five or six years of prosperity

[2] *Statistical Abstract of the United States, 1935*, Table No. 399, p. 353, and *1938*, Table No. 424, p. 370. Government Printing Office, Washington, D. C.

in that decade, many families found that the automobile had become to them a necessity as important as adequate food and clothing. To the salesman, good-looking clothes are no more important than a good-looking car. To the carpenter, a car which will take him to his work is just as important as the tools with which he will work after he gets there. To the whole family, the ownership of a car may be more important than the quality of shelter, for the ownership of a car makes it possible for the whole family to spend more time away from the home.

It is now possible to secure at very moderate cost compact, well-equipped house trailers which provide the small family with a portable home that in a mild climate, at least, is not at all inadequate for year-round living. If an industrial people must be a nomadic people, here may be one solution for the problem of mobility of whole family groups which our present economic order presents.

Expenditures for automobile maintenance. *National totals.* Because of the recent introduction of the automobile, there are no adequate records of the amounts individual families spend for the maintenance of the family car. There are, however, a number of estimates of total national consumption which indicate the relative amount of consumer income which goes for automobile maintenance and operation. Of these Miss Hoyt's 1926 estimate [3] (see page 177), attributing 5 per cent of total consumer outlay to automobile expense, is typical.

These estimates have been made from statistics of automobile production, and statistics of sales of gasoline, oil, tires, batteries, and automotive services. Production figures include output for business and professional as well as for family use. There is no way to tell, even from registration figures, what proportion of the cars are used primarily for business and what primarily for family needs. Since many family cars are used part of the time at least for business purposes, and many cars registered under firm names are put occasionally to private use, since there is no way to determine the amount of gasoline or oil that is bought for business and the amount that is bought for family use, it has been necessary to determine probable

---

[3] See Elizabeth E. Hoyt, *The Consumption of Wealth*, Table IX, p. 275, and the discussion on p. 284. The Macmillan Co., New York, 1928.

See also William H. Lough, *High Level Consumption*, Table 10, p. 53. McGraw-Hill Book Co., Inc., New York, 1935. This table shows that for the years 1923-27 American consumers spent 8.7 per cent and in 1931, 8.8 per cent of their total outlays for transportation. This does not distinguish between expenditures for automobile maintenance and other transportation items.

family outlay by using some arbitrary assumption as to the proportion of these outlays which should be allotted to business costs, and the proportion which should be counted as family expenditures.

In all probability these studies, most of which were made in the late 1920's, underestimate rather than overestimate the proportion of total automobile expense which must be met by the family. In many occupations it is now assumed that since the family will have a car anyway, the fixed charges involved in the purchase and ownership of the car will be borne by the family and not by the employer.

From the point of view of the family, these assumptions regarding the proportion of expenditures which should be charged to business and to family use are not significant. If it is necessary for the head of the family to provide an automobile for business use, the money spent by the family for the maintenance and operation of its automobile must be provided out of family income. Whatever can be secured from business expense accounts only helps to repay in part the outlays advanced by the family.

Individual family expenditures. Studies of total expenditures for automobile maintenance show only the proportion which expenditures for automobiles represent in the national total of consumer outlay. They tell nothing about either the amount or the proportion of individual family incomes which go for the maintenance and operation of the family car.

Suppose we assume that automobile expenditures represent somewhere between 6 and 7 per cent of the national total of consumption. If, as registration figures indicate, one-third of the families in the United States do not own cars, then the two-thirds of the families who do own cars must make all of this outlay. For the two-thirds of the families who do own automobiles, automobile expense will represent on the average not 6 or 7 per cent, but more nearly 8 or 9 per cent of their individual expenditures.

There is little evidence, however, of any uniformity either in the amount or the percentage of the individual family income actually spent for the family car. The amount of expenditure seems to depend not so much upon the amount of the family income as upon the type of car owned, the amount and kind of use, and the extent to which the family is dependent upon commercial services for repair and upkeep.

Further, for the same family, the amount of expenditure for

automobile maintenance varies markedly from year to year. In the years in which a family buys or trades for a new car, the current outlay is heavy. In the years in which they make the old car do, they pay only for current upkeep and garage rent, and the annually recurring charges for license, insurance, and taxes. The only families whose expenditures for car maintenance run at about the same level from year to year are the families who each year trade in the old car for a later model.

An analysis of the expenditures of a small group of families of moderate income,[4] living in moderate sized communities, indicates that a great many families are able to operate a car on an amount which represents as little as 5 per cent of the family expenditures. This same study shows, further, that if they buy a car only once in three, four, or five years, as many of them do, the year they replace the old car with a later model, automobile expenditures may amount to 15, 20, 25, or even 30 per cent of their current expenditures. The family that trades for a new car every year may spend anywhere from 10 to 20 per cent of its income for automobile expense, depending, of course, upon the amount of the family income, the kind of car it buys, and the amount and the way it uses the family automobile.

Automobile costs. There are a number of items which must be included in computing the cost of owning and operating the family car. There are certain fixed charges which every car owner must meet, regardless of how much or how little he drives his car. These include annual payments for taxes, license fees, and insurance, and monthly payments for garage rent, when necessary, together with adequate allowances for depreciation, obsolescence, and interest on the family's investment in the automobile.

It is possible of course to consider the original purchase price of the car as a single large item of cost. But most families consider the purchase of a car in the nature of an investment in family capital. In estimating the cost of owning an automobile, they simply charge up each year the decrease in the value of the car due to depreciation and obsolescence. For most families this item of depreciation involves no current outlay, since they do not set aside as part of their savings a fund specifically to cover depreciation, but they pay for

---

[4] H. F. Bigelow, *Unpublished Study of Middle-class Families.*

accumulated depreciation when they trade for a new car. Similarly, because they pay themselves no interest on their family capital, few families count interest on their investment in the car as part of its annual cost. This item should be included, however, in determining the actual cost of maintaining the family car.

The amount for fixed charges is determined at the time the family buys a car. The value of the car, its weight, and its horsepower determine the annual taxes which the owner must pay. The value of the car and its rating by insurance companies determine to a large extent the cost of insurance. (See Ch. XIX, p. 473.) The type of car, the amount of the original investment, and the trade-in value determine the amount which must be allowed for interest and for depreciation. There is no way to reduce fixed charges once the family has bought its car.

In addition to fixed charges, there are operating costs. These include direct costs, the amount spent for gasoline and oil and for greasing and parking charges, which vary directly with the amount a car is used; and overhead expense, the amount spent for anti-freeze, tire chains, repairs, washing and cleaning, tire and battery replacements, and similar items which are needed from time to time but cannot be charged directly to any particular type of use.

Both direct and overhead operating costs are determined in part by the make of the car, its weight, lines, and mechanical efficiency. Ordinarily the larger and heavier the car, the higher are its operating costs.

There is, of course, significant variation in the cost of operating individual cars, even of the same make and model. Gasoline and oil consumption depend upon the condition of the motor. Repairs depend upon the mechanical perfection of the individual car. Under present standardized manufacturing conditions, most cars give average performance. But every manufacturer inevitably, by the laws of chance, turns out an occasional "lemon," and every manufacturer, by those same laws of chance, occasionally turns out a car which will give much better than average performance.

Further, the cost of operating an individual car depends to a considerable extent upon the kind of care which it has had, and the way it has been used or abused. An automobile is a machine. Proper care is essential to efficient and economical operation. Serious accidents, or even minor accidents, may add a great deal to subsequent operating costs.

Operating costs depend also upon the conditions under which a car is driven. Both gasoline and oil consumption vary with traffic conditions. Ordinarily a car will use less gasoline per mile on long drives at moderate speeds in the open country than it will when driven at high speed or in congested traffic. It is usually possible to get more mileage from a set of tires that is worn out in a single year than from a set that is worn out over several seasons. Tires wear out faster in city driving and on unimproved country highways than they do when driven at moderate speeds over improved roads. A family driving over all kinds of roads in all kinds of weather will need to spend a good deal more for washing the car than will a family that does most of its driving on paved highways in fair weather. If a family drives a great deal over icy roads, it may need a set of tire chains twice in one winter. If it drives only occasionally when the roads are icy, it may find that a set of chains will last as long as the car.

Every family should understand the various elements which enter into the cost of owning and operating an automobile. Since these elements are variable, each family must determine for itself the probable cost of operating its own car under the conditions involved in its own types of use.

Some problems of car ownership. *Should the family own a car?* There are a number of problems connected with car ownership which every family must work out for itself, taking into account all of the elements in its individual family situation. In the first place, every family, whether it now owns a car or not, should from time to time consider carefully the wisdom of owning and operating an automobile.

For in spite of the fact that for many families an automobile is actually a necessity, and in spite of the fact that once a family has become adjusted to car ownership, it can do without a car only after extensive rearrangement of its whole manner of living, not every family should own one. Yet this is not a question which can be settled once and for all. For as conditions change, the family without an automobile may find it wise to buy one. And occasionally the family with one may decide to dispose of it and depend upon other means of transportation.

In deciding whether or not it is wise to own a car, there are a number of factors to be considered. A family must, of course, be sure that there are funds available both to buy a car which is suited to the family's needs and to maintain and operate it once it has been paid for.

The family must consider the amount of use it will make of a car. There are many elderly people who have never learned to drive; there are many women, and some men, who do not care to be bothered with the care of an automobile. They prefer to call a taxi for local transportation, and for longer trips to hire a car and driver or to go by rail or by air.

Families whose members go about for the most part in the congested areas of large cities find less advantage in the use of a car than do families living in moderate sized cities outside the larger metropolitan areas, since the larger cities are reasonably well supplied with rapid local transportation. Traffic is heavy. It moves slowly.[5] It is subject to many necessary restrictions. Parking must be paid for. Garage rent is high. The car requires more for upkeep when it is driven in heavy traffic. Gasoline mileage is lower, tires wear out sooner, brakes must be relined at frequent intervals. Fenders are often dented, and bumpers and finish scratched. Because of the higher accident and theft rates, insurance costs are higher. Ordinarily, then, the larger and more congested the district, the smaller is the advantage of using an automobile. The smaller and more isolated the community, the more necessary and frequent is the use of an automobile. In the open country, for most families, the family car is the only available means of rapid transportation.

Finally, in deciding whether or not to own a car, the family must determine the total cost involved in owning and operating an automobile. It must compare its expenditures for transportation with and without the use of the family car. And since the ownership of a car may bring great changes in the way the family lives, it must go still further. It must consider all the ways in which the ownership of a car will change the manner of the family's living. It must consider all the expenses it will add—for trips that the family without an automobile cannot conveniently make and does not plan, for additional expenditures for clothing, and for supplementary recreational

---

[5] In inter-city driving on business trips in northern New Jersey, one driver was able to average 30 miles an hour. In inter-city driving on similar business trips in western Illinois and Iowa, the same driver was able to average 45 miles an hour.

expenditures. It must consider all the outlay that the ownership of a car will save, such as making it possible for the family to live in the suburbs where it can get larger quarters for lower rent, where it can have a garden, where it can be near the children's school, and where it can get away from complete dependence upon commercial recreation.

In determining whether or not to own a car, the family income alone is no criterion. Some families of modest means find it absolutely essential to own a car. Other families with generous incomes decide that for them there are many other more desirable expenditures. A family must make its final decision only after careful consideration of the comparative cost of living with and without a family car, and of the relative desirability of the two patterns of living.

Selecting the family car. In buying a car, a family must decide first how much it can afford to pay. Then it must determine the general style, the body type, and the mechanical features which will most nearly fill its needs. It must compare the reputation of various makes of cars as to operating economy and resale value. It should buy from a dealer with a good reputation for efficient and economical service. If it plans to drive a good deal away from home, it should select a car which is widely distributed, and which has high standards for service. And finally, the family must decide whether it can get most nearly what it needs for the price it can afford to pay in the new- or the used-car market.

New cars vs. used cars. Many families prefer to buy an inexpensive or moderate priced new car. Others prefer a used car from a higher price class. Some families are not able to buy a new car at all, but are able to find on the used-car market plenty of cars that will give them many miles of good transportation for a good deal less than the cost of a new car.

If fashion is important, a family will buy a new car of the very latest model. If it wants individuality, it will buy either a car in a high price class or a new de luxe model with striking accessories and a distinctive color scheme. If it wants dependability, unless it knows how to judge the mechanical condition of used cars, or knows that it can depend absolutely upon the word of the dealer, it will probably buy a new car. But it should buy a model which has been on the market for some months, and preferably one which contains no major mechanical changes.

If the family wants a low operating cost, it had better buy a new car, but not necessarily a new model. It will be more sure of getting a car which will be economical to operate if it buys a model which has demonstrated its economy in the hands of actual consumers. On the other hand, if the family wants to keep its fixed charges at a minimum, if it is interested in low depreciation and obsolescence, it may buy a used car on which the original owner has already taken the heavy initial depreciation.

If the members of a family can do their own repair work, it may be possible to buy an old used car, repair it with second-hand parts, and provide a good deal of transportation for a minimum of cash outlay. If, however, the family must pay for its repair work, it will probably be cheaper in the long run to buy an inexpensive new car or a used car in good mechanical condition.

When to use the family car. The way a family uses the family car is, and should be, largely a matter of habit. For families are much too busy to be bothered with constant decisions in matters of everyday use. Since it is easy to get into the habit of always using the car whenever any member of the family wants to go anywhere, since it is easy to get into the habit of driving many unnecessary miles doing many unnecessary errands, if the family is to use its automobile efficiently and economically, it must consciously form wise habits. It must take time to determine deliberately the uses to which its car is to be put.

This involves the making of a whole series of decisions as to whether or not the car is to be used for specific purposes. The family must decide, for example, whether to make a practice of driving downtown on a shopping trip, or of riding on a bus; whether to make a practice of driving or of walking about the neighborhood to call on friends; whether or not to make a practice of taking the family for a ride on warm summer evenings and bright fall Sunday afternoons; whether to make a practice of driving the car on business trips to a city a hundred miles away or of riding on the train.

In deciding whether or not to use a car for a specific purpose, the family ordinarily considers only the additional immediate cost which this use will involve, and it ignores fixed charges entirely. It thinks of the cost of a shopping trip in terms of additional direct costs, of a few cents for gasoline, plus a small parking fee. It thinks of the cost of a ride in the evening in terms of a half-dollar for gasoline, and perhaps a few cents for oil. It thinks of the cost of transportation for an occasional business trip in terms of the actual outlay for gas and oil, with an additional allowance for mechanical check-over before making the trip.

If a particular use increases the mileage driven enough to necessitate noticeably more frequent replacement of tires, or relining of brakes, or motor overhaul—if, for example, frequent business trips increase by several thousand miles the mileage driven in the course of a year—the family includes as part of the cost not only direct expenditures for gas and oil, but an amount equal to the probable increase in these occasional operating costs. It usually includes in its cost estimates a part of the fixed charges only if the use in question is responsible for a major part of the mileage driven during the year, or if the use noticeably decreases the trade-in value on the car, or necessitates replacement earlier than would otherwise have been the case.[6]

It will make its decision after comparing the cost and convenience of driving the car with the cost and convenience of using some other means of transportation. If it finds that it costs a little more to drive downtown on a shopping trip, it may decide to use the car when there are many packages to bring home, and to use the bus for other trips. It may decide that it is better to walk about the neighborhood when the weather is fair and to use the car when the weather is threatening. For while shoe leather is cheaper than gasoline, the cost of gasoline used will be much less than the cost of pressing a suit of clothes or having a dress cleaned.

The family may find that it is cheaper for one member of the family to make a business trip on the train. The railroad fare for one person may be less than operating expenses plus parking charges for a car. But if it is necessary to go about a good deal in the city,

---

[6] Because the decrease in the value of a car from year to year is due in part to physical deterioration or depreciation, and in part to obsolescence, increasing the mileage driven may or may not add to the amount which must be allowed for decrease in trade-in or resale value. If the car is driven a very great deal, it may wear out more quickly than it passes out of style. If, on the other hand, it is driven only a little, it loses in value because it is no longer the latest model, either in style or mechanical design. Increasing the mileage driven may or may not increase the amount which must be allowed for depreciation. Decreasing the amount a car is used will not decrease loss of value from obsolescence. Increasing the mileage driven always increases operating expenses. Ordinarily, therefore, the more a family drives during the year, the higher is the total cost of car ownership and operation. At the same time, the more the family drives, ordinarily the lower is the cost per mile for transportation.

driving the car may save enough in taxi fares to make it cheaper and more convenient to use the automobile. Again, while it may be cheaper for one member of the family to go by train, for a slightly larger expenditure for gasoline, it will be possible for the whole family to spend a day in the city.

If the family is to get the largest possible satisfaction from the family car, it must be constantly on the alert for new uses which are in the nature of by-products of car ownership.

There are many families that are not justified in maintaining a car solely for occasional pleasure trips. But if the head of the family must have a car to use in his business, the family can easily afford the small additional cost of using it for recreation. For very little extra the whole family can take a ride in the country, which may provide much more enjoyment and cost much less than a trip to the movies. If the family owns a car, by taking thought it can at only moderate additional expense make it possible for the children to visit many places of interest not simply for their recreational value, but for the broadening effect upon the children's experience. It is often possible for the whole family to take a rather extensive vacation trip in the car for no more than it would cost for the father and mother alone to go by train.

There are also some by-products to be had from using the car to reduce other expenditures. The car may be used to bring home vegetables bought direct from the grower on the farmer's market, or for buying groceries on sale at the cash-and-carry store. When out for a ride in the country, the family may buy eggs at a farm on the way. A car may be used in many ways to secure small savings in other expenditures at little additional cost.

The family must understand, of course, that every time it uses the car it adds to the operating costs. But if the family has money to spend for automobile operation, it will find it good business to use the family car in every case in which the satisfaction secured from its use is equal to or greater than the satisfaction which would be secured if the money actually expended for these additional outlays were put to some other use.

When to trade for a later model. Every car-owning family from time to time must decide whether it is better to trade for a later model or to make the old car do. There is no common practice to guide them. Some families trade every year, as soon as the new models are available. Others trade every year, but wait until the end of the season, when dealers are giving unusually generous trade-in allowances to clear out the last few cars of the current model. Some families trade once in two years, and others only at much longer intervals.

When the individual family should trade for a later model depends in part upon what the family expects to get from a car, and in part upon the comparative cost, in their particular case, of trading for a new car and of making the old car do for some time longer. If style is important, the family will want to trade every year for the latest model. If the family must have dependable and rapid transportation, it should trade for a new car as soon as its present car begins to need frequent mechanical adjustments. If economy is important, the family will decide largely upon the basis of the comparative cost of maintaining and operating the old car and buying and operating the new. If lowest current outlay, rather than lowest long-time cost, is essential, the family may continue to drive the old car, making a minimum of repairs, and putting up with somewhat higher operating costs in order to save the immediate outlay involved in trading.

It is not always more economical either in long-time cost or in current outlay to make the old car do. If a family drives a great deal, it may actually require a smaller outlay during the year to trade for a new car than to spend what is necessary to keep the older car on the road. Suppose, for example, that a family drives its car 25,000 miles a year. By the end of the first year, the car will need a complete set of tires. It should have a thorough mechanical check-up. If it is to be put into condition for another 25,000 or 30,000 miles of driving, it may need rather extensive repairs, new pistons and rings, new brake-linings, and a number of minor replacements and adjustments. Usually the operating cost of a car is higher for the second 25,000 miles of its life than for the first. It can hardly be expected to be quite so efficient in its performance. It may use more oil. It may not give as good mileage on gasoline. Even though it is put into good condition at the beginning of the year, in all probability it will need an increasing amount of mechanical attention during a second year of hard use. But at the end of the first year, as far as style is concerned, it is still a new car. It has a high trade-in value. If the family compares the cost of necessary repairs and the higher operating cost of the old car the second year with the lower operating costs and higher depreciation of a new car, they may often find that it will require a smaller expenditure in the course of the year to trade for a new car.

On the other hand, if the family drives only 5,000 or 10,000 miles in the course of a year, it may find it much more economical to drive the old car for several years before trading. At the end of the first year, the tires will still be in good condition, the motor will be just nicely broken in, and the car will be in substantially new-car condition. And yet its trade-in value will be little if any more than that of a car which has been driven three or four times as far. Operating costs do not begin to increase noticeably until the car has run at least 20,000, and in some cases 30,000, miles. The family driving only a few thousand miles a year usually finds it good economy to drive a car as long as it gives satisfactory service, and to trade only when it begins to need extensive repairs.

In a few cases, if a family has an old car with a low trade-in value, and does not have the money necessary for the purchase of a newer car, it may be wise to spend some money for extensive repairs on the old car. A family may be able to spend $100 for a thorough overhauling of the old car, though it does not have $500 to spend for a new one. It must remember, however, that repairing an old car ordinarily adds very little to its trade-in value. It is wise to spend money to put an old car in condition only if the family plans to drive it long enough to get back its money in actual use.

In general, then, it is wise to trade for a new model if the total cost of owning and operating the new car is no more than the total cost of owning and operating the old one. And even though trading for a new car costs a little more than driving the old one, if the family has the money available for the expenditure, it is usually desirable to trade for a new car whenever the additional satisfaction the family secures from it in style, in comfort, or in dependable service is more than sufficient to offset its higher cost.

Financing automobile expenditures. Owning and operating an automobile involves three types of expenditure: First, there is the initial investment in the automobile; or, for the family which already owns a car, the difference which must be paid whenever the family trades for a later model. Second, there are occasional expenses, some large and some small. A number of these, such as the annual license fee and the premium on the automobile insurance policy, come at regular intervals, and can be definitely planned on in advance. Others, like the replacement of tires and occasional repairs, come only at irregular intervals. Sometimes it is possible to anticipate them; sometimes it is not. Third, there are regular running expenses, for gasoline, oil, greasing, washing, minor repairs, and garage rent. For many families, these running expenses vary only a little from month to month, depending upon the amount the car is used at different seasons of the year.

Since there are all these varied types of expenditure to be provided for, obviously the problem of financing the family car is not the simple problem of setting aside a certain number of dollars each month, or even of appropriating a predetermined proportion of the family income each year for automobile expenditure. Instead the family must determine as definitely as it can in advance exactly what outlays it will be necessary to make during the year, and, what is even more important, exactly when it will be necessary to make them.

Financing the purchase of the family car. For most families the purchase of an automobile is a major outlay, but one which need not be made every year. Financing the purchase of the family's first car presents the most difficult problem. To buy a new car, even in a moderate price class, takes a substantial sum of money. If the family is to pay cash, it must save the entire purchase price in advance. If it buys on the instalment plan, it must save at least one-third of the purchase price for a down payment, and be able to complete the balance of the payments within a year. In order to keep the amount of their original investment within reasonable limits, many families find it necessary to buy an inexpensive used car for their first venture in car ownership.

Once the family owns a car, the problem is not so difficult, for it is no longer necessary to provide the entire purchase price of the new car, but simply the difference between the trade-in value of the old car and the price of the new one. And, if the family cares to pay for its new car on the instalment plan, unless it has driven the old car until it is completely worn out, it can usually use the trade-in value of the old car as a down payment.

The desirability of buying an automobile on the instalment plan is one of the most discussed questions in the whole problem of family finance. In deciding whether to save and buy, or to buy and pay, the family must compare the importance of immediate purchase with the cost of instalment credit. Automobile financing charges usually are not less than 7 per cent of the face of the instalment contract. But 7 per cent of the face of the contract is not 7 per cent but more nearly 17 per cent in annual interest on the actual unpaid balances advanced by the financing company.[7] If by immediate purchase of the car the family can reduce other expenditures by an amount equal to the financing charges, it may be good business to buy the car at once, and pay for the car as it uses it. If the family needs a new car for some special purpose, even though no cash is saved by immediate purchase, it may be willing to pay the extra cost of financing for the privilege of immediate use. But if the family does contract to pay for its car on the instalment plan, it must be sure that it will have the money needed to meet each payment as it comes due. And it must have this money over and above the amount it will need to operate the car.

But even though a family believes that the immediate purchase of a new car is worth the extra cost involved in instalment buying, there is no good reason for paying more for financing the purchase than is necessary. In buying a car on credit, the family should use the most economical form of credit which is available. If it will be able to complete its payments in three or four months instead of ten, the family may be able to borrow at a commercial bank or the dealer may be willing to accept bankable personal notes on which is paid only 6 or 7 per cent annual interest. If the family has funds which it is saving for some other purpose, it may decide to divert its own savings temporarily to the purchase of the car, paying back into the savings fund the amount of the instalment payments, and saving the financing charges. Or it may decide to borrow part of the loan value of a life insurance policy, repaying the loan as rapidly as possible.

The most economical way to buy a car is to save and pay cash. This eliminates the necessity of paying interest. If a family has a monthly surplus sufficient to meet instalment payments, by deferring the purchase and depositing the amount of these payments in a savings account it can have its growing fund earning interest which will defray part of the cost of buying the car. After the family has its first car, the plan of saving and depositing each year an amount

[7] See Ch. XVIII, p. 424.

equal to that year's depreciation will provide at any time the sum needed, beyond the trade-in value, to buy a new one.

Financing occasional expenditures. There are a number of other smaller outlays which, like the purchase of a car, come at occasional intervals. But, unlike the purchase of a car, most of these cannot be postponed. They must be made at once if the family is to continue to operate the automobile. For example, a family cannot drive a car legally without a license. This license must be renewed each year. A family cannot safely drive a car without insurance, to protect it against damage to the car, and liability which may arise from its use. The annual insurance premium must be paid upon the anniversary of the original policy. In case of mechanical breakdown or tire failure, it is impossible to continue to drive the car without immediate expenditures for replacement and repair. It is absolutely essential that the family have funds available for all of these occasional expenditures at the time when the expenditure must be made.

There are a number of these occasional outlays for which the family can plan definitely in advance. It knows both the amount of the annual license fee and the date at which the plates will be on sale. It knows the day upon which its automobile insurance policy will expire. It must make provision for these fixed charges in making its annual budget. If there is current income available in the months in which these expenditures must be made, they can be treated like any other current expenditures. If they require a larger outlay than can be made from a single month's income, it will be necessary to accumulate the needed money in advance.

For such occasional expenditures as it is impossible to anticipate, the family must hold some funds in reserve. It may be wise to have a small savings account upon which to draw if current income is insufficient to meet these occasional and unexpected expenditures. It is often possible to buy new tires or a new battery on the instalment plan. It is sometimes possible to finance extensive repair bills in the same way. But instalment financing always costs money. It is much better, if the family can possibly do so, to maintain reserves adequate to cover any possible expenditure.

Financing running expenses. Running expenses involve small but frequently repeated outlays week by week and month by month throughout the year. Usually they are paid out of current income. In most cases they call for cash outlay, although a few families find it convenient to establish their credit with a company operating a chain of conveniently located stations giving rather complete service, charge their purchases, and settle the bill once a month.

To determine the amount which will be needed for running expenses, a family should determine how many miles the family will probably drive each month in the year. Then it can estimate, on the basis of its own experience, how much money must be provided each month for gasoline and oil, for washing, greasing, and minor repairs. These amounts it can then set up and provide for along with other current outlays in the family budget.

If it can afford to operate a car at all, the family with a small but regular income can usually take care of regular running expenses out of current income. But it may find it necessary to set aside in advance enough to care for the annual license fee and the insurance premium. It must, if possible, maintain adequate reserves for unexpected occasional expenditures. For if it does not, it will be forced to pay the extra cost of financing these occasional large expenditures on the instalment plan.

The family whose income is received in occasional large increments, on the other hand, must be careful to set aside enough out of each instalment of its income to care for current operating expenses. It can plan to take care of predictable occasional outlays, both for the purchase of a new car and for operating expense, out of current income. It must maintain reserves sufficient to provide for any expected outlays.

If a family is to maintain and operate an automobile, it must be prepared to make every expenditure which car ownership involves. Often a family finds it difficult to provide funds for automobile expenditures, not because it does not have sufficient income, but because it has never taken the trouble to find out how much the ownership and operation of an automobile actually costs, and when these expenditures must be made.

If the family must have a car, it must provide funds for automobile maintenance and operation. If necessary, it must rearrange and reduce its expenditures for other items in order to assure adequate funds for all the expenses of automobile maintenance, whenever those expenditures must be made. If, as is the case in a good many families, these expenditures are being made and have been made for some years, what is necessary is not so much to rearrange family expenditures as to adjust the family's thinking about its expenditures to the new pattern of living which the ownership of an automobile brings with it.

Every family must, of course, carefully analyze both the costs and the satisfactions of car ownership. It must decide whether or not the ownership of a family car is worth the price. If the family decides that it is, it should stop worrying about what the car ought to cost, make adequate provision for financing automobile expenditures, and proceed to enjoy to the maximum the ownership and use of the family car. If it decides that it cannot afford to maintain a car, it must make whatever changes in its manner of living are necessary in order to do without it, and use the money saved for other more satisfying expenditures.

QUESTIONS

1. What proportion of families of your acquaintance own automobiles? Buy them new? Used? For cash? On the instalment plan? Is this typical of the entire community?

2. Describe in detail all the ways in which three families of your acquaintance use their automobiles. What members of the family drive? For what purposes? How many miles a year? What restrictions, if any, do these families place upon the use of the family car?

3. How much do families of your acquaintance spend for the family car in the course of a year? Secure actual records of automobile expenditure from at least three families. Compare your records with those gathered by other members of your class. What conclusions about costs can you draw from a study of the records of actual expenditures? For example, under what conditions would you say that it is more economical to own and operate a new car? A used car? A car in a low-priced group? A car in a moderate or high-priced group?

4. A friend comes to you for advice about the selection of a car. Work out a list of points which he should consider.

5. What types of used cars are in most active demand in your community? How does this demand compare with the demand in other communities with which you are familiar?

6. Under what circumstances do you consider it absolutely necessary for a family to own and operate an automobile? Under what circumstances is it desirable? Under what circumstances is car ownership unnecessary? Undesirable?

7. List all the ways in which a family that needs a car may effect economies in the cost of owning and operating an automobile.

8. Should your family own a car? If so, what kind? In what price class? For what purposes should it use the car? Under what conditions should it trade for a new car? How should it finance its automobile expenditure?

REFERENCES

Automobile Facts and Figures. National Automobile Chamber of Commerce, New York City.

An annual handbook giving statistics for the automobile industry, registration figures, estimate of the life of an automobile, production records, digest of state and federal tax laws affecting the automobile owner, and facts of interest to the student of family finance.

Consumers' Research, Inc., *Annual Handbook* and *Special Automobile Supplement.* Washington, N. J.

This material, available to members of Consumers' Research, gives detailed evaluation of current models and compares delivered costs and trade-in values as well as engineering features. The material includes suggestions as to the way to analyze market offerings in relation to use, suggests possible economies, and points out current fallacies in advertising copy.

Nystrom, P. H., *Economic Principles of Consumption,* Ch. XII, pp. 277-298. The Ronald Press Co., New York, 1929.

The author describes the place of the automobile in a number of typical 1924 levels of living.

Willey, Malcolm M., and Rice, Stuart A., "The Agencies of Communication," in *Recent Social Trends in the United States,* Ch. IV, pp. 172-180. McGraw-Hill Book Co., Inc., New York, 1933. (See also the Index.)

Wolman, Leo, "Consumption and the Standard of Living," in *Recent Economic Changes,* Vol. I, Ch. I, pp. 59-62. McGraw-Hill Book Co., Inc., New York, 1929. (See also the Index.)

These references describe briefly the place the automobile has come to fill in modern American life. Further interesting comment on the social and economic implications of the automobile can be found by using the index.

CHAPTER XIII

HEALTH, EDUCATION, AND RECREATION

HEALTH

The family's health program. In recent years it has become increasingly evident that adequate provision for the health of the family involves much more than provision of medical care during incapacitating illness. The medical profession has done a good deal in recent years in the development of preventive medicine. Recent research has demonstrated the importance of mental as well as of physical health. It is now clearly evident that the maintenance of health involves the whole life of the family.

Adequate provision for health includes at least three types of expenditures: First, in case of incapacitating illness, there must be expenditures for adequate medical care. Second, there should be some expenditures for preventive medicine. Third, many of the family's ordinary expenditures should be made only after careful consideration of their relation to the maintenance of the health of the members of the family. Most families are conscious of the importance of healthfully adequate food and clothing and of shelter that provides an environment which is conducive to good health. Heating, lighting, and air conditioning all involve health values as well as comfort. Proper recreation is especially important in the hurry and strain of modern urban civilization. Even the purchase of a set of new tires for the family automobile, or the relining of the brakes, or any other repairs or adjustments which may increase safety of operation have a direct bearing upon the maintenance of the good health of the family.

Expenditures for medical care. In this chapter we are concerned primarily with the expenditures for preventive and curative medical care. Medical care always costs money. Although knowledge of the existence of preventive medicine, and of the modern methods of treating disease is becoming increasingly widespread, recent studies of the cost of medical care show that only a small minority of even the informed families in this country are in a position to avail themselves of the latest types of treatment. We are making progress with the simpler forms of preventive medicine, but there is still a serious lag between medical progress and the general availability of modern medical care.

There are a number of reasons why families find it difficult to provide adequate medical care for their members. In the first place, it is not easy to estimate in advance the expenditures which will be necessary. Most major expenditures for medical care come at unpredictable intervals. Then, too, not all families must make equal expenditures. Some families go for years without any serious illness, while others suffer from a whole series of accidents and ailments. In addition, every family finds that its expenditures vary from year to year. There are some small expenditures for medical advice and dental care and for drugs and sundries which can be counted upon every year. Other demands depend largely upon the place of the family in the family life cycle. The birth of children should involve adequate pre-natal and post-natal care and, whenever desirable, hospitalization at the time of delivery. Pre-school years involve expenditures for medical advice, even in the case of reasonably healthy children. In these years comes the expense of vaccination against smallpox and inoculation against diphtheria. When the oldest child starts going to school the family can count on the usual run of children's diseases.

Then in most families follows a period of better than average health. The children are subject to minor ailments such as indigestion, "colds" and sore throats, and influenza. The more daring may suffer from cuts and bruises and an occasional broken bone. But unless the family is unusually unfortunate it finds that doctor's bills drop for a time.

As the family grows older, the parents themselves begin to suffer from the degenerative diseases of middle and later life. The general breaking down of health that comes with age sooner or later in every family brings increasing expenditures for medical care.

While most families make provision for the recurring outlays for medical advice and drugs and medicines, and for regular visits to the dentist as part of their regular expenditures, they can pay for adequate medical and surgical care in case of serious illness only by greatly reducing the family's customary manner of living. Since many families escape these heavy expenditures, there is a tendency to set up such moderate reserves for hospitalization and medical care as can be established without encroaching on the family's manner of living; and in case an emergency situation actually arises, to compromise between a sacrifice of standards of medical care and of other elements in the family's living standard.

The result is, therefore, that most families set aside for health expenditures an amount adequate to cover ordinary demands, estimated on the basis of the family's usual health experience. They try to take into account any element in the situation which they know will bring unusual demands for expenditures for health. If the family is expecting a new baby, it sets aside in advance enough to cover the expenses of confinement. If the oldest of the children is to enter school in the fall, it plans on a run of children's diseases in the next year or two. If the parents use glasses and are approaching forty, they plan for an examination at the oculist's upon the first indication of eye strain and set aside funds for the purchase of bifocals. For the rest, the family tries to add a little to its savings each year and hopes that these savings will be sufficient to provide adequate and up-to-date medical and hospital care in case an emergency arises.

Health insurance. Recent studies indicate that ordinarily 40 per cent of the families pay 90 per cent of the cost of medical care. For the 40 per cent, medical care is a heavy burden. In many cases these families are unable to have as much care as they need, simply because they cannot afford to pay what high-grade service costs.

For the 60 per cent, on the other hand, medical care is comparatively a minor item. But the 60 per cent never know when they will find themselves among the 40 per cent who are in need of medical care. If they could pay for medical service when they do not need it, pay in advance in a way which would eliminate the cost of credit, they would be able to afford more adequate medical service when need arises.

Various schemes have been proposed for providing adequate medical service at moderate cost. They range from individual insurance schemes to comprehensive plans sometimes dubbed "state medicine." So far very little has been accomplished in this direction.

There are a number of reasons why it is difficult to apply the insurance principle to the provision of funds for medical care. On the basis of present information, it is very difficult to estimate accurately the cost of adequate medical care. It is possible to estimate the amounts now being spent, but present care in many cases is far from adequate. Many people are doing without needed medical and surgical attention because of lack of funds. Until the total cost of adequate care can be definitely determined, it is impossible to work out any actuarially sound basis for payments.

It is usually difficult to interest the healthy individual in insuring against a risk he does not feel in his own case to be very great. In order to spread the cost of medical care, it is necessary to have contributions by both the 40 per cent who need it most and the 60 per cent who need it least. But in order to make such insurance attractive to the healthy individual, even in order to make it worth while for any individual to take care of his health expenditures in advance, it will be necessary to work out a sliding scale of rates based upon the risk actually assumed in the individual case. This is a difficult problem at best, but is especially difficult in so personal a matter as medical care.

The application of the insurance principle is difficult because of the personal nature of the work involved. Personal considerations loom large in the selection of a physician. He must have definite ability. He must have a personal interest in his patients and must understand them thoroughly, and they must have confidence in him.

The individual is not sure that he will get adequate care from a company physician. He is afraid that the company will be inclined to slight him to save expense. And yet if he is allowed to select his own physician, there is always the risk of connivance between the doctor and the patient to draw unnecessarily upon the insurance fund.

At the present time many families use health and accident insurance to help them provide funds for emergency expenditures for health. But health and accident insurance as it is now written is *loss of income* insurance, not insurance of the cost of medical care. Health and accident insurance is ordinarily available only for individuals who are gainfully employed, and then in amounts not to exceed 80 per cent of their income. A health and accident policy will provide the family with some income during the period in which the head of the family is unable to earn, but only if his salary continues during his disability will the policy provide any money to apply on the cost of medical care. This insurance does not help at all in case of an accident to or the illness of any other member of the family. It is ordinarily available only in case of the disability of an individual who is contributing to the family's money income.

At present the need for a certain amount of medical care seems inevitable. Some illness is due to inherited weakness. More is due to living and working under conditions to which members of the family are not well adapted. Some is due to the necessity for long periods of hard work, involving great physical or mental strain, and some to too strenuous or unwise recreation. The nature of modern employment, the rush of modern traffic, and even the use of modern equipment in the home involve accident hazards.

It is important, therefore, that every family should make adequate provision for reasonable expenditures to safeguard the family's health. It would help a great deal if the family could secure at reasonable cost insurance which would provide medical care and hospitalization for any member of the family. Until it is possible to work out the problems involved in providing such care in return for small regular payments, each family must set up its own reserves for the care of the health of its members. In setting up these reserves, it must balance as well as it can the desirability of accumulating funds in advance against the common practice of securing medical care on credit and spreading at least part of the payments over a period of years.

Medical care always costs money. Even preventive medicine requires money outlay. The only way a family can save money in medical expenditures is by so ordering its whole life as to reduce both illness and accident hazards to a minimum. This involves care in the selection of food, clothing, shelter, recreation, and as far as possible, the community in which the family lives and the occupations in which its members work, with due regard to individual health limitations.

EDUCATION

The increasing importance of education in modern life. Education is becoming an increasingly important factor in modern life. Modern industrial conditions have necessitated the passage of child labor laws which have had the effect of making a four year high school course the minimum of formal education in many industrial centers. Today the college degree represents about the same amount of preparation above the minimum as did the high school or academy diploma of a generation or two generations ago. Today, if a family wishes to provide its children with more than the minimum of formal education, its plans must include college education for them.

Education is an important factor in the life of the modern family. For many families education is the best possible stop-gap between adolescence and employment. For many more, education, particularly a college education, is the only feasible means by which the parents can give their children a little better start in life than they had themselves. For all families, education is important if the individual is to understand the nature of the world in which he lives. Recent scientific developments have surrounded us with forces which we must understand if we are to use them well. Recent developments in transportation and communication have brought us into such close contact with the world about us, that we must understand the problems of our immediate neighborhood, the problems of our own state or nation, and in addition have at least some knowledge of the social and political and economic forces at work in the entire world.

Ordinarily we think of education as a formal process consisting of formal schooling and of private lessons. While we must realize the increasing importance of this sort of education, we must not overlook the importance of many of the everyday experiences of family life which are definitely a part of the educational process. Reading, sewing, cooking, drawing, gardening, running errands, helping about the house, helping in the care of the younger children, working with tools of one sort or another, and most types of play activities have definite educational value. Many of these educational by-products can be secured from the family's ordinary expenditures for other purposes, simply by taking thought, and without any considerable additional money outlay. On the financial side, therefore, most families are primarily concerned with the problems involved in providing funds for the children's formal education.

Characteristics of educational expenditures. Ordinarily these problems have a number of rather definite characteristics. The time at which expenditures must be made for the children's education is determined for the family by the age and the interests of the child. Educational opportunities must be provided for each child whenever he is ready for them; otherwise the opportunity is lost.

Most educational expenses come at the peak of the demands upon the family's income. Both high school and college education must be provided at the period in the life of the family when the cost of physical maintenance is at its maximum, and when social as well as physical elements in its living standard are most important.

Most families of moderate means make large use of public facilities for education. They ordinarily send their boys and girls through the local high school. In many cases they take advantage of the locally supported junior college, or of the state-supported colleges and university. In this way they pay for the children's education indirectly through taxes. They pay on the basis of their ability, not on the basis of their use of public educational facilities. Instead of paying for education in full at the time the children are in school, they spread their share of the cost of support of public education over the entire life of the family.

Most families find it desirable to supplement public school training with private instruction. They want to give their children some special training in music, art, dancing, language, or sports. If the child has special abilities which should be developed, private lessons are desirable. If the child does not adjust well to the public school situation, it may be desirable to send him to a private school or provide other special educational facilities.

Most families find it desirable to supplement the formal educational work of the private teacher and the public school with other opportunities in the home. There are many things which can be learned best in the home situation, and it is important to provide the necessary facilities and direction for these activities. The family should provide magazines, books, drawing materials, music of some sort, handicraft materials, and equipment for sports and games, all selected with due regard to educational as well as recreational values. Even the amount and administration of the children's allowances should be determined not entirely on the basis of the amount the family can spare for them to spend for whatever they please, but in part at least upon the basis of the educational values the handling of money provides.

How much to spend for education. The amount a family should spend for education depends upon the abilities, the interests, and the needs of the children, and, in part, upon the occupations they are planning to follow. It also depends to some degree upon the social group in which they expect to move. Each family must study the needs and the abilities of each of the children. Then it must take stock of the educational facilities which are available. It must consider the public school, library, college, and professionaι or trade school within the community. It must consider the additional values which the children can get if for at least part of their education they attend school away from home. Once the family decides what sort of an education will best provide for the needs of each child, it can employ social-use facilities in so far as they are available and suitable. Anything beyond this must be provided through family expenditures.

It is impossible to set down any amount which ought to be adequate to provide for high school or college or professional education for even any one member of a family. There are a number of estimates which can be secured from various schools and college. Most of these estimates give both maximum and minimum costs. Expenses vary a great deal in different schools and different sections of the country. The incidental expenses vary even more than do the actual expenses for tuition. Board and room varies with the taste and income of the student. Fraternity expenses vary considerably both from one school to another and among fraternities on the same campus. The amount it is necessary to spend for clothing depends a good deal upon the school and its location, and even more upon the group with which the individual student is associated. Ordinarily, if a college student moves in the same sort of group in college as at home, his incidental expenses will not be very much different from what they would if he were living at home. On the other hand, his board and room always cost more than food and lodging at home.

It is possible to spend almost any amount the family desires upon a college education. If there is a good college in the community, the college course will cost not much more than another few years of high school. Tuition fees are larger, books are more expensive. A little more money is needed for social affairs and extra-curricular activities. But that is about all the additional outlay required. On the other hand, if the family desires to secure for its children the additional advantages which come from attending college away from home, they can spend as much more as they desire. It would be conservative to estimate the variation in costs from $500 to $2,500 per year. In the early 1930's there were many college students who worked for their board and room, and went to college for as little as $250 a year.

Financing the children's education. *Public school education.*
Public school education is ordinarily paid for by taxes, either directly
by home owners, or indirectly by families who rent their homes, as
an element in rent. If the public schools are financed in part by state
or federal aid, the family makes its contribution either directly through
income or sales taxes, or indirectly through the prices it pays for
many of the commodities it buys.[1]

Most families find that even public school education involves some
expenditures in addition to the payment of taxes. In many school
districts the parents must provide school books and supplies. In most
school systems there is a chance to spend some money on athletic
events and school parties and other extra-curricular activities. Most
families feel that it is necessary to spend a little more on the children's
clothing when they are in school than when they are at home. In
many communities, there is some expense for transportation to and
from school. This is not an important item in smaller communities,
nor in most primary schools. But in the larger cities, car fare or
other transportation costs are an important item for many families
with boys and girls in junior and senior high schools. And in most
cases where it is necessary to provide the children with car fare, it is
also necessary to provide them with at least some money for their
noon lunch. While none of these items is large in itself, the total
for school expenses for a family with two or three children in school
is enough to demand definite attention.

Private lessons. Private lessons for music, art, dancing, language,
or other special training always require cash outlay. They must be
paid for in full as the training is secured. If a child has any special
ability to be developed, it is important to secure a well-qualified
teacher. And ordinarily the rapid progress under a good teacher is
little if any more expensive than slower progress under a lower priced
but less capable instructor.

Each family must decide for itself how much it can afford to pay
for private lessons of one sort and another for the children by balancing all the advantages to the individual child against the expense to
the family. It must remember that a certain amount of this sort of
expenditure is necessary if the family is to find out the abilities of the
children. Some exploratory opportunities are now provided in music
and art and physical education in group classes in the public schools.

[1] See Ch. VII, esp. pp. 166 ff.

Many of these are organized on a low tuition basis as extra-curricular activities.

Some expenditure for private lessons is justified simply on the basis of providing worth while leisure time activity for the child. For example, many children get enough benefit from the interest and the activity involved in taking music lessons for a few years to justify the expenditure. The experience in itself is a worth while form of recreation even though they do nothing with music in later years.

College education and professional training. There are comparatively few families with incomes generous enough to enable them to pay for a college education or for professional training for even one or two children without careful planning. There are several ways of defraying the cost of a college education. In a few cases the family may be able to provide funds out of current income. By planning they may be able either to anticipate or defer many of the family's regular expenditures, leaving a large part of the family's current income available for college expenses. This is ordinarily possible, however, only if the family income is generous, if the head of the family is at or near the peak of his earning power, if the family is small, and if there is not more than one person in college at a time.

A family may provide funds for college education from savings. Most families with small regular incomes, families of salaried workers, of the higher grade skilled wage earners, of small business men, and of professional men who reach the peak of their earning power only after they have reared their family, find it necessary to save for some years in advance if they are to have available the funds necessary for college expenses without reducing too greatly the family's living standards.

It is possible for the college student to finance part or all of his college expenses by working his own way. Many college students earn a part or all of their college expenses. They may limit their contribution to what they can earn during the summer vacation, or they may supplement their summer earnings with part-time work during the school year.

There is, of course, a point beyond which it is not wise for a student to go in earning his way through college. The time he spends working outside reduces the time available for study and college activities. He cannot get the same sort of an education that he would have if he should concentrate fully upon his college career.

On the other hand, few college students do put all the time they might upon the constructive side of college life. Many students who must work their way learn valuable lessons in the use of time, in concentrating upon the job in hand, and in weighing the relative values of various types of activities. These go far to offset the loss of other values which greater leisure might bring. It is important, however, for the student who is working his way to avoid loading up with too heavy a schedule. If he tries to crowd too much into his years in college, he may easily miss much that college should bring, and he must constantly be on his guard against overwork to an extent which will permanently injure his health. A student working his way may find it wise to spend five years doing the regular four years of college work.

Most families find it wise to use a combination of these ways of financing a college education. They plan their expenditures so as to provide as much as possible out of current income. They make the old car do another year or two, postpone major repairs and improvements to the home, and use up their inventories of household linens, china, and other supplies, postponing major replacements to the family's furniture or equipment. They divert the amount they ordinarily would spend for these purposes to expenditures for education.

In addition they draw upon the savings they have accumulated, planning carefully in order to make them last through the entire period involving expenditures for education. They divide these savings as equitably as they can, giving each child his or her share. Any money needed beyond this they expect the members of the family in college to earn for themselves.

If the college student is living at home, the family frequently makes its contribution to educational expenditures in the form of a living, while the individual student works enough to finance his direct expenditures for books and tuition, for fraternity dues, for amusement and for extra-curricular activities.

If the college student is living away from home, he may work for board and room, while the family makes its contribution in money for books and tuition and other college expenses.

The educational savings fund. There are a number of ways by which families provide funds through savings. Many families use funds accumulated as part of the family's regular savings program. They set aside from year to year as much as the family is able to spare from immediate current expenses. They assume that when the need arises the family will withdraw from this accumulation whatever is necessary to provide the children with a college education and necessary professional training.

Other families prefer to set up a special fund for education which they administer separately from the family's other accumulations. They invest their savings for educational expenses in a form which will be available at the time the children will be ready for college.

Still other families use endowment insurance policies to insure the provision of funds for the children's education. Some families use the standard endowment insurance policy, selecting one which will mature at the time when the children are ready to enter college. Others use a special educational insurance policy, which matures the year the child is ready to enter college. The ordinary endowment policy is usually paid in a lump sum. The special educational policy usually contains provisions for payment either in four annual instalments, or in monthly payments during the school year.

The use of insurance in connection with savings for the children's education has much to commend it. This plan provides funds for education even in case of the death of the chief wage earner. In such a case, the endowment policy becomes payable at once, and can be used for whatever expenses the family feels to be most important. The special educational policy ordinarily is available only for educational expenses. In some cases it pays a moderate amount during the college preparatory period. In other cases, it is not available until the boy or girl is ready to enter college.

Some families prefer to insure their educational fund, but to separate the savings and the insurance features. If a family is in a position to invest its current savings to good advantage, it may set aside a savings fund sufficient to provide for college education if the head of the family lives, and supplement this fund with a term-insurance policy which will provide the money needed to carry out the educational program in case the head of the family dies before the last child has finished college.

It is highly important that every family give careful thought to the provision of funds for educational expenditures. The sort of education a family is to provide for its children is an essential part of its standard of living. Under modern conditions, adequate education is fundamental in the life of every child. Since these expenditures come at the most expensive period in the life of the family, most families find that definite provision for the education of the children must be made some time in advance.   These expenditures are sufficiently important so that it is entirely justifiable to draw on the family's savings in order to meet them.   For educational expenditures, properly made, should and usually do represent simply a transfer from investments in stocks and bonds to an investment in the next generation.

RECREATION

The importance of recreation in modern life.   The pressure of modern life makes it imperative that every family work out for itself a well-balanced recreational program.   Many families think of recreation in terms of commercial amusement, sports, parlor games, or listening to the radio; many include reading for pleasure, and the use of the family car as a recreational facility.   Only a few, however, think of recreation in its broadest sense, as including all the great variety of activities in which people engage after working hours for the sake of the recreative values they provide.

In providing recreation for its members the family should consider all the recreational possibilities in its situation.   It should include the whole range of available commercial amusements, from grand opera, the theater, and the concert hall, through the movies, dancing, the baseball game, the bowling alley, and the amusement park.   It should canvass the various community facilities for recreation.   City parks provide golf courses for the parents and tennis courts for the older boys and girls; playgrounds provide teeters, sandboxes, and slides for the younger ones.   The public library and the museum provide opportunity for less strenuous types of recreation.   Civic and social organizations, such as the Y.M.C.A. and the Y.W.C.A., the Boy and the Girl Scouts, public school gymnasiums, factory baseball leagues, handicraft classes, all may play a part in the family's recreational program.

The family should pay special attention to the recreational activities which can be carried on in the home.   The radio brings a variety of music and entertainment into the home.   Symphony, grand opera, and vaudeville are all available at a turn of the dial.   Periodically there is a revival of what used to be known as parlor games, which provide desirable and inexpensive activity for both children and grown-ups.   Even the family living in a small apartment can find room to entertain a few friends informally at an evening of cards.

The family must work out its recreational program by selecting from the list of available facilities those which are best suited to the interests, tastes, and needs of the various members of the family. The recreational activities selected should complement the everyday tasks of each member of the family. For example, the housewife whose duties keep her closely at home needs recreational activities which will take her away from home at regular intervals. Her husband, on the other hand, may find the rest and relaxation he needs in the quiet of the home, where he can get away from the noise and hurry of the world in which he must work. The children need a chance for vigorous activity after a day in school. Then, in the evening, they need some quiet relaxation, with music or games or a book.

In the rush and hurry of modern life it is especially important to give sufficient place to the quieter types of recreational activity, in which an individual can engage by himself. Reading for pleasure has definite recreational value. Solitaire and jig-saw puzzles and repetitive activities like knitting and tatting require just enough concentration to take the mind off the day's problems. The constantly repeated activity they involve serves as an outlet for pent-up nervous energy.

In working out the family's recreational program it is important not to overlook any desirable form of recreation. For rest, relaxation, diversion, and participative activity, both physical and mental, all are essential to the maintenance of the physical and mental health of all the members of the family.

The family's recreational standards. Every family should have some consciously thought out standards to guide it in working out its recreational program. These recreational standards should be recognized as an essential part of the family's standard of living. They include not only the type of recreation in which the family is to engage, but also the ways by which it is to be provided.

In working out its recreational program the family must decide the extent to which it should follow the latest recreational fads. All of these fads provide the essential element of novelty. Some of them are very good diversion. It must decide whether to play golf for the sake of the game, or for the sake of membership in an exclusive country club; whether it will get more pleasure from two shows viewed from inexpensive seats or from one seen from the dress circle. Every family must decide, largely on the basis of the personal preference of the members of the family, whether it will get more pleasure from a number of trips to the neighborhood movies, or from perhaps half as many trips to concert or theater.

In most cases the family will get more actual recreation if it selects its recreational activities not on the basis of the latest fad, not on the basis of pecuniary emulation, but upon the basis of personal preference and intrinsic recreational values. This does not mean that its recreation will always be "high-brow." On the contrary, while there is a place for the more intellectual types of recreational activity, there is also a large place for activities which involve for the most part pure diversion.

Financing the family's recreation program. Unlike medical care and formal education, recreation does not necessarily involve the expenditure of large sums of money. Recreation lends itself well to production for use at home. It is entirely possible to provide a variety of recreational activities with a minimum of expenditure.

On the other hand, recreation is sufficiently important to justify the careful expenditure of whatever funds the family has available for it. Here, as everywhere else, it is important for the family to get its money's worth, to spend for the things which will give it the most recreational value for the money.

Most families find it worth while to spend something for commercial amusement. Many families make plans for regular expenditures for vacation and week-end trips in the family car. But not all families realize the recreational values which can come from spending money for materials and equipment with which to have a good time at home. They do, of course, plan to buy some toys for the children, but they are not always familiar with the recreational possibilities of various types of materials and equipment for older boys and and girls and for the adults. By spending a comparatively small amount for carefully selected equipment a family can make its home into a very satisfactory recreation center for all the members of the family and for their friends. If a little more money is available, an attractive recreation room can be made in the basement. If there is plenty of room in the basement, or a heated garage is available, a home workshop can be arranged which not only will provide a place for worth while recreational activity, but which can be made to pay its way in by-products. What is fun for father and the boys may result in toys for the younger children. And the same equipment which is bought primarily for its recreational value can frequently be used in making repairs about the house.

In selecting recreational equipment, the family must consider first of all the suitability of the equipment for the individuals who are to use it. It must consider durability. If money cost is an important consideration, it must select as far as possible equipment which can be put to a variety of uses. It is well in this connection to consider not only the recreational values which the equipment affords, but any other practical by-products which may come from use of the equipment.

In purchasing equipment it is important to supplement commercial and community recreational facilities. A family having access to a good public library may decide to spend but little upon books and magazines. A family living in an isolated rural community may find that the gradual accumulation of a library of good books will give them more satisfaction per dollar of expenditure than any other use they can make of their money.

In selecting equipment it is important to provide both for active participation and for passive enjoyment. A family interested in music should provide instruments and a library of music which will make it possible for the members of the family to participate actively in musical expression. At the same time they must not neglect the radio and the phonograph and some expenditures for concerts which give an opportunity to develop and deepen their appreciation of good music.

When it is necessary to reduce expenses most families think first of cutting down expenditures for recreation. But they must be careful not to eliminate or even greatly reduce recreational opportunities. Even though it may be necessary to cut down severely on recreation expenditures during periods of depression, when income is inadequate, when the family is conscious of financial and other sorts of mental strain, it is especially important to continue provision for recreation.

If it is necessary to economize on recreational expenditures, the family will find that it can secure these economies without reducing the opportunities for recreation, if it changes somewhat the nature of its recreational program. It can economize by reducing its expenditures for the more evanescent types of commercial amusement, and spending what funds it has available for the sort of equipment which can be used over and over again by the family. Properly selected equipment will provide for a variety of activities. A deck of cards, or a checker-board and a box of checkers or a set of chess men will provide many evenings of recreation for the adults. A few games from the five-and-ten-cent store will provide hours of fun for the younger children.

If the family has already accumulated a considerable amount of equipment, it can plan to make more extensive use of this equipment. And it can frequently supplement its own equipment by exchanging with friends. During the bank holiday in 1933, no one had very much money to spend for jig-saw puzzles. And yet many people found that these very puzzles were an important factor in keeping their minds off their troubles, and keeping them mentally on an even keel. In many communities, each family bought one or two puzzles, put them together once or twice, and then exchanged with their friends. The same thing can be done with books, phonograph records, and games.

When it is necessary to cut down expenditures for recreation the family should plan to make more extensive use of the recreational facilities the community affords. It can substitute books from the library for trips to the movies. It can substitute a walk in the park for a ride in the car. It can if necessary withdraw from the country club and play golf on the municipal golf course. It can substitute a camping trip in state and national parks for a more expensive vacation in a resort hotel.

When it is necessary to economize on expenditures for recreation, the important thing is to plan to take advantage of all the inexpensive opportunities for recreation in the family situation. Ideas are more important than money. A little money helps, of course, but it is possible to provide a variety of types of recreational activity with a very small expenditure of money, if it is supplemented by a generous expenditure of thought.

A picnic out on the hills at the edge of town, or up in the orchard, costs no more than a meal served at home on the dining room table. A well-selected radio program which will have in it something of interest for every member of the family costs no more in money than the too frequent hit-or-miss listening to whatever happens to be coming in on the nearest and loudest station on the air. An evening spent with friends sitting round the fire talking about what is going on in the world costs very little, even if the hostess serves inexpensive refreshments toward the end of the evening. A little time spent showing the small boy how to build some new kinds of buildings with his set of blocks or showing the small girl a new way to make dresses for her paper doll takes no money. And yet an occasional suggestion of new ways to use his present play equipment will start a boy on a whole new series of enterprises which will occupy him for days at a time. It will give the girl new ideas which she can work out over and over again in a variety of ways.

The working out of the family's recreational program provides one of the best possible examples of the importance of taking thought about the family's spending problems. Especially in connection with recreational activities is it true that ideas are more important than money in providing every member of the family with what he enjoys and needs.

QUESTIONS

HEALTH

1. Compare the expenditures for health made by a number of families of your acquaintance. How do you account for the variation in both the amount and the type of outlays they involve?
2. Compare the extent to which these families practice preventive medicine.
3. What public health facilities are available to the families in your community? What types of families does each of these facilities serve? Along what lines should the health services in your community be extended? How should the costs of these services be defrayed?
4. Investigate and report upon the relative desirability of various plans providing for group payments for medical care. From the point of view of the family with a moderate income, what should such plans include?

EDUCATION

1. List the educational facilities, both public and private, which are available in your community. To what extent do families of your acquaintance avail themselves of each of these facilities?
2. Estimate as closely as you can the costs involved in providing a grade and high school education for a boy or girl in your community. Include both payments by parents and costs borne by the public through taxation. What portion of the tax costs will be paid by the family during the years in which the child is in school?
3. Under what circumstances do you believe that a family should provide private instruction in the various arts for members of its family? How much would such instruction cost in your community?
4. In what ways are families of your classmates financing their college education? If your family were to start over, in what ways could they lessen

the burden of educational expense by using other methods of financing your education?

5. What facilities for "adult education" does your community afford? To what extent do families of your acquaintance avail themselves of these facilities? What benefits do they derive? Are these benefits worth the cost?

6. A young couple of your acquaintance have two children, three and five years old. Work out for them a detailed plan for financing the children's education.

RECREATION

1. Work out a detailed description of the leisure time activities of a family of your acquaintance. Include an analysis of the time and money spent for each type of activity. Analyze the program with regard to the personal preferences of the members of the family. Make a supplementary list of recreational activities in which this family might engage. Include an estimate of the time, equipment, and money each of the supplementary activities requires. What improvements, if any, could you suggest in their recreation program?

2. Make a list of inexpensive recreational activities centering in the home, together with an inventory of the equipment and supplies each activity requires. How much of this equipment must be purchased? How much can be homemade?

3. How many families of your acquaintance engage in reading as a recreational activity? What do they read? How many magazines do they buy regularly? How many books do they buy? Borrow from public library or commercial circulating libraries? How much time do they spend in recreational reading?

4. Make a list of the books, toys, and other play equipment provided for children of various ages in families of your acquaintance. Estimate the cost of this play equipment. How much is purchased by the family? How much is given to the children by friends and relatives outside the home?

5. In what sports or other outdoor recreational activities do the members of your family engage? Compare the cost of these various activities. Work out a program which will provide adequately for the needs of each member of your family for active recreation.

6. Describe the ways in which families of your acquaintance use the family automobile for recreational activities. How much do these uses add to the cost of operating the family car?

7. Plan a week's radio programs which will allow each member of your family to listen to the programs he likes best, with a minimum of interference with the activities of other members of the family.

REFERENCES

Andrews, B. R., *Economics of the Household*, Revised Edition. The Macmillan Co., New York, 1935.

Ch. XXI, "Family Health, Sickness, and Death Costs," pp. 536-551, gives a careful analysis of the burden of providing for family health needs, with special attention to voluntary group payment plans and preventive public health activities. Ch. XX, "Personal Advancement Expenditures," pp. 517 ff., contains a discussion of educational expenditures as well as expenditures for other leisure time activities.

Nystrom, P. H., *Economic Principles of Consumption*. The Ronald Press Co., New York, 1929.

Ch. XVII, pp. 419-436, presents an analysis of the problems involved in securing adequate provision for health needs, especially among families of low and moderate income. Ch. XVIII, pp. 437-483, is an analysis of the various leisure time activities now available, and a consideration of the ways in which the amount of leisure may be increased and the quality of enjoyment may be improved.

Recent Social Trends in the United States. McGraw-Hill Book Co., Inc., New York, 1933.

(a) Moore, Harry H., "Health and Medical Practice," Ch. XXI, pp. 1061-1113. A description of the various facilities now available for care of health and an analysis of present needs. For a more detailed discussion of problems involved in adequate care of the family's health, see the complete report of the Committee on the Cost of Medical Care, many sections of which are referred to in the footnotes in this reference.

(b) Judd, Charles H., "Education," Ch. VII, pp. 325-381. A discussion of recent developments in public education. Interesting background material, showing educational opportunities available to American families.

(c) Steiner, J. F., "Recreation and Leisure Time Activities," Ch. XVIII, pp. 912-957. Keppel, Frederick P., "The Arts in Social Life," Ch. XIX, pp. 958-1008. A description of recent developments in family, commercial, and community recreational facilities.

(d) See also Lynd, Robert S., "The People as Consumers," Ch. XVII, pp. 857-911.

PART IV
THE STRATEGY OF FAMILY FINANCE

CHAPTER XIV

FAMILY BUDGETING IN THEORY
AND PRACTICE

The need for a comprehensive spending plan. Planning
is required whenever it is necessary to co-ordinate spending by a
number of individuals for a variety of items all of which must contribute to the accomplishment of a common purpose. It is not enough
to work out as a separate problem the best way to satisfy each one
of the family's long list of wants. These wants vary in intensity, in
importance, in the amount of money and time and effort necessary
for their satisfaction. Some of them cannot be satisfied until others
have been provided for. Many can be satisfied only through the
co-ordinated activities of a number of individuals. It is absolutely
essential that the family work out all of its specific spending problems
as part of a carefully integrated spending plan. A family budget is
such a spending plan.

Actual vs. theoretical budgets. It is important at the outset
to get clearly in mind the distinction between actual and theoretical
budgets. Actual budgets are never exactly alike. No two families
need exactly the same spending plans. Even for the same family, no
two years in the life of the family call for exactly the same budget.

Theoretical budgets are more or less arbitrarily determined budgets
designed to represent typical or desirable spending plans for groups of
families living on given social and economic levels. There are a number of types of theoretical budgets, worked out for a number of purposes, and expressed in a variety of terms. There are average
budgets and typical budgets, standard budgets and ideal budgets.
There are budgets expressed in terms of dollars, budgets expressed in
terms of percentages of family income, and budgets expressed in
terms of the quantity and cost of a long list of items which a family
is assumed to buy.

Average budgets and typical budgets are devices for describing,
analyzing, and comparing the expenditure patterns of families in
given economic and social groups. Average budgets are worked out

by averaging the actual expenditures of a group of families for various commodities and services. Typical budgets are statements of what the author of the budget considers to be typical expenditures for the families in the group. Frequently they are based upon the study of a large number of actual family budgets, but they usually represent the mode rather than either the median or the arithmetical average of all expenditures. The average and the median expenditures give a composite photograph of the expenditures of a group of families. The typical budget gives an artist's conception of the essential elements in their expenditure pattern.

A standard budget is an average or typical budget designed to represent the spending plan of the average family in a given social or economic group. It is intended to be used as a guide in working out actual budgets for families living under similar though hardly ever identical conditions. An ideal budget represents the author's idea of the best possible way to spend a given amount of money under an assumed situation. Usually it assumes more income than most families in similar situations have available; it assumes ideal rather than actual market situations, and greater knowledge and foresight and intelligence than are available for any actual family.

A quantity and cost budget is a convenient device for estimating the cost of providing a family with a given list of commodities and services under local market conditions. The list of commodities included in such a budget depends upon the purpose for which the budget is to be used. If it is to be used to measure more accurately than do index numbers the cost of living in a given community, it will include a list of items of expenditure typical of that community. If it is intended to show the need for higher wages for a given group of workers, it will include a complete list of the items for which the families of workers in that group can reasonably expect to spend their money.

By pricing the items in quantity and cost budgets from time to time, it is possible to get a fairly adequate idea of changes in living costs. But when these budgets are designed to indicate actual living costs, they are open to the criticism that they usually include less than families actually enjoy, and cost more than families actually spend. This is inevitable, for quantity and cost budgets assume the purchase of everything the family has to use. There is no way for these budgets to make adequate allowance for savings by better than average buying, or for home production activities.

Some misconceptions of the budget. Because they fail to distinguish between actual and theoretical budgets, for many people the term "budget" has a number of unfortunate connotations. They think of some arbitrarily determined budget they have seen, which obviously does not fit their situation. Or they think of some "ideal" spending plan, which is far beyond their reach. Or they think of some "budget book" recommended to them as a help in planning their expenditures which turned out to be a set of directions for keeping a complicated and tiresome set of household accounts. In much of the literature on budgeting there has been too much emphasis upon writing down round numbers in advance, too much emphasis upon entering the details of expenditures after they have been made, and not enough emphasis upon working out in advance a carefully considered and realistic spending plan.

There are many families that live according to a budget, though they never put pencil to paper from one year's end till the next. The members of the family talk over their spending problems occasionally. They decide upon what they can afford and what they cannot. They decide how much they can spend for their various needs and wants, and they spend accordingly. Their method works very well if the group is small, if there is perfect understanding between the individuals, if their planning is based upon long experience, and if spending according to the family planning is firmly grounded as a habit with each member of the group.

What a family budget is and what it is not. Because there are current so many misconceptions about budgets, every family before it begins to work out its own budget must have clearly in mind what a budget is and what it is not. A family budget is not a classified system of household accounts. It is not an arbitrary division of each month's income. It is not a hard-and-fast list of predetermined expenditures, an ironclad arrangement allowing for no variation or flexibility in the use of income. The family budget is a spending plan. It is a tentative estimate of the family's income and of the family's expenditures for a realistic list of items. It is a guide to intelligent spending.

A budget will not spend the family's income for it. It will not help the family to get more than a dollar's worth in return for each dollar it budgets. A family budget will help the family to spend its money for the things it wants most. It will help the family to get a dollar's worth for each dollar it spends.

Budget headings. In making a budget it is usually customary to classify expenditures under a number of budget headings. There are several reasons for this practice. A system of classification helps to divide a long list of heterogeneous and apparently unrelated items of expenditure into workable units. A system of classification breaks the problem up into a series of smaller problems. Within the limits of these smaller problems it is possible to work out the details of expenditure with sufficient care to be sure that no important item is overlooked. And finally, the process of classification itself into major and minor items, into headings and sub-headings, leads to consideration of the relative merits of the various items and makes it easier to determine the proper proportion of expenditure to be devoted to each division and to each item within each division in the finished budget.

Budget headings, then, are simply a convenient means of grouping the long and varied list of items to be included in the budget so that the family may be sure that it has taken care of all the probable demands upon its income. There is nothing sacred about any of them. There is no one best system of classification. Each family must work out for itself the sort of classification which will fit its own spending problems, and will best enable it to see all its expenditures in their proper relationship to each other.

There are some groups of items, such as food, clothing, and shelter, for which every family spends its money. These general headings appear in all standard classifications. A family can well make use of a few of these general headings in order to be able to compare its proposed expenditures with the expenditures of similar families in larger groups.

The Bureau of Labor Statistics of the Department of Labor computes index numbers for food, clothing, shelter, fuel and light, furniture and furnishings, and miscellaneous expenditures. If the family plans to use these figures in estimating probable changes in its living costs, it should use a set of budget headings from which totals can easily be taken to compare with the Department of Labor indexes. Miss Hoyt's classification of consumer outlays, given in the table on page 177, indicates the sort of divisions used in more detailed discussions of budgeting. The authors of "budget books" offered by various organizations for the use of their clientele have devised a great variety of budget headings. It is interesting to compare a number of these budget books to see the extent to which the nature of the organization influences the type of classification used and the relative emphasis which is placed upon different items of expenditure.

The following table shows a long list of items which might be included as budget headings and sub-headings. No one family will need to use all these headings. The list is intended to suggest a great variety of possible items which a family may wish to include in working out its own set of budget headings. The individual family may select from this list the items which fit its needs.

SUGGESTIONS FOR BUDGET HEADINGS

Food
- Groceries
- Meats
- Baked goods
- Fresh fruits and vegetables
- Butter
- Eggs
- Milk
- Meals purchased outside home

Clothing
- Wraps
- Outergarments
- Undergarments
- Hosiery
- Shoes
- Hats
- Accessories
  - *or*
- Husband
- Wife
- Each child

Housing
- Charges on rented home:
  - Rent
  - Repairs paid by tenant
  - Other expenses paid by tenant

Rent for garage
Charges on owned home:
- Payments on principal
- Interest charges
- Taxes
- Special assessments
- Insurance
- Repairs
- Depreciation allowance

House Operation
- Public utilities:
  - Water
  - Gas
  - Electricity
- Fuel:
  - Coal
  - Wood
  - Fuel oil
  - Kerosene
  - Gasoline
- Ice
- Telephone and telegraph:
  - Phone rental
  - Extension phones
  - Toll charges
  - Telegrams

House Operation (Cont.)

Garbage removal

Service:

  Resident service

  Non-resident service:

    Regular

    Occasional

Supplies:

  House-cleaning supplies

  Stationery and postage

Furniture, furnishings, and equipment

Laundry service:

  Laundry

  Dry cleaning

Transportation

Automobile:

  Initial expense

  Upkeep and operating expenses

  Insurance

  Allowance for depreciation

Carfare:

  Car fare

  Bus fare

  Taxi fare

  Railroad fare

Personal Expenditures

Personal supplies

Tobacco

Tonsorial

Allowances

Health

Fees for physician

Fees for dentist

Fees for specialists

Drugs on prescription

Eyeglasses

Hospital expense

Nursing

Education

School expenses:

  Tuition

  Books

  School supplies

  Car fare to school and return

Periodicals

Daily papers

Books

Private lessons

Recreation

Amusements for the family

Entertainment of others

Children's toys and play equipment

Vacation expense

Organization Memberships

Church

Professional organizations

Labor unions

Fraternal orders

Social clubs

Savings, Investments, and Insurance

Real estate

Stocks and bonds

Building and loan association

Savings account

Life insurance

Health and accident insurance

Insurance on household goods

Other insurance

Interest on borrowed funds

Payments on principal of loans

Expenditure for Others

Charity

Dependents outside home

Gifts

Occasional

In working out the list of budget headings, it is important to make the list of items reflect the family's actual expenditures. Especially in working out the details of expenditures under each of the main headings, it is well to put in the actual items for which a family spends its money. While it may be worth while, in planning the details of food expenditures, to make separate estimates of the amount to be spent for milk, meat, cereals, fruits, vegetables, and fats, in planning the budget it is more helpful to classify expenditures on the basis of the place where they are made. Under food, for example, might be the headings, grocery, meat market, milkman, bakery, purchases at door, eggs from the country, and so on. Under clothing there may be sub-headings for each member of the family, or for each type of clothing to be purchased. Under shelter, if the family owns its own home, there should be items for taxes, repairs, and improvements. If the family is buying its home there should be, either under shelter or under savings, provision for the payments of principal and interest. If the family is renting a heated, lighted, and furnished apartment, it will not need any item for fuel or public utilities. The single item for rent will include all that.

The important point is that when a family gets through working out the list of items included in its system of budget headings, the list should not sound like a statistical cost of living study, or like someone's budget book, but rather should picture the everyday expenditures of a wide-awake and up-to-date American family. At the same time, if the job is properly done, it will be possible to use the totals under the general headings for purposes of comparison with standard budget studies, and it will be possible to use the Department of Labor Cost of Living Index as a guide in working out estimates involving probable price changes.

Two ways to build a budget: The "live-within-your-income" method. When budgeting is mentioned, most people think of the traditional "live-within-your-income" method. In working out a budget by this method the procedure is as follows: First, estimate the family's income for the coming year. Second, divide this income roughly among the principal budget headings. Third, spread the money assigned to each of the principal divisions of the budget over as many items as it will cover. Fourth, in case the appropriation for any budget division is obviously inadequate to take care of the essential items within that division, find another heading from which some funds may be diverted.

This method works fairly well for beginners. It is valuable for a family that has very little idea of what a given income will do in providing for a family's varied needs. It is particularly worth while for the newly established family that is engaged in working out the standard by which it is to live for some years to come. For this method emphasizes the limits within which the family must confine its expenditures. It definitely guards against setting a standard higher than the family will be able to maintain.

But this budget is negative rather than positive in its operation. It is chiefly concerned with "Thou shalt nots." There is nothing about it which looks positively to the future. The family with a well-established standard, that has been operating for some years on an unwritten budget, instinctively avoids this type of spending plan.

Two ways to build a budget: The "make-life-what-I-would-like-it" method. The family with a positive outlook on life, with well-established standards, with definite long-time aims, prefers the more positive and more realistic "make-life-what-I-would-like-it" method of working out a spending plan. The outstanding characteristic of this method is that it allows a family to begin as all wide-awake American families begin, by considering what it wants to do. The procedure is as follows:

First, list the actual items for which the family is to spend its money. Put under each principal budget heading, in considerable detail, a long list of actual items of expenditure. Under clothing, for example, list the actual garments to be bought for each member of the family. List them not as "father, so much," "mother, so much," "son, so much," and "daughter, so much," but as "a pair of everyday shoes for father," "a pair of high-tops for son," "some dancing slippers for daughter," "three house dresses for mother," "a suit of clothes and six shirts for father," and so on. Instead of a lump sum in the budget for shelter, list rent, or, if the home is owned, taxes, redecoration of two bedrooms, a new cupboard in the kitchen, and an allowance for the annual overhauling of the heating plant.

In making out this list of proposed expenditures, deliberately include more items than can possibly be provided with the income available in the period under consideration. This should be done for several reasons. It helps the family to get away from too great dependence upon habit in planning its expenditures. It brings constant pressure for the reduction of unnecessary costs, by suggesting desirable alternatives. It keeps constantly before the family the importance of intelligent choice when living in a world so full of worth while things to buy and have and do.

Second, arrange the items under each budget heading in the order of their relative importance. Fundamental necessities, such as a minimum of food, clothing, and shelter, and fixed charges, such as rent, payments on instalment purchases, insurance premiums, club dues, and church pledges, come at the head of the lists in which they occur. But not all items of food, not all articles of clothing, not all obligations to social, civic, and charitable organizations are equally important. An adequate amount of food is absolutely essential. Elaborate Sunday dinners or after-the-theater suppers are not. Certain minimum payments must be made for shelter, for heat, light, repairs, and the like. Expenditures for other highly desirable but less important items in each of these groups can be made or not as necessity demands. The completed list under each budget heading should be so arranged that if the family begins at the top and goes down the line as far as its income will permit, it will be spending, in so far as that group is concerned, for the most important of its wants.

Third, estimate as accurately as possible the probable cost of each item in the classified list. Fixed charges are determined definitely in advance. Many other expenditures vary only a little from year to year, and so are easy to estimate. If prices are rising, initial estimates should be made generous enough to take care of probable price increases. There are a few highly important items for which it is very difficult to estimate accurately in advance, like medical services, drugs, hospital and nursing care, under health; emergency repairs, under shelter; replacements of children's caps and gloves and rubbers, under clothing; and allowances for entertaining guests who drop in unexpectedly from out-of-town, under recreation. The family must be guided by past experience in deciding upon the amount which should be kept in reserve for each of these unforeseeable expenditures.

It simplifies the problem of final selection a good deal if instead of listing the allowances for all these expenditures in one column they are listed in some one of three columns as given in the form on page 348. In column 1, the family puts the amounts which must be spent if the family is to maintain for the next budget period the same scale of living to which it has been accustomed in the past. This list of estimates naturally will include all the fixed charges which the family must meet. In the second column the family puts all estimated allowances for expenditures which represent improvement in the family's situation. Some of these will be additional allowances for items for which some provision has already been made in column 1. Some will represent allowances for specific expenditures, a new piece of furniture, or some new gadget for the kitchen, some nice but unnecessary addition to the wardrobe, an allowance for a vacation trip, or even provision for additional savings or additional life insurance should the funds be available. In the third column the family puts estimates for unforeseen and unpredictable expenditures. These items may be much larger than the family's expected outlays. But they represent the amounts that the family must be able to raise if the need should arise. In working out the completed budget, a single item for contingent reserves may be set up against the allowances in column 3. This will not need to be as large as the total of all these estimates, because while all of these things may happen, and while some of them are sure to happen, it is only rarely that all, or even many, of these emergencies do happen in any one year. This item is not intended to take care of all possible emergencies, but to provide sufficient leeway in the budget to meet any unforeseen demands which are important enough to take precedence over most other items in the budget.

SUGGESTED FORM FOR ESTIMATING EXPENDITURES

Item	Allowances for Essentials and Fixed Charges	Allowances for Improvement in Living Levels	Reserves for Contingent Expenses
Budget Heading Item Item Item Item Item Budget Heading Item Item Item Item Item	Put here allowances for all items necessary to maintain family's present standard of living, including allowances for all fixed charges.	Put here allowances for other worth while expenditures, indicating the order of their importance.	Put here adequate allowances for the unforeseen and unforeseeable expenses which may be necessary.

Fourth, estimate the amount of money income which will be available in the period under consideration. Income from some sources is easy to estimate. If the chief wage earner is employed in an industry in which employment is regular, if his position is reasonably secure, his wages or salary can be definitely counted upon. Interest on sound bonds can be depended upon. Rents from long-term leases to well-established business concerns come in regularly year after year. There are even a few common and preferred stocks in companies with regular earnings and a long unbroken dividend record that, for at least a year in advance, can be counted upon to pay dividends regularly.

Other income, however, is not so easy to estimate. If the chief wage earner is employed in an industry in which operations are irregular, and wage rates are uncertain, if he depends for any considerable portion of his income upon commissions or bonuses, it is possible to estimate his income only roughly, making allowances for probable variations from yearly averages on the basis of current business prospects. The same is true of business and professional incomes of all kinds, and of most incomes from rents and from dividends.

In some cases it is difficult to separate family income and business income. This is the case with farm income, with income from a family business, with income from boarders and lodgers, and in some cases with supplementary income from rented properties. If it is possible to separate business and family income, it is usually better to handle by themselves the expenses incidental to securing the income and to count as part of the family income only such net income from the business or investments as is available for family expenditure.

For example, it is much more businesslike for the family with income from rented property to keep separate account of taxes and repairs and other expenses incidental to the maintenance of that property, paying them out of the rent which it receives, and turning over to the family only the net income from the property.

But it is not always possible to do this. It is impossible for a family with a single boarder or lodger to separate the extra expense involved from the general family expenditures. There is no practical way for a family living in one apartment of a two-apartment building and renting the other with heat and utilities furnished to separate from the family's expenditures that part of the expenses for fuel, for water, for light, for repairs, and for taxes which is involved in securing the family's rental income. All these expenditures must be met out of family funds, from the general family income. And since they are incidental to securing a considerable part of this income, they must take precedence over many ordinary items of family expenditure. It is important, therefore, in all cases in which it is impossible to separate business and family income, to include in the family budget adequate provision for all expenses which are involved in securing this income. In comparing family expenditures with the expenditures of other families, only the expenditures made by the family for itself, and only the income actually available for family use, should be considered.

Just as it helps to classify expenditures in the order of their relative importance, so too it helps to classify income on the basis of its certainty, putting at the head of the list all income which can be definitely counted upon, putting next the additional income which the family will probably receive, and putting last the income which the family may possibly receive, but upon which it cannot place any dependence.

If this is done, it will be possible to work out a spending plan in which minimum essentials and fixed charges and other items of major importance are taken care of out of assured and probable income, and in which the less important items are set up in the order of their relative importance to be purchased with such other income as may become available.

Some families have found that the problem of estimating income is simplified by the use of a three-column form which classifies income as assured, probable, or uncertain, as given below:

SUGGESTED FORM FOR ESTIMATE OF EXPECTED INCOME

Source	Assured	Probable	Uncertain
Salary or wages Earned by: (List employed members.) Commissions or bonuses Interest on bonds and mortgages (List bonds and mortgages.) Rent from real estate (List properties.) Dividends on preferred stocks (List stocks.) Dividends on common stocks (List stocks.) Miscellaneous income	Put here income which you are reasonably sure you can count on.	Put here income you will probably get, but which may be affected adversely by uncertain business conditions.	Put here income which might materialize, but which probably will not.

Fifth, total all the estimates for minimum essentials, and fixed charges, and for the more important items under each budget heading, and compare the total of estimated expenditures with the estimate of assured and probable family income. If the job of estimating has been well done and if there is adequate allowance in the preliminary estimates for unforeseen as well as for foreseen expenditures, in all probability the total of proposed expenditures will be considerably larger than the available income. This is as it should be. For it brings pressure to bear to secure all reasonable economies. It emphasizes the importance of eliminating all waste, and of getting full value in want-satisfying goods and services for every dollar expended.

Sixth, balance the budget. Bring expenditures into line with income. This should be done constructively, so that every possible worth while expenditure will be provided for in the completed budget.

There are two ways to go about balancing a budget. The first is to increase the family's money income. For families in the lower income groups particularly, even a small increase in money income is sufficient to make possible a definite increase in the family's standard of living. A few dollars a week from part-time employment, from a roomer, or even from a paper route, will greatly increase the possibilities for constructive economy. It is worth while, therefore, for every family to consider carefully all possible expedients for increasing its money income.

But this method of balancing the budget has some disadvantages. Too much emphasis upon increasing the number of dollars to be handled sometimes removes the emphasis from satisfying wants. The family is interested primarily in want-satisfying commodities and services, and only incidentally in the amount of its money income.

The second method of balancing a budget is to reduce expenditures until they are in line with expected income. The common method is simply to eliminate one or more of the least important items under each of the principal budget headings. The constructive way to balance a budget, however, is to eliminate whole items only as a last resort, and to begin reducing expenditures by reducing the cost of the individual items.

This can be done in a number of ways. The family should check over its buying practices to discover new ways of buying to better advantage. It should consider the possibility of finding less expensive articles than it had originally intended, which will do reasonably well for the purpose it has in mind. It should consider the reductions in cost to be effected by the purchase of materials and the production of finished articles in the home, and should canvass the possibilities of performing for itself services which cost money if purchased in the market. It should plan to use to the best possible advantage the family's existing stock of capital goods. It should consider ways of making more extensive use of the various facilities and services provided by the community.

Constructive balancing of a budget involves a great deal of attention to detail. It is necessary to scrutinize every item in the budget to see if it is essential, and to see if there is some equally satisfactory way of providing it at a lower cost. It is helpful to estimate the cost of doing a great many of the things the budget calls for in a variety of ways. It is necessary to consider possible economies even in items which must be included in the budget regardless of cost, in order that savings on essentials may free some funds for other items which are not on the essential list.

In studying comparative costs, it is important to consider both the present savings from lower current outlay, and the long-time savings to be secured from lower cost. If by spending one-third more for a winter coat it is possible to buy a garment which will last two years instead of one, the cost of the coat over a two-year period will be one-third less. Or again, the purchase of an electric refrigerator involves the immediate current outlay of a couple of hundred dollars. On the other hand, over a ten-year period, the lower operating expense of the electric unit may considerably reduce the cost of the family's refrigeration.

In making out the family budget it is necessary to decide upon the relative importance of low current outlays and low long-time costs. Few families are able to make the current outlay necessary to secure everything they need in the way which will give them the lowest long-time costs. They must decide which items involve large enough long-time economies to justify a heavy immediate investment, and which items they should buy on the basis of low current outlay.

It is impossible to lay down definite rules for a family to follow in balancing its budget. Every family must use its own ingenuity to devise methods which in its own case will enable its members to do most nearly what they want to do. Whether the family will find it easier to bring the budget into balance by increasing the family income or by reducing its expenditures will depend to a large extent upon the opportunities for employment and the earning power of the members of the family. If it is easy for members of the family to obtain remunerative employment, if their earning power is greater when they are working for others than when they are working for themselves, they will more easily bring the budget into balance by working to increase the money income.

If, however, either earning power or opportunities for employment are limited, the family will be able to bring the budget into balance more easily by spending time in various ways making the most of the family's present income. If, for example, a housewife can save $5 on the cost of a dress by buying materials and making it for herself at home, she is just as truly adding $5 to the family's income as if she added $5 in money earned by working outside the home.

Constructive economy of all sorts takes time. In balancing its budget, the family must keep in mind not only the limits to its money income, but the limits to the time available for practicing the economies for which it plans. No family can expect to practice every possible economy. It must plan to practice those economies which in its own case will give it the greatest savings possible with the time at its disposal.

Seventh, check for solvency. Solvency is the ability to meet all obligations as they fall due. Even though its total assets may be greater than its total liabilities, a business can be brought into court, declared insolvent, and thrown into receivership if it is unable to pay its current bills. Families similarly may find themselves in a position of considerable financial embarrassment if they are not able to buy and pay for the things they need when they need them.

Many families have difficulty with their expenditures, not because their yearly income is less than their yearly expenditures, but because expenditures cannot be made before income is available. Income cannot be used until it is received. But many goods must be paid for at the time when they are purchased. Bills must be paid when they fall due.

In order to be sure that funds will be available with which to make each of the expenditures as planned in the year's budget, work out a spending plan for each month in the year. To do this, list expenditures month by month as they are to be made throughout the year. Similarly, estimate the monthly income which will be available for use in making these expenditures. Then balance each month's budget. This is easy enough if for the first few months of the year income is greater than expenditures. The heavier expenses to be met in later months can be taken care of out of the surplus accumulated earlier in the year. If, however, the first few months

call for more expenditures than the income will permit, it will be
necessary to make special provision for financing them. This can
be done by drawing temporarily upon savings, by using credit, or by
postponing some expenditures.

Although it takes a little time, the preparation of such a budget is
not such a difficult problem as at first it might seem. No month
will be burdened with all the big items in the budget. There will
be taxes to pay in January and July, a license to buy for the car near
the first of the year, insurance premiums on the anniversary of the
purchase of the insurance, clothes to buy just before Easter, coal to
buy in the fall, a vacation trip in July or August, wedding presents
for friends in June, Christmas presents in December, repairs to the
house in the spring and summer, and the purchase of a new car
whenever it seems most convenient. If these occasional purchases
which call for considerable outlay are fitted into the budget first,
then the other variable expenditures can be worked around them until
for each month there is worked out a clear-cut spending plan which
will be sound in itself and at the same time fit in perfectly with the
yearly budget.

*Eighth, work out a system of positive checks upon expenditures
which will make it easy to keep the family's expenditures within the
limits set in the family budget.* These should be mental checks,
rather than bookkeeping checks, preferably the sort of restraints that
become family habits.

It is not necessary to work out special devices for checking every
item in the budget. Fixed expenditures will take care of themselves. Rent must be paid the first of every month. Public utilities
cost only about so much, and these bills must be paid promptly to get
the discounts they carry. Insurance premiums when once provided
for in the monthly budget are easy to remember. It is the items of
more frequent expenditure, the variable items, the items for which
it is easier to spend more than to spend less, that require watching.

For example, a family with a food allowance of $45.00 a month
has divided its food money as follows: 2 quarts of milk a day, at 10
cents a quart, $6.00; meats, $7.50; groceries, $30.00; incidentals,
$1.50. It is easier to keep track of expenditures if the housewife
thinks of her meat allowance not as $7.50 per month, but as $1.75
a week; if she thinks of her grocery bill not as $30.00 per month,
but as $1.00 a day; if she thinks of her margin for incidentals not as
$1.50 a month, but as 35 cents a week.

If the family pays cash for all its food purchases, it may be convenient to set aside $10.50 every week for food, and limit food expenditures to that amount. If the family runs monthly bills, it is easy to check up on food expenditures two or three times a month. On the tenth of the month, for example, the bill at the grocery should run not far from $10.00, and at the meat market not far from $2.50. If on the tenth the bill is running below the scheduled amount, the family can buy a little more generously. If the bill is larger than it should be, the family can cut down its food expenditures.

In the same way, a family can check up on its automobile expense. License, taxes, and insurance are fixed charges which can be definitely counted upon. There is no danger of spending too much for any of them. Heavy expenditures for repairs or overhauling cannot be foreseen in advance. They must be taken care of out of reserves for unforeseen expenditures. The danger point in the automobile expenditures comes in connection with those expenditures involved in day-to-day operation. The best way to check up on this part of the budget is to limit the amount to be spent each week for gasoline. If the price of gasoline is low, it will be possible to use the car a little more than usual. If the price increases, spend the same amount for gasoline each week. Then keep the mileage down to what a week's gasoline money will provide. This will keep the family within budget limits in its automobile expenditure.

By such means as these it is possible to operate within the limits of a carefully-thought-out budget with a minimum of bookkeeping. If a family cares to do so, it is instructive to keep an accurate set of books covering much of the detail of the family's expenditures. If a family has little or no idea where its money has been going, it is wise to keep accurate accounts of all its expenditures for a few months, or even for a year, in order to get a definite idea of the points at which expenditures are likely to overstep the limits set up in the budget.

But when these danger points have once been located, the family needs, not records, but some workable check upon each of these expenditures. It helps very little to write down extravagant expenditures after they have been made. Every successful budget must include these positive checks as safeguards against unwise and unplanned-for expenditures.

Finally, check the finished budget against the family's long-time plans. Go over the finished budget to see that it is entirely consistent with the family's underlying philosophy, its long-time aims, as well as its more immediate objectives. Just as each month's expenditures must be worked out as an integral part of the year's budget, so each year's budget must fit into its place as part of the family's long-time program. It is especially important to check over items like insurance and savings, to see that they are adequate to assure the carrying out of the family's long-time program. It is equally important to check over the fixed charges which the family has assumed, or is planning to assume during the year, to make sure that they help rather than hinder the working out of the family's long-time plan. And it is important to see that the budget provides adequate reserves for unforeseen and often unforeseeable expenditures, for emergencies and contingencies which every family must face, so that no ordinary uncertainty which it is reasonably possible to guard against can upset the family's steady progress toward the attainment of its ultimate objectives.

Why budgets fail. *Underestimating expenditures.* One reason why family budgets fail to work out as they should is that most family budgets are stated in too general terms. They are not realistic. They overlook important items of expenditure. They pay too little attention to the actual details of prices and costs. They underestimate the actual expenses involved. They ignore entirely the inevitable incidental expenses always connected with major items of expenditure.

For example, in planning to buy a new car, it is important to keep in mind incidental expenses for accessories, license, insurance, and interest on instalment payments. It is important to remember that repairs for a large car cost more than repairs for a small one, that the amount spent for gasoline and oil and anti-freeze for the radiator will be considerably larger for an expensive car than for a moderate priced one.

Or again, the purchase of new evening clothes involves more than the suit. The old shirts look shabby, new shoes are necessary, and the wife must have a new evening gown—and then the family must spend enough money to go to places where evening clothes are worn.

Overestimating income. There is a tendency to overestimate the amount of income the family will have available for expenditure. This is true during periods of prosperity, when wages and salaries are high, when employment is assured and promotions are in order, when business is brisk, when dividends are regular, when interest even upon low-grade bonds can be definitely counted upon. During prosperity, families are not even content to limit their plans to spending current income. They anticipate increases in income as a matter of course.

During depression, families are inclined to overestimate available income for other reasons. They know that all incomes are uncertain. But since many families go through a depression with only moderate reductions in their income, and since any considerable reductions in expenditures involve upsetting changes in family habits, many families deliberately take a chance that they can get through the depression without much loss of income. Other families fail to face the facts about their incomes. They refuse to reduce their living standards until their incomes are actually cut off.

Then, again, many families overestimate their income because they fail to distinguish between business income and family income, between income from investments and repayments on principal, between current receipts which represent income and receipts which are in fact repayments of the family's invested capital. In making their budgets many families plan to use all the income they receive from rented properties, from business ventures, and from payments on mortgages and contracts without making any provision for reinvestment of principal or the expenses incidental to securing income.

Assuming too heavy fixed charges. Families have a tendency to assume too heavy fixed charges. They buy homes and cars beyond their means and assume a life insurance burden that they are unable to carry. They commit themselves to too many recurring payments at one time. They are not content to wait until they have paid for one thing before they buy another. At the end of every period of prosperity, many families find themselves faced with commitments that must be met, regardless of changes in income or of changes in the demands upon the family funds. At the end of 1929, for example, a year in which our total national income amounted to not far from 90 billion dollars, there were outstanding consumer obligations of something over 11 billion dollars. In other words, had prosperity continued and the 1930 income been equal to 1929, at least one-eighth of the next year's income would have been needed to liquidate all of these outstanding consumer obligations within the year. Families with excessive fixed charges find themselves involved in an inflexible spending plan which cannot be easily adapted to changing conditions. Eventually they reach a point beyond which it is impossible to continue as they had planned. Then they find it necessary to overhaul their entire spending program, to liquidate what it is possible to save out of their outstanding obligations, and in many cases to lower, definitely and uncomfortably, their accustomed standard of living, in order to be able to live within their current income. Only by keeping a considerable unencumbered margin above fixed charges is it possible for a family to adjust to changing conditions without completely overhauling the family's spending plan.

Inadequate contingent reserves.[1] Many budgets fail to work out as they should because they plan in advance for spending too large a proportion of the available income. There is not enough left in a general fund for the host of unforeseen and in many cases unforeseeable expenses that inevitably arise, and that are actually more important than many items which have been included in the budget. Most budgets are devoted exclusively to foreseen expenditures. They neglect entirely the unforeseeable demands which must be met when they come, regardless of savings or other plans for the improvement of the family situation.

Most budgets are uncomfortably restricting because not enough is left in unallocated funds to be spent as fancy dictates. They make no provision for even a few definitely unpremeditated but at the same time highly desirable expenditures. In the attempt to get as much immediate improvement in the family situation as possible, most budgets neglect entirely the setting up of reserves adequate to cover emergency outlays and provision for a reasonable amount of impulsive spending.

Building a workable budget. It takes time to build a workable budget. If a family is to make a budget which will help its members to do what they want to do with their income and to make their family life what they would like to make it, it must be willing to put many hours of work scattered over several days into working out the details of the initial spending plan. Then, every month, it is wise to go over the details of the next month's budget, making such changes as are necessary in the light of recent events, adding a little to this expenditure and cutting down on that, adapting the plan to current needs, and getting before the members of the family the

---

[1] For a discussion of the problem of reserves, see Ch. XIX, pp. 444, 446 ff.

things which must be bought, the limits to various items of expenditure, and the amount of unappropriated income which is available.

A corporation executive who knows that he must run his department on the funds provided in the next year's budget, is careful to present every possible item of expenditure for consideration, and to see that all estimates of costs are as accurate as it is possible to make them. Altogether, weeks of work and thought and planning on the part of a group of executives go into the making of an effective corporation budget.   If a family budget is to have an equal chance of success, all the members of the family must exercise equal care in making up their lists of proposed expenditures, in estimating costs, in estimating income, in planning the details of financing each expenditure, and in devising positive checks to keep the family from spending more than has been planned.

QUESTIONS

1. How many families of your acquaintance practice budgeting as it is defined in this chapter? How many work according to an informal or unwritten budget? How many work out detailed spending plans? How many keep accurate account of their expenditure?

2. Work out a set of budget headings for each of the following families:

Family A: A man, age 25, and his wife, age 23, living in a furnished apartment in a large eastern city. Both are employed, the husband as teller in a bank, the wife as clerk in a department store. The family's income is not far from $3,500. They own an automobile, have a good many meals away from home, and go about a good deal with a young married set.

Family B: Husband, age 45, a business man in a city of 750,000; wife, age 42; boy, age 15; and girl, age 12. Income from employment is $3,600, and from investments is $600. The family owns its home, drives a car, carries life insurance, is saving for the college education of the children, entertains some, and enjoys the theater. Business takes the husband to a nearby city three or four times a year. His wife usually accompanies him, leaving the children in the care of a middle-aged woman who helps with the housework two days a week.

Family C: An elderly couple, man 70 years old, wife 65, retired and living in a small town on an annuity of $1,200. They own their home, have a car and garden, hire heavy housework done, send the laundry out, enjoy good books, concerts, and the theater in the nearby city.

Family D: A college student.

Family E: Your own family.

3. Bring to class one or more "budget books" or family account books put out by various organizations in your community. Secure also a number of typical family bookkeeping systems. Compare these devices in detail, evaluating both the accounting forms and the budgeting suggestions they include.

4. Select one of the families described in question 2. Work out a simple but workable set of forms for planning and keeping track of essential family expenditures.

5. Give original examples of the way actual families of your acquaintance balance their budgets.

6. How do families of your acquaintance check their spending plans to be sure they will have money available to make all expenditures as planned?

7. What devices do the families of your acquaintance use to keep actual expenditures within the limits set up in their spending plan? List at least 10 devices for checking expenditures without the use of a complicated bookkeeping system.

8. Work out tentatively a year's budget for your family; or, if you are living away from home, for your own personal expenditures. Try out the various suggestions in this chapter, and any other budget practices with which you may be familiar. Work out the budget both on a yearly and a monthly basis. Test for solvency. Set up wherever necessary positive checks against specific expenditures. Try spending according to your plan for a two months' period. Then revise your budget in the light of your experience.

9. What kind of budget best suits your personal needs? Point out a number of specific ways in which this budget insures your securing the maximum of satisfaction from the money income and other resources at your disposal.

10. What proportion of the expenditures of families of your acquaintance goes for fixed charges which cannot be reduced without radically changing their manner of living?

11. In families of your acquaintance, which member or members of the family group make the final decisions in planning family expenditures? What seem to be the advantages and disadvantages in each case? How can a budget be devised which will care adequately for the necessary common wants of a family, and at the same time allow each individual the largest possible amount of freedom in satisfying his personal preferences?

REFERENCES

Andrews, B. R., *Economics of the Household*, Revised Edition, Ch. XXII, pp. 552-578. The Macmillan Co., New York, 1935.

A brief discussion of budgeting, with a thorough explanation of the details of household accounts.

Donham, S. Agnes, *Spending the Family Income*. Little, Brown and Co., Boston, 1933.

The whole book is worth reading. See especially Ch. XII for Miss Donham's method of budget building.

Donham, S. Agnes, *A Case Book in Family Budgeting*. Boston Cooking School Magazine Co., Boston, 1937.

Cases illustrating a wide variety of financial problems faced by every family, drawn from real life, are accompanied with reading references to aid in their solution. Excellent material for use in studying the technique of family financial planning.

Friend, Mata Roman, *Earning and Spending the Family Income*, Unit III, pp. 103-143. D. Appleton-Century Co., New York, 1930.

An interesting and detailed discussion of financial planning written for high school students.

Hoyt, Elizabeth E., *The Consumption of Wealth*, Ch. XXVIII, pp. 302-315. The Macmillan Co., New York, 1928.

Emphasizes materials available for use in working out the individual family budget.

Kyrk, Hazel, *Economic Problems of the Family*, Ch. X, pp. 166-187, and Ch. XX, pp. 398-415. Harper and Bros., New York, 1933.

Ch. X, "The Control of the Purse," is an excellent discussion of the principles involved in effective control of expenditures in the democratic American family. Ch. XX presents Kyrk's analysis of budgeting and account keeping.

Reid, Margaret G., *Economics of Household Production*, Ch. XIV, esp. pp. 223-238. John Wiley and Sons, Inc., New York, 1934.

Both Kyrk and Reid discuss in some detail the aims and values to be obtained from budgeting as well as the technique which successful budgeting involves.

CHAPTER XV

THE LONG-TIME PLAN

The need for a long look ahead. For a number of years we have been hearing about the importance of long-time planning. Recent proposals have been confined for the most part to grandiose schemes for large-scale social planning. There is nothing essentially new in the idea of long-time planning. These recent proposals are simply well-advertised applications on a colossal scale of the sort of thing that well-managed businesses and forward-looking individuals have always been doing.

Many families plan for the future as a matter of course. They work quietly and unostentatiously from one immediate objective to another toward the ultimate ends they have set out to attain. Sometimes it is a home, sometimes a new car, sometimes a college education for the children. Sometimes it is the accumulation of a fortune which will make the family independently wealthy for generations to come, and sometimes it is simply to maintain the family's normal standards of food and shelter and clothing during a period of unusual financial strain.

It is not enough to work out week by week or month by month the details of everyday expenditure. Every family needs a yearly budget to give direction to the working out of each month's spending plan. And in the same way, every family needs a definitely thought out long-time plan to guide it in working out its yearly budget. No plan for family spending will work well unless there is, on the one hand, adequate provision for the careful working out of every day's expenditures, and on the other, provision for co-ordinating all the daily details into a unified long-time plan, which is definitely directed toward the ultimate objectives which represent the family's idea of the good life for all its members.

Is it possible to plan for the future? Most people recognize the futility of planning for the present alone, and yet, when conditions all over the world are changing rapidly, as they have been ever since the outbreak of the World War, it often seems impossible to make plans for more than the very immediate future. Whatever we plan to do we may be forced to do differently than we intended. Unforeseen changes in the business or family situation may even make it necessary to set aside all our plans, and begin over again. In periods of widespread uncertainty there is a strong temptation to stop planning. Every family is inclined to drift for a time with the tide of circumstance.

There is, without question, some validity in such an attitude. There are changes occurring in the world over which no single individual or family has any control. And there always will be. We have long since learned that it does no good to try to control the weather. Instead, we adapt ourselves to it as best we may. If we live in a climate where it is cold in winter, we build well-insulated houses and equip them with storm windows and an efficient heating plant. We buy warm clothes to wear when we go outdoors. We equip our automobiles with heaters and anti-skid chains, fill the radiator with some sort of anti-freeze solution, put lighter oil in the crank case and transmission and differential, and go about as we please, regardless of the weather. We adapt—we do not try to control.

But when it comes to our economic and social environment, we are not content to adapt to conditions as they are. We find it difficult to reconcile ourselves to playing the game of life according to the rules. We frequently assume obligations we have no reasonable chance to fulfill. In times of prosperity, our desire for large and immediate returns on our investments helps to create an unsound financial situation. When, as a result of the accumulated effects of our individual actions, depressions occur, instead of recognizing and paying for our mistakes, instead of learning by experience, instead of making the best of a bad situation we have created by our own short-sightedness, we spend our time working for all sorts of political and social panaceas which we hope in some mysterious collective way will save us from the results of our individual folly.

Why some plans fail. There are a number of reasons why our long-time plans fail to work out as we intend. In the first place, we overestimate our capacity to bring about immediate fundamental changes in our economic and social environment. We see all around us the results of scientific discovery. We see that increasing knowledge makes possible continued progress in extending our control over the physical world about us. But we overestimate our power to use this knowledge to make our existing economic and social environment quickly into the environment in which we would like to live.

We do not realize how long a time economic and social changes require. It was thirty years after men began to experiment with horseless carriages, and almost twenty years after Henry Ford made a car which would run a mile a minute, that automobiles came into general use. Although the annual output of motor cars passed the 3 million mark in 1923, the social and economic and political effects of the general adoption of the motor car are still working themselves out. Land values are only gradually adjusting themselves to the implications of automobile transportation. Tax systems are in the process of rebuilding. Marketing channels are changing. Railroad rate structures are being adjusted to new highway competition. Traffic regulations are being framed and reframed. Safety habits are being developed. Social customs are undergoing change, and our whole horizon is being broadened. All these changes have been in the making for more than a generation. It may take another ten, fifteen, twenty, or even thirty years before our social, political, and economic adjustment to the automobile is completed.

Obviously, we should use our increasing knowledge in every way that we can to improve our environment. But improving our environment is a long-time process. Only future generations will reap the full benefit of our efforts. Immediate improvement in present-day family life will come for the most part in making successful adjustment to conditions as they now are. Our long-time plans must always make allowance for the possibility of change, but they will have a better chance for success if they count upon the fundamentals of the general situation as continuing in substantially their present form in the years immediately ahead.

We do not understand the nature and the possibilities of constructive adaptation. We take it for granted that the lower animals must adapt themselves to their environment or die. We know that man is the most adaptable animal. We know that the family is the most adaptable of our social institutions. But we fail to realize fully the degree to which the conscious, reasoned, active adaptation of intelligent human beings is superior to the passive, instinctive, unconscious adaptation of plants and animals. Animals must adapt themselves as best they may to the situation in which they find themselves. Men may anticipate a situation before it arises. Their adaptation is more effective because they can plan in advance their adjustment to a new situation.

Many of our long-time plans fail because we confuse means with ends. We become so enamored with the details of our planning that we confuse the ultimate end, which is the attainment of happy family life, with the means by which we attain it. Too often we feel that successful family life depends entirely upon living on a certain street in a certain town. We feel that we can secure a livelihood for the family only by working at a chosen job. We feel that stability of family life depends upon the ownership of an expensive home, that the enjoyment of pleasant social relations with our friends depends upon being able to drive an expensive car, that getting the necessary amount of physical exercise to keep ourselves in good health depends upon maintaining a membership in an exclusive country club. We make our plans in terms of means, rather than of ends. And when changed conditions place these means obviously beyond our reach, we abandon as a failure the whole idea of long-time planning.

Many of our long-time plans fail because we are unable to bring ourselves to face any facts which we do not like. Most of us are incurably romantic. When we are satisfied with our present situation, we refuse to recognize the possibility of any change. When we are not satisfied with some features of our situation, we refuse to face the possibility that they may remain unchanged for some time to come. In many cases the failure of our long-time plans is due not so much to our lack of foresight as to our refusal to face facts that are staring us in the face.

The fundamentals of successful long-time planning. *Adequate information.* The first fundamental for successful long-time planning is adequate information. In working out any plan, it is highly important to have available all the information which may have a bearing upon the problems to be solved. In working out its long-time plan, a family needs a great variety of information. It is important to know about all the significant factors in the family situation.[1] It is essential to know about business conditions, particularly those which affect directly either the family's income or its

---

[1] See Ch. XVI.

expenditures. It is important to know about the changes which inevitably come with changes in the business cycle. It is necessary to keep in mind fundamental economic and social trends, the long-time trend of prices, the growth and decline of specific industries, the discovery, utilization, and exhaustion of natural resources, the rate of population growth, changes in life expectancies, and urban growth and decline.[2] Much ingenuity is frequently required to discover all the information which may have a bearing upon the family situation. Sometimes there are factors of fundamental importance which seem very far removed from present family life. And yet in long-time planning, the degree of success a family can attain depends upon the amount and accuracy of the information it possesses.

Analysis in the light of the family situation. Nor is it sufficient simply to gather together a mass of more or less relevant information. The second fundamental for successful long-time planning is to consider carefully just how the family will be affected by each of the forces—physical, economic, social, and personal—which are at work in the complex environment in which the family lives. Each family must decide for itself which factors it must regard as of fundamental importance, and which factors it can safely ignore in working out its long-time plans.

For example: There is no longer a demand for the product of a once prosperous industry. One by one the plants in the industry close their doors. This is of no particular importance to families who no longer want the product the industry once provided. But to the families whose investments are centered in the industry, and to the families whose wage earners are dependent upon the industry for wages or salaries, the decline of the industry is a factor of first importance.

When the automobile and the motor bus supplant interurban lines, to many families it is simply one more reason for buying a motor car. But to families with money invested in electric railway securities, it means the loss of a large part of their invested capital. To the families of men employed by interurban lines, it means an inevitable shift in employment, with the probability of lower earnings on the new job, and the possibility of a long period of unemployment while the change is being made.

[2] See Ch. XVII.

Proper timing. In working out a long-time plan for a family, the third essential is to estimate as accurately as possible the times when specific needs will arise, when income and other resources will be available, and when reserves will be needed, either for unusually heavy expenditures or against declining income.

In order to estimate the timing of important changes in needs, the family should consider its position in the family life cycle.[3] To estimate the timing of increases and decreases in income, the family should consider probabilities for promotion, the period of maximum income, and the usual retirement age in the occupation of the chief wage earner. In estimating probable changes in prices of the commodities it must buy, and in the value of property it owns, the family must consider long-time price trends and the ebb and flow of the business cycle.

It is impossible to predict the exact time at which many elements in any situation will develop, or when a period of prosperity will end and a depression begin, or a depression end and recovery begin. It seems to be impossible to determine any changes in the long-time trend in prices till the new trend has been in effect for several years. It is impossible to predict exactly when the family must draw upon unemployment reserves, or plan for permanent retirement. For all these reasons, the family must learn to judge the speed at which various tendencies are developing, and make its plans flexible enough to adjust to coming changes as developments become apparent.

Successful long-time planning, therefore, involves timing various adjustments which must be made between income and outgo so that it will be possible to provide for the family's needs at the time when they are most acute, and to provide the various goods and services a family wants at the time when these goods and services are most desired.

Planning for the normal. Finally, because of the great variety of factors to be considered and co-ordinated, the fourth essential in long-time planning is to assume a reasonably normal course of events as far as the progress of the family through the usual family life cycle is concerned. It is important, of course, to recognize the possibility of unforeseen elements arising in the family situation. The variable factors for which it is impossible to predict accurately in advance must be kept in mind. It is absolutely essential to leave adequate margins

---

[3] See Ch. I, p. 15.

for these uncertainties. But on the whole, long-time plans will have a much better chance of success if they are based upon the usual situation, and then are made flexible enough to permit adjustments to unusual conditions if and when those conditions actually arise.

It is equally essential to assume a reasonably normal course of events in the world outside the home. A family must refuse to be stampeded into abandoning or completely overhauling its long-time plan by every pronouncement of a new social order. There is no reason for believing that we have as yet discovered a way to eliminate the ebb and flow of the business cycle, nor to get away from the operation of the forces underlying long-time price trends. Every war brings with it inevitably a period of pronounced inflation. After every war, deflation is equally inevitable. There is no good reason to believe that this deflation can be avoided. It may be postponed. But if it is postponed by resorting to further inflationary devices, additional deflation eventually must follow.

It is possible by careful study of the operation of economic laws throughout many years, to develop some basis for judgment as to the probable course of events in years ahead. Economic forces, however, do not work out unhindered. The problem is complicated, among other things, by the effect of political measures designed to direct economic developments along lines which will benefit some special interests, sometimes debtors, rarely creditors, almost never the family in its capacity as a consumer.

Fundamentally, then, the problem of long-time planning resolves itself into this: The family must determine as closely as it can some time in advance what is necessary if it is to live the sort of life it would like to live in the world as it now is. Then it must estimate, again as closely as its situation makes possible, the probable income it will have available with which to carry out these plans. And it must proceed to work out a long-time plan which will be within the limits set by the family income and other resources and at the same time will come as near as possible to providing the family with the sort of life it desires.[4]

How to proceed in working out a long-time plan. How should a family proceed in the construction of a workable long-time

---

[4] Some families find it helpful to work out a number of alternative plans, each to be used in case of a possible change in the family's situation. Some families whose income is uncertain, work out one plan to follow if they receive all their anticipated income, another to guide their expenditures if their income is cut 10 per cent, another to use in case their income is cut 25 per cent, and still another to use if their income is cut 50 per cent.

plan? The first step is to take stock of all of its financial and personal assets, to estimate at least in general terms the income and other resources which it will have to work with in the years ahead.

The second step is to set up certain broad aims toward which it is to work—adequate provision for immediate necessities like food and clothing; desirable additions to the family's present way of living, such as larger allowances for worth while amusement and recreation, or a better car; additions to the family's permanent equipment, some new furniture, more up-to-date home equipment, or even a home of its own; some provision for the future which will guarantee the children a high school or college education and be adequate for the needs of the parents in their declining years. These broad aims should state in concrete terms the fundamentals of the family's standard of living.

The third step is to translate these broader aims into a series of definite and immediate objectives, expressed in terms possible of early accomplishment. The purchase of a home may be a long way in the future; it is possible to open a savings account with some of this month's pay check. Refurnishing a home frequently calls for a larger outlay than can be made with the money available in any one year. But it is possible to decide on what is needed and then plan to buy a rug this month, a new chair next, and to set aside a little for several months more until enough is available for new dining room furniture.

The object of any plan is to facilitate steady and consistent progress toward the ultimate attainment of the more distant aims the family has in view. The fourth step in the family's long-time plan, therefore, must be to arrange the immediate objectives in a series of steps, so that each readily obtainable objective leads easily on to the next. It is well to provide early in the plan for those things which relieve the everyday strains on the family income, and in this way release funds for carrying out the next part of the plan. It may be good policy to buy first a washing machine or a sewing machine, which reduce family expenditures, and then use the money saved on laundry or the making of clothing for the purchase of a new radio, or the financing of a larger car, which add to rather than reduce current outlay.

The last step is to check over the long-time spending program to make sure that it provides the flexibility necessary to enable the family to meet any unforeseen changes in its immediate situation without endangering the ultimate aims of the plan. If a plan lacks flexibility, the chances are that the family is attempting too much—that its aims are almost impossible of attainment.

How will such a plan look on paper? For the first year it will look much like any ordinary budget, with definite amounts set down for definite expenditures. The same sort of procedure will be possible for a good many of the second year's items, though there will be less provision for the details of expenditures. For the third, fourth, and fifth years, it will be possible to outline the plan only in a more general way, setting aside a reasonable amount for food, clothing, shelter, current operating expenses, life insurance premiums, ordinary amusements, and the like, and concentrating attention on the more important items of occasional expenditure to be included each year.

Suppose that the family usually trades automobiles every third year. It bought a new car last year. This means that in the second and fifth years there must be provision for the purchase of a new automobile. A washing machine is to be purchased new the first year of the plan. With proper care it ought to last for five years. There need be no provision for replacing it until the sixth year. The family is living in a rented house. It has been paying on shares in a building and loan association for three years. These shares will mature in three years more. Then the family can buy or build a permanent home. This means that the budget for the fourth year must include an allowance for moving expenses, and some funds for new furnishings or additions to present equipment.

Will such a plan work? Will any family at the end of five or ten years find itself at the place it started to attain? Probably not. Some will find part of their program necessarily postponed. Some will have accomplished even more than they hoped. Most of them will have modified somewhat their original ideas of what they wanted. But all of them, if they have worked out their original plans carefully, and modified and adapted them thoughtfully to conditions as they developed, will find that they have attained much more than they would have done through random spending.

The long-time plan will be worth while if it does no more than give perspective and direction to current spending. The long-time plan will have accomplished its primary purpose if it enables the family to see its life as a whole, and to see each immediate problem in its relationship to the long life of the family.

QUESTIONS

1. Give some original examples of passive, active, unconscious, and conscious adaptation of families to the environment in which they find themselves.

2. List a number of objectives which families can attain only by long-time planning.

3. Compare the certain elements and the uncertain elements in the situation of two families of your acquaintance.

4. List five points about which you can be reasonably certain, and five points which are definitely uncertain in the social, economic, or political situation at the present time. What is the significance of each of these points to your family in working out its long-time spending plan?

5. Give some original examples of the importance of timing in family planning.

6. Work out a five-year plan for a young couple who are planning to be married in June. If you have no actual couple in mind, work out your plan for the following family: Both man and girl are college graduates. He is 27 and she is 25. He has been out of school five years, and has worked up to a position as minor executive in a manufacturing plant. She is employed as secretary to the executive vice-president of a bank in the same community. At the present time his salary is $50 a week. Her salary is $1,800 a year. They each own a car. Their combined savings amount to $2,000.

REFERENCES

Bristol, L. M., *Social Adaptation*, pp. 5-11. Harvard University Press, Cambridge, 1921.

This book should be consulted for a statement of the theory of adaptation.

Bushee, Frederick A., *Principles of Sociology*, Ch. IV, pp. 34-41. Henry Holt and Co., New York, 1923.

Gives a statement of the theory of adaptation.

Carver, Thomas Nixon, *Sociology and Social Progress*, pp. 9-10. Ginn and Co., Boston, 1905.

Also presents a statement of the theory of adaptation.

Donham, W. B., *Business Adrift*, Ch. II. McGraw-Hill Book Co., Inc., New York, 1931.

Suggests a method of predicting the timing of economic and social change. The foreword to this volume is an essay on *Foresight* by Alfred Whitehead.

CHAPTER XVI

ADJUSTING FAMILY EXPENDITURES TO CHANGES IN FAMILY NEEDS

What does a family need? In planning for the future, there are at least three ways to approach the problem of determining what the family will need. One is to estimate in round numbers the probable cost of providing everything necessary to maintain the family at its usual standard over a period of years. A second is to devise some sort of index which will show the comparative burden of family expenditure as the size and make-up of the family changes from year to year. A third is to work out in terms of actual goods and services the needs of the family as it proceeds through the various stages of the family life cycle.[1]

All three of these methods are valuable. By comparing estimates of total living costs with estimates of probable total income over a twenty-five or thirty year period, it is possible to set reasonable limits to the scale of living a family should try to maintain. By comparing the yearly burden of expenditures with estimates of the amount of income which will probably be available from year to year, it is possible to anticipate periods of unusual financial strain. It is these periods for which provision must be made in advance if the family is to maintain its usual scale of living. By using the family life cycle method of analysis it is possible not only to point out peaks of expenditure and periods of varying financial strain, but also to indicate the nature of the problems the family must face, and the methods by which these problems can best be met.

Cost of living studies. Because of the time involved and the detail which must be included in working out in objective terms a satisfactory description of the needs of a family over a period of years, most families prefer to begin by using some simpler form of estimate. Especially families just starting out in life, whose members have little idea as to what various items ought to cost, may learn something about the relative cost of various items in their budget from material given in recent cost of living studies.

---

[1] A detailed description of the stages of the family life cycle is given in Ch. I, pp. 15 ff.

But cost of living studies show only average expenditures. In most cases they do not distinguish between the expenditures of large and of small families, nor do they indicate the variations in expenditures for families at various stages of the family life cycle. They do, however, give some estimates in round numbers of the amounts families with given incomes do spend for the groups of items under the more usual headings in the family budget.

Dublin and Lotka,[2] of the Metropolitan Life Insurance Co., in their book, *The Money Value of a Man,* have worked out living costs for families living on three income levels, $2,500, $5,000, and $10,000 maximum yearly income. They have carried the cost of living estimates a little farther than do most studies, and have worked out tables showing the estimated cost of living for an individual for each year of his life.

Their estimates are in terms of 1929 prices, and assume large city living costs. These estimates were worked out, not to be used in estimating future cost of living, but to determine the cost of bringing a man to maturity, and of maintaining him during the productive years of his life. They are interesting, but rather arbitrarily determined, estimates of what able statisticians consider to be typical living costs for families in the three income groups for which they have prepared estimates. The estimates assume rather larger savings than most families in these income groups feel they are able to make unless they curtail the size of their families to one or at the most two children.

Dublin and Lotka's method of estimates is worth studying as one device for estimating roughly in advance the probable cost of family maintenance and support.

Adult male maintenance units. Because of the difficulty in applying results of cost of living studies in estimating living costs for actual families, there have been a number of attempts to work out some simple but accurate index which can be used to estimate the differences in living costs for families of various sizes with members of various ages. Obviously the size and age of the members of the family affect directly the amount which must be spent for food. Engel worked out a scale of "quets" originally based on food consumption, which he used to estimate the relative cost of maintaining

---

[2] L. I. Dublin and A. J. Lotka, *The Money Value of a Man.* The Ronald Press Co., New York, 1930.

families of different sizes, with members of different ages. There have been a number of similar and more accurate food scales worked out for use in this country.

On the basis of these scales of food units, Ogburn worked out a series of regression equations for estimating the variation in the proportions of their incomes families of varying sizes would spend for each of the principal groups of items in their family budgets. His equations are a little too complicated to be of use to the ordinary family in working out plans for its own expenditures.[3]

About the same time that Ogburn was working out his regression equations, two men in the United States Public Health Service, Edgar Sydenstricker and Willford I. King, devised a scale of consumption units designed to show the relative demands of individuals of different ages and sexes upon the family income. They worked out their scale from budgets showing in detail the actual expenditures of a group of families living in South Carolina cotton mill towns in which they were conducting a public health survey. Their scale of consumption units was "intended to represent approximately the *relative demands* in terms of money value for food, clothing, and miscellaneous individual requirements all combined. Expenses incurred for these articles together constitute about 89 per cent of the total family expenditures; hence it seems certain that the scale is fairly representative of all expenses for the families considered."[4]

Since their units were designed to represent the relative cost of maintaining individuals of different sex and age, and were expressed in terms of a unit which represented the total expense of "adult male maintenance," Sydenstricker and King called their consumption units "ammains."

The table on page 375 gives Sydenstricker and King's ammain table as it was finally completed. The authors of the ammain scale were chiefly interested in working out a device which would allow them to measure the relative demand upon the family income made by families of different sizes and with members of different ages.

[3] Ogburn described his method in an article in the *Quarterly Publication of the American Statistical Association*, June, 1919, under the title, "Analysis of Standard of Living in District of Columbia in 1916."

Andrews has a brief statement of the trends in proportionate expenditure for different items as family size changes and as income changes, as revealed by Ogburn's equations. See B. R. Andrews, *Economics of the Household*, Revised Edition, Ch. VII, pp. 142 ff. The Macmillan Co., New York, 1935.

[4] E. Sydenstricker and W. I. King, *A Method of Classifying Families According to Incomes in Studies of Disease Prevalence*, Public Health Reports, Vol. 35, No. 48, November 26, 1920, pp. 2829-2846.

The next table, page 376, shows how the ammain scale may be used to compare the relative cost of maintaining a given standard of living for four families of different ages and sizes.

The group of families from whose expenditures this ammain scale was devised had small incomes. At no time could they buy more than the immediate necessities of life. The figures in the ammain table, therefore, assume that everything the individuals in the various families use will be purchased as needed. Because this table does assume that everything will be bought from day to day, it gives a fairly accurate basis for predicting the probable cost of providing the necessities of life for families living near the subsistence level.

TABLE OF AMMAINS [5]

A Scale of Consumption Units Showing Relative Expenditures for Persons of Different Sexes and Ages

Age in Years	Male	Female	Age in Years	Male	Female
Under 1	0.22	0.22	41	0.93	0.74
1	.24	.24	42	.93	.73
2	.28	.28	43	.92	.73
3	.31	.31	44	.92	.72
4	.33	.33	45	.92	.72
5	.35	.35	46	.91	.71
6	.38	.38	47	.91	.71
7	.40	.40	48	.90	.70
8	.42	.41	49	.90	.70
9	.44	.43	50	.89	.69
10	.47	.45	51	.89	.69
11	.50	.48	52	.88	.69
12	.54	.51	53	.87	.68
13	.59	.55	54	.86	.68
14	.66	.60	55	.85	.67
15	.74	.65	56	.84	.67
16	.81	.71	57	.83	.67
17	.88	.74	58	.83	.66
18	.93	.76	59	.82	.66
19	.96	.78	60	.81	.66
20	.98	.78	61	.81	.65
21	.99	.79	62	.80	.65
22	.99	.79	63	.80	.65
23	1.00	.79	64	.79	.65
24	1.00	.79	65	.79	.64
25	1.00	.79	66	.78	.64
26	1.00	.78	67	.78	.64
27	.99	.78	68	.78	.63
28	.98	.78	69	.77	.63
29	.98	.78	70	.77	.63
30	.97	.78	71	.76	.63
31	.97	.77	72	.76	.63
32	.96	.77	73	.76	.63
33	.96	.77	74	.75	.62
34	.95	.76	75	.75	.62
35	.95	.76	76	.75	.62
36	.94	.76	77	.75	.62
37	.94	.75	78	.75	.62
38	.94	.75	79	.74	.62
39	.93	.74	80	.74	.62
40	.93	.74			

[5] E. Sydenstricker and W. I. King, op. cit., p. 2843.

In using the ammain scale to estimate the needs of middle-class families, it is necessary to keep in mind the importance of additional allowances for such items as medical expenses, music and dancing lessons, concert and theater, college education for the children, and

RELATIVE COST OF MAINTAINING A GIVEN STANDARD OF LIVING FOR FAMILIES OF VARIOUS SIZES, COMPUTED IN AMMAINS [6]

FAMILY I			FAMILY II		
	Age	Ammain		Age	Ammain
Man..............	38	.94	Man..............	30	.97
Wife.............	35	.76	Wife.............	28	.78
Boy..............	12	.54	Boy..............	5	.35
Girl.............	9	.43			
Total ammains..................2.67			Total ammains..................2.10		

FAMILY III			FAMILY IV		
	Age	Ammain		Age	Ammain
Man..............	43	.92	Man..............	45	.92
Wife.............	38	.75	Wife.............	40	.74
Boy..............	15	.74	Boy..............	15	.74
Girl.............	12	.51	Girl.............	11	.48
Grandfather.........	75	.75	Boy..............	7	.40
Grandmother........	72	.63			
Total ammains..................4.30			Total ammains..................3.28		

Assume that Family I has an income of $2,000. This means they can spend $\frac{\$2,000}{2.67} = \$750$ per ammain. If the other families in this group are to spend the same amount per ammain, they will need the amounts determined in each case by multiplying the total ammains by $750.

Total ammains 2.67 ×$750	Total ammains 2.10 ×$750	Total ammains 4.30 ×$750	Total ammains 3.28 ×$750
Necessary income......$2,000	Necessary income......$1,575	Necessary income......$3,225	Necessary income......$2,460

the family automobile. Because the scale was prepared for families near the subsistence level, it probably underestimates rather than overestimates the expenses which middle-class families must meet in the most expensive periods in rearing children.

[6] Example computed by the author.

The table on page 378 shows how the ammain scale may be used in predicting the changing cost of the necessities of life for a family as it passes through the usual life cycle. In computing this table it is assumed that the family consists of a man and wife, who marry when he is twenty-five and she is twenty-three years of age. They bring up two children, a boy born at the end of the second year, and a girl born at the end of the fourth year of their married life.

The next table compares the total annual unit cost for this family (as Family B) with similar costs for a family rearing three children (Family A), a family rearing one child (Family C), a family without children (Family D), and a family rearing two children born ten years apart (Family E). The chart on page 382 is a graphic representation of the figures given in this table for Families A, B, C, and D. In this chart it is easy to see at a glance the relative cost of rearing a family of one, two, and three children.

The chart on page 383 is a graphic representation of the annual unit costs for Family B and Family E. This chart shows clearly the difference in the problems faced by a family with children close together, and those faced by a family in which the children come at longer intervals. Similar computations can be made from the ammain table to estimate the relative burden of various spacings in the birth of children.

There are a number of things which can be learned better from the use of the ammain method of analysis than perhaps in any other way. This method indicates clearly the time at which various items of family expenditure must be prepared for. It shows clearly periods of unusually heavy expenditure. It indicates the wide variation in the annual demands upon a family income. It emphasizes the fact that if a family is planning to rear two or three children, unless it can expect its income to more than double in the first twenty years of its life, it must make provision of some sort in the early years for the funds with which to meet demands at the peak of its expenditures.

From a study of these ammain charts it is easy to see why families living close to the subsistence level so uniformly sink into poverty during the years when they are rearing their families.[7] It is easy to see also why it is necessary for most families living on moderate incomes to reduce their living standards somewhat during this period.

[7] E. Sydenstricker, W. I. King, and Dorothy Wiehl, *The Income Cycle in the Life of the Wage-earner*, Treasury Dept. Public Health Reports, Vol. 39, No. 34, August 22, 1924, pp. 2133-2140.

Relative Annual Cost of Supporting a Family for Thirty Years, Computed in Ammains

The family consists of a husband and wife, married when he is 25 and she is 23, who bring up two children, a boy born at the end of the second year, and a girl born at the end of the fourth year of their married life. It is assumed that the family supports each of its children for 19 years, providing them with a high school education. On the 19th birthday, each child leaves home and becomes self-supporting.

	1st Year		2nd Year		3rd Year		4th Year		5th Year		6th Year	
	Age	Unit Cost	Age	Unit Cost	Age	Unit Cost	Age	Unit Cost	Age	Unit Cost	Age	Unit Cost
Husband.............	25	1.00	26	1.00	27	.99	28	.98	29	.98	30	.97
Wife.................	23	.79	24	.79	25	.79	26	.78	27	.78	28	.78
First child, boy......	..	....	..	....	−1	....	1	....	2	.28	3	.31
Second child, girl....	..	....	..	....	..	.22	..	.24	−1	.22	1	.24
Total.............		1.79		1.79		2.00		2.00		2.26		2.30

	7th Year		8th Year		9th Year		10th Year		11th Year		12th Year	
	Age	Unit Cost	Age	Unit Cost	Age	Unit Cost	Age	Unit Cost	Age	Unit Cost	Age	Unit Cost
Husband.............	31	.97	32	.96	33	.96	34	.95	35	.95	36	.94
Wife.................	29	.78	30	.78	31	.77	32	.77	33	.77	34	.76
First child, boy......	4	.33	5	.35	6	.38	7	.40	8	.42	9	.44
Second child, girl....	2	.28	3	.31	4	.33	5	.35	6	.38	7	.40
Total.............		2.36		2.40		2.44		2.47		2.52		2.54

13TH YEAR

	Age	Unit Cost
Husband..........	37	.94
Wife..........	35	.76
First child, boy....	10	.47
Second child, girl....	8	.41
Total..........		2.58

14TH YEAR

	Age	Unit Cost
Husband..........	38	.94
Wife..........	36	.76
First child, boy....	11	.50
Second child, girl....	9	.43
Total..........		2.63

15TH YEAR

	Age	Unit Cost
Husband..........	39	.93
Wife..........	37	.75
First child, boy....	12	.54
Second child, girl....	10	.45
Total..........		2.67

16TH YEAR

	Age	Unit Cost
Husband..........	40	.93
Wife..........	38	.75
First child, boy....	13	.59
Second child, girl....	11	.48
Total..........		2.75

17TH YEAR

	Age	Unit Cost
Husband..........	41	.93
Wife..........	39	.74
First child, boy....	14	.66
Second child, girl....	12	.51
Total..........		2.84

18TH YEAR

	Age	Unit Cost
Husband..........	42	.93
Wife..........	40	.74
First child, boy....	15	.74
Second child, girl....	13	.55
Total..........		2.96

19TH YEAR

	Age	Unit Cost
Husband..........	43	.92
Wife..........	41	.74
First child, boy....	16	.81
Second child, girl....	14	.60
Total..........		3.07

20TH YEAR

	Age	Unit Cost
Husband..........	44	.92
Wife..........	42	.73
First child, boy....	17	.88
Second child, girl....	15	.65
Total..........		3.18

21ST YEAR

	Age	Unit Cost
Husband..........	45	.92
Wife..........	43	.73
First child, boy....	18	.93
Second child, girl....	16	.71
Total..........		3.29

22ND YEAR

	Age	Unit Cost
Husband..........	46	.91
Wife..........	44	.72
First child, boy....	..	..
Second child, girl....	17	.74
Total..........		2.37

23RD YEAR

	Age	Unit Cost
Husband..........	47	.91
Wife..........	45	.72
First child, boy....	..	..
Second child, girl....	18	.76
Total..........		2.39

24TH YEAR

	Age	Unit Cost
Husband..........	48	.90
Wife..........	46	.71
First child, boy....	..	..
Second child, girl....	..	..
Total..........		1.61

25TH YEAR

	Age	Unit Cost
Husband..........	49	.90
Wife..........	47	.71
Total..........		1.61

26TH YEAR

	Age	Unit Cost
Husband..........	50	.89
Wife..........	48	.70
Total..........		1.59

27TH YEAR

	Age	Unit Cost
Husband..........	51	.89
Wife..........	49	.70
Total..........		1.59

28TH YEAR

	Age	Unit Cost
Husband..........	52	.88
Wife..........	50	.69
Total..........		1.57

29TH YEAR

	Age	Unit Cost
Husband..........	53	.87
Wife..........	51	.69
Total..........		1.56

30TH YEAR

	Age	Unit Cost
Husband..........	54	.86
Wife..........	52	.69
Total..........		1.55

RELATIVE ANNUAL COST OF SUPPORTING FIVE FAMILIES FOR FIFTY YEARS, COMPUTED IN AMMAINS

Family A consists of a husband and wife who bring up three children, a boy born at the end of the fourth year, and a girl born at the end of the second year, a girl born at the end of the fourth year, and a boy born at the end of the sixth year of their married life.

Family B consists of a husband and wife who bring up two children, a boy born at the end of the second year, and a girl born at the end of the fourth year.

Family C consists of a husband and wife who bring up one child, a boy born at the end of the second year of their married life.

Family D has no children.

Family E, like Family B, brings up two children. But in this case, the boy is born at the end of the second year, and the girl at the end of the twelfth year of their married life.

It is assumed in each case that the husband and wife were married when he was 25 and she was 23, and that each family supports each of its children for 19 years, providing them with a high school education. On the 19th birthday, each child leaves home and becomes self-supporting.

The computation of unit costs for Family B for thirty years is shown in the table on pp. 378-379.

UNIT COST

YEAR IN LIFE OF FAMILY	AGE OF CHIEF WAGE EARNER	Family A	Family B	Family C	Family D	Family E
1	25	1.79	1.79	1.79	1.79	1.79
2	26	1.79	1.79	1.79	1.79	1.79
3	27	2.00	2.00	2.00	1.78	2.00
4	28	2.00	2.00	2.00	1.76	2.00
5	29	2.26	2.26	2.04	1.76	2.04
6	30	2.30	2.30	2.06	1.75	2.06
7	31	2.58	2.36	2.08	1.75	2.08
8	32	2.64	2.40	2.09	1.74	2.09
9	33	2.72	2.44	2.11	1.73	2.11
10	34	2.78	2.47	2.12	1.72	2.12
11	35	2.85	2.52	2.14	1.72	2.14
12	36	2.89	2.54	2.14	1.70	2.14

13–50	37–74					
13	37	2.96	2.58	2.17	1.70	2.39
14	38	3.03	2.63	2.20	1.70	2.44
15	39	3.09	2.67	2.22	1.68	2.50
16	40	3.19	2.75	2.27	1.68	2.58
17	41	3.31	2.84	2.33	1.67	2.66
18	42	3.46	2.96	2.41	1.67	2.76
19	43	3.54	3.07	2.44	1.66	2.82
20	44	3.77	3.18	2.53	1.65	2.93
21	45	3.95	3.29	2.58	1.65	2.99
22	46	3.11	2.37	1.63	1.63	2.06
23	47	3.20	2.39	1.63	1.63	2.08
24	48	2.49	1.61	1.61	1.61	2.09
25	49	2.65	1.61	1.61	1.61	2.12
26	50	1.59	1.59	1.59	1.59	2.14
27	51	1.59	1.59	1.59	1.59	2.15
28	52	1.57	1.57	1.57	1.57	2.22
29	53	1.56	1.56	1.56	1.56	2.27
30	54	1.55	1.55	1.55	1.55	2.29
31	55	1.53	1.53	1.53	1.53	2.29
32	56	1.52	1.52	1.52	1.52	1.52
33	57	1.50	1.50	1.50	1.50	1.50
34	58	1.50	1.50	1.50	1.50	1.50
35	59	1.49	1.49	1.49	1.49	1.49
36	60	1.47	1.47	1.47	1.47	1.47
37	61	1.47	1.47	1.47	1.47	1.47
38	62	1.46	1.46	1.46	1.46	1.46
39	63	1.45	1.45	1.45	1.45	1.45
40	64	1.44	1.44	1.44	1.44	1.44
41	65	1.44	1.44	1.44	1.44	1.44
42	66	1.43	1.43	1.43	1.43	1.43
43	67	1.42	1.42	1.42	1.42	1.42
44	68	1.42	1.42	1.42	1.42	1.42
45	69	1.41	1.41	1.41	1.41	1.41
46	70	1.40	1.40	1.40	1.40	1.40
47	71	1.39	1.39	1.39	1.39	1.39
48	72	1.39	1.39	1.39	1.39	1.39
49	73	1.39	1.39	1.39	1.39	1.39
50	74	1.38	1.38	1.38	1.38	1.38

The charts on pages 382 and 383 show graphically the material in the table. The first chart shows the relative unit cost of families with three, two, one, and no children. The second chart compares the peak and duration of the burden of bringing up two children, when the children are born within two years of each other, and when they are born ten years apart.

RELATIVE ANNUAL COST OF SUPPORTING FOUR FAMILIES
FOR FORTY YEARS, COMPUTED IN AMMAINS

Family A consists of a husband and wife who bring up three children, a boy born at the end of the second year, a girl born at the end of the fourth year, and a boy born at the end of the sixth year of their married life.

Family B consists of a husband and wife who bring up two children, a boy born at the end of the second year, and a girl born at the end of the fourth year of their married life.

Family C consists of a husband and wife who bring up one child, a boy born at the end of the second year of their married life.

Family D has no children.

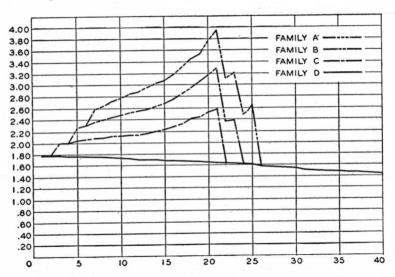

It is assumed in each case that the husband and wife were married when he was 25 and she was 23, and that each family supports each of its children for 19 years, providing them with a high school education. On the 19th birthday, each child leaves home and becomes self-supporting.

This chart shows graphically the comparative cost of bringing up to age 19 one, two, or three children. The cost line for a family with no children is introduced for purposes of comparison. In estimating costs by the ammain method, it is assumed that each family will buy each year everything it consumes in that year. There is no allowance made for possible savings from quantity buying or from additional production for use in the larger families.

RELATIVE ANNUAL COST OF SUPPORTING TWO FAMILIES
FOR FORTY YEARS, COMPUTED IN AMMAINS

Family B consists of a husband and wife who bring up two children, a boy born at the end of the second year, and a girl born at the end of the fourth year of their married life.

Family E consists of a husband and wife who bring up two children, a boy born at the end of the second year, and a girl born at the end of the twelfth year of their married life.

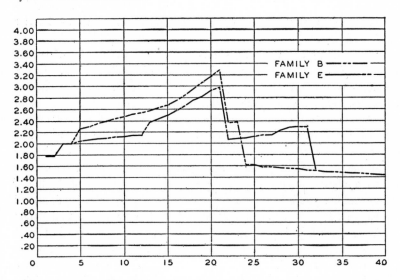

This chart shows graphically the relative severity and duration of the burden of bringing up two children, when born two years, and when born ten years, apart.

Reduction of living standards during the years when children are being reared is inevitable if the family is inclined to spend all its money each year for current expenses. The greatest value of the ammain method lies in its emphasis upon the importance of starting out upon a standard somewhat lower than that which might be maintained, in order to avoid the very unpleasant necessity a few years later of greatly reducing the family's standard of living.

In order to determine roughly the amount which a family should plan to spend for current expenses in the early years of its married life the procedure is as follows: First determine the total cost in

ammains of maintaining the family during the years in which it will
be bringing up its children.   Second, determine the total amount of
income the family will probably have available to spend during this
same period.   Then divide the total anticipated income by the sum of
the ammains.   This will give the cost per ammain which the family
can plan to spend year by year for current expenses.   Then multiply
the number of ammains of expense for the coming year by the cost
per ammain, to determine the amount available for current expenses.
The balance should be saved or spent for durable equipment which
will lighten the burden of family support in years of heavier
expenditure.

The chart on page 385 shows graphically the results of such a
comparison of family income with the cost of family support.   In this
chart, cost figures were computed for Family B.   For the income
figures, Dublin and Lotka's estimate of the annual earning power of
a man with a maximum earning power of $2,500 was used for the
first 45 years.   It was assumed that the head of the family retired
at 70.   After age 70 (beginning with the 46th year of the life
of the family), the family income consisted of interest on savings
accumulated between the 22nd year and the 45th year of the life of
the family.   (The 22nd year was the year in which the family passed
the peak of its burden of family support.)   For the detailed tabulation
from which this chart was drawn, see the following insert chart.

In using the ammain method of analysis, it is especially important
to remember that this very definitely stated cost index can be assumed
to be an accurate measure of relative costs only for individuals living
in the same sort of families as those for which the scale was determined, and that it can be assumed to be accurate for those families
only as long as price relationships remain substantially the same as
they were in 1916.

Because this ammain scale was worked out for families living near
the subsistence level, it overestimates somewhat the relative importance of the primary necessities of food and clothing, and underestimates the other expenditures—for recreation, for medical care, for
education, and the like.   It can be considered reasonably accurate
only in so far as necessities are concerned.

However, it does give a family something to begin with.   And
because it is stated, not in dollars, but in terms of relative cost, it is
less subject to inaccuracy because of price changes than are most cost

THE VARYING BURDEN OF FAMILY SUPPORT

A Comparison of Family Income and the Cost of Family Support

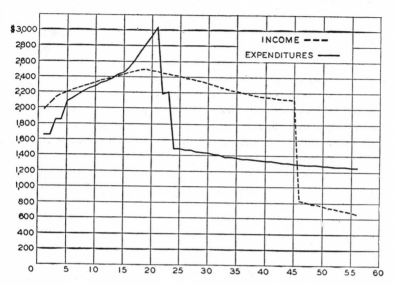

Family income, for 45 years, is Dublin's estimate [9] of the annual earning power of a man with a maximum earning power of $2,500.

Family income after retirement consists of interest on accumulated savings.

Family cost is the cost of supporting a family and bringing up two children, computed in ammains. See Family B, page 380.

This chart is represented in tabular form in the preceding insert chart.

of living studies. It suggests the importance of making some expenditures in anticipation of future need, and of postponing other less important things the family would like to do until a time when there will be more income or less demand upon the family's resources. The method emphasizes the importance of seeing the life of the family not as a day to day or week to week or year to year affair, but as a whole. The ammain method of approach gives perspective. It provides a pattern to follow in planning expenditures throughout the entire life of the family.

The family life cycle method. To be of maximum value the outline which the ammain method of analysis provides should be

---

[9] Louis I. Dublin and Alfred J. Lotka, *op. cit.*, Table III, p. 42.

filled in by careful detailed studies of what the family will need during each of the stages of the family life cycle. At first sight it seems an impossible task to make a comprehensive list of all the goods and services a family will need in the twenty-five or fifty years of its life as a family. But by considering in turn each one of the stages in the usual family life cycle, it is possible to break the one impossibly complex problem into a series of problems, each one of which can be solved. By analyzing in specific terms the needs of the family in each of these stages, it is possible to see clearly the characteristic details of the problems each stage involves. By studying these problems as phases of a cycle, it is possible to see them not as isolated problems but as steps in a progression, which must be worked out in their proper order, if the family is to continue to live a good life as years go by. As a result of such analysis it is possible to plan for the present and the immediate future with the long-time well-being of the family clearly in mind.

How can a family just starting out in life find out what it will need in the way of goods and services in each of the stages of the cycle through which a family ordinarily passes? Most people have grown up in families. They know from experience what they enjoyed, and what they wanted but could not afford during each of a number of the stages of the cycle. Most people know one or more families now living in each stage of the family life cycle. By observing these families, it is possible to determine definitely what problems arise in each stage of the cycle. A young couple can project both their experience and their observation into the future through conscious use of constructive imagination. In this way they can determine with considerable accuracy most of the problems which they themselves will face in the years ahead.

Of course it is important to remember that many families will not follow exactly the cycle outlined in Chapter I.[10] The family without children (what Groves calls the *arrested* family) [11] faces some peculiar problems of its own. It does not have to provide funds for food and clothing and education and all the rest of the expenses which children always entail. But it must make adequate provision for its own old age from its own invested savings. And it will want all along the line to spend money for many interesting things with

---

[10] See pp. 15 ff.
[11] E. R. Groves, *The American Family*, pp. 228 ff. J. B. Lippincott Co., Chicago, 1934.

which to fill the time which other families spend caring for and enjoying their children.

The family with more than the average number of children, on the other hand, faces an entirely different set of problems. It must practice all possible economies in the use of its money income in order to provide for the family as many as possible of the things which the standard of the group calls for. It must choose between severely curtailing its current living standards and postponing its savings program until after the children are self-supporting. However, it can safely postpone its accumulation for old age, because if worst comes to worst it can fall back upon the combined earnings of several children for support in old age. It will be forced to forego much of the commercial recreation small families can enjoy. It will plan to make its contribution to community affairs in the form of personal services rather than of cash. And it will find its time for such contributions, as well as its money income, limited.

The family with elderly dependents faces a different sort of demand upon its income for a limited period of years. It is usually possible for a family to judge in advance the probability of some members of an older generation becoming partially or totally dependent. By taking into account their resources, the health, the age, and the life expectancy of the members of the older generation, it is possible to judge within a few years the period of dependency and to make plans in advance for the care of the individuals in the family or for their support in homes of their own.

The broken family in its turn must do the best it can to provide for its children as nearly as possible the equivalent of a normal environment. And it must try to make this provision in most cases with considerably curtailed resources. If the wife is left with children to rear, her earning power is almost always less than was her husband's. If the husband is left with motherless children, he must buy with money as nearly as he can the equivalent of the work and service and child care which the mother usually contributes. It is almost never possible to anticipate the contingency of a broken family. Adjustments must be made when the situation arises. But the problem of making suitable adjustments is simplified if the family has had clearly in mind what it wants to accomplish. It is in a position to proceed immediately with intelligent and constructive adjustments to the new situation which it must face.

Analyzing the needs of the family in terms of its progress through the family life cycle, then, has a number of definite advantages. It breaks the seemingly impossible problem into a series of problems each one of which is entirely possible of solution. It brings into clear relief not only the usual problems which normal families must face, but the special problems of families with some unusual elements in the family situation. It emphasizes the importance of the long look ahead. It sets up a long-time program not in terms of dollars, which are often of changing value, but in terms of the actual goods and services which a family should have during the years. At the same time that it keeps constantly before the family the importance of planning to live within its means, it places the emphasis not upon the money cost of living, but upon living.

Estimating family income: Using income statistics. As was indicated in the discussion of family incomes in Chapter III, there are no really reliable statistics of individual earnings in the various industries and occupations. The Department of Labor publishes from time to time estimates of average wage rates and of average hours of employment, and in some cases estimates of average weekly earnings in various industries. But these figures tell nothing at all about the actual earnings of individual workers.

Willford I. King, in his study, *The National Income and Its Purchasing Power*,[12] has some interesting tables showing the median yearly incomes of workers in a number of groups of industries. His estimates do take account of the usual amount of unemployment in each occupation, but they tell nothing of the range of incomes on each side of the median given. They make no distinction between the earnings of men and of women. They tell nothing about relating the age to the earnings of the individual workers.[13]

The table on page 389 was compiled from Dublin and Lotka's estimates of the annual earning power of a man with maximum annual earnings of $1,000, $2,500, $5,000 and $10,000. These are estimates of typical or average earnings rather than records of the earnings of heads of actual families. They are intended to indicate the relative earning power of men of different ages. Therefore they are expressed in terms of the amounts a man would earn

---

[12] W. I. King, *The National Income and Its Purchasing Power*, pp. 144 ff. and 157 ff. National Bureau of Economic Research, Inc., New York, 1930.
[13] The tables in Ch. III give some typical income statistics. The problem facing the family in planning its individual expenditures is to determine as accurately as it may from figures such as these what its probable income will be.

ANNUAL EARNINGS OF A MAN WITH MAXIMUM ANNUAL EARNINGS OF
STATED AMOUNTS [14]

Estimates in Terms of 1929 Earning Power; Wage Levels Assumed to Be
Those of the Larger Cities

1 Age	2 $1,000	3 $2,500	4 $5,000	5 $10,000
18	385	963	910	1,150
19	450	1,125	1,040	1,300
20	520	1,300	1,170	1,475
21	585	1,463	1,352	1,660
22	650	1,625	1,534	1,875
23	715	1,788	1,690	2,090
24	755	1,888	1,742	2,275
25	790	1,975	1,924	2,420
26	820	2,050	1,976	2,520
27	850	2,125	2,158	2,640
28	870	2,175	2,314	2,770
29	880	2,200	2,392	2,925
30	890	2,225	2,548	3,100
31	900	2,250	2,652	3,310
32	910	2,275	2,730	3,545
33	920	2,300	2,860	3,825
34	930	2,325	3,016	4,160
35	940	2,350	3,068	4,550
36	947	2,368	3,198	4,990
37	954	2,385	3,328	5,455
38	963	2,408	3,380	5,950
39	972	2,430	3,536	6,430
40	981	2,453	3,640	6,900
41	989	2,473	3,744	7,360
42	997	2,493	3,900	7,800
43	1,000	2,500	4,004	8,300
44	992	2,480	4,186	8,725
45	988	2,470	4,264	9,100
46	980	2,450	4,524	9,400
47	975	2,438	4,732	9,640
48	969	2,423	4,888	9,780
49	963	2,408	4,992	9,890
50	957	2,393	4,940	9,950
51	951	2,378	4,888	9,990
52	944	2,360	4,855	10,000
53	937	2,343	4,820	9,820
54	929	2,323	4,775	9,640
55	920	2,300	4,730	9,460
56	910	2,275	4,680	9,280
57	901	2,253	4,635	9,100
58	892	2,230	4,585	8,920
59	887	2,218	4,560	8,740
60	881	2,203	4,530	8,560
61	876	2,190	4,505	8,380
62	869	2,173	4,470	8,200
63	864	2,163	4,445	8,020
64	860	2,150	4,420	7,840
65	857	2,143	4,405	7,660
66	854	2,135	4,390	7,480
67	851	2,128	4,375	7,300
68	848	2,120	4,360	7,120
69	845	2,113	4,345	6,940
70	842	2,105	4,330	6,760
71	839	2,098	4,315	6,580
72	836	2,090	4,300	6,400
73	833	2,083	4,285	6,220
74	830	2,075	4,270	6,040
75	827	2,068	.....	......
76	824	2,060	.....	......
77	821	2,053	.....	......
78	818	2,045	.....	......
79	815	2,038	.....	......
80	812	.....	.....	......

[14] Compiled from various tables in Louis I. Dublin and Alfred J. Lotka, *The Money Value of a Man*. The Ronald Press Co., New York, 1930.

each year if wages were at 1929 levels. When expressed in current dollars, the earnings of individual workers would seem to vary more than these figures indicate. But when allowances are made for changes in purchasing power, these estimates may be taken as fairly typical. They do not, of course, take into account relative wage and salary levels in cities of various sizes, or in various industries. They do give a set of income figures which the family can use as a starting point in working out estimates of its own future income.

Estimating family income: By analysis of the family situation. In estimating the family's probable income over a period of years, the family may use available statistics of income for what they are worth. But in most cases it can learn more about its future income from a careful analysis of its own family situation, in each stage of the family life cycle. In making such an analysis it must canvass all the possible sources of income which this particular family has available, from earnings of its members, from business ventures, and from family investments. In doing this, it must estimate as closely as possible the probable earnings of the husband through the years. It must determine what proportion of these earnings will probably come in the form of regular wages or salary, and what proportion will be received as a bonus or commission or as a share in business profits. It must consider the usual trend of earnings, opportunities for promotion, regularity of employment, and the usual retirement age in his present occupation. It must consider his chances of finding some other employment in case he loses his present position.

It must consider the possibility and the desirability of supplementing the income of the chief wage earner with the earnings of other members of the family. It must decide whether or not the wife is to continue to work for money outside the home during the first few years of married life, and if she does, how much she will be able to add to the family's money income. It must determine whether or not the family is to plan upon some supplementary income from her earnings during the high school period, the college period, or any other period when the family's expenses are greater than its regular income. It must determine whether or not the family is to plan upon using some income contributed by the children in the first few years after they begin earning for themselves. The family must consider also the income which it can count upon from investments. It must take inventory of the family's present investments, and consider the dependability of each of them as a source of future income. It must consider the possibility of savings and the probability of inheritances with which to supplement the family's earnings.

A family must consider all the sources of real income which will be available during each of the stages of the family life cycle. It must consider the specific skills and abilities possessed by each of the members of the family. If the husband is handy with tools, he can make many minor repairs around the house that other families must pay for. If the wife can cook and sew, she can make many things that other families must buy with money. The family with a number of children can count upon some contributions from them as they grow older and are able to take on their share of family responsibilities. The family that owns its own home and has an adequate stock of furniture and equipment can count upon using up some of these resources during periods of financial strain. The family with a few acres of ground or a country home has here a resource to fall back upon in case of unemployment or loss of investment income.

By comparing the needs and the income of the family in each successive stage of the family life cycle, the points at which there must be planned adjustment of income and expenditures become clearly apparent. The family is thus in a position to work out the specific adjustments that are necessary if the family is to finance the expenditures which must be made in each stage of the family life cycle.

Methods of adjusting expenditures to needs and incomes. There are a number of devices which can be employed to bring into line with available income the expenditures necessary to meet the varying needs of the family as it passes through one after another of the stages in its inevitable life cycle.

As families grow and the children mature, it is reasonable to expect some increase in the family's money income. The head of the family in many cases is in line for promotion to a better paying position. In other cases, where wage rates are fixed by custom or by trade union agreement, the middle-aged worker finds his earnings are increased because he secures the regular employment often reserved for the dependable family man. In the professions, there is opportunity for the successful doctor or lawyer to build up his income as the demands of his family increase. And whether or not it is desirable for the wife to seek employment outside the home, the shorter working day and the five-day week are making it easy for her to do so.

It is possible to level off the peaks of expenditure by drawing upon savings accumulated when current demands were less than the current family income. Either the income from invested savings, or if necessary the savings themselves, may be used to provide the things the family needs during the period of maximum expenditure. For example, the cost of confinement and of pre-natal and post-natal care may be financed from savings made for the purpose during the first year or two of married life. More of the savings may be used, if necessary, for extra help in the home during the period when the children are small. It is possible to finance the heavy expenses involved in a college education from savings or endowment insurance set aside over a period of years in anticipation of this specific need.

Inadequate income may be supplemented by borrowing. Temporary deficits may be taken care of in this way. In some cases it is wise to use credit rather than to disturb the family's investments. Some families find it is wise to place a mortgage on the family home, or to borrow against life insurance to allow the last of the children to complete the last year or two of his college or professional training. But borrowing is feasible only if the family can see in the near future a sufficiently adequate income to enable it to pay off its obligation within a reasonable length of time. Borrowing early in a period of financial strain is unwise, for it only serves to add interest charges to the already too heavy expenditures.

A family may level down peaks of expenditure by producing for use in the home many of the things which at other times it would purchase in the market. Particularly for families with growing children, who are old enough to do a good deal for themselves but who are barred from gainful employment by child labor legislation, there is a chance to provide worth while activity of a definitely educational nature and at the same time to reduce demands upon the family income.

A family may level off many of the peaks of the demand upon the family income by what may be termed "planned expenditure." In using this method the family deliberately buys many of the things it must have some time in advance of its greatest need. It builds up inventories of household supplies, china, silver, linen, and even some types of clothing. It invests a considerable part of its surplus over immediate needs in durable goods, like furniture, a car, a washing machine, a radio, or the home itself. Then as current demands upon its income increase, it gradually shifts a larger and larger proportion of its spending to current necessities. It reduces its inventories, wears out many of its pieces of equipment, defers maintenance on the rest, and plans to replace the worn-out furniture and equipment, and to rebuild its inventories during the next period of adequate income.

There are many families with little surplus and less inclination for saving who find it almost impossible to accumulate any cash savings, but comparatively easy to buy and pay for many of the more durable things a family needs. Most families find that they can provide for the peak of expenditures with less reduction in the family's current living standard by investing their surplus above current needs in inventories of household supplies and in permanent equipment from which they can get some immediate benefit than they can by setting aside in the bank a similar amount of money income.

To whatever extent it proves to be impossible for a family to care for the peak of its expenditures by these means, it must deliberately reduce its standard of living sufficiently to bring expenditures into line with available resources. But such a reduction should be made only as a last resort. And if it must be made, it should be with care, eliminating only the least essential items, postponing them rather than doing without them entirely, in order that the family may retain just as far as possible all the worth while things its ordinary standard calls for.

QUESTIONS

1. Using the ammain table on page 375, work out a curve showing the relative annual cost your parents incurred in rearing their family. Did the family income increase as rapidly as unit costs? If not, by what devices did your family provide for periods of unusually heavy expenditure?

2. Does the ammain curve you have constructed show with reasonable accuracy the changing burden involved? At what points in the life history of your parents' family does the ammain method overestimate and at what points does it underestimate the costs actually involved? What is your estimate of the value of the ammain curve as a method of predicting family expense?

3. A young couple described in question 6, page 371, want advice in working out a financial plan for their family. Using the family life cycle method, indicate for them the probable expenses they must provide for in each of the stages of the family life cycle.

4. What devices should each of the families described in question 10, page 81, use in adjusting their expenditures to changing family needs? Work out in detail a plan for the next five years for one of these families.

5. How do Dublin and Lotka's estimates of the earning power of a man check with the experience of some of the older men of your acquaintance? Remember that these figures state incomes in terms of 1929 incomes, not in terms of wages and salaries over a long period of years. In what ways do you believe these estimates are helpful? What are the limits to their use by actual families?

6. What is the difference between earning power of a man and family income? What is the significance of this distinction in adjusting family expenditures to family needs?

REFERENCES

Douglas, P. H., *Wages and the Family*. University of Chicago Press, Chicago, 1927.

An analysis of the varying burden of family support, together with a description of the family allowance system of wage payments adopted in a number of European countries as a means of solving the problem for families at the subsistence level.

Dublin, Louis I., and Lotka, Alfred J., *The Money Value of a Man*. The Ronald Press Co., New York, 1930.

In working out a method for estimating the money value of a man, the authors have devised interesting tables showing the relationship of earning power and living costs to the age of the individual. The study includes a number of estimates for typical income groups.

King, W. I., *The National Income and Its Purchasing Power*. National Bureau of Economic Research, Inc., New York, 1930.

A thorough analysis of national income. Interesting here for the occasional tables estimating average annual earning of individuals in various occupations. See Index and Table of Contents.

Kyrk, Hazel, *Economic Problems of the Family*, pp. 214-225. Harper and Bros., New York, 1933.

A discussion of the relation between family needs and family income. Includes interesting statistics of earnings at various ages for groups of skilled workers and professional men.

Monroe, Day, *Chicago Families*. University of Chicago Press, Chicago, 1932.

Chs. V, VI, VII, and VIII contain interesting material upon the general situation of the group of Chicago families studied by Miss Monroe. Of special interest is the author's comment as to the changing burden of child dependency (pp. 121 ff.) and the ways in which the number and personnel of the family wage earners change with the age and make-up of the family group (pp. 154 ff.).

Nystrom, P. H., *Economic Principles of Consumption,* Ch. IX, pp. 185-214. The Ronald Press Co., New York, 1929.

A description and critical analysis of the various attempts to measure the relationship of living costs to the size of the family and the ages of its members, together with a statement of the practical value of such measurements in family budget studies.

Sydenstricker, E., and King, W. I., *A Method of Classifying Families According to Incomes in Studies of Disease Prevalence.* Public Health Reports, U. S. Treasury Dept., Vol. 35, No. 48, November 26, 1920.

A description of the development and use of the ammain table.

Sydenstricker, E., King, W. I., and Wiehl, Dorothy, *The Income Cycle in the Life of the Wage Earner.* Public Health Reports, U. S. Treasury Dept., Vol. 39, No. 34, August 22, 1924.

A description of the varying burden of family support at various stages in the life of North Carolina cotton-mill families.

CHAPTER XVII

ADJUSTING FAMILY EXPENDITURES TO CHANGING BUSINESS CONDITIONS

How changing business conditions affect the family. Every family must from time to time adjust its financial program to changing conditions in the world outside the home. Changing business conditions affect the prices a family must pay for the goods and services it purchases in the market, and the income which it receives from employment and investments. Such conditions affect the kind, the quantity, and the quality of goods offered for sale in the market, as well as the opportunities for employment, for saving, and for effective investment of family funds. Changing business conditions affect the age at which marriage is economically feasible and the size of the family which it is wise to rear. They affect the length of the effective earning period of the members of the family, and the age at which retirement is imperative or financially possible.

These changes may be specific, affecting the price of some one article which the family must buy, or the income which it receives from some one source, or they may be general in character, affecting all prices, regardless of conditions of supply and demand for a particular commodity, and all types of income, no matter from what sources it may be received. Most families are accustomed to watching for any changes which will directly affect the prices of the goods they must buy. They know that a severe drought will necessitate definite adjustments in their food purchases. They know a prolonged strike in the coal fields may increase sharply the price of coal. They know that the general introduction of a labor-saving machine or a new production process ought to reduce definitely the price they should pay for automobiles, or radios, and they are, if anything, even more on the alert for similar changes which will affect either earnings or employment in the industry or occupation in which the family's members or money are employed.

But most families do not understand so clearly the nature or the significance of the more fundamental changes which affect whole groups of prices, and make their influence felt in one way or another upon all types of income. It is impossible to understand specific changes apart from their relation to general trends.

The better and more widespread is the understanding of the business cycle, the less severe will tend to be the successive swings from prosperity to depression. If consumers as well as producers are on guard against the overspending and the overexpansion which mark the period preceding a depression, if the more intelligent consumers refuse to overmortgage their future, no matter how high is the sales pressure which the less intelligent business men place upon them, if they stop buying at the first indication of an unnecessary widening in the spread between costs and prices, business will not reach dangerously high peaks of false prosperity. And these same consumers, refusing to be stampeded into making commitments of future earnings when prices are unreasonably high, will be able to start buying again as soon as prices swing into line with reasonable costs, with the result that many depressions will prove to be but temporary recessions from a more permanent prosperity.

The better and more widespread is the understanding of the nature and causes of long-time trends in prices, the more intelligent can be the adjustments which both producers and consumers make to these underlying forces. Both producers and consumers will be on guard against assuming too heavy fixed charges late in a period of rising prices, or early in a period of falling prices. They will be less hesitant to secure the advantages which come from assuming reasonable obligations early in a long period of rising prices.

The better and more widespread is the understanding of the futility of inflation and the inevitability of deflation, the less easily will nations be stampeded into the acceptance of money-tinkering as a panacea for all their ills.

The nature of the business cycle. The name *business cycle* has been applied to the periodic ebb and flow of business which recurs at more or less regular intervals. There are four stages which are usually recognized in the description of the cycle: prosperity, crisis or liquidation, depression, and recovery. Some descriptions divide the period of prosperity into two parts, prosperity proper and a later period of financial strain which immediately precedes the period of liquidation.

Some descriptions distinguish between depression and recession.

They use the terms liquidation and depression for downward swings in business activity which last for several years, and use the term recession for minor readjustments which are completed within a few months. Other descriptions distinguish between major and minor cycles. They consider that the minor declines are simply less severe manifestations of a complete cycle.

The stages of the business cycle. Each stage of the business cycle has its own peculiar characteristics. The prosperity stage is a period of widespread business activity. Under the stimulus of growing demand prices rise gradually. In order to secure the economies which can be had by anticipating these price increases, both producers and consumers buy a little in advance of their current needs. Employment increases. Wages and salaries are raised. Interest rates and earnings increase. Plants operating at or near capacity expand to be able to care for their growing business. Security values advance in line with current trends of earnings. All seems well with business.

But sooner or later in the prosperity stage of the cycle, unmistakable signs of financial strain begin to develop. First one and then another takes stock of his situation and finds his current needs are well cared for without immediate purchases. Then follows widespread use of high-pressure salesmanship, in an attempt to attain and maintain the volume of business necessary to operate enlarged plants to capacity. There develops extreme emphasis upon fashion, which spreads to more durable goods like automobiles, bathrooms, home furnishings, and even to houses. There is a deliberate attempt to get people to discard many goods before they are worn out, and to buy the many new commodities which expanded plant capacity is able to produce. To make it easy for the consumer to buy, he is offered all kinds of goods on easy credit. These methods do stimulate sales for a time. People are attracted by the new designs, and because their incomes have been steadily increasing they are willing to mortgage a part at least of their future income.

Eventually, however, even the consumer reaches his limit. He refuses to react any longer to sales stimulants. He decides to pay for what he has bought, rather than to contract for any more goods at their present high prices. The producer too finds that he must retrench. Because of the cost of his new sales methods, and because of the expense of frequent and radical changes in his models, his costs are increasing faster than his sales. The speculator discovers he has pushed stock prices to levels which shrinking earnings make it impossible for him to maintain. The banker becomes worried and begins to try to collect his credits, and the period of liquidation sets in.

The liquidation stage is a short period of rapid changes. The fact that it is sometimes spoken of as a crisis indicates that in many ways it is the most upsetting part of the entire cycle. Usually in two or three months comes the greater part of the deflation of security values, although they may continue to decline all through the depression stage which follows. Demand falls off markedly; orders are canceled; wholesale prices fall; production is curtailed; work forces are greatly reduced; and unemployment, which was beginning to appear late in the period of financial strain, becomes a serious problem. With the decline in productive activity, consumers further curtail their buying, many because their needs are well provided for, others because they have lost their jobs, and many more because they have lost heavily from reductions in dividend rates and the decline in security values.

Then depression sets in. Security values continue to decline. The trend in wholesale prices is definitely downward. The retailer, however, has heavy stocks of goods on his shelves, purchased at prosperity prices, which he is anxious to dispose of at a reasonable profit. As a result, retail prices remain for some time at or near prosperity levels. But sooner or later, faced by the fact that most of his customers have only curtailed incomes with which to buy, every merchant brings his prices into line with lowered costs. Even falling retail prices bring out only a limited amount of buying at first; but gradually, in spite of the fact that consumption is much below normal, stocks of goods are reduced, and consumers begin to buy a little here and a little there, as their needs develop. Eventually, retailers are forced to replenish their reduced stocks, and place orders for merchandise, cautiously at first, but gradually gaining confidence as consumers' purchases continue to increase. Wholesalers' orders in time reach the manufacturers, and industrial employment picks up, bringing new purchasing power into many families that for months have been in want.

So finally recovery appears. As demand develops, price declines are checked first in one line and then in another. Output increases, employment picks up, profits again appear, dividends are resumed. Production is kept closely in line with current demand, but business gathers momentum, and sooner or later prosperity again returns.

Causes of the business cycle. There is no one simple explanation of the causes of the business cycle. In part it is a psychological phenomenon and in part a phenomenon of unbalanced production and consumption. During prosperity the current mood of optimism leads business men to produce more than they can sell. It leads consumers to buy more than they need. It leads business men and consumers to borrow more than they can repay. It leads bankers and investors to lend more than they can recover. Once the spell is broken, the psychology of depression brings just the opposite reaction. People buy less than they need, make less than they might sell. They borrow less than they can repay, lend less than enough to finance the business necessary to supply actual needs. People everywhere do without things they would like to have. Those who have money neither spend it nor invest it. Those who are unemployed have little or nothing with which to buy. When they get a job they are afraid to spend more than is necessary of their meager earnings. Business men and consumers are held back for some time after fundamental conditions begin to improve by the unreasoning mood of pessimism which everywhere prevails.

But if the business cycle is in part a psychological phenomenon, it is so only in part. It is impossible to bring back prosperity by hoping for it. For during prosperity, especially late in prosperity, conditions develop which cannot be wished away. During prosperity industry produces more than families consume. Stocks of goods accumulate. Eventually a point is reached at which consumers are no longer willing to pay higher prices for commodities of which they already have enough. As production gets out of line first with consumption, and then with sales, unemployment begins to develop. Then numbers of consumers become unable to buy. And as prices weaken, still others become unwilling to buy. They have enough for current needs, and are able to wait for lower prices. As depression continues, on the other hand, faced by curtailed incomes, families gradually use up stocks of surplus commodities. They wear out their more durable equipment. They exhaust their inventories. They consume what is currently produced, and use up what they have left over from the preceding period of prosperity as well. It is only after consumption has caught up with production that it does very much good to talk about recovery.

The swing of the cycle depends not alone upon domestic conditions, but upon world conditions as well. Although cycles do not proceed at the same pace or swing at the same time from one stage to another in every country in the world, they are definitely interrelated. For just as it is necessary to keep domestic production in line with domestic consumption, so there is the same fundamental need of keeping production and consumption reasonably in line throughout the entire world.

In our complex world-wide economic organization, it is impossible to keep production always perfectly adjusted to consumer demand. We cannot hope, therefore, completely to eliminate the business cycle. But it is possible greatly to reduce the severity of the swings of the cycle if business men plan their production always with due regard to consumer demand, and if the consumer consciously plans his expenditures, and estimates his future earnings with due regard to the inevitable swings of the business cycle.

Adjusting family expenditures to changes in the business cycle. Every family can reasonably expect to live through a number of complete swings of the business cycle. It is not possible to tell years in advance the exact timing of the successive swings of the cycle. It is possible, however, to determine approximately the number of complete cycles through which the family will live in the period covered by its life span.

For example, a family consisting of a man, twenty-five years old, and his wife, twenty-three, planning for the future of their newly established family, should look at least fifty years into the future. It will be impossible for them to tell exactly which years of the life of the family will be lived in periods of prosperity and which will be lived in depression, but they can predict with a considerable degree of accuracy the number of cycles through which they will live. If they assume an average length of seven years for each cycle, the family may expect to experience seven complete swings of the cycle. They will live through seven or eight periods of prosperity, and they will weather seven or eight periods of depression if they live to celebrate their fiftieth wedding anniversary. They must remember that some cycles last longer than others, and that generally it is the periods of depression rather than the periods of prosperity which are unusually prolonged. They must understand that some swings of the cycle are much more severe than others. They need not feel discouraged if they spend the first cycle or two acquiring experience which they can use to advantage in planning for the swings of the later cycles. They will probably succeed better in planning their affairs if they ignore any predictions that the business cycle has been eliminated, and assume that business cycles will continue to come and go in the future much as they have in the past.

Families are not all affected in the same way by the successive swings of the cycle. Each family must plan its adjustments to these changes on the basis of its own individual situation. If the family income swings with the cycle, it will have plenty of money to spend during prosperity. It can enjoy the exhilaration which prosperity brings. But it must not neglect to conserve a considerable portion of its prosperity income for use during the leaner depression years.

If a family is living on a fixed income, on the other hand, from salary or income from bonds, annuities, or long-term leases, unless its income is generous, it will be burdened by the constant stimulus to spend during prosperity when prices are high, for its income fails to keep up with that of other families of its acquaintance. Such a family will feel less burdened early in depression, as social pressure is relaxed and prices decline.

The family living on fixed income can ease the pressure somewhat by building up an inventory of needed goods early in prosperity. It must deliberately ignore the high-pressure salesmanship, extreme emphasis on fashion, and excessive obsolescence during the period of financial strain. It must get its satisfaction during these periods from more permanent and less immediately expensive values.

If a family can count upon its earning members being regularly employed throughout the depression stage of the cycle, it will find little difficulty in making both ends meet. For its own peace of mind it will want to accumulate an unemployment reserve early in the depression. It should not wait too long to set up this reserve, but should anticipate wage and salary reductions which usually come in the later years of the depression.

If a family must expect that its income will be curtailed by underemployment or complete unemployment of some of its members, it must plan definitely to accumulate unemployment reserves during prosperity. If the husband is unemployed the wife may seek part-time or full-time employment. Or if this is unwise or impossible, the family may stretch its unemployment reserves over a longer period by producing for its own use many of the things which it is accustomed to buy during more prosperous times. If it is planning to supplement its depression income with production for use, it should deliberately acquire during prosperity the equipment it is going to need.

In general, families should buy as their incomes permit early in the prosperity stage of the cycle. With the first signs of financial strain they should put their affairs in order. They should plan to complete the payment of whatever obligations they have outstanding. If a family is buying a home on the instalment plan, it should if possible protect its equity by refinancing in such a way as to be able to pay the interest only during the depression stage of the cycle. It should go over all its investments carefully, disposing of such securities as are of doubtful value, and shifting part at least of its investment in stocks to sound interest-bearing securities.[1]

During the liquidation stage of the cycle, the family should conserve its resources. It should watch for signs of weakness in any of its investments. It should study carefully the financial condition of the banks in which it has deposited money. It should be on the alert for opportunities to buy needed goods at bargain prices. But it should remember that sacrifice sales in consumer goods seldom develop to any considerable extent in retail trade until the depression is well under way.

As the country settles down to a period of depression, the family will probably live for a time upon its prosperity accumulations, buying only for its most imperative needs. But it should constantly be on the alert for opportunities to buy both needed commodities and sound investment securities at bargain prices. It must make such purchases only when it is convinced that the prices represent sound long-time values. It must not rush in and spend all its available money too early in the depression. It must be constantly on guard against false recovery.

Once recovery is well under way, however, it should begin stocking up with the goods necessary to replace those worn out during the depression period. It should anticipate the return of prosperity in so far as possible in making repairs to its home, and in buying those commodities which usually rise most in price during periods of prosperity. Late in depression and early in recovery, when the family's income is reasonably assured, it is often wise to use credit for some necessary

---

[1] For a detailed discussion of the problems involved in adjusting the family's saving and investment program to changing business conditions see p. 465.

purchases if the family can secure economies from lower prices which will more than offset the interest charges which the use of credit involves.

Once prosperity has clearly returned, the family should buy for long-time needs in order to be able to diminish its buying as prices trend upward.

In adjusting to the successive swings of the cycle, one thing only is important: to look forward, and not back. The family must plan its adjustments not on the basis of what has recently passed, but upon what the future holds.

Long-time price trends. But it is not enough simply to plan with regard to the business cycle. If a family is to plan its affairs intelligently it must understand that the cycle itself is affected by underlying long-time or secular trends in prices. In the later 1920's many people who were familiar with the theory of the business cycle were misled by the fact that during nearly five years of prosperity, prices did not rise. As a result they assumed that prices were stable. They believed that by one means or another we had been able, once and for all, to eliminate in our financial set-up the periodic swings of the cycle. They made this mistake because they did not understand the influence of long-time price trends upon the course of prices during the business cycle. They did not realize that in 1920 at the end of the period of post-war inflation, there had begun a long-time downward trend of prices sufficiently pronounced to offset the usual cyclical price increases. Nor did they realize that the stationary prices of the middle '20's were the result of the same cyclical forces that produced rapidly rising prices when the trend of prices was gradually upward in the years before the war. It was only after two or three years of the secondary post-war depression had passed that business men generally came to realize that prices do inevitably trend downward for a number of years following a prolonged war with its attendant and widespread inflation. Only after two or three years of the secondary post-war depression had passed, did business men generally become familiar with the fact that in the past century or more for which we have reasonably adequate statistics, following every war which was sufficiently prolonged to result in any substantial amount of inflation, prices have trended downward for a number of years. It was only when prices continued to fall well into the third year of the depression that they began to believe that in spite of the existence of superior

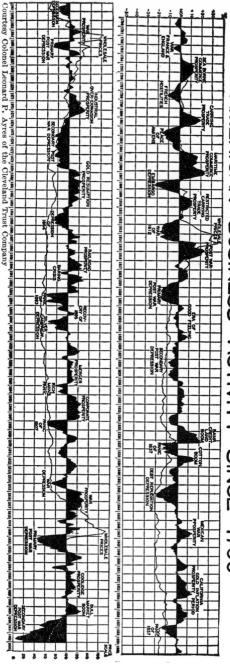

AMERICAN BUSINESS ACTIVITY SINCE 1790

Courtesy Colonel Leonard P. Ayres of the Cleveland Trust Company

The dotted line represents changes in wholesale prices. Prior to 1930, there were only two periods of depression lasting six years—one in the 1840's, the Debt Repudiation Depression, and one in the 1870's, which lasted until the country returned to the gold standard in 1879.

facilities for controlling money and credit, perhaps the World War would prove to be no exception.

The course of wholesale prices. The chart on page 405 shows the changes which have taken place in American business activity since 1790. During this period there have been three major wars. The War of 1812 was the American phase of the Napoleonic Wars. The War of the Rebellion in the United States was not far removed in time from the Franco-Prussian War in Europe. The World War involved all the major nations of the Western world before its conclusion in 1918. Each of these three major wars was accompanied by marked inflation, and was followed by a period of gradually declining prices.

Following the War of 1812, the secular trend of prices was downward until the middle 1840's. Following the Civil War, the secular trend of prices was downward until the middle 1890's. In neither case, however, was the rate of decline continuous, nor was the course of prices identical during these two periods. In the 1830's, following the secondary post-War of 1812 depression, price declines were checked by the bank-credit land boom with its attendant borrowing for canals and other public improvements. But this period of temporary credit inflation was followed by a "debt-repudiation" depression, in the years following the panic of 1837. In the period following the Civil War, price declines continued until the return to the gold standard at the end of the secondary post-Civil War depression in 1879. They rose somewhat in the early 1880's, only to resume their downward drift with the swing of the cycle at the end of the period of gold-resumption prosperity. At the end of the World War prices declined markedly in 1920 and 1921, rose a little in 1922, leveled out in 1923, and declined again in the early 1930's.

Between the three periods in which the long-time trend of prices was downward, there were two periods when the trend of prices was definitely upward. Following the discovery of gold in California in 1849, the long-time price trend was upward until the outbreak of the Civil War. Beginning about 1897, soon after the discovery of gold in Alaska and South Africa, the long-time trend of prices was upward until the outbreak of the World War in 1914.

Causes of secular price trends. Business cycles are the result of current developments. Secular price trends, on the other hand, are due to fundamental changes in the economic system. Of the explanations which have been offered for these long-time trends in prices, one turns upon the quantity theory of money. This theory seems to explain rather satisfactorily the reason for a rising secular trend of prices, and for the price increases which inflation involves. Another explanation turns upon the concept of "normal price." This theory seems to account for some of the features of a long-time declining price trend, which cannot be satisfactorily explained by monetary theory alone. Neither is a completely satisfactory explanation of long-time price trends. In all probability there is an element of truth in both.[2]

Briefly, the quantity theory of money is as follows: The price of an article is by definition the amount of money which would be given for one unit of it. But money is, by definition, simply another commodity which is so generally acceptable in exchange that it has been legally designated as money. The dollar contains so many grains of gold of a specified fineness. If the quantity of gold increases, the effect upon the value of gold is just the same as if the quantity of any other commodity had increased. Its power to command other commodities in exchange declines. But since prices are expressed in terms of gold, a decrease in the value of gold results in an increase in prices to correspond to the increase in the amount of money which must be given in exchange. Suppose we apply this theory to the long-time trend of prices. Whenever gold is discovered, and there is a marked increase in its production, it declines in value, relative to other commodities, and their prices rise.

In recent years, we have actually passed very little gold from hand to hand in the course of trade. Instead, we have used other forms of currency, issued by the government, and except for a few short periods in the past, redeemable in the standard monetary commodity. Or we have used bank credit, paying our bills by checks, which in turn could be turned into currency upon demand at the bank upon which they were drawn. In order to make allowance for the extension of the use of credit in recent years, the simple statement of the relationship between the quantity of gold and prices of commodities has been replaced by the "Equation of Exchange": $MV + M'V' = PT$. This is simply a statement of an obvious fact. If M equals the quantity of money, and V equals the velocity of its circulation, if M' equals the amount of credit available and V' equals the velocity of its circula-

---

[2] For a more detailed discussion of these theories, see any standard text in principles of economics.

tion, then the total amount of money and credit multiplied by the number of times it is used within a year must necessarily equal the volume of trade carried on multiplied by the prices at which the exchanges were made. The quantity theorists hold that there is a normal relationship between the quantity of gold, the quantity of currency, and the quantity of bank credit in existence.

The quantity theory concludes, therefore, that if the amount of money or the amount of credit is increased, other things being equal, a given volume of trade will be carried on only at higher prices. If, however, the quantity of money and credit is decreased, then a given volume of trade can be carried on with this money only at lower price levels.

The quantity theory also helps to explain the decline in prices which follows every war. In the years following a prolonged war, these normal relationships between gold and currency and credit are often upset. Gold is not evenly distributed among the countries of the world. At the close of every war, there are outstanding large numbers of government bonds and of private obligations which are the result of war-time business activity. These obligations can be used as security for bank loans, and usually are in the period of postwar prosperity. But in the years following the war, gradually the government pays off its outstanding obligations, business reduces its outstanding funded debt, and gold finds its way back to goldless nations. The basis for bank loans and currency expansion is reduced and the general effect upon prices is the same as though there had been a reduction in the amount of money in circulation. Like the reduction of the war debt, the period of readjustment spreads over many years. This is one explanation which has been offered for the decline in prices following every war.

There are some elements in a long-time declining trend of prices which can be explained more satisfactorily by the "normal price" theory of prices. This theory holds that prices in the long run tend to follow cost of production. There are a number of forces at work during every war which tend to raise production costs. There is an unusual demand for goods of all kinds, together with a shortage of labor. There is an enormous demand for capital, followed by the actual destruction of much of this capital in the conduct of the war. For a few years following the war these forces making for high prices continue. There is a delayed peace-time demand for many essential commodities. There is a tendency for costs to remain for some time at high levels, owing to the shortage of capital and the permanent destruction of a large part of the labor supply.

Then follows a long period of readjustment. High interest rates stimulate saving. Paying off the government war indebtedness frees capital for investment in business. The labor supply is gradually restored as a new generation comes to maturity. Productive efficiency is increased. Labor-saving devices, encouraged by the war-time shortage of labor and by the necessity of economizing for some years in the use of available labor, reduce costs. This reduces the demand for labor, and wages and prices trend downward.

Adjusting family expenditures to long-time price trends. Since long-time price trends are due to fundamental conditions existing deep down in the structure of the economic system, they are an important part of the business situation to which the family must adjust. Experience seems to show that following every war, prices tend to decline for twenty-five or thirty years, and then rise again for twenty or twenty-five years until the next major political disturbance brings on another period of inflation and another period of post-war readjustment. On the basis of the experience of the last century, a family starting out in life can expect that if its members live for fifty years, they will have lived through not far from twenty years in which the secular trend of prices was rising, and not far from thirty years in which the long-time trend of prices was downward.

For example, suppose a family started out in life in 1866, just at the close of the Civil War. The husband was twenty-five. When he retired at seventy in 1911, he had lived through thirty years when the secular price trend was downward, and through fourteen more years of definitely rising prices. If he lived ten years in retirement, he saw the purchasing power of his savings cut to less than half by the inflationary rise in prices from 1917 to 1920. But when he died in 1921, prices had declined enough so that his estate could afford him a decent burial.

Suppose another family started out in 1890. In this family the husband was thirty. When he retired in 1930 he had lived through six years of declining prices, twenty years of rising prices, three years of war-time inflation and deflation, and ten years of declining prices. His children, born before 1897, were out of college before the worst of the war-time inflation. Relieved of the burden of bringing up his family, he was able to get along comfortably during the war period, and after the first post-war readjustments, to save a substantial sum for his old age. The money was carefully and conservatively invested. As a result of the continued decline in prices in the years following 1930, he was able to live with increasing ease on his fixed income.

It is important for every family to consider how these long-time trends in prices will affect family expenses and family income during the various stages of the family life cycle. If a family is living during a period of rising prices and the head of the family plans to retire when prices may be expected to reach their peak, it will be necessary to save and invest a much larger amount than if the head of the family were planning to retire during a period of declining prices when a much smaller amount of savings would yield a satisfactory retirement income. Similarly, if the family will come to the peak of its expenses toward the end of a period of rising prices, it must make much more generous provision for the heavy expenses those years will bring. If the family is carrying life insurance for protection against the death of the chief wage earner, it must carry more insurance to provide adequate protection during a period of rising prices than it will need if the trend of prices is definitely downward.

In making long-time commitments the family must keep in mind the underlying force of long-time price trends. If the family buys at high prices late in prosperity, on a rising price trend, the next swing of the cycle will more than make up for the decline in value during intervening depression years. But if a family pays too much for anything at any stage of the cycle when the secular trend is downward, its present mistake will become a steadily magnified loss. For example, a family buying a home may well consider the timing of the purchase with regard to long-time price trends. If the family pays a little more than a house is worth on a rising price trend, the increase in dollar values soon makes up for the mistake. If the family pays too much for a home when price trends are downward, however, the mistake once made will not be rectified simply by waiting for values to catch up with the price the family paid. If in a period of rising prices a family agrees to pay more for a home than it can easily spare, increases in income soon relieve the family of a major part of the burden. If, on the other hand, the family buys in a period of declining prices, it may soon find that falling prices have greatly reduced the value of the property it has purchased and that declining income has made it difficult, if not impossible, to continue payments as agreed.

Inflation. By definition, inflation is an increase in the amount of money, either gold, currency, or bank credit, without a corresponding increase in the production of commodities. In the popular mind, inflation involves an increase in the circulating medium sufficient to cause a rapid and marked increase in prices.

Inflation may be of three types. It may be gold inflation, caused by the increased production of gold, or, during a war, by the rapid flow of gold into some one or two countries which are engaged in the production and sale of war supplies, or by reduction in the gold content of the monetary unit.

It may be paper money inflation. This occurs during a prolonged war in a country drained of its gold by the necessity of buying war supplies abroad. Paper money is used to provide a domestic medium of exchange in place of the gold which is needed for foreign trade. Once a country has been forced off the gold standard, the value of its money depreciates, and prices inevitably rise to offset the loss of confidence of the people in the ultimate redemption of the circulating medium. This means that in order to carry on a given volume of business, more money is needed. More is printed. It depreciates still further in value. Prices continue to rise, and a cycle is started which often is checked only by complete abandonment or drastic devaluation of the currency. It is this type of paper money or currency inflation which is synonymous with inflation in the popular mind.

Or it may be credit inflation. Credit inflation is caused by expanding credit faster than the actual production of goods and services. During a war, there is a rapid expansion of bank loans to finance the increased war-time business activity. As the war continues, the government becomes a heavy borrower. Often it borrows directly from the banks. The banks pass on the government obligations as rapidly as possible to the investing public. These government bonds are used by the public as collateral for more loans, and thus provide the basis for further increase in deposit currency. Bonds held by the banks are often used as collateral for bank notes, which circulate as part of the country's currency. Ordinarily, credit inflation does not proceed to the heights of currency inflation, but it does cause marked increases in prices. Credit inflation, like paper money inflation, is inevitably followed by a period of deflation. Individual loans mature and must be repaid. Government obligations are gradually reduced. If credit inflation has been very marked, some obligations never can be met, and the severity of the deflation is increased by wholesale default and by the voluntary scaling down of obligations.

Inflation in history. The chart on page 405 shows three periods of pronounced inflation, during the three major wars. This inflation took various forms. Inflation during the Civil War was paper money inflation. Inflation during the World War, as far as the United States was concerned, was in part gold and in part credit inflation. There have been at least two periods in peace-time in which credit expansion approached the popular conception of inflation levels. In the 1830's there was a period of credit inflation caused by speculation in western lands. This was followed by wholesale default on obligations by many of the middle western states. In the 1920's there was some evidence of credit inflation, especially loans for real estate development and stock market speculation. This overexpansion of credit was not sufficient to cause marked rise in prices of goods, but it did delay for some years the decline of prices which seems to be an inevitable part of post-war readjustment.

Inflation is dangerous. Inflation is dangerous because it looks attractive. Once started, it cannot be stopped without deflation and its attendant economic losses. Inflation does bring a temporary increase in business activity. In the early stages, inflation increases profits, for prices usually increase faster than wages and interest charges. But profits early in inflation prove to be but temporary. Since prices are increasing faster than production, it is not long before output begins to outrun demand. Then follows the demand for more inflation. As prices rise to higher levels, another period of activity follows. Prices rise faster than wages. The increase in employment is not enough to make up for the loss of purchasing power of the money in the pay envelope. People begin to buy at once to protect themselves against further price increases. This still further stimulates business. Prices continue to rise. More money and credit is needed to finance business at higher price levels, prices rise higher, consumers borrow to buy more. Prices rise higher and higher, and more and more money and credit must be had. Inflation once well under way can hardly be stopped without disaster.

Who benefits from inflation? Because of the widespread and insistent demand for inflation which arises from time to time, it seems that there must be a considerable group who feel that they will benefit from inflation. For the most part, these are people who owe money or who stand to benefit from the temporary increase in profits which a little inflation brings. They feel that it would be easier to pay off their accumulated obligations, which can be satisfied in dollars, if prices would rise enough for them to get more dollars to use. Business men are usually not averse to a little inflation. They have stocks of goods on hand to turn into commodities they would like to sell at higher prices. They know that the prices they receive will for a time at least increase faster than production costs. Farmers are business men with crops to sell. Like other business men they benefit temporarily until the prices they must pay for the goods they buy rise enough to offset their own personal gains.

Who loses by inflation? The creditor loses because he is paid in dollars of decreasing purchasing power for both the income and the principal of his debt. The salaried man loses because prices rise faster than salaries. The wage worker loses, unless the initial impact of inflation increases employment enough to offset the decrease in the purchasing power of the dollars he receives. But wages never increase as fast as prices during a period of inflation. Almost all families in the lower income groups lose from inflation, for their incomes come from wages and salaries which never increase as fast as prices, and from some small amounts of interest from fixed income securities.

Who loses by deflation? Debtors obviously are heavy losers by deflation. They must pay inflated debts in deflated dollars. The creditor loses, because debtors are not able to pay and so default. The worker loses from unemployment, which, during a period of rapid deflation, increases more rapidly than the increasing purchasing power of the dollar in his pay envelope. The business man loses, for prices tend to decline faster than wages and salaries. He buys raw materials at high prices, makes them up, and sells them for less than they cost.

Protecting the family against the dangers of inflation. There is little that a family can do to protect itself against the dangers of inflation. If it buys in anticipation of rising prices, it only adds to the speed with which those prices rise. If it does not buy everything it can afford with its available income, it will be forced to pay higher prices later on. If it borrows to anticipate price increases, it will find difficulty in repaying its loan, because still further price increases will wipe out the margin it had counted upon to repay the obligation it has assumed. If it does not borrow, it will be forced to curtail its consumption at some time in the very near future anyway, because prices will have gotten out of line with its income. If inflation is too long continued, it may lose all its savings, either because it must spend them for current needs, or because of investment losses in the succeeding period of deflation which will inevitably follow.

The family feels helpless in the face of the possibility of inflation. But there is something that it can do that is at least partially effective. Before inflation gets well under way, it can stop buying in so far as possible whenever prices begin to get even a little out of line with its income. But families everywhere must put the brakes on rising prices early in inflation, before fear of loss has completely demoralized the situation. For it is this desperate fear of the inevitable consequences of inflation and the madly futile attempt to postpone impending disaster, that makes it so difficult to stop inflation once it is well started.

A family can minimize its losses from deflation by making just as few commitments as possible at high prices. It can protect its investments in part by buying property that will have use value in case of complete demoralization of security values. In some cases it can gain by buying sound bonds at low prices, which will increase in value as deflation proceeds, and offset part of the loss the family must take on its investments in stocks and in property.

Consumers alone may not be able completely to eliminate inflation with its attendant deflation. The necessities of a great war can be provided for in no other way. But consumers can hold peace-time inflationary tendencies in check, just to the degree that they are able and willing to refuse to buy as prices rise. The earlier they apply this check upon inflationary tendencies, the less severe will deflation need to be. Once people generally understand that in the long run the great majority lose much by inflation, while only a few gain even temporarily, inflation will no longer be a politically popular proposal. If, when inflation is proposed, consumers everywhere become vocal in opposition and back up their words by refusal to buy at inflated prices, it may be possible to avoid the wilder types of inflationary excesses in the future.

Long-time trends of rent, interest, and wages. Families are interested not only in the trend of prices which they must pay for the commodities they purchase in the market, but also in trends in wages, salaries, rents, and interest rates, which affect the amount of the family's income.

During the last three quarters of a century, wages have followed prices up during periods of rising prices. They have lagged markedly during periods of sharp inflation. But they have never declined as far as have prices during periods when the long-time trend of prices has been downward. After each primary post-war depression, wages have leveled out at a point not far from the peak reached during the inflationary years. Salaries, in general, have followed the trend of wages, with fewer minor variations. In the years since the World War, they have lost some of the advantages they held over wages previous to 1914. Wage earners lose in purchasing power during periods of rising prices because prices rise faster than wages. They gain during periods of declining prices because wages decrease more slowly than do prices.

Interest charges have followed prices up and down. They have increased markedly during every war. They have declined gradually in the years that followed as the accumulations of capital gradually made up for war-time losses.

Rents have tended to increase with the increase of population all through the history of the country. But this increase has not been uniform. Every improvement in transportation has made new land available. It has increased rents in locations served by the new facilities. It has tended to reduce rents in the formerly more favored regions. The development of the automobile has tended to check somewhat the rise of rents, both urban and agricultural. In cities, the use of the automobile has made it entirely possible for families to live farther and farther from the center of the city. It has decreased the tendency to congestion. It has checked the increase in rents for property located close to centers of employment. It has increased the value of land in the outskirts. The shift from horse-drawn to motor transportation has freed for the production of food for human use millions of acres of land formerly used to provide hay and oats for horses. The use of the automobile and the motor truck has greatly increased the acreage of land which is within economical reach of central markets.

Current wages, interest rates, and rents depend upon immediate conditions of supply and demand for labor, capital, and land. The long-time trends can better be explained by what economists call the *law of proportionality*. According to this law, any social change which reduces the ratio of one factor to other factors used in production, increases the share of the common product going to each unit of that factor.

If, for example, the population increases, and capital accumulation increases, this decreases the relative amount of land available for use, and increases the importance of each acre of land used in production. Rents, therefore, tend to increase. If capital is destroyed in a great war, this creates a scarcity of capital relative to existing land and labor, and results in an increase in interest rates paid for each dollar of capital. If population increases faster than capital is accumulated, and the land area remains the same, rents tend to rise, interest rates to increase, and wages to fall.

During the last seventy-five years, the increase in wages and salaries in the face of a growing population can be explained largely in terms of the rapid increase first in land area and then in available capital. Since the World War, wages and salaries have increased, in part because of the decline in population growth, and in part because of rapid capital accumulation.

Adjusting family expenditures to changes in rent, interest, and wages. The adjustment to changes in wages, interest rates, rents, and profits must be worked out by each individual family in the light of its own immediate situation, using methods similar to those that are effective in the case of the business cycle and long-time price trends.

Fundamental social changes. Finally, it is important for the family to consider fundamental social trends. There are many of these trends. Population changes are a significant example. Changing distribution of the population among the various age groups has a good deal to do with opportunities for employment, the demand for labor of various sorts, and the age to which it will be possible for an individual to find employment. For many years the birth rate has been declining. In the first few years of the century, this decline was offset by immigration. For a generation there has been a decline in the death rate. Part of this has been due to a reduction in the rate of infant mortality. Part of it has been due to control and prevention of the degenerative diseases of middle life. As a result the American population now contains more than the usual number of people in the middle years. This present preponderance of people in middle life means that in the years ahead there will be a larger proportion than formerly of older people in our population.

It ought also to mean increased demand for younger workers, and for workers in active middle life. It may necessitate industrial reorganization so that more work can be done by older men. It may involve shifts in employment from industries serving younger families to those satisfying the wants of older people. It may mean a postponement of the retirement age. It may mean a relaxation of child-labor laws, and a reduction in the period of education.

In determining the effect of these changes upon the individual family, it is necessary to consider both the present age and the life-expectancies of the members of the family, and to prepare them for occupations which will continue to be in demand in an aging population. If the shortage of younger people becomes great enough, it may be necessary for both husband and wife in the younger families to find employment outside the home in order to carry their share of the common responsibility for the older people in the population.

This is but one example of changing social conditions which may be significant to the family. The family should watch also such trends as the rate of city growth, urban growth or decline, the drift of production to the factory or back to the home, tendencies toward centralization or decentralization in industry, and trends in the popular attitude toward the increase or relaxation of political control.

The problem of adjusting family expenditures to changing business conditions is not a simple one, but it is a problem which is highly important. It calls for a great deal of constructive imagination. The more a family knows about and is aware of conditions in the world outside the home, the more alert it is to anticipate changes as they occur, the more successful it will be in adjusting its affairs satisfactorily to changing conditions in the world in which it lives.

QUESTIONS

1. Make a list of all the elements in the current business situation which families should consider in planning their expenditures for the next month; in working out their next year's budget.

2. Find out the specific ways in which a number of families adjusted to the last complete swing of the business cycle.

3. In what stage of the business cycle are you now living? Are prices rising

or falling? Is the secular trend of prices up or down? Is either inflation or deflation in immediate prospect? How do you tell?

4. In question 8, page 80, are described the experiences of four families during the first four years of the secondary post-World War depression. Compare the ways in which these families should adjust to the depression phase of the cycle.

5. Compare the significance of long-time price trends to the families described in question 10, page 81.

6. A young couple are planning to be married next June. Draw a diagram indicating the number of complete business cycles through which they can expect to live in the next fifty years. Indicate in your diagram the long-time price trends which will probably be operative during this same period. Point out a number of ways in which your diagram will help the family to adjust its expenditures to changing business conditions.

REFERENCES

Hoyt, Elizabeth E., *The Consumption of Wealth*, Ch. XII, especially pp. 127 ff. The Macmillan Co., New York, 1928.

A brief discussion of the effect of business cycles upon consumer demand.

Kyrk, Hazel, *Economic Problems of the Family*, Ch. XVI, pp. 294-310. Harper and Bros., New York, 1933.

A discussion of the causes, measurement, and effect of changes in the general price level and of the way in which these changes affect the individual and the family.

Nystrom, P. H., *Economic Principles of Consumption*, Ch. XX, pp. 508-547. The Ronald Press Co., New York, 1929.

A description of various business indexes, designed to determine the effects of changing business conditions upon consumption.

Waite, W. C., *Economics of Consumption*, Chs. IV and V, pp. 35-61. McGraw-Hill Book Co., Inc., New York, 1928.

A description of methods of measuring price changes, a description of the business cycle, and a discussion of changes in the cost of living and their effect upon the consumer.

CHAPTER XVIII

THE PLACE OF CREDIT IN FAMILY FINANCE

The purpose of credit in family finance. In the long run, a family's expenditures, including its investments, must be approximately equal to its income. But most families, like most businesses, find that it is impossible to maintain continuous equality between income and expenditure. Changes in family needs, changes in prices, changes in income, all the ebb and flow of the business and the family cycles call for continuous adjustment of income to expenditure. In fact, the major part of the strategy involved in family finance consists in devising ways and means by which funds will be available when expenditures must be made. There are two ways of keeping income in line with expenditures. One is to set aside some current income in anticipation of future expenditures. The other is to anticipate future income by the use of credit. If a family is to make expenditures out of savings it must accumulate some readily available family capital. It can buy on credit only if someone else has accumulated capital which the family can use for its immediate expenditures.

Wise use of credit is mutually advantageous both to borrowers and to lenders. A mutual building and loan association is a good example of an organization which is built upon this mutual advantage. In such an organization, some people are saving, others are borrowing. The borrowers get homes of their own sooner than they could if they had to save the entire cost of a home first. The lenders also get homes sooner than they otherwise could, for the interest paid by borrowers cuts down the total amount which lenders must accumulate out of their own funds. In an association of this sort, the mutual benefit to borrowers and lenders is clearly evident. It is also clearly evident that this mutual benefit exists only if borrowers can repay their loans by the time the lenders want to use their own savings. The fundamental purpose of credit, then, is to make it possible for people who want things more in the present to use the funds already accumulated by other people who want things more sometime in the future, and to make it possible for people who want things more in

419

the future to get more in the future than they would otherwise be able to obtain.

The basis of credit. The word *credit* comes from the Latin word *credo,* meaning "I believe." A merchant will allow a customer to get goods now and pay for them in the future only if he believes that the buyer will pay for them as he promises. A lender will make a loan only when he believes that the borrower will repay the money he borrows. It is possible for a family to use credit only if someone, merchant or lender, believes that the family will meet promptly and in full the obligation which it assumes.

It is sometimes said that an individual's credit is determined by four C's: character, capacity, capital, and collateral.

Character means willingness and determination to repay a loan as agreed, even though it be at greater cost and inconvenience than the borrower anticipated.

Capacity means the ability to meet an obligation when it is due. Ordinarily capacity depends upon income. It is important to understand that the capacity of a family to repay a loan depends not so much upon total income as upon the available margin over and above necessary expenses. The capacity of a family to repay a loan is determined by the difference between what the family receives and what it spends.

Capital means net worth. A family's capital is determined by the difference between what it owns and what it owes. The existence of this capital provides a margin of safety for the lender, since if the family's income proves to be inadequate to repay its loan, the family can draw upon its invested capital.

Collateral consists of specific units of capital which are pledged as security for a given loan. Usually these units are placed in the possession of the lender, with the understanding that if the borrower fails to pay his loan as he has agreed, the lender is to reimburse himself in so far as he can from the sale of the pledged collateral. Pawn shops sometimes advertise as collateral loan banks. In the later 1920's commercial banks favored collateral loans secured by listed securities. But their experience indicated that collateral alone is not sufficient security for any credit obligation. The existence of character, capacity, and other capital is equally important. Even today, however, there is a tendency for banks to demand not only character and capacity but marketable collateral as well. From the point of view of the consumer, therefore, the possession of some property of a type which makes good collateral security aids in establishing credit and in borrowing on reasonable terms.

Trade credit vs. money credit. There are two principal ways in which a family may secure credit. It may use trade credit; that is, it may buy goods and pay for them at some time in the future. The individual who sells the goods extends the trade credit to his customers. Or the family may use money credit; that is, it may borrow money from an organization making a business of lending money, and pay cash for the goods it buys. In either case the family assumes an obligation to pay a certain sum of money at a given time.

Lump-sum vs. instalment payment. There are two ways in which a family may pay off the obligations it assumes. One is to repay the entire amount of a loan at one time. This is technically known as *lump-sum liquidation*. The other is to repay the loan a little at a time in a series of payments. This is *piecemeal liquidation*, or what is ordinarily known as instalment payment.

Retail stores and commercial banks ordinarily assume that the obligations of their customers will be settled at a definite time in a single payment. Stores selling goods on the instalment plan, and industrial banks and personal finance companies assume that their customers will settle their obligations in a series of small payments. Families with generous incomes, and families receiving moderate incomes in large increments at irregular intervals, ordinarily find it to their advantage to settle their obligations in a single payment, when they receive their incomes. Families with small but regular incomes find it more convenient to pay on the instalment plan, for they can use their small margin above current necessities to pay a little at a time upon the loan. However, it costs more to collect obligations in a series of payments than to collect the same amount in a single sum. There is always the risk that unforeseen circumstances may wipe out the small margin which the family must use to make its instalment payments. As a result, instalment payment contracts usually carry a higher rate of interest than loans to be liquidated in a lump sum.

Long-time vs. short-time credit. If credit is to be of maximum value to a family, the family must be able to buy when its need is greatest, and be allowed to pay when its income is most easily available. As a result, families want to borrow for varying lengths of time. Ordinarily credit granted for a year or less is considered to be short-time credit. Credit granted for from one to five years is called intermediate credit. Credit granted for more than five years is considered long-time credit. In connection with consumers' credit, however, any obligation running more than one year is considered to be a long-time obligation. Because of the personal nature of the character and capacity back of family credit, there is a very definite relationship between the length of time credit is extended and the risk which is involved. It is unwise to grant credit to a family for as long a time as is safe in lending to a well-established corporate enterprise. Because of the uncertainties of family life, it is equally unwise for any family to assume many obligations running over a period of years.

The cost of credit. There are three factors which determine the cost of credit. They are interest, risk, and the expense of making and collecting the loan. The interest charged for the use of advances of capital, whether in the form of money or in the form of goods, is determined by the amount of the advance and the length of time for which it runs. The risk depends in part upon general business conditions, and in part upon the length of time the loan is to run, but primarily upon the character, capacity, and capital of the borrower. The expense of making and collecting the loan depends upon the credit standing of the borrower, the method of repayment, and the type of collateral or other security back of the loan.

Every borrower assumes that he must pay a reasonable rate of interest for the use of someone else's money. Most borrowers realize that if a lender advances money to a group of borrowers, he is entitled to the return of the capital he advances. Since there is a chance that some members of the group of borrowers will fail to repay their loans, the lender must add to the amount he advances, in addition to the interest rate, a charge large enough to insure his recovering the total amount he loans.

Every credit transaction involves a certain amount of expense. The lender must investigate the credit standing of his customer. He must keep a record of the transaction. He must send a notice to the borrower whenever a payment is due. In case the borrower fails to pay as he has agreed, the lender must send out a collector to secure the payment by personal solicitation. If the borrower defaults on the obligation, the lender must go into court and establish his claim, and he must recover and sell any property posted as security for the loan.

It costs more to make a loan to a new customer than to an individual with well-established credit. It costs more to collect a loan in instalments than to collect a loan settled in a single sum. It costs more to collect from customers who are "slow pay," who must be solicited personally for every payment, than to collect from the borrower who brings in his payments promptly when they are due. In case of default, it costs more for the lender to recover and realize upon chattels, household goods, radio, washing machine, or automobile, than to realize upon negotiable securities. The cost of foreclosing a mortgage upon real property varies from state to state, depending upon the length of time involved in the initial foreclosure proceedings, the length of the redemption period, and the date at which the creditor can secure possession of the property.[1]

Because most credit charges are expressed in terms of a percentage of the amount of the loan, most people think of interest as the only element in the cost of credit. They are willing to pay a *reasonable* amount of interest for the credit which is extended them, but they think of reasonable rates as 5 or 6 or 7 per cent. Because customers object to paying what low-grade instalment credit actually costs, and because in some cases at least merchants wish to make some profits from extending credit as well as from the sale of goods, many instalment houses and many other credit institutions use a variety of devices to conceal actual credit charges.

It is important, therefore, for the family to know how to determine the actual cost of any credit which is offered them. Seven per cent may mean 7 per cent a year, $7\frac{1}{2}$ per cent a year, 17 per cent a year, or almost any other annual interest rate, depending upon the terms of repayment and the other charges which are added to the initial discount on the loan. Even the 5 per cent interest on repair loans offered to home owners by the Federal Housing Administration turned out to be a little more than 9 per cent for the capital actually advanced to the borrower.

There are many cases in which it is legitimate to charge more than 6 or 7 per cent for the use of money, and in which the consumer can afford to pay more than 6 or 7 per cent for the use of credit. But the consumer ought to know just what his credit is costing him. In buying goods on credit, he ought to know how much of the price he

---

[1] The total time involved in foreclosure proceedings ranges from thirty days to two years. The shorter the redemption period, the more generous are the terms and the lower the interest rate upon mortgage loans.

is paying covers the cost of the merchandise, and how much is for credit charges. He should be definitely suspicious of any concern that advertises goods for sale on the instalment plan with no financing charge. In almost every case firms advertise no financing charge because they know that their customers would consider the actual financing charges excessive.[2]

How to estimate the cost of credit. The essential problem in comparing the cost of credit offered the family by various agencies is to reduce the great variety of credit terms to some common denominator. The most satisfactory common denominator is the annual interest rate. Suppose a family borrows $100 for one year at 7 per cent interest, payable at the maturity of the loan. At the end of the year it returns the $100 together with $7.00 interest. The family has the use of $100 for a year. The annual interest rate in this transaction is 7 per cent.

Suppose, however, the family borrows $100 with interest at 7 per cent payable in advance. This is commonly known as bank discount. At the end of the year it returns $100. The family has the use of $93.00 for the year. In other words it pays $7.00 for the use of $93.00 for one year. The annual interest rate in this transaction is 7½ per cent.

Suppose, again, the family borrows $100 from a Morris Plan or Industrial Bank. The charge for the loan in this case is 7 per cent of the principal of the loan plus 2 per cent of the principal of the loan as a credit investigation fee, payable in advance. The family repays the loan in twelve monthly instalments. Four of these instalments are $8.34, and eight are $8.33. In this case the family actually has the use of $91.00 for one month, $82.66 for one month, $74.33 for one month, $66.00 for one month, $57.66 for one month, $49.33 for one month, $41.00 for one month, $32.66 for one month, $24.33 for one month, $16.00 for one month, $7.66 for one month, and 33 cents for one month. Altogether, then, it has had the use of $542.63 for one month, or (dividing by 12) of $45.22 for one year. In other words, the family pays $9.00 for the use of $45.22

---

[2] As a result of an investigation of credit charges in Boston, Mass., there is under way a movement to require the statement of all credit charges in terms of the annual interest rate. How successful this movement will be will depend on the extent to which consumers insist upon knowing what they are paying for credit. Unless consumers themselves insist on knowing, unless they take the time to compare quality and price in cash and credit stores, unless they are willing to do a little simple arithmetic to find out what they actually are being charged, legislation will help but little in reducing charges for low-grade credit.

for one year. The annual interest rate in this transaction therefore is 19.9 per cent.

Or take the case of a college student who buys a portable typewriter on the instalment plan. The cash price of the typewriter is $60.00. The financing charge for instalment payments is $5.00. The terms are $5.00 down and $5.00 a month for twelve months. If you consider the initial $5.00 payment as the payment of the financing charges, then the buyer has $60.00 of the seller's capital for one month, $55.00 for one month, $50.00 for one month, $45.00 for one month, and so on. He has the use of $390 for one month or of $32.50 for a year. On the other hand, if the initial payment is the first payment upon the typewriter, and the last payment is the $5.00 financing charge, then the buyer has had the use of $55.00 of the seller's capital for one month, $50.00 for one month, $45.00 for one month, $40.00 for one month, and so on. He has had the use of $330 of the seller's capital for one month, or $27.50 for one year. In the first case, the charge of $5.00 for the use of $32.50 for a year would be 15.4 per cent. In the second case, the charge of $5.00 for the use of $27.50 would amount to an annual interest charge of 18.2 per cent.

A student faced with the alternative of renting a typewriter for $3.00 a month does not consider the charge of $5.00 excessive, whether he calls the annual interest rate 15 or 18 per cent. However, the comparison of charges in terms of annual interest rates will let him determine whether or not he has some more economical way of financing the purchase of the typewriter.

To determine the cost of credit, then, the procedure is as follows: First determine the total amount of money actually advanced to the borrower for a year. ($60 for two months equals $10 for a year.) To do this in the case of monthly payments, determine the amount of the principal sum (not principal and interest charges) remaining unpaid each month. Add and divide by twelve. To do this in the case of weekly payments, determine the amount remaining unpaid each week, add, and divide by 52. Second, determine the total amount in dollars and cents charged for the use of the money. Include the actual number of dollars charged for interest or discount, for credit investigation fees, for premium for securing funds, for penalties, or for any other purpose.

In the case of instalment purchases, compare the total cost of the goods purchased on the instalment plan with the cost of goods of similar quality purchased for cash. In case of goods advertised for sale on a credit basis with no financing charges, find out how much less similar goods would cost if purchased in stores doing business on a cash basis.

Third, divide the total cost of credit by the total amount of money actually advanced to the borrower for a year. This gives the annual interest rate.

Sources of consumer credit. When borrowing is mentioned, most people of moderate means think of borrowing from a commercial bank. But commercial banks have never been much interested in lending money to consumers. The smaller banks have made accommodation loans for consumption purposes to a few of their depositors, but at no time have more than 15 per cent of the families in the United States been able to secure loans at commercial banks. As a result, for many years consumers were limited to the use of trade credit. If their credit was good, they could buy either on open account, or on the instalment plan. If not, they were forced to fall back upon the pawn shop or the loan shark.

In recent years, however, there have been developed a number of agencies granting credit to consumers. Because of the variety of these institutions, and because of the differences in their charges, it is important for the family to know about all the sources to which they may turn for funds.

Trade credit. A family can use trade credit in two ways. It can buy on open account from stores which extend credit to their customers. Usually these accounts are supposed to be settled in full every thirty or sixty days. Or it can buy what it needs and pay for it on the instalment plan. Automobiles, furniture, clothing, jewelry, radios, musical instruments, washing machines, sewing machines, vacuum cleaners, oil burners, stoves, mechanical refrigerators, and even roofs and insulation and plumbing can be purchased on the instalment plan. In some of the larger cities there are department stores, complete even to the grocery department, which will sell a family a complete outfit of everything it needs, including a week's groceries, and let it pay for it a dollar down and several dollars more every week.

The charges for this trade credit vary from a very nominal mark-up in high-grade grocery and department stores that extend

credit only to a selected list of customers to as much as 200 per cent
in the case of low-grade credit houses selling cheap merchandise to
poor credit risks "without a financing charge." It is impossible to
make any general statement as to the probable cost of trade credit.
The cost of instalment credit varies with the commodity sold, the
terms of the sales contract, and the type of customer with whom the
seller deals. Every family must analyze for itself the cost of credit
in the various stores in its own community. It must decide whether
or not the trade credit which is available is worth what it costs.[3]

Short-time money loans. *Commercial banks.* There are a
number of institutions from which a family can borrow money in
small amounts for short periods. There is a small group of families
that can secure loans for from sixty to ninety days at a commercial
bank. Usually, however, these accommodation loans are limited to
business and professional men who have a line of business credit at
the bank. Usually banks making these accommodation loans, while
nominally they make the loans on a character basis, insist on the
deposit of some high-grade and easily marketable collateral to secure
the loan. If the bank has a personal loan or industrial loan division,
it usually insists that families borrow from the personal loan department and pay higher interest charges for the privilege of instalment
payment. As a result, the strictly commercial loan from the commercial banks is beyond the reach of all but a few American families.

Insurance policy loans. In recent years many families have found
that the most convenient and most economical loans they could make
were life insurance policy loans. Every whole life or investment
type of life insurance policy has both a cash and a loan value. Most
high-grade insurance companies upon a few days' notice will loan
their policy holders any amount of money they need up to the loan
value of the policy. In most cases they charge 6 per cent interest for
the loan. The policy holder can pay any amount he pleases, or he
can pay his loan in full at any time. He is charged interest only for
the time he actually uses the money.

Industrial banks. In recent years there has been a rapid growth
of Morris Plan or Industrial banks. These banks lend money to con-

---

[3] Evans Clark estimates that in the larger cities families in the lower income groups can buy on
the instalment plan not much more than 10 per cent of the goods and services they need. For the
rest they are limited to not more than thirty days' credit on open accounts. And workers' families
often are unable to secure this type of trade credit. As a result, in case of any emergency, they
must fall back upon money credit. For his discussion see *Financing the Consumer*, pp. 194 ff.
Harper and Bros., New York, 1930.

sumers in small amounts. Unless his credit is unusually good, the borrower must furnish the written guarantee of two responsible persons that both the loan and the interest will be paid. The loans are payable on the instalment plan. The charges range from 6 to 12 per cent of the principal of the loan plus a 2 per cent credit investigation fee, both payable in advance. Computed on an annual interest basis, charges range from 17 to 34 per cent. Industrial banks try to keep their discount rate the same as that of the commercial banks in the community. If banks are charging 7 per cent for loans, industrial banks advertise loans at 7 per cent discount. Then they add their credit investigation fee, in many cases even though the borrower is known to the bank. Many industrial banks add penalties for delinquent payments. Few allow any credit for unearned interest in case the loan is paid before it matures. Nevertheless, many people borrow at least once from an industrial bank before they find out that 7 per cent is not 7 per cent but 17 per cent instead. The chief criticism of industrial banks is not that their charges are unreasonable for the services they render, but rather that they try to conceal their actual charges in order to give the impression that their loans cost no more than do loans from commercial banks.

Personal finance companies. For families that are unable or unwilling to secure two guarantors for a loan, there is another type of organization which has had a very rapid growth in the last few years. This is the personal finance company. Personal finance companies are organized under laws sponsored by the Russell Sage Foundation. They are intended to provide credit for low-grade credit risks, who otherwise would be forced to borrow from pawnbrokers or unlicensed lenders. They are limited by law to loans of $300 or less. Usually they require a chattel mortgage as security and in some cases take an assignment of wages to protect themselves in case the borrower defaults upon the loan. But they value their good will too much to foreclose upon a mortgage or use an assignment of wages except as a last resort. They prefer to work with the family to help it pay off its loan as it has agreed.

Charges for loans are limited by law in some states to 3 per cent and in some states to 3½ per cent per month on unpaid balances. They can make no other charges. To people who are accustomed to borrowing from commercial banks at 6 per cent, their charges seem outrageous. But to families that have been forced to borrow in emergencies from a pawnshop or a loan shark, these charges seem more reasonable. The companies state frankly that the rate they are allowed to charge determines the kind of credit risk they can assume. The higher the legal rate of interest, the larger the group of low income families they can serve. At the same time, companies like the Household Finance Corporation have adopted a graded scale of charges, loaning at 2½ per cent per month to families that borrow more than $100 and pay promptly. They have found that at 2½ per cent per month they can compete very definitely with industrial banks, for many people prefer to borrow where they can secure money on their own credit, without being forced to provide co-signers as is required by most industrial banks. In 1929 personal finance companies made loans totaling not far from $500,000,000, as compared with $360,000,000 loaned by industrial banks.[4]

Credit unions. Credit unions are legally chartered mutual savings and loan associations. In the United States they are usually organized by workers in a single industry. The employer provides office space, does the bookkeeping, and supervises the work of the plan. Loans are made by a board of directors elected by the workers. Members may deposit regular sums which are applied to the purchase of shares in the credit union. These shares may be used as security later on in case the member needs to borrow money for a short time. Credit unions usually charge interest at the rate of 1 per cent per month on unpaid balances. Loans are made only to members of the credit union, and only upon the recommendation of a loan committee appointed by the board of directors. The security for the loan may be either shares in the credit union or a co-signer who is a member of the credit union.

These credit unions work very well in industries in which employment is regular, and in which the workers remain for many years in the employ of the same company. But they are limited to a comparatively small group of workers. However, for the families with workers eligible for membership in a credit union, they provide the cheapest form of instalment loan.

The first table on page 430 gives Evans Clark's classification of the small loan public. It is interesting to see the wide range of occupations included in the group without commercial banking connections.

The second table on page 430 gives Evans Clark's estimate of the

[4] See the table on page 430.

The Small Loan Public [5]

Occupational and Economic Status of Customers		Average Income	Average Loan	Agencies Serving
1. Lowest	Laborers Factory Workers Machine Hands Chauffeurs Truckmen, etc.	up to $30 a week	$20 to $125	Personal Finance Companies Credit Unions Pawnshops
2. Middle	Clerks Salesmen Gov't. Employees Buyers	$30-$50	$125 to $250	Personal Finance Companies Pawnshops Personal Loan Departments Industrial Banks Credit Unions
3. Highest	Foremen Business Men Professional, etc.	Above $50	$250 to $1,000	Industrial Banks Personal Loan Departments Credit Unions

The Small Loan Agencies [6]

	Estimated Amount of Loan Funds Employed	Per Cent of Total	Estimated Total Loans Advanced	Per Cent of Total	Estimated Number of Borrowers
1. Unlicensed lenders	$125,000,000	9.6	$750,000,000	28.9	3,000,000
2. Pawnbrokers	400,000,000	31.1	600,000,000	23.2	17,000,000
3. Personal finance companies	294,000,000	22.9	500,000,000	19.3	2,000,000
4. Industrial banks ...	240,000,000	18.7	360,000,000	13.9	1,000,000
5. Commercial banks					
Small loan depts.	....	....	40,000,000	....	....
Non-specialized .	....	....	150,000,000	....	....
Total, commercial banks	110,000,000	8.6	190,000,000	7.3	500,000
6. Credit unions	40,000,000	3.5	62,500,000	2.4	200,000
7. Remedial loan societies	32,000,000	2.5	60,000,000	2.3	500,000
8. Axias	30,000,000	2.3	50,000,000	1.9	100,000
9. Employers' plans ..	10,000,000	0.8	20,000,000	0.8	50,000
Grand total	$1,281,000,000	100.0	$2,592,500,000	100.0	14,350,000

[5] Evans Clark, *op. cit.*, Table 29, p. 181.
[6] Evans Clark, *op. cit.*, Table 3, p. 30. These figures, especially on number of borrowers, are rough estimates and should be used with extreme caution.

Charges, Interest, and Cost to Borrower of Small Loans
(Rates Based on Loan of $100)

Agency	Charges as Levied	Usual Loan Period (Months)	Annual Interest Rate (Per Cent)	Cost Rate to Borrower * (Per Cent)	Usual Collateral Required
Credit Unions:					
Lowest Legal Max. (N. C.)	6% per yr. (N. C.)	10.	6.0	6.0	Shares or Co-maker Note
Usual Legal Max.	1% per mo. on balances	10.	12.0	12.2	Shares or Co-maker Note
Highest Legal Max. (Va. and W. Va.)	1½% per mo. on balances	10.	18.0	18.6	Shares or Co-maker Note
Personal Loan Departments:					
Lowest Rate (3 banks)	6% discount, 3% interest on repayments	12.	9.4	10.3	Co-maker Note
Typical Rate (6 banks)	8% total discount and investigation fees in advance	12.	17.3	18.1	Co-maker Note
Highest Rate	8% discount plus 2% fee (10% in advance)	12.	22.6	23.7	Co-maker Note
Industrial Banks:					
Morris Plan Rate (N. Y.)	6% discount plus 2% fee (8% in advance)	12.	17.3	18.1	Co-maker Note
Highest Rate	12% discount plus 2% fee (14% in advance)	12.	34.9	36.1	Co-maker Note
Remedial Loan Societies:					
Lowest Rate (Provident Loan)	12% per yr.—paid at term's end	12.	12.0	12.0	Pledge
Average Rates (Pledge)	1.3% per mo. (at end)	12.	15.6	15.6	Pledge
Average Rates (Chattels)	1.5% per mo. on unpaid balance plus 3.1% fee	12.	18.9	22.5	Chattel Mtge.
Highest Rate	3% per mo. on unpaid balances	12.	36.0	36.0	Chattel Mtge.
Axias:					
Usual Rates	8% discount plus 4% fee (12% in advance)	12.	28.5	29.6	Co-maker Note
Personal Finance Companies:					
Household Corp.	2½% per mo. on unpaid balances	10.	30.0	30.5	Chattel Mtge.
3% States	3% per mo. on unpaid balances	10.	36.0	36.6	Chattel Mtge.
3½% States	3½% per mo. on unpaid balances	10.	42.0	44.8	Chattel Mtge.
Pawnbrokers:					
Lowest Legal Max. Rate (Minn.)	1% per mo. at term's end	12.	12.0	12.0	Pledge
Usual Legal Max. Rate	3% per mo. at term's end	12.	36.0	36.0	Pledge
Maximum Legal Rate (N. M.)	10% per mo. at term's end	12.	120.0	120.0	Pledge
Unlicensed Lenders:					
Usual Rates, larger loans	20% per mo. (end of term)	½	240.0	240.0	Wage Assignment
Usual Rate, smaller loans	40% per mo. (end of term)	½	480.0	480.0	Wage Assignment

* Based on $100 loan for full loan period.

7 Evans Clark, op. cit., Table 13, p. 128.

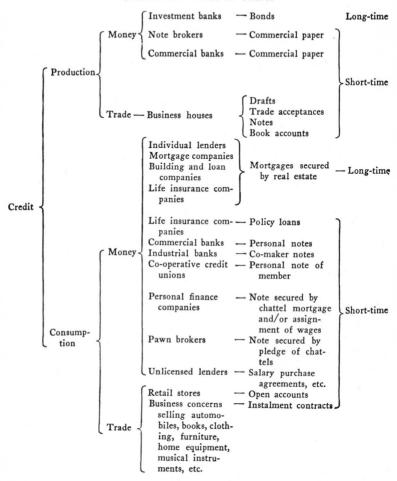

SOURCES AND TYPES OF CREDIT

relative amount of business done by the various small loan agencies in 1929.[8] It is interesting to see the large volume of business still being done by unlicensed lenders, whose charges run anywhere from 20 to 40 per cent per month. It is clear that families should, if possible, so handle their affairs that they will not be forced to resort to borrowing even for emergencies on terms such as these.

The table on page 431 is Clark's "The Borrower's Guide." This

[8] See table, "Current Family Financing," p. 68.

THE COST OF CONSUMER CREDIT [9]

Credit Agency	Annual Interest Charges
Trade Credit	
Book accounts	No measurable charges
Instalment contracts	12–200%
Money Credit	
Life insurance companies' policy loans	6%
Commercial Banks	
Commercial depts. (lump sum settlement)	6– 7%
Personal loan depts. (instalment settlement)	9– 23%
Credit unions	6– 18%
Industrial banks	17– 35%
Personal finance companies	30– 42%
Pawnbrokers	12–120%
Unlicensed lenders	240–480%

table shows the charges, interest, and cost to borrower of small loans from various small loan agencies.

Long-time loans. A family needing money for a period of years can borrow money by giving a mortgage upon its home as security. It can borrow for a definite period of years and repay the whole loan in a lump sum, or it can borrow on a reducing mortgage and repay the loan in instalments.

A family may use mortgage credit to finance the purchase of its home. If it borrows upon a reducing mortgage, it can make its payments in regular monthly instalments, gradually reducing its indebtedness. This is equivalent to buying its home on the instalment plan.

A family owning its own home free from any incumbrances may use mortgage credit to secure money for emergencies, or for current expenses during a period of several years in which expenditures will run ahead of income. In this case it usually finds the lump-sum method of settlement more convenient, for this enables the family to use the mortgage money until the period of heavy expenses is past, by paying only the annual interest charges.

If a family is to secure money for current expenses by mortgaging its home, it should secure all the money it needs with its first mortgage, for it is not easy to increase the amount of a loan secured by a mortgage. And second mortgage interest charges are usually higher than are the charges for a first mortgage.

There are a number of agencies to which the family can go for

---

[9] Adapted from Evans Clark, *op. cit.*

mortgage credit. Life insurance companies, building and loan associations, and mortgage companies will allow borrowers to repay their loans in instalments. Commercial banks and most individual lenders prefer the lump-sum method of settlement for their mortgage loans. Because individual lenders find it difficult to reinvest small amounts of capital, some mortgage loan agreements definitely specify that there can be no payments upon the principal until the end of the period for which the money is advanced. If a family wants to be able to reduce its indebtedness before the end of the loan period, it should see that definite provision is made for the privilege in the original loan contract.

The interest rate upon mortgages is usually limited by the state usury laws. Usually the maximum contract rate of interest ranges from 6 to 12 per cent. This rate is lower in the North and East and higher in the South and West. Because of these legal limits upon the interest which can be charged, lenders increase their charges for second mortgages, not by charging more than the legal rate of interest, but by charging a premium for finding the mortgage money. In determining the cost of credit, the family must be sure to take into account not only the legal interest rate but all other charges connected with the making of the loan.

The table on page 432 gives the place of consumer credit in the general credit structure. The table on page 433 shows in summary form the comparative cost of credit from each of the agencies extending credit to the family.

Legitimate uses of family credit. *Emergencies.* In every family there are occasional emergencies which throw the family's income and expenditures out of balance. A severe illness, a death in the family, an automobile accident, fire loss, or other heavy property damage, or even unexpected repairs or replacements in the home may necessitate unexpected and heavy expenditures. Or the family may be faced with interruption or loss of expected income. The chief wage earner may lose his job. Stocks may pass their dividends. There may be loss of business income due to business depression or crop failure. In all such emergencies, families may find it wise to use credit for a time until they can once more bring income and expenditures into line.

Anticipating assured income. Many families find it convenient to use credit to anticipate assured income. A family with irregular income, received in large amounts at considerable intervals, may use credit for regular current expenses until the next instalment of income becomes available. An elderly couple, living upon the income from investments in stocks and bonds, receives most of its income in quarterly dividends and semi-annual interest payments. There are frequently two or three months at a time when the family has no current income. They find it desirable to anticipate an unusually large increment of income following a long interval without funds, by running accounts for a month or more at the grocery, the drug store, and the department store. In this way they can buy what they need when they need it without waiting until their income actually arrives.

Similarly, families with regular income, but with only a small margin above current expenses, may use credit to make occasional large purchases, paying on the instalment plan. A family is faced with immediate and heavy repairs upon the old car. It must have a car to use. The repairs amount to three months' payments upon a new car. They decide it is best to buy a new car. But they can do so only if they can spread the payments over several months. There is no one month or two months or three months in which they have a surplus above necessary expenses sufficient to pay cash for the car the family wants to buy. This does not mean that every family with a small regular income should buy a car on the instalment plan. But if in the light of all the circumstances the immediate purchase of the car is important enough to justify the additional cost of instalment credit, a family may decide it is wise to use credit and buy the car.

Financing the family's investment program. Families frequently find it pays to use credit to advance their investment program. In some cases by buying securities on credit, it is possible to invest small increments of savings to better advantage. For example, a family has $250 in a savings account drawing 3 per cent interest. This money is earning $7.50 a year. They borrow an additional $250 and buy a $500 bond paying 5 per cent interest. The bond pays them $25.00 a year. If they pay 6 per cent interest on their loan for an entire year, it will cost them only $15.00. This will leave them $10.00 income on their own $250, or 4 per cent instead of the 3 per cent the bank would have paid them. And as fast as they reduce the principal of their obligation they can invest their own money, not at 3 per cent but at 5 per cent.

There are some people who find it easier to save money if they have obligated themselves to make regular payments. These families accumulate more if they buy sound securities on credit than they would if they tried to save first and then invest. Some families find it wise to use credit to introduce diversity into their investment program. For example, a family may have money enough accumulated to pay for a home. But they do not feel it wise to tie up all of their savings in a single investment. In order to leave part of their savings in easily available form, they convert part of their savings, use them for a down payment upon their home, and finance the balance with a mortgage. Of course they must pay interest on the mortgage. In some cases this interest is a little larger than the returns they are getting from their investments, but in case they should need some money for emergencies, they have part of their family capital in a form upon which they can realize more easily than they could if it were all invested in a home.

Convenience in buying. Many families find it wise to use credit because of its convenience. By using credit the family avoids the necessity of paying every day for daily purchases. It avoids the necessity of carrying large sums of money. Itemized bills are a definite convenience as records of expenditures. The use of credit saves time in shopping. The credit customer has telephone order privileges at the grocery and department store. He can secure goods on approval more easily than can the customer who always pays cash. He can often get better adjustments than can the cash customer if the goods he purchases prove unsatisfactory. The credit customer is often given advance notice of sales. He frequently gets better service from sales people than do cash customers, not because there is any deliberate intention of slighting the occasional buyer, but because the sales people can learn the wants of credit customers who are definitely affiliated with their organization.

Some people feel that if they must buy in stores granting credit, they might just as well use credit because they are being charged for it anyway. This, of course, is not a reason for using credit. The logic of the situation is this: There are certain conveniences which come from the use of credit. If they can be secured at no additional cost, there is no reason why the family should not take advantage of them.

Establishing the family as a buyer in the community. The use of credit frequently establishes the position of the family as a buyer in the community in a way which is otherwise impossible. By using a charge account, the family gets the volume of its business before a store, while the occasional customer does not. It may be that the cash customer buys just as much in the course of a month, but the management has no way of seeing his purchases as a whole.

From the point of view of the store, too, the credit customer becomes a little more closely and a little more permanently identified with the organization than does the cash customer. In case of doubt as to the relative value of two commodities, the family usually buys where it has credit, because it knows by experience that it is easy to get satisfactory adjustments. In case of temporary financial stringency, the family buys at the store where it has credit. Because it expects the store to extend credit when family funds are low, the family ordinarily feels some obligation to buy from the store whenever it can find goods which satisfy its needs.

Using credit to establish credit. Many people feel that it is worth while to use credit in order to have it established in case of emergency. The easiest way to establish one's credit is to buy on credit at a time when there is no question of being able to pay obligations as they fall due. In case of some widespread emergency, such as the bank holiday in 1933, the store with credit facilities is inclined to confine its extension of credit to its regular customers. Many stores have learned from experience that it is dangerous to extend credit to the individual who ordinarily pays cash, because the only time he asks for credit is when he is not in a position to make payments. Since credit is easier to establish when the family is sure of its income, it is wise for the family that may occasionally need credit to use its credit enough to keep in good credit standing. It is interesting to compare the list of legitimate uses of consumers' credit given in the preceding discussion with the results of Evans Clark's study as given in the table on page 438. This table is based on a study of loans made by personal finance companies. This represents, of course, the lower grades of consumer credit, but it indicates clearly the sort of use families do make of existing credit facilities.

	Per Cent
Current expenses	36.44
Household and miscellaneous 19.35	
Repairs on home 3.75	
Moving expenses and rent 3.20	
Furniture and furnishings 2.16	
Coal 1.97	
Clothing 1.94	
Travel and vacation 1.59	
Christmas gifts 1.53	
Repairs on automobile .... .74	
Wedding expenses .... .23	
Liquidation of other debts	32.36
Consolidation of several 15.70	
Taxes 5.78	
Other debts 4.61	
Payments on home 3.24	
Payments on automobile 2.51	
Insurance .... .52	
Expenses arising from illness or death	10.99
Physicians, dentists, hospitals 9.85	
Funeral expenses .... .71	
Confinement expenses .... .43	
Business expenses	10.03
Combination of purposes	8.02
To assist friends and relatives	1.55
Miscellaneous	.61

Dangers in the use of credit. There are, of course, some
dangers to guard against in the use of credit. The family must remember that there is an essential difference between buying on
credit and being sold by credit. A family should never buy something just because it can get it now and pay for it later. A family
should never be blinded by the lure of easy payments and persuaded
to pay more than the commodity is worth. And in determining
whether or not a commodity is worth the price, the family must
remember that the price of the article includes not only the amount
actually charged for the commodity itself, but also the amount of
credit charges. A family should never buy an article on time unless
the article is actually worth all that it costs.

The family must always keep in mind the fundamental fact that
using credit to secure goods is not paying for the goods. It is deferring payment. When a family defers a payment it goes in debt.
It assumes an obligation which must be met at some time in the

---

[10] Evans Clark, *op. cit.*, pp. 180-181.

future.   Today's credit purchases are tomorrow's bills.   An instalment contract signed today becomes a fixed charge in next month's budget.

In using credit a family must be careful not to overestimate its future income.   It must be constantly on guard against underestimating the uncertainties in its situation.   It must leave an adequate margin for future contingencies, and still have in sight enough to pay the bills it assumes.

The family must remember that no matter how great is the pressure of today's demands, tomorrow will bring with it its own needs. In the presence of immediate necessity it is important to keep in mind also the needs of the future.   It may be wise to use credit to care for some present necessities.   But today's credit purchases will take precedence over tomorrow's pleasures.   In using credit, therefore, a family must be careful not to buy more today than it can pay for tomorrow without exhausting the margin above necessities which represents its capacity to pay.

The wise use of credit.   If a family is to use credit wisely in financing family expenditures, it must make a thorough and discriminating appraisal of what credit is, of the types of credit that are available for the use of the family, and of the legitimate uses of credit in financing family expenditures.   Since the use of credit tends to remove some of the usual restrictions upon buying, it is most important to be hard-headed and practical in making decisions involving the use of credit.

A family should decide whether or not to borrow money on the basis of the answers to these questions: Is there reasonable assurance of having the money available with which to pay off the loan?   Are the things which the family can do with this money worth all that the money costs?   Can the funds be secured elsewhere on more favorable terms?

A family should decide whether or not to buy on the instalment plan on the basis of the answers to these questions: Does the family need the articles offered for sale?   Are they worth the price asked? Will the money be available with which to meet the payments?   How much would these goods cost if purchased for cash?   Is the immediate purchase of these goods worth the additional cost involved in buying them on the instalment plan?   Is there any more economical way to finance the purchase of these goods?

There are a number of cases in which it is clearly wise to use credit. It is well to use credit to purchase an article when the savings from the use of the article will repay the loan. If by buying a washing machine and doing the washing at home enough can be saved on the cost of laundry to meet the payments on the machine, the purchase of the washing machine becomes a self-liquidating investment. It may be wise to buy goods on credit on a rising market. The higher price that the buyer would pay a few months hence may more than offset the credit charges. The family must always remember, however, that the converse is equally true, that it is not wise to buy on credit on a falling market. A family should use credit to anticipate price increases only when the rising market trend is clearly defined.

It is worth while to use credit if the convenience involved is worth the cost of credit. Sometimes this convenience is simply the convenience of using telephone order and delivery privileges. Sometimes it is the convenience that comes from being able to get an article now instead of later. There are many cases when an article is actually worth much more in the present than at any time in the future.

In using credit, a family should always borrow upon the best terms that are available. If it can secure trade credit on favorable terms it should use trade credit. It should borrow money and pay cash, if credit can be secured more economically in that way.

The individual with a good character, adequate capacity, plenty of capital, with certain kinds of easily salable collateral is a good credit risk. If he pays promptly, collection costs are low. He should borrow in so far as he can from institutions in which the interest charge constitutes the chief cost of doing business. On the other hand, the individual who has little in the way of collateral, who has a small and uncertain income, and who cannot be depended upon to make his payments regularly, will find that he can borrow only from institutions which are equipped to handle collections by personal solicitation and that must charge enough to cover the loss which comes inevitably in dealing with low credit risks.

In general, then, a family should borrow for as short a time as possible, in order to keep interest charges at a minimum. It should pay promptly in as few instalments as possible, in order to keep collection costs at a minimum. It should use as high-grade credit as possible, in order to avoid unnecessary payments for risk.

QUESTIONS

1. List all the agencies for consumer credit in your community. Describe the terms on which credit can be secured from each. Compute the cost of credit from each source in terms of an annual interest charge.

2. Is it good business for a college student to buy a typewriter on the instalment plan? To borrow money from a friend for tuition and other necessary college expenses? To borrow from a student loan fund? To run up a board bill? To buy clothing on the instalment plan? To borrow money from a friend to finance a week-end date?

3. Give examples of wise and of unwise use of credit by families of your acquaintance.

4. It is possible to buy a diamond ring at a credit jewelry store advertising no credit charges for $125, $5 down and $10 a month for twelve months. A similar ring could be bought in a cash store for $75. Compute in terms of an annual interest charge the cost of buying the ring on the instalment plan.

5. Explain how a new family can establish its credit in a department store in your community.

6. What types of credit should be used by each of the families described in question 10, page 81?

REFERENCES

Andrews, B. R., *Economics of the Household,* Revised Edition, Ch. X, pp. 221-231. The Macmillan Co., New York, 1935.

A concise analysis of the family's credit problems.

Clark, Evans, *Financing the Consumer.* Harper and Bros., New York, 1930.

A thorough study of facilities for financing the consumer. This study describes the various credit agencies, analyzes their costs and charges, and estimates their relative share of consumer credit financing.

Donham, S. A., *Spending the Family Income,* Revised Edition, Ch. XVII, pp. 187-205. Little, Brown and Co., Boston, 1933.

An analysis of the advantages and disadvantages of paying cash and buying on credit, with a number of rules governing the wise use of credit.

Kyrk, Hazel, *Economic Problems of the Family,* pp. 424-433. Harper and Bros., New York, 1933.

A brief discussion of the problems involved in wise use of credit by the consumer.

CHAPTER XIX

PROVIDING FOR THE FUTURE

SAVINGS

The purpose of saving in family finance. We hear inter-minable arguments about the importance of saving and the importance of spending. On the one hand, we are told that unless a family saves a given proportion of its income every month or every year of its life, it is doomed to failure. On the other, we are told that unless every family spends every cent of its current income as fast as it is received, the country will be thrown immediately into the depths of a business depression.

These arguments have made but little impression upon the intelli-gent American family. From the point of view of the individual family there is only one reason for spending. That is to provide the members of the family with the goods and services which will satisfy their present wants. There is only one reason for saving. That is to provide, at some time in the future, for wants which the family considers to be more important than any present wants it could satisfy with the same income. The purpose of saving is to provide out of present income for the satisfaction of future wants which it would be impossible to satisfy with future income alone. From the point of view of the family, saving, like credit, is simply another (and often more economical) way to even out inequalities between income and expenditure.

Evening out inequalities between income and expendi-ture. *Current inequalities.* It is impossible for the ordinary family to live from one pay-day to the next without setting aside something out of today's income to be spent tomorrow and the day after. It is impossible for most families to balance their year's budget without occasionally setting aside some current funds to be used for expendi-tures a few weeks or a few months in the future. The family with a small but regular income must accumulate small increments of current income if it is to pay cash for articles which cost more than the small margin above fixed charges which it has available for occasional expenditures. The family whose income is received in occasional large increments at irregular intervals must save enough out of each instalment of income to care for continuing expenses for current needs until the receipt of the next instalment of income. Most families take such saving as a matter of course.

Inequalities due to the family life cycle. Most families find that just as there are weeks and months each year in which current income is less than adequate, and other weeks and months when current income is more than adequate for current needs, so there are longer periods in the life of the family in which current income is less than adequate and other periods in which current income is more than adequate to maintain the family's usual standard of living. Thoughtful families are finding that they can more easily meet the heavy demands upon current income which inevitably come in certain stages of the family life cycle if they set aside funds for the purpose in earlier stages of more adequate income. Only the few families whose income can definitely be depended upon to increase more rapidly than the demands upon it, can safely spend current income without regard for the future. Even these few families, if they are counting upon substantial yearly increases in income from the increasing earning power of the head of the family, must spend some current income for insurance in order to guarantee the continuance of an income in case of his incapacity or death.

Inequalities due to the business cycle. Just as the adequacy of the family income varies from one stage to another of the family life cycle, so also does it vary from one stage to another of the business cycle. For most families, in some one or two stages of the business cycle, current income is more than adequate for current needs, while in other stages it is far from adequate. But not all families are affected in the same way by the changes in the business cycle. In families of business and professional men, salesmen selling on commission, wage earners in industries in which employment is responsive to general business conditions, and in families dependent for a considerable part of their income upon investments in common stocks or business enterprises, income ordinarily increases faster than prices during periods of prosperity, and declines more than living costs during the depression stage of the cycle. On the other hand, in families depending upon the earnings of salaried employees, and in families living on income from investments in bonds, mortgages, and other fixed-income securities, income fails to keep pace with the increase in prices during prosperity, but ordinarily decreases less than do living costs during periods of business depression.[1] Few families have income from such a variety of sources that they are completely secure from the effects of changes of the business cycle. Most families will find that if they are continuously to maintain a given level of living, they must, in the stages of the business cycle in which their income is more than adequate for current needs, accumulate enough savings to provide for their needs during those stages in which their expenditures usually run ahead of their income.

Inequalities due to unforeseeable contingencies. Well-established families know from experience that from time to time emergencies arise which necessitate unanticipated but heavy expenditures, or which sharply curtail anticipated income. In order to meet these emergencies without lowering its usual level of living, every family must, in periods of adequate income, set up reserves against the time when these unforeseeable emergencies may arise. A family may accumulate its own reserves for the peculiar contingencies which it faces as an individual family, or by purchasing insurance it may share in the common reserves accumulated by many families against common contingencies. Every family should consider both its individual savings for a rainy day and its payments of insurance premiums for protection against common risks as an integral part of its savings program.

Saving to create an estate. Many families, who feel that their income is more than sufficient to maintain a desirable level of living, plan to accumulate some funds with which to create an estate or add to an existing estate. These families try to save enough so that they will need to use only the income from their investments to even out inequalities in current expenditures. They consider the principal of their accumulation as set aside to provide a continuing source of income for the present and for future generations.

Saving money to make money. Still other families—though perhaps these families, nowadays, are in the minority—plan to save money to use to make more money. They definitely include plans for accumulation of a fund for investment in business ventures, or

---

[1] The tables on pages 65, 66, and 67 suggest the way family incomes from different sources may be affected by the business cycle. From time to time the National Bureau of Economic Research (New York) publishes the results of research showing the effect of changing business conditions upon incomes. See Bulletin 49, June 7, 1934, for example.

for speculative purchases of real estate, commodities, and securities. This, too, is a legitimate reason for saving. Every family that is saving money to make money must distinguish clearly between the savings it is to use for business ventures, and the other funds which it needs to even out inequalities between income and expenditure, or to create an estate. Too many families speculate with all of their savings. As a result, too often an unfortunate speculation wipes out not only the fund they have set up to use to make more money, but their entire estate and reserves as well.

The place of saving in the family spending plan. If a family is to handle its savings intelligently, it must set up a comprehensive savings program as an integral part of its long-time spending plan. It must determine as definitely as it can in advance the items requiring large outlay, the periods of heavy expenditure, and the periods of inadequate income for which funds must be provided. It must decide which, as well as how many, of its future needs are to be financed from savings. It must include in its plan the accumulation of adequate reserves for specific contingencies. It must be sure that it is making proper provision for the payment of necessary insurance premiums. If the family plans to establish an estate or add to an existing estate, it must make definite provision for the accumulation of the original fund and for the use of the income from these investments. If it is planning to save money to make money, it must plan definitely for the handling of these funds as a separate unit in its long-time spending plan. And finally, it must determine, as closely as it can, not only how much and for what, but when, its savings are to be made, and when they are to be drawn upon and used for the purposes for which they were accumulated.

Saving for planned expenditures. Most families find it better to save for specific purposes than for long periods of heavy expense. It is much more interesting to be saving for a new car, a new home, a vacation trip to Europe, a college education for the children, or even for extra money for groceries, extra allowances for clothing, or extra money for gasoline or recreation than simply to be saving for some vague future period of unusually heavy expenditures. In addition, planning savings in terms of specific future expenditures is more valuable than planning savings in general terms, because a detailed savings plan acts as a guide not only to saving but also to the investment and spending of the savings as well.

If a family works out its savings program in terms of specific expenditures, it will find that the objects for which the family is saving, like its current expenditures, will change from year to year. The family just starting out in life may be saving for furniture. If it has enough accumulated at marriage to buy furniture, it may be saving for a home, or for a new car, or for medical care and hospitalization, and all the other expenses involved in the birth of the children. When the children are well started in school, most families begin to accumulate funds with which to finance their education. After the children leave home and become self-supporting, the parents may concentrate upon the accumulation of money upon which to live in their declining years. And if their income is at all adequate, they usually try to accumulate a little more than they themselves will need, which they can use during their lifetime as an additional reserve against emergencies and leave behind them as an estate, in order that their children may have a little more in the way of resources, a little more as a margin above current necessities than did their parents.

Setting up reserves for contingencies. Just as a family plans its savings in terms of a definite list of future expenditures, so it should set up its reserves with regard to a definite list of specific contingencies. There are a number of these common contingencies against which reserves should be set up. The family dependent for most of its income upon the earnings of one wage earner should have some reserves to fall back upon in case the bread winner loses his job. The better the position he holds, the larger this reserve should be. The man working at semi-skilled or common labor has a much larger range of occupations open to him than does the man of unusual ability holding a highly specialized job for which long training is required. There are many positions open to the wage earner which he can take without much loss in earning power. But the corporation executive, even the minor executive, may find that six months or a year may elapse before he can find another position as good as the one he previously held. Even the man of more than average ability will find his bargaining power is much better if he has sufficient reserves so that he obviously is not forced to take the first job that offers. It has been suggested that a fund equal to six months' income may be an adequate unemployment reserve for families in the lower income groups. Families in the upper income groups, on the other hand, should maintain an unemployment reserve equal to not less than a year's income.

Most families need reserves for unexpectedly heavy expenditures for medical care. In almost every family expenditures for the care of health vary a great deal from year to year. Every family should, of course, make adequate provision for routine care of health in its yearly budget. But few families have incomes large enough to defray from current income the cost of a disabling accident or an emergency operation or a long and serious illness. Unless they maintain reserves to use in such emergencies, they must either radically adjust their present mode of living, or be burdened for several years by the obligations such emergencies always involve.

If prices are fluctuating widely, families find it easier to maintain their usual living standards if they maintain reserves upon which to draw in case prices rise rapidly. Families dependent upon wages and salaries or fixed-income investments almost always find that prices go up faster than do their incomes. A family can frequently use some of its reserve to advantage to make necessary purchases before prices advance too far. Or it can use these reserves to supplement budget allowances from ordinary income.

A family needs reserves to draw upon for a whole list of unexpected but essential expenditures. Home owners always face the possibility of emergency repairs. Families living in rented homes need reserves for moving expenses. These must be sufficient not only to cover the actual cost of moving the family's household goods to the new home, but to pay the usual fees for moving the telephone, installing the gas stove and the electric refrigerator, hooking up the radio, and connecting the electric, gas, and water services. This reserve must be large enough to cover repairs to furniture damaged in moving, and the replacement of pieces which do not fit the new apartment. Like the home owner, the car owner must always be prepared to pay for unexpected repairs and replacements. Parents of boys and girls of school age must set aside something with which to buy new books and caps and gloves and rubbers and other equipment to replace the articles children are always losing. They need reserves for shoes which wear out unexpectedly, and for clothing torn in play. And if the family includes boys, it may find it necessary to set up some reserves to replace the neighbor's broken windows and to repair other property damage.

This long list of unexpected expenditures may include many pleasant as well as unpleasant contingencies. Accepting an invitation to a formal reception may necessitate the purchase of a new evening gown or the replacement of evening clothes. The marriage of a friend calls for the purchase of a suitable gift. The arrival of guests from out of town necessitates unplanned-for expenditures for entertainment. Bargain sales occasionally present opportunities for the family with available cash to secure something it has long desired but never before felt it could afford.

Determining the amount of reserves. No matter how carefully a family plans, it can never foresee all the demands upon its income. Few families can accumulate adequate reserves for these contingencies in a single year. And yet when these demands arise, it must have funds to use if it is to provide for all its needs and make the most of its opportunities.

A family can determine how large its reserves should be only after a careful consideration of the particular contingencies it must face. Most families find that their incomes are not large enough to let them maintain completely adequate special reserves against all possible emergencies. Because they do not understand the difference between saving for definitely planned expenditures and setting up reserves for possible contingencies, many families are constantly worried about their apparent inability to maintain adequate safeguards against the uncertainties of the future.

Reserves for contingencies differ from savings for planned expenditures in one important particular. A family expects to use all of its savings for planned expenditures for the purpose for which they are being accumulated. It hopes it will not need to draw upon the reserve it is accumulating for emergency expenditures. Nevertheless, any of the contingencies for which it is planning may occur. Some of them without question will occur. However, it is highly improbable that any family will ever be called upon within a single year to meet all the emergencies against which reserves are maintained.

In determining the amount of reserves to be accumulated against the uncertainties of the future, therefore, it is not necessary to set aside each year a fund large enough to cover all possible contingencies. It is necessary only to have enough savings available to meet those unforeseen expenditures which may reasonably be expected to occur at any given time in the life of the family.

How to handle reserves. There are two ways by which a family may provide for future contingencies. It may carry insurance against certain risks which it has in common with many other families, or it may set up its own reserves against these as well as its peculiar personal and therefore uninsurable risks. In deciding whether or not to purchase insurance against common risks, each family must compare the amount of the premium charged for adequate insurance with the amount it would need to set aside to provide similar protection from its own reserves. In some cases insurance provides more complete protection than the family could possibly provide for itself, and at much lower cost. In other cases, a family may be able to maintain more economically by its own savings all the reserve that it can afford.

There are two ways in which a family may handle its own reserves. It may set up special reserves for specific contingencies. Or it may accumulate one fund large enough to cover all probable demands for unforeseen expenditures. There are some advantages to each method. Setting up special reserves emphasizes the importance of maintaining a continuous reserve against each specific contingency. Setting up special reserves emphasizes the importance of replacing as soon as possible any amounts which may be withdrawn, in order to have money available when next a similar emergency may arise. Maintaining special reserves indicates definitely the amount which is necessary to provide adequately for a specific future contingency.

In our modern industrial society, unemployment is a continuing risk which most families must face. At the same time, it is a contingency which may arise only at long intervals. It may be wise, therefore, to invest the unemployment reserve as a separate fund, to be maintained in addition to all other reserves, to be used only in case of unemployment, and to be replaced as soon as possible after new employment is secured.

On the other hand, there are many minor hazards which call for only small expenditures at irregular intervals. Most families need to draw upon their reserves first for one emergency and then for another. Unless a family has a considerable amount available for investment in reserves, it usually finds it more convenient to set up a single contingent reserve fund, to make this fund as nearly adequate as the family income will allow, and draw upon it for whatever emergency arises. A single large fund can usually be invested to better advantage than can a number of smaller funds. If the amount of the single fund is determined by an accurate estimate of the specific uncertainties for which reserves must be provided, and if the family never draws upon this fund for any other purposes than those for which it was created, the single fund will work as well as a series of special funds, and is usually much easier for the family of moderate means to manage.

How much to save. What amount to save is an individual problem which each family must work out for itself. There is no general rule which can be easily applied to determine arbitrarily the amount a family should save.

How much a family should save depends in part upon the specific future needs for which funds must be accumulated. It depends in part upon the uncertainties in the family situation for which reserves must be provided. The amount which must be set aside out of current income for contingent reserves depends also upon the reserves the family already has available in its present investments.

How much a family should save depends in part upon the importance to that family of saving money to make money. Saving for that purpose may be relatively unimportant for the family of a salaried man in a relatively secure position. It may be absolutely impossible for the family of a wage earner. It may be of primary importance to the family of a man who is planning to enter or is now engaged in business for himself.

How much a family should plan to save depends in part at least upon the importance the family places upon creating an estate or adding to an existing estate. In a large family it may be desirable to add considerably to the family's present investments in order that each of the children may have as good a start in life as did their parents. In a family with considerable property, and with only one or two children, especially if the family is in line to receive additional inheritances, it may seem better to liquidate part of the family's present investments for present needs, rather than to lower the family's living standards to add to an already adequate estate. On the other hand, if a family is responsible for the care of someone who is permanently either partially or entirely dependent, it may be necessary to make many current sacrifices in order to accumulate enough to assure the dependent a continuing income.

And, finally, how much a family should save depends to a large extent upon the attitude with which its members face the future. It depends upon the relative importance to the members of the family of future security and of present needs. Some families want security in the future, even at the cost of a very low level of living in the present. Other families definitely prefer to live as well as they are able in the present, and let the future take care of itself.

Most families find that they must do the best they can to strike a balance between present and future expenditures. Few families are able to live as well as they would like in the present. Not many families are able to accumulate all the reserves they would like, to plan to do everything they would like in the future. Only a few families have a sufficient margin above current necessities to insure the future maintenance of their present level of living. There are not very many families with incomes generous enough even to guarantee absolutely the provision of minimum essentials throughout the whole life of the family.

Most families, therefore, are forced to take a chance upon some of the contingencies of life. If a major disaster, like prolonged unemployment, or sickness, or serious accident, or the death of the chief wage earner befalls them, they recognize the fact that they will be compelled to make definite and major adjustments in their manner of living.

The essential thing, therefore, in determining how much to save, is to set up sufficient savings and reserves to provide for all the expenditures in the future which are obviously more important in the long life of the family than are any present expenditures which might be made with these savings. The essential thing is to set aside enough for the future to reduce to a minimum the events which may necessitate the complete replanning of the family's manner of living.

When to save. Similarly, when to save is an individual problem. Obviously, there is no one amount, there is no one percentage of the family income which should arbitrarily be set aside for savings every year during the entire life of the family. Each family must determine for itself when it can best make its savings. In some years it may save half or more than half of its income for future needs. In other years it may save little or nothing. In still other years, it may draw upon its savings for the purposes for which they were accumulated.

It is not always wise for two families of the same size and with the same income to set aside each year the same amount of money. Each family must work out its own savings policy, taking into account not only the size of the family and its present income but the stage of the family in the family life cycle, and the way in which its needs and its income will probably be affected by long-time price and employment trends, and by changes in the business cycle.

For example, most families find that in the period when they are establishing the family current expenses for immediate needs are low. In this period, a considerable part of the family income can well be used to accumulate a stock of furniture and permanent equipment, to build up the family inventory of china, silver, and linens, and to make a substantial start toward the accumulation of a fund to be used a few years later for the purchase of a home. In this period, also, many families plan to save money to be used in making more money. In this period many families try to set up a substantial backlog of investments to provide an adequate unemployment reserve. And toward the end of this period most families try to save enough to defray at least partially the extra expenses involved in the birth and care of small children.

During the years when the children are small, on the other hand, most families find it advisable to cut down their savings program considerably. If they are planning eventually to buy a home, they will if possible continue regular payments to a savings account, or to a building and loan association, in order that their money may accumulate at compound interest. To provide added protection while the children are small, they may buy additional life insurance in its cheaper forms. For the most part, however, the period when the children are small is a period in which extra funds may well be invested in the children themselves, either in preventive medicine, or in play equipment, or in household help which will free the mother for care of the children in order to insure their normal physical and mental development in the pre-school period.

As soon as the children are well started in elementary school, more generous savings may again be possible. If the family is permanently located in a community, it may decide to buy a home of its own, using the savings begun earlier in the life of the family for a down payment, and completing the payments out of current income during the next few years. During this period, it may begin saving for the children's education. It may be setting aside some money for the repair or replacement of the furniture, which will inevitably soon show the wear and tear involved in the bringing up of small children. If the family already owns its own home, it may be saving some money for repairs, redecoration, expansion, or alterations. In most families this is a period when extensive saving is imperative. This is the period in which the family must anticipate the heavy demands which inevitably come at the peak of the family life cycle.

During the high school and college period, the family income may increase rapidly enough to allow for some savings. But many families find that during these years it is necessary to draw upon past savings for current expense. And the period of college education is one in which most families use up a considerable amount of their earlier accumulations.

After the children have left home, or, if still living at home, after they have become self-supporting, comes a period in which savings again may take a large part of the family income. If the earning power of the head of the family is still unimpaired, it may be possible to set aside as much as half the family income for savings. Some will be invested to provide funds upon which to live after retirement. Some may be used to add to the family estate.

Finally in the period of retirement, some few families may have an income from earlier investments large enough to allow them to continue their accumulation. Families are doing much better than the average, however, if they are able to live upon only the income from their investments. After retirement most families must draw upon their principal for living expenses.

Obviously, then, when to save depends upon the relative importance of present and future needs as the family passes through the successive stages of the family life cycle. Similarly, it depends upon the relative adequacy of present and future income, as determined by long-time price trends and the swing of the business cycle. Most families are fortunate if they come to the peak of demands upon their income during a period of moderate prosperity. It is not so easy for them to adjust their expenditures at the peak of their needs either to boom prices or to a curtailed depression income. It is obvious, therefore, that the savings program not only must be timed with regard to the immediacy of the family's needs and the adequacy of the family's income, but also must be adjusted from time to time to the peculiar coincidence of the family life cycle and the business cycle.

There are a few families, usually of business or professional men, whose incomes increase more rapidly than do their expenses. These few families may find it feasible to save a definite amount each year, which they invest and allow to accumulate at compound interest. These families may determine the amount of income they desire at retirement. They then set aside each year for the purchase of a deferred annuity the amount necessary to provide them with the desired income. Or, if their income is large enough, they may personally invest in sound securities a given proportion of their current income, plus the interest from their already accumulated savings. Then when they approach the retirement age, they can use the income from their investments to provide what they formerly bought with their earnings.

Saving, then, is an individual problem, which each family must work out for itself on the basis of its own resources, its own needs, its own philosophy of life. The savings program must be developed as an integral part of the family's spending plan. For after all, saving is different from other spending only in that it is spending for wants which must be satisfied not in the immediate present but at some time in the future. Each family must therefore work out for itself an individualized savings plan. It must decide how much it is to spend for present wants, and at the same time it must determine how much it is to set aside for more important wants in the future. It must plan carefully in advance the timing of both the accumulation and the spending of its savings. It can do this intelligently only if it considers the accumulation of funds not as something which is worth while primarily for its own sake, but as a highly important and effective device for the enrichment of living.

INVESTMENTS

How to invest savings. There are three principal ways in which a family may invest its savings. First, it may invest money in such a way as to have money to use in the future. This may be done either by the purchase of income-producing securities which will provide the family with a regular money income from the earnings of the investments, or by depositing in a savings bank, by investing in a building and loan association, or by buying readily marketable securities from which both principal and interest can be secured when needed for current expenditures.

Second, a family may invest its money savings in a stock of durable goods, or in an inventory of supplies purchased in anticipation of future needs. In this case it is accumulating family capital, which will not yield a money income, but will yield dividends in use and will eliminate an equivalent amount of necessary expenditure in the future.

Third, a family may invest in insurance. This will provide, not future income for ordinary expenditures, but definite amounts of money for specified future contingencies.

Investing in order to have more money in the future. It is the setting aside of money in the present in order to have more money to use in the future which people usually think of as saving. It is the handling of money savings which is usually discussed in standard treatises on investment. The management of investments is a whole field in itself. In a book on family finance there is no room for a thorough discussion of the principles of investment or for a detailed description of the great variety of investment opportunities available and their relative desirability.

Few families are in a position to select securities without competent advice. In recent years it has not been easy to find qualified, unbiased, and conscientious investment counsel. A family must, therefore, learn enough about the relative merits of various investment opportunities to be able to judge the soundness of such counsel as is available. It must check for itself upon specific recommendation, by using some standard securities rating service, of which Moody's [2] is probably the most generally available. It must make the final decision as to the advisability of each specific investment, in terms of its intrinsic merits, the purpose for which the funds are to be used, and the place which the specific security must fill in the family's investment program.

It is worth while, therefore, to suggest a few fundamental principles involved in the selection of investments, to point out their application to the individual savings program, and to show how some of the more common types of investments may be used in working out the family's savings and investment program.

---

[2] *Moody's Investors' Service*, New York.

Some points to consider in making investments. *Safety.*
The ownership of anything involves risk. Property in our own possession may be destroyed. Property let out of our possession may never be returned. Money savings, hidden around the house, may be stolen. Invested, they may be lost. No family can afford to take unnecessary chances with its savings. If it does, it may be unable to carry out as planned its long-time spending and savings program.

Two types of risks may be incurred in making investments. If the family purchases income-producing property, it assumes responsibility for management, and all the risks involved in the conduct of a business enterprise. If, on the other hand, the family lends its money to others, it assumes the risks inevitably involved in the granting of credit.

For example, suppose a family uses its savings to buy a well-located apartment house. It must either spend considerable time upon the management of the property, negotiating leases, supervising and paying for necessary repairs and alterations, collecting rents, and evicting non-paying tenants, or it must pay someone else to do the work of management for it out of the income from the property. Further, as owner, the family is responsible for all debts, taxes, or other obligations arising out of the ownership or management of the apartments. In return, however, the family receives whatever remains of the income from the property after all expenses, taxes, and other obligations are met. If the demand for apartments increases, and rents advance, the owner benefits from the increase in income. If rents decline, the owner is still responsible for all the expenses involved in the upkeep and ownership of the property. If real estate values increase, and the family is able to sell the property for more than was paid for it, the profit belongs to the family. If, on the other hand, property values decline, and the property must be sold for less than was paid for it, the family as owner of the property must assume the loss. If the family does not own the property outright, but has borrowed on mortgage security part of the money it has invested, it is responsible for the payment of both interest and principal on the mortgage, as part of the obligation ownership entails. If it fails to meet these obligations, it may lose title to the property, which according to the terms of the mortgage agreement may be sold for the benefit of the mortgagee.

In this example, the risks the family assumes are obvious enough.

That families purchasing stock in a corporation are assuming similar risks is not always so clear, since so many minority stockholders seem to do nothing but receive their dividend checks at regular intervals. Nevertheless it is equally true in the case of the corporation, as in the case of the apartment house, that if the business prospers, profits belong to the stockholders; if the business fails, it is first the income and then the capital of the stockholder which is lost in the failure.

When a family buys stock in a corporation, therefore, it must consider the investment as the purchase of a share of a business. The purchase of stock in a corporation does not, of course, involve direct participation in the management of the affairs of the concern. It does, however, imply responsibility for the payment of the officers and employees who carry on the corporation business. It does imply opportunity to participate in stockholders' meetings and to vote for the directors who shape the policies of the corporation, but the average stockholder has no real voice in management. Even if, in order to reduce somewhat the risk it is assuming, the family buys preferred stock instead of common stock, it must remember that it is still one of the owners of the corporation, whose position is preferred as to income and principal, but who, nevertheless, has no guarantee other than the earning power and assets of the business of either income or the principal of its investment.

Suppose that instead of buying a share in a business, a family lends its accumulated savings. If it lends money to an individual or to another family, taking in return a personal note with a mortgage upon a piece of real property as security, the risks it runs are obvious enough. The borrower may be unable to repay the loan as he agrees. He may be unwilling to pay either interest or principal, and may make it very difficult for the family to collect either income or principal on the loan. If the lender tries to force repayment, he may find that the collateral posted as security is worth less than the amount of the loan, and that the expenses of collection and foreclosure eat heavily into the amount finally obtained.

A family is taking similar risks when it buys bonds or notes issued by business corporations. It is taking similar risks, which differ only in degree and not in kind, when it invests in the bonds or notes of municipal, state, or federal governments, or when it purchases endowment insurance or annuities, or deposits in a savings account in a commercial or industrial bank. In all of these cases, the family must consider the character, the capacity, the capital of the borrower, for these determine his willingness and ability to repay the loan as he has agreed. And it must consider also the collateral posted as security for any loan made, for this determines in large measure what the lender will be able to recover if the borrower is unwilling or unable to repay the loan.

A family must select its investments with due regard to both the amount and type of risk it is willing to assume. It must recognize that every investment involves some risk. It must realize that some investments involve a great deal more risk than do others. It must understand that this is true both of credit and of business risks. It is ordinarily believed that credit risks are better risks than business, or ownership, risks, that well-secured bonds are better risks than preferred stocks, and preferred stocks better risks than common stocks. It is generally assumed that obligations of the federal government are safer than obligations of state or local governments, and that all government obligations are safer than the bonds and notes of business corporations. In general this is true.

At the same time it is true that common stocks in conservatively managed corporations may actually involve less risk, not than bonds in the same sort of companies, but than a great many bonds offered to the small investor. Sound industrial bonds may be safer than bonds secured by mortgages on overvalued real estate. Underlying bonds secured by operating properties of railroads or privately owned public utilities may be safer than the bonds of bankrupt municipalities.

In making its choice of investments, a family must consider, not the general desirability of a general class of securities, but the specific risks involved in a single security or a specific group of securities it has under consideration. The investment it selects must first of all measure up to the rigid standards it has set for the safety of its principal and the certainty of its income, and at the same time give it the other features which will best fit into its general investment program.

Availability. A second fundamental consideration in the selection of investments is availability. A family must select investments which will be available both as to principal and income when the family needs to use the money. If the family is investing primarily for income, it will consider the time of interest or dividend payment. If it is accumulating funds for specific objectives at some definite time in the future, it will consider the maturity of loans, and the marketability of income property or corporation securities. Funds used as reserves, whether for remote or immediate contingencies, must be so invested as to be readily convertible into cash whenever needed, without loss of principal or too great sacrifice of current income.

For example, a family building up investments designed to provide income upon which it is to live in old age will want to select a number of securities with a variety of interest payment dates, so that it will have some income every month of the year. On the other hand, a family planning to reinvest the income from its investments may prefer to receive the income from all of them at the same time, so that it will have enough to invest to good advantage, promptly, and without loss of interest.

Savings for definite objectives several years ahead, such as the purchase of a home, the provision of funds for a college education for the children, a trip to Europe, or the needs of old age, may be invested in mortgages or sound bonds, maturing at the date when the funds will be needed. Or they may be invested in building and loan shares or in annuity contracts maturing at the desired date. Or these funds may be invested in seasoned long-term bonds for which there is a ready market. In a few cases, if it is absolutely necessary to guarantee the availability of funds at a definite time, it may be wise to purchase endowment insurance, though of course this requires the payment of a premium for protection in addition to the necessary investment.

In planning for objectives to be attained only at some time in the future, it is often worth while to take advantage of the power of compound interest. Many families prefer a type of investment in which interest is compounded regularly, for two reasons: first, because reinvesting the interest reduces the amount which the family must divert from current income, and second, because if the income is reinvested automatically, there is never any temptation to use it for current expenditures. If, however, a family prefers to invest in bonds or mortgages, rather than in building and loan shares or annuities, it can secure the advantage of compound interest by reinvesting the income from its investments as fast as it is received.

In investing savings for contingent reserves, it is important to put at least part of the reserves into a savings account where it will be always available. Because savings accounts pay only a low rate of interest, some people prefer to invest most of their reserves in high-grade readily marketable bonds paying a somewhat higher rate of interest. They believe that this is sound investment policy, provided they confine their investments to high-grade government issues and well-seasoned listed municipals and high-grade rails and utilities. This may be a safe enough way to invest reserves when the investment market is strong. But whenever the securities market shows any signs of weakening, a number of these securities should be converted into cash, even at the sacrifice of most of the interest. After the World War, Liberty Bonds sold for as little as 85 cents on the dollar. During the depression years in the 1930's, many inherently sound bonds could not be sold for more than half their long-time value, and at times were difficult to market at any figure. Families that were forced to draw upon their reserves during these years lost heavily in realizing on the principal of their investment.

Obviously, then, it is highly important for the family always to invest its savings with definite thought as to the time and the purpose for which they are to be used. Every investment should be made only after careful consideration of the time at which principal and income must be available. It is always well for the family to keep enough of its money readily available in a bank account to avoid the forced liquidation of any of its securities.

Convenience in management. A third factor to consider in the selection of investments is convenience in management. This is important, because for most families management of investments is and must be only incidental to the more immediate task of providing for the family's everyday needs.

Convenience in management involves convenience in making the investment. A family must select investments which can be bought with the amount of money the family has to invest. If the family has only a small amount to invest at regular intervals, it must use the savings bank, the building and loan association, or the annuity contract. In some cases, when it has secured enough for a substantial down payment, it may be able to buy real property, and occasionally corporate securities, on the instalment plan. A family can secure a few government bonds in denominations as low as $100. If it has $500 to invest, it has a somewhat larger selection. Most bonds, however, are issued only in denominations of $1,000, and are not available to the ordinary family until it has made a substantial start upon its savings program. Stocks, on the other hand, are available in odd lots. It is often possible to purchase as little as a single share of stock in a corporation, though it will be necessary to pay the higher commissions charged by brokers for such odd-lot transactions.

Convenience in management involves convenience in supervision of the investment, and convenience in collection of the income and the principal when it falls due. Corporate securities are popular because they require so little of the investor. He may put his bonds into his strong box, clip the coupons twice a year, and cash them at his own bank. If he wants to realize on the principal of his investment, any reputable broker will be glad to sell a listed bond for him. If he has invested in stock, his shares are registered on the transfer books of the company, and the dividend checks are mailed to him from time to time. If he cares to participate in the management of the concern, he can attend the annual stockholders' meetings; or he can send in a proxy to be voted as he directs.

If, on the other hand, he invests in mortgages, he must collect his own interest. He must check from time to time to see that the mortgaged property is kept in proper repair, that taxes are paid upon it, and that fire insurance is kept in force. In case of default he must institute and carry through foreclosure proceedings, and stand all the costs that are involved.

Investments in rental real estate or in business enterprise involve, of course, all the management problems which come with the conduct of any business. If some member of the family has the time to devote to their management, they may be a suitable source of investment. But they do not rate high in convenience of management. Mortgage loans and business investments are usually convenient only for the family that is permanently located in a community, that has, and is reasonably sure to continue to have, time to attend to all the details that such investments involve. Most families find savings accounts, building and loan shares, annuity contracts, and listed government or corporate securities are a much more convenient type of investment. Most families prefer the type of investment into which they can put their money and forget about it. The only danger from the use of these more convenient forms is that the family will be inclined to devote too little time to the supervision of its investments.

Yield. Every family is interested in securing as large a return upon its investment as is consistent with safety of principal and certainty of income. The return upon stocks, bonds, notes, and mortgages is usually stated in terms of percentages of the par value or face value of the security. If a stock has no par value or only a nominal par value, earnings may be stated as so many dollars or so many cents per share. What the family wants to know, however, is not the rate of return upon a par or a nominal value, but rather the percentage the security will yield them upon the amount they have actually invested.

Suppose a family wants to compare the yield of securities which can be bought upon the following terms: Security A pays at the rate of 5 per cent upon a par value of $1,000. It can be purchased for $1,000. Security B pays at the rate of 6 per cent upon a par value of $1,000. It can be purchased for $1,200. Security C pays at the rate of 4 per cent upon a par value of $1,000. It can be purchased for $800.

The procedure is as follows: (1) Determine the amount of income received from the security in a single year, by multiplying the par value of the security by the rate of return. (2) Divide the yearly income by the purchase price. The resulting percentage is the yield. That is:

Security A: $1,000 × .05 = $50; $50 ÷ $1,000 = .05, yield on security A.
Security B: $1,000 × .06 = $60; $60 ÷ $1,200 = .05, yield on security B.
Security C: $1,000 × .04 = $40; $40 ÷ $ 800 = .05, yield on security C.

In this case, although the rate of return on Security B is higher than on Security A, and the rate of return on Security C is lower than on Security A, the purchase prices vary so that the three securities yield the same amount upon the actual investment. This procedure may be expressed as a formula as follows:

$$\frac{\text{Par value} \times \text{Rate}}{\text{Amount Invested}} = \text{Yield}$$

For fixed-income securities having a definite maturity date, the process of estimating yield is not quite so simple as this. Suppose the three securities are bonds, which mature ten years from the time the family buys them. If the family buys Bond A, the $1,000 it invested will be repaid at the maturity of the loan. If it buys Bond B, however, it will be paid, not the $1,200 which it originally invested, but the $1,000 which is the principal amount of the loan. If it buys a **bond** at a premium, therefore, it must subtract enough from each year's income to make up for the loss which it must take when it cashes in its bond at maturity.

Suppose, on the other hand, it buys Bond C, and holds it till maturity. In this case it will receive $1,000, which is $200 more than the amount which it originally invested. This $200 represents an amount which can be added to the income from the bond in computing the yield during the years the family holds it.

In computing the yield upon a bond bought at a premium, it is necessary to subtract from each year's income enough to make up for the loss which it will take on the principal of the investment at the maturity of the loan. In computing the yield upon a bond purchased at a discount, it is necessary to add a proportionate part of the discount to each year's income. The formulæ to use in this case are as follows:

For bonds bought above par:
$$\frac{\text{Par value} \times \text{Rate} - \dfrac{\text{Premium}}{\text{Term}}}{\text{Amount Invested}} = \text{Yield}$$

For bonds bought below par:
$$\frac{\text{Par value} \times \text{Rate} + \dfrac{\text{Discount}}{\text{Term}}}{\text{Amount Invested}} = \text{Yield}$$

The return upon any investment is compounded of a number of elements. One is the payment of interest upon the money invested. Another is a payment sufficient to compensate the investor for the risks he assumes. If the management of the investment involves any unusual costs, or puts the investor to any considerable inconvenience, there may be in addition a payment sufficient to cover these costs of management. In the case of a few securities, such as amortizing mortgages and mining stocks, part of the return represents repayment of part of the original investment.

Relation of risk and yield. By comparing the yields of a number of investments involving similar management costs, the family can determine the market estimates of the amount of risk each investment involves. If the other elements in the situation are equal, it is easy to see that the higher the yield, the higher is the risk which the investment involves.

Many people take it for granted that risk varies proportionately as well as directly with the yield. Actually, however, because payment for risk is only one element in the return, the payment for risk increases faster than the total return upon the investment.

For example: Suppose that at a given time investments involving a maximum of convenience and a minimum of risk, such as long-time government bonds, are yielding 3 per cent upon the investment. A 4 per cent bond involving similar management costs would represent a payment of 3 per cent for interest and management and 1 per cent for risk. A 5 per cent bond would represent 3 per cent for interest and management and 2 per cent for risk. A bond yielding 6 per cent would represent a payment of 3 per cent for interest and management and 3 per cent for risk.

In this case, the return from the 5 per cent bond would be 25 per cent more than the return from the 4 per cent bond, but the payment for risk would be increased 100 per cent. The 6 per cent bond would yield 50 per cent more than the 4 per cent bond, but it would involve three times the risk.

In determining risks by comparing yields, some people are careless enough to assume that an investment yielding 5 per cent involves only 1 per cent more risk than a 4 per cent investment, and that a 6 per cent investment involves only 1 per cent more risk than an investment yielding 5 per cent. Obviously, this is not so, for the return upon an investment yielding 5 per cent is 25 per cent more than the return from the 4 per cent investment.

Families frequently get into difficulties because they assume that a given rate of return represents a given amount of risk. Because at one time they were able to buy 6 per cent bonds giving them the desired degree of safety, they assume that at any time a 6 per cent bond will give them the same degree of safety. They do not realize that the interest rate changes from time to time with changes in the demand for loans and in the supply of funds offered for investment. They do not understand that the $60 return upon a $1,000, 6 per cent bond issued when the interest rate is 4 per cent represents a payment of $40 for interest and $20 for risk, while the $60 return upon a $1,000, 6 per cent bond issued when the interest rate is 3 per cent represents a payment of only $30 in interest and $30 for risk.

There are even a few people who do not understand that a $1,000, 6 per cent bond selling for $800 involves more risk than a 6 per cent bond of similar maturity selling for its face value. If they would compute the yield upon a bond selling at such a discount, and compare it with the yield of securities involving a minimum of risk, they could more easily see the risk experienced investors believe is involved in the purchase of securities for less than their face value.

Suppose, for example, that the 6 per cent bond selling for $800 had 10 years to run. Using the formula for computing the yield of bonds purchased at a discount:

$$\frac{\$1,000 \times .06 + \dfrac{200}{10}}{\$800} = 10 \text{ per cent}$$

If the going rate of interest for investments involving a minimum of risk is 3 per cent, the bond selling at a 20 per cent discount involves more than twice the risk that a bond yielding 6 per cent does. It should be compared in desirability, not with bonds yielding 6 per cent, but with stocks and other speculative securities yielding 10 per cent upon the investment.

Adjusting the investment program to changing business conditions. Since the relative desirability of investments, both as to safety, availability, and yield, changes materially from time to time with changes in the general business situation, every family must adjust its personal investment program to changes in business conditions. If a family is to make the most of available investment opportunities, if it is to keep the yield of its investments at a reasonable figure, and at the same time keep the risks it assumes at a minimum, it must appraise the effect of economic, social, and political developments upon the particular properties in which it has investments. It must be constantly on the alert to anticipate changes in the business cycle. It must keep in mind, not only the immediate business situation, but also underlying and fundamental long-time trends. It must make each of its investments, especially those upon which it is planning to realize some years in the future, only after careful consideration of the significance of the underlying long-time or secular trend of prices.

Older families, with years of experience in handling their investments, have learned the importance of keeping abreast of industrial developments, shifting investments from one industry to another as new lines of business develop and older lines decline. For example, the development of motor transportation has made available many new investment opportunities. At the same time it has reduced markedly the value of many railway securities. It has completely wiped out many investments even in the underlying bonds of electric railways. The general adoption of the private motor car has caused many shifts in real estate values. It has facilitated the development of suburban subdivisions. It has greatly reduced the value of much older residential property. The shift from horse-drawn to motor vehicles has freed millions of acres of land for the production of human food at the same time that the restriction of immigration and the decline in the rate of population growth has put an end to the assumption that any business dealing with the necessities of life can count upon a constantly expanding market. It is absolutely essential that every family keep always in mind the possible effect of such current developments, no matter how remote they may appear to be, upon the industries in which it has invested its savings.

In recent years people generally have learned a good deal about adjusting their financial affairs to changes in the business cycle. They now understand the danger of investing heavily in stocks or income properties at peak prices toward the end of a long period of prosperity. They have come to realize the importance of keeping their affairs in such shape that they will not be forced to liquidate any substantial part of their investments at depression prices.

But for the most part it is only a few of the older families who have learned from the experience of thirty or forty years the fundamental importance of adjusting investments to long-time price trends. They know that if during a period of rising prices they invest in fixed-income securities, the money income they receive from such investments will buy less and less as the years go by. They know that when such an investment matures, even though they are sure to receive the same number of dollars of principal, because of higher prices these dollars will not buy as much for the family as they would have when invested.

Looking back over the period from 1897 to 1920, many families discovered that if they had invested a considerable part of their savings in common stocks of well-established, conservatively-managed corporations, both the earning power and the market value of their investments would have increased with the general rise in prices. As a result of their observations, in the late 1920's they invested heavily in common stocks and income real estate.

In the middle 1930's, after some fifteen years of declining prices (the secular trend of prices turned downward in 1920), these same families are learning the value of owning fixed-income securities during a period of falling prices. They have found that in spite of the losses from default of some of the lower grades of fixed-income investments, on the whole well-seasoned, long-term bonds in essential industries have made a better showing, both as to regularity of payment of income and market value of principal, than have common stocks. The experience of the last thirty-five or forty years indicates clearly the importance of planning a family investment program with due regard for changing business conditions.

There are two ways in which a family may adjust its investment program to the changes in the business cycle. It may watch carefully for coming changes, shifting its investments from time to time, anticipating as far as possible the swing of the cycle. Or it may hedge against these short-time changes by investing part of its funds in seasoned long-term, fixed-income securities and part in high-grade common stocks in a number of essential industries.

The first method is satisfactory for a family with considerable money to invest and plenty of time to devote to the management of its investments. During the recovery stage and early in the prosperity stage of the cycle, such a family may invest most of its funds in carefully selected common stocks, rental real estate, or other business property. Late in the prosperity stage, the family will make its new investments in high-grade bonds. At the first sign of financial strain, heralding the approach of another depression, it will sell the majority of its stocks, dispose of a good deal of its business property, and shift the bulk of its investments to sound bonds or other fixed-income securities. If these are properly selected, they will yield a steady income during the depression years, and as stocks lose their attractiveness to less foresighted investors, they will tend to appreciate somewhat in value. But depressions do not last forever. Sooner or later business will begin to improve. When recovery is well under way, the family will again shift to stocks, in order to benefit from the increase in yield and appreciation in value which will come as prices rise with the return of prosperity.

The second method of adjusting investments to the swing of the business cycle is better for the family with small savings and for the family which cannot follow closely the changes in business conditions. The family of modest means feels the pressure of rising prices which tend to reduce materially the buying power of their investments. These families may find it wise to put part of their funds into fixed-income securities, and part into sound common stocks. During the up-swing of the cycle, the increase in the earnings of their stock holdings will offset in part at least the loss in purchasing power of their bonds and mortgages. During the depression stage of the cycle, on the other hand, the decline in earnings of their common stocks will be offset in part at least by the increased buying power of the regular income they continue to receive from their fixed-income securities. If for any reason it becomes necessary to sell part of their investments, they can select the securities which can be marketed to best advantage in the current stage of the cycle.

In adjusting to the secular trend of prices, families may follow similar procedure. A family making frequent changes in its investments will shift more of its investments into stocks during the periods in which the long-time trend of prices is upward. When the secular trend is downward, it will keep a larger proportion of its funds invested in long-term bonds and other fixed-income securities. A family making more permanent investments will put a slightly larger proportion of its funds into common stocks during a period of rising prices. It will hedge in common stocks with a much smaller proportion of its savings when the long-time trend of prices is downward.

Whichever plan a family follows, it must keep in mind one fundamental of all successful planning. It must look ahead and not back. It must plan on the basis of what is to be in the future, not on the basis of what has been in the past five, ten, or twenty years. At the same time it must be careful to distinguish between temporary flurries and fundamental changes. It must not be drawn this way and that by every eddy in the business current.

Because safety is more important than yield, a family must not wait to extract the last cent of profit from increases in the market values of its securities. It must not rush back into the market until it is sure that the bottom has been reached, and that a permanent up-swing is under way. There may be months at a time when a family will find it wise to keep a considerable portion of its funds in a savings account, investing in more lucrative securities only when it can see clearly what the future holds.

And at all times the family must keep in mind the purposes for which it is saving and investing. It must never allow itself to become so intrigued with the management of its investments that it works out its investment program as something worth while for its own sake. It must always see its investments in securities yielding a money income in proper perspective along with investment in needed commodities and in insurance. For money investments is only one of three ways in which savings may be used to make certain in the future a richer and more satisfying life for all the members of the family.

Investing in needed commodities. Since the primary purpose of saving is to provide for the future needs of the family, it is entirely legitimate to invest present income in articles the family will need at some time in the future. Every family must, of course, have a moderate amount of money available for future expenditures. But once a minimum of future income is assured, a family can often provide more effectively for its future needs, not by saving more money to spend in the future, but by the purchase of commodities.

Building up household inventories by buying permanent equipment and non-perishable commodities in advance of need is a practical method of anticipating a period of increasing expense in the family life cycle. Investing in needed durable goods is always worth considering late in a period of depression or early in recovery, when the investment market is still unsettled and increases in prices are in prospect. Purchase of commodities in advance of need is usually profitable early in any period of rising prices. If prices increase as much as 5 per cent a year, funds invested in present purchases will earn 5 per cent in savings in future outlay.

If the family is to secure the maximum benefit from the purchase of permanent equipment in advance of need, it must be sure the articles it buys are truly durable in material and workmanship, in style, and in suitability to family needs. In building up inventories of supplies, the family must be careful to buy articles which will keep until they are needed. It must select goods of needed qualities. It must determine the quantity to purchase only after careful consideration of both future needs and future price trends.

For example: If the family is investing in life-time furniture, obviously each piece must be well made. It must be conservatively styled, and inherently in good taste. Only pieces which are permanently useful can be considered to be good investments.

If a family invests in a home, the lot should be well located, and the house must be well planned and honestly constructed. It should be made of durable materials which will involve a minimum of future outlay for upkeep. It should be so designed as to make possible considerable flexibility in use. It must be suited to the future as well as to the present needs of the family.

In building up an inventory of household linens, the family should determine the quantity of tablecloths and napkins and sheets and pillow cases and towels to be purchased with the needs of the family definitely in mind. It should select articles of a quality which will be sure to last until the next period of low prices, or until it is convenient for the family to spend money to replace them.

Working capital. In addition to purchasing durable commodities and building up inventories of imperishables a year or more in advance of need, a family can frequently set apart some of its savings to good advantage as working capital to be used to enable the family to buy to good advantage.

A family can frequently save a good deal more than the going rate of interest by taking advantage of seasonal price changes, buying a generous supply of goods in the season in which prices are low. For example: A family uses ten tons of coal a year. Suppose coal sells in winter for $10 a ton, and can be bought in the summer for $9. If the family sets aside $90 to purchase coal at lowest summer prices, and puts back into the coal fund the amount it would pay for coal if bought as needed in the winter, it will find that the $90 has earned more than 10 per cent upon the investment.

Quantity buying requires the maintenance of somewhat larger inventories than are necessary if the family buys goods only as needed. This, of course, ties up some money which otherwise might be invested in interest-paying securities. But if it is possible to get a 10 per cent discount by buying a six months' supply of canned goods, and the money can be so invested twice a year, it can be made to earn at least 20 per cent, not in additional cash income, but in the form of present money income which is freed for other expenses.

A family can make a revolving fund of working capital pay returns simply by taking advantage of cash discounts. Suppose electric current consumed by a family costs $5.00 a month, if the bill is paid before the discount date, and $5.50 if payment is delayed until the end of the month. It requires the investment of $5.00 to prepay the electric light bill. But this $5.00 so invested will save 50 cents each month, or $6.00 a year, a return of 120 per cent upon the $5.00 originally invested.

Buying on the instalment plan involves the payment of financing charges. The minimum charges for monthly payments usually run from 17 to 23 per cent, when figured in terms of annual interest charges. If a family sets up part of its savings in a fund which it uses to pay cash, and to which regular payments are made from month to month out of current income, as they would be if the family were buying on the instalment plan, its own savings can be made to pay the family similar rates of interest upon its own investment.

A family frequently can make its money earn good returns by using part of it to finance the purchase of materials and equipment for production-for-use at home. Many families find that the saving in the cost of home-canned over commercially-canned goods pays good returns upon the money invested in home-canning equipment. Often the saving on a single garment will pay the interest and depreciation involved in the ownership of a sewing machine for an entire year. The purchase of a good radio to which the family will listen an evening or two a week instead of going out for commercial entertainment will often save enough in recreational expenses to pay very good interest on the investment.

Every family obviously finds desirable some investments which will yield a regular money income, and which can be converted into cash when needed. But no family can afford to overlook the opportunities to invest money in the family business. A family with adequate working capital is able to save much more than the going rate of interest on investments from the increased buying power which ready cash can give. A family can secure for money put into essential commodities purchased in anticipation of future needs, a yield, not in money income, but dividends in use which eliminate the necessity of future expenditure. If the commodities which they buy are carefully selected, with an eye to present as well as to future needs, they can be made to pay a high dividend in the satisfaction which comes from present use as well.

INSURANCE

A third way in which a family may use its savings to provide for future needs is by purchase of insurance. The purpose of a family in buying insurance is not to save money for definitely foreseen expenditures. Rather it is to secure adequate contingent reserves against possible eventualities at lower cost than would be required should the family maintain similar reserves with its own savings.

Insurance is based upon the law of large numbers. Individual losses are uncertain and impossible to predict definitely; total losses to a group are more definite and predictable. By combining a large number of individual risks the element of uncertainty may be removed. The reserve necessary to compensate for the losses actually incurred by individuals is accumulated by contributions from all the members of the insured group.

In most cases the total reserve which an insurance company must maintain in order to compensate individual policy holders for their losses is much smaller than the total of reserves which would be necessary if each individual were to provide himself with similar protection.

For example: Suppose that the owners of 1,000 homes, each valued at $5,000, want to protect themselves against loss by fire. Assume that they know from experience that 10 houses out of each 1,000 will be completely destroyed each year, and that 100 more will suffer partial losses averaging $500 each. No one family can tell whether its home will be one of those damaged or completely destroyed by fire. If each of these 1,000 families were to protect itself adequately against possible fire loss, it would need to maintain a reserve of $5,000. This would require savings totaling $5,000,000.

If these families combine their risks, however, it will still be true that 10 homes will be completely destroyed and that 100 more will suffer partial losses averaging $500 each. The total fire loss for the 1,000 home owners is still $100,000. But since they combine their risks, a reserve of $100,000 will be adequate to protect all of them against possible fire loss. Under these circumstances the payment to a common reserve fund of $10 per family, or $2.00 per $1,000 of property covered by insurance, would be ample to take care of all the losses which would be incurred. Obviously, in such a situation, it would be much more economical for a group of families to protect themselves against possible fire loss by the use of insurance than it would be for each family to set up adequate individual reserves.

In the preceding example, for the sake of simplicity, we have assumed that each family presents exactly the same amount of risk, and needs exactly the same amount of protection. In actual life, of course, different families live in homes of different value. They wish to purchase different amounts of insurance. In order to make it possible to compute easily the amount individual policy holders should pay in premiums to the common fund, rates are usually stated in terms of so-many-dollars-per-thousand, or so-many-cents-per-hundred dollars of protection provided.

How insurance rates are determined. In determining the amount which policy holders must pay for each unit of insurance, the first step is to estimate the total losses which must be met by the insurance company out of its common reserve funds. This is usually done on the basis of past experience. Fire insurance companies, writing insurance for many years, have accumulated records which show the losses which have actually occurred in each of a great variety of classes of fire risks. Automobile insurance companies know how much it has cost them each year to pay the losses incurred by their policy holders. Life insurance companies have compiled complicated mortality tables showing the number of deaths which occur at each age each year. Accident insurance companies have records of the amounts they have paid to large numbers of individuals in a great variety of occupations. On the basis of these records, they can predict with reasonable accuracy the losses they will incur if they agree to insure a large group against any of these rather common hazards.

To the total of these losses must be added the costs which are inevitably involved in the operation of an insurance company. There are costs of management and administration, salaries to executive officers, commissions to salesmen, and the payment of adjusters who attend to the actual settlement of claims. There are payments for rent, office equipment and supplies, electric light and telephone bills, taxes, and all the other expenses inevitably involved in the operation of any business.

On the other hand, most insurance premiums are paid in advance. Fire insurance companies write much of their insurance for three- or five-year periods. A good deal of health and accident insurance, and most automobile insurance contracts call for the payment of premiums for a year in advance. The great majority of life insurance policy holders accumulate their reserves by premium payments over many years. The insurance company has the use of these prepaid premiums until such time as it is necessary to pay them out in compensation for losses. The earnings of these funds offset in part the cost of losses and expenses of administration.

The rate which must be charged for a given amount of insurance is determined by adding together the total losses and cost of administration, subtracting the probable earnings of reserves built up out of prepaid premiums, and dividing by the total amount of insurance in force. The amount which an individual policy holder must pay for his insurance is then determined by multiplying the amount of insurance he carries by the rate charged for his particular type of coverage.

Merit ratings. There is often a considerable difference in the amount of risk involved in insuring individual policy holders. For example: Families living in well-built houses with solid brick walls, concrete floors, hollow tile partitions, and slate roofs, in all probability will suffer much smaller losses from fire than will families living in flimsily built frame structures with partitions of inflammable wallboard, poorly constructed heating plants, and highly inflammable roofs. Young men in good health are a much better risk for a life insurance company than are older men, or men of the same age suffering from some chronic organic ailment.

In computing rates, insurance companies ordinarily must assume a normal distribution of risks. When they come to write insurance they find that individuals who know that they present more than the average amount of risk are anxious to secure the protection insurance affords, while individuals who feel that they are better than average risks are not much interested in buying insurance. In order to encourage individuals who present less than average risks to protect those risks by insurance, it is customary for insurance companies to classify risks, computing a separate rate for each class, which is based upon the losses each group of risks will probably involve. The policy holder who presents a better than average risk is given a reduced rate. The policy holder who presents an unusually large risk is charged enough more to cover the cost which the assumption of his risk actually involves.

In buying insurance, a family must be sure it is given as favorable a classification as it is possible to obtain. It should find out what will make it a preferred risk. For often at comparatively small cost it can qualify for a more favorable classification, in which the saving in premiums will pay good interest on the amount invested to secure a more favorable rating.

Moral hazard. Insurance inevitably involves what is technically known as "moral hazard." When an individual or a family knows that it is protected by insurance, it is inclined to neglect safety measures which it would be sure to take if it were carrying its own risks. In most cases it is not intentionally careless, but unconsciously it takes more risks. The family completely protected against all fire losses does not deliberately pile hot ashes against a wooden partition, or allow large quantities of highly inflammable waste paper to accumulate in the basement near the furnace. But it is a little more careless about where it lays down lighted cigarettes. The automobile owner with complete coverage is inclined to take a few more chances on minor collisions which may dent a fender. The individual whose income is insured by a health and accident policy does not deliberately malinger, but he may take a little more time for convalescence than he would if he were not insured.

There are a number of ways in which an insurance company protects itself, and its policy holders as well, against these inevitable moral hazards. It may insist that the individual policy holder must stand some small part of every loss. It may do this by limiting the amount of insurance it will write on any risk. It may write only deductible insurance, in which the individual policy holder must pay part of every loss. Or it may use merit ratings, reclassifying individual policy holders from time to time on the basis of their individual experience, raising the rates charged policy holders whose losses run above the average, and granting lower rates to policy holders who prove to be better than average risks.

Every family must do all that it reasonably can to keep losses at a minimum. It must be constantly on the alert for preventive measures which will eliminate or reduce risks. Especially must it be constantly on guard against contributing by carelessness to the moral hazard, for the cost of insurance inevitably depends upon the amount of risk involved.

Mutual vs. "old line" insurance. There are two types of companies from which a family may secure insurance. These are mutual insurance companies and stock companies. A mutual insurance company is organized by a group who want insurance. Each policy holder is a member of the company. As such he must pay his share of the losses incurred, and is entitled to a share in any profits which may result from the conduct of the company's affairs.

The simplest form of mutual insurance company is the assessment type of company. In the assessment type of company each policy holder agrees to share in the losses incurred by members of the group. As the losses occur, they are pro-rated upon the entire membership of the company in proportion to the amount of insurance they are carrying.

The assessment type of mutual is a simple organization, involving a minimum of administrative expense. The members of the company secure their insurance at actual cost. They pay only for expenses of administration and for the losses actually incurred. This type of company has proved satisfactory in the case of a group of carefully selected preferred risks.

But to the family which is trying to plan carefully its future expenditures, the assessment type of mutual is subject to one serious disadvantage. There is no way to determine in advance the amount which the family must pay for a given amount of protection. Given favorable experience, the cost will be very low. But assessments may be made at times which prove very inconvenient to the family. The assessment company is subject to the further disadvantage that every member must pay his full share of the losses which are incurred by the members of the group. If a mutual group contains a number of poor risks, the cost of insurance may prove to be unreasonably high. If the group contains some members who are unable to meet their assessments, the entire burden of losses must be borne by those members of the group who are financially responsible.

In order to eliminate as many as possible of the obvious disadvantages of assessment insurance, in recent years there have been organized many legal-reserve mutuals which issue non-assessable policies to their members. These companies charge rates which are more than adequate to cover their probable losses. Out of these premiums they set up adequate reserves from which to pay all claims. Then from time to time they return to their policy holders, as stockholder-owners of the company, any profits which may have resulted from a favorable loss record, earnings of invested reserves, and from the efficient management of the insurance business.

The legal-reserve mutual with its non-assessable policy obviously has many advantages over the assessment type of mutual group. In this type of company the family still gets its insurance at actual cost. But because the policy is non-assessable, it knows definitely in advance the maximum cost of its insurance. There may be two disadvantages to this type of insurance. In some cases the premiums charged may be higher than those charged by stock companies for similar coverage. This may make the initial cost of the insurance higher. The long-run cost, however, is determined by the premium paid minus the dividends paid back out of the profits of the company. Further, in case of the failure of the company, there may be certain liabilities for outstanding obligations which attach to the policy holders as owners of the insurance business. These liabilities are usually much more limited in the legal-reserve company than are the liabilities of the policy holder in the assessment type of company.

The "old line" or stock insurance company is a corporation organized for profit by a group of individuals who invest their own capital in the stock of the firm. The funds put into the company by the stockholders are used to guarantee payment of claims to policy holders. They are so used, of course, only if reserves accumulated from premiums prove to be insufficient to meet unexpectedly heavy losses, or if the company loses heavily from unfortunate investments of its reserves. In case of more favorable experience, whatever remains of the premiums above the amount necessary to maintain legal reserves and to pay policy holders according to the terms of their insurance contracts goes to the stockholders as dividends upon their investment.

Participating policies. In order to compete with mutual companies in which policy holders share in the earnings of the company, some stock companies, especially life insurance companies, write participating policies. In the participating policy, the owners of the insurance company share the earnings with the policy holders after a stated dividend has been paid upon the stock of the insurance company. Competition for business ordinarily keeps the rates of legal-reserve mutuals and stock company participating policies very closely in line.

If a family purchases insurance from a stock company, the cost of its insurance is definitely determined at the time the policy is purchased. There is no chance for further charges either in the form of assessments or stockholder's liability. On the other hand, except in the case of participating policies, there is no refund of part of the profits, there is no dividend to reduce the cost of the insurance. Since the stock company assumes all of the risk, whatever profits there may be belong to the stockholders as owners of the company.

Determining the risks to insure. It is possible nowadays to purchase a great variety of types of insurance. Many of these policies have been designed to meet the needs of business concerns rather than families. But even the kinds of insurance available to the family have been increasing in recent years.

Insurance men classify insurance as life insurance, casualty insurance, and marine insurance. Marine insurance is written upon goods in transit, and so is of little or no interest to the ordinary family. Most families do find it worth while to carry some form of life insurance, and a few types of casualty insurance. The most common types of casualty insurance carried by families are fire insurance, either upon the home or household goods, and automobile insurance, covering losses and liability incurred in the ownership and use of the family car. A considerable group of families carry health and accident insurance upon the chief wage earner. Families with valuable personal property sometimes carry burglary insurance. In a few cases families employing household help protect their workers against work accidents with workmen's compensation insurance.

Families usually purchase insurance for one of two principal purposes. Either they want to guarantee in advance the existence of a predetermined amount of income with which to make definitely planned expenditures, for some special purpose like the payment for a home, the purchase of an automobile, or the provision of a college education for the children, or for the ordinary running expenses of the family. Or they wish to be assured of the existence of funds sufficient to meet heavy future expenses arising out of possible contingencies like the damage to or destruction or loss of the family property, or any unusual claims which might possibly be brought against them.

Ordinarily families carry insurance either upon the person of the members of the family, or upon the family's property. Life insurance, life annuities, and health and accident insurance are usually written upon the person of the members of the family. Life insurance is ordinarily used to guarantee the continuation of a certain amount of income in case of the death of the insured. Life annuities are written to guarantee the existence of an income adequate for living expenses after the retirement of the annuitant from active employment. Health and accident insurance is intended to guarantee the receipt of a definite sum for a certain period during disability from specified causes. Families carry fire insurance, windstorm insurance, hail insurance, earthquake insurance, burglary insurance, or public liability insurance upon the home, household goods, the family automobile, or any other personal property. This insurance provides funds for repair or replacement in case of loss or damage to the property covered by the policy, and funds for the payment of claims for damages which may be brought against the family as a result of its ownership and use.

Few families find it worth while to buy all the kinds of insurance which are available. Each family must decide, after a careful analysis of its own situation, which risks it should insure and which risks it should provide for with personal reserves. In general it is wise to carry insurance against risks from which the family may suffer occasional heavy losses. In the case of these risks, while individual losses may be large, the total loss to the insurance company each year is relatively small. As a result, the premium paid by the individual family is very small compared with the amount which would be required to provide the family with adequate protection from individual reserves.

It is not necessary to carry insurance against risks involving very small losses which can easily be absorbed out of current income. There is little advantage in carrying insurance against risks in which annual losses vary but little from year to year. Where individual losses are very evenly spread, there is little advantage in combining them. The premium which the individual would pay for insurance would not be much lower than the heaviest loss he would run in any single year. By setting up individual reserves against risks of this character, the family saves the management costs which insurance inevitably involves.

It is not possible in a single chapter to discuss in detail the problems involved in every type of insurance available to the family. It is worth while, however, to analyze in some detail the problems involved in the selection and use of a few of the more common types of insurance in order to suggest the type of analysis which should be made of every sort of policy which is offered to the family.

Life insurance. Life insurance is ordinarily used for two purposes. Families with small incomes often carry small amounts of life insurance as burial insurance upon each member of the family. They may carry one hundred or two hundred dollars upon the wife and each of the children, and in some cases as much as five hundred dollars upon the head of the family. This money is intended to be used to defray the cost of the last illness and death, which it is often impossible for families of modest means to meet from current income.

Most of the burial type of life insurance is written as "industrial" insurance. Premiums are quoted as so-many-cents-per week. The insurance companies employ collectors who call in person every pay day to collect the premium. Because of the cost of writing insurance in small amounts, and the expense involved in collecting premiums on these small policies, the cost of the industrial type of life insurance is somewhat higher than insurance written in larger amounts, on which premiums are paid quarterly, semi-annually, or a year in advance. Nevertheless, industrial insurance does fill a real need among families in the lower income groups, that need small amounts of insurance but find it impossible to accumulate at any one time the money necessary to pay for insurance on a semi-annual or annual basis.

Families with larger incomes, who can defray burial expenses from current income, or from the estate of the deceased, usually buy life insurance in order to guarantee to the family the continuance of a money income, in case of the death of the insured. The family may be paid the amount stipulated on the face of the policy in a lump sum, or in instalments paid over a period of years. In either case, the money received from the insurance policy is used to replace in part the contribution, either in money or personal services, which the insured has been making to the family income.

Since this life insurance is intended to protect the family income, ordinarily it should be carried only upon members of the family who are gainfully employed. Usually, if only limited funds are available for the purchase of insurance, it is wise for the husband as chief wage earner to carry most of the insurance. In some cases, however, it may be wise to carry some insurance upon the wife in order to provide, in the event of her death, funds with which to defray the extra expenses involved in running the home with a hired housekeeper. In some cases, too, it is wise to carry some insurance upon the older children, either to enable a boy or girl to secure favorable rates for insurance which he will want to carry as soon as he begins to earn for himself, or to assure the family of a partial return of the money invested in the children's education. If it is necessary to borrow to secure funds to enable a boy or girl to complete professional training or a high school or college education, the family may purchase insurance upon the boy or girl sufficient to repay the amount of the loan in case death should prevent the student from repaying the loan from his own earnings after he completes his education and becomes self-supporting.

Types of policies. Most life insurance companies write four standard types of policies: term, ordinary or whole life, limited payment life, and endowment insurance. These policies vary in cost. They combine in varying quantities protection and investment features.

Term insurance. Term insurance is written on the same basis as fire insurance. It provides the insured with protection only. If the insured dies within the term for which the policy runs, his beneficiary receives the amount indicated on the face of his policy. If he outlives the term for which his life is insured, he has received the protection he paid for and has no further claim upon the insurance company. Term insurance is written both on a yearly-renewable and on a level-premium or unchanging annual cost basis. Level-premium term insurance is usually written for five, ten, fifteen, or twenty years. It may be purchased for any stated period.[3]

The cost of term insurance is determined by the life expectancy of the policy holder. In the case of yearly renewable term insurance, rates are determined by computing from life expectancy tables the probable number out of a group of 100,000 individuals of the same age who will die during the year. On this basis the insurance company can compute the probable cost of paying $1,000 to each individual who dies during the year. By adding to these death losses the cost of administration, and then dividing by 100,000, the insurance company can determine how much it must charge each individual in this age group for $1,000 of insurance for the coming year. Since the mortality rate among each 100,000 individuals of a given age increases with advancing age, the rate which the policy holder must pay for yearly renewable term policies increases each year. Up to the age of forty, the cost is moderate. In later years, however, death

---

[3] A few companies write level-premium life-term insurance. This coverage differs from ordinary or whole-life insurance chiefly in that it has no cash or loan value. The premium charged is sufficient only to pay the death losses of the members of the group. There are no additional reserves accumulated to be returned to the policy holder who discontinues his insurance. (See p. 483.)

losses mount rapidly until in the sixties and seventies the cost of yearly renewable term insurance becomes almost prohibitive.

Level-premium term insurance. Because the cost of insurance increases each year, when written on a yearly renewable term basis, most families prefer the level-premium type of policy. Under the level-premium plan the insured pays the same premium each year as long as the policy is in force. The determination of the rate in the case of level-premium insurance is not a simple matter. Suppose we take for example a level-premium, five-year-term policy. The insurance company must compute the premium for this type of policy somewhat as follows: It is assumed that 100,000 men of a given age buy a five-year-term policy. During the five-year period in which this insurance is in force, the mortality tables show that there will be a given number of death losses. As in the case of yearly renewable term insurance, the total amount of these losses, plus the cost of administration, must be met by the policy holders. Therefore the total cost of insuring this group is pro-rated by dividing by 100,000. But this insurance is to run for five years. The individuals in the group wish to make their payments in five equal annual instalments. This cost to the individual must, therefore, be divided by five to determine the annual premium.

However, some of the individuals in the group will die during the first year. They will make only one payment for their insurance. Others will die during the second year. They will pay only twice, instead of five times, on their policies. Enough must be added to the total cost of insurance so that the amount paid by the survivors will make up for the premiums lost by the death of part of those insured.

On the other hand, not all of the first year's premiums will be used to pay death claims arising in that year. Part can be invested at interest until it is needed. The earning power of the prepaid premiums— that is, premiums paid in advance of losses—must be deducted from the cost of the insurance, in determining the actual level-premium to charge.

When a family buys a level-premium term policy, it is investing in prepaid insurance. If the insured dies during the first year or two in which the policy is in force, the insurance will cost more on a level-premium than it would on a yearly renewable term basis. If the insured dies late in the period for which the policy was written, or outlives the term of the policy, the outlay for insurance will be less under the level-premium than it would under the yearly-renewable term basis, because the earnings of the earlier payments will offset part of the premium which must be paid on the yearly-renewable term basis.

Ordinary or whole-life insurance. Ordinary life insurance, or whole-life insurance, is written on the assumption that the individual carrying this type of policy will carry it during his entire life. The policy is written on a level-premium basis. Premiums are usually somewhat higher than in the case of the level-premium life-term policies. After two or three years the holder of a whole-life policy is credited with part of the prepaid reserves in the form of a cash value. In case he decides not to carry the policy throughout his entire life, he is entitled to receive back the unused portion of those reserves which he has been setting up to cover the heavier cost of protection in the later years of his life.

The reserves which accumulate as cash value on an ordinary or whole-life insurance policy may be used in a number of ways. If the policy holder wishes to discontinue his insurance, he may receive in cash the cash-surrender value of his policy. If he wishes to keep the insurance in force, he may borrow the major portion of this cash-surrender value, paying interest upon his loan until such time as he is able to repay the amount he has borrowed. Or if he is unable to continue to pay the annual premiums necessary to carry his insurance he may use this cash value to buy a paid-up insurance policy for a somewhat smaller amount, or to keep the original policy in force for a stated period.

Limited-payment life insurance. Like ordinary life insurance, limited-payment life insurance is carried for the entire life of the insured. But instead of agreeing to pay a stated premium every year during his entire life, the holder of a limited-payment policy agrees to pay a somewhat larger premium for a stated number of years, sometimes ten, sometimes fifteen, sometimes twenty, sometimes thirty. The rate for limited-payment life insurance is fixed at a point at which the reserves accumulated out of the premiums will provide protection for the insured during his entire life. Limited-payment policies have the same cash-surrender, loan value, and extended insurance features as whole-life insurance. These values are larger than in similar whole-life policies, for at the end of the limited payment period, the insured has paid enough for his policy in premiums to pay for extended insurance for his entire life.

Endowment insurance. Endowment insurance differs from limited-payment life insurance in this way: If the policy holder is still living at the end of the period for which the policy is written, he will receive in cash the face amount of the policy. If he dies at any time before the maturity of the policy, the entire amount of the policy will be paid to his estate or to a named beneficiary. In the case of endowment insurance, the insured must pay in premiums an amount which if invested at compound interest will amount to the face of the policy at its maturity. In addition, he must pay enough for protection to cover the payments to the individuals in the group who die before the maturity of the contract. For people in earlier age groups, endowment insurance is primarily a method of making an insured investment. The small additional payment for protection is included to insure the accumulation of the funds as contemplated in the contract.

Special policies. In addition to the four standard types of policies, various companies offer from time to time special policies designed to meet special needs. These policies they call by a variety of descriptive names in order to attract attention and facilitate the sale of the insurance. Most of these policies are simply modifications or combinations of the standard types of policies.

For example: One type of educational policy is an endowment policy which matures at the time when a child will be ready to enter college. The face of the policy is usually paid in four equal annual instalments, or in ten monthly instalments each year for the four years of a college course, or in some other way which will make the money available as needed to defray the student's expenses. The premiums upon such a policy cease with the death of the chief wage earner. In some cases there is provision for beginning at once payments to the child named as beneficiary of the policy, usually a smaller amount during the elementary and high school grades, and the stated amount during the four-year college course. In other cases, the money is not available until the child is ready to enter college. In a few cases these educational policies include burial insurance, in the form of an amount which is paid in case of the death of the beneficiary before the policy matures.

The family's life insurance program. A family should select the type of life insurance policy which is best suited to its personal needs. Most families find it wise to make ordinary or whole-life insurance the backbone of their insurance program. Over their whole life as a family, ordinary life insurance will give them a maximum amount of protection at a minimum of cost. Its level-premium feature makes it possible to compute accurately in advance the maximum amount which will be required to carry the insurance. If it is taken out comparatively early in the life of the family, the rate for whole-life insurance is low. Yet there is no increase in the cost of this insurance during the peak of the family life cycle.

In addition, the loan value of the ordinary life policy provides a fund from which the family can borrow at any time when it is temporarily in need of funds, either to pay insurance premiums or for other expenses. During the life of the insured the cash value of the policy provides supplementary savings which can be used in case an emergency should arise which is sufficiently serious to justify the sacrifice of the protection the policy affords.

If the head of the family, upon whom the insurance is carried, lives to the retirement age, he can continue to pay the premiums upon his policy and add the face of the policy to his estate. He can use the cash value to purchase an amount of paid-up insurance somewhat smaller than the death or face value of the policy. He can cancel the policy and add to his investments the accumulated cash value, which will at age sixty or sixty-five ordinarily amount to a substantial sum. He can use the cash value to buy a life annuity which will guarantee him an income for the remainder of his life. Or, in many companies, instead of receiving a cash settlement in a lump sum he can receive a settlement in the form of an annuity which will pay him a guaranteed monthly income for life.

A family usually finds it worth while to supplement whole-life insurance with other types of policies. Many young men take out a fifteen- or twenty-payment life policy when they become of age, in order that they may have a minimum amount of insurance available regardless of what happens to their earning power later on. By taking out a limited-payment policy some years before they marry, they can complete the payment for a substantial part of their insurance program before their family reaches the peak of its expenditures.

The limited-payment life policy is ordinarily advantageous only for the individual whose family and personal history indicates a longer than average life expectancy. The long-lived individual will benefit from the freedom from payment for insurance for many years. If he faces a long period of retirement, he can use the larger cash-surrender value to advantage in purchasing a life annuity upon which to live in his declining years.

The individual with less than the average life expectancy, on the other hand, may not live long enough to benefit from the premiums he has prepaid. He needs the maximum amount of present protection and can afford to put up with a minimum amount of savings in his insurance program.

Many families use a five- or ten- or fifteen-year-term insurance policy to provide with a minimum of current outlay the additional protection they need during the years of heavy expense at the peak of the family life cycle. Families paying for a home on the instalment plan may use a term insurance policy to guarantee the completion of the payments, in case of the death of the head of the family.

Endowment policies are in effect instalment savings contracts plus a term insurance policy which guarantees the completion of the savings program and makes the fund immediately available in case of the death of the insured. These policies can be used to insure the existence of the exact amount of money needed at a given time or for a given purpose.

For example, a family may take out an endowment policy upon the head of the family for an amount adequate to cover the cost of a college education, maturing when a child will be ready to enter college. The child for whose education the proceeds of the policy is to be used can be named as beneficiary. Or the proceeds can be made payable to the insured, the fund to be handled as a discretionary trust in case of his death.

As long as the policy holder lives he may from time to time change the settlement options to adapt his protection to changing family needs. In general, unless there are specific contingencies to be provided for, it is well to leave the terms of settlement in a form which will give the beneficiaries some voice in the terms to be followed in settling the policy.

The family may, of course, supplement its ordinary life insurance with any one of a number of special policies. In determining the value of a special policy, it is usually wise to compare its provisions with the provisions of a similar standard policy. If the special contract does just what the family needs to have done, it may be wise to buy that type of policy. But unless it exactly fits the family's needs, it will probably be better to stick to standard types of contracts.

Annuities. Annuities are contracts which call for the payment to an individual called the annuitant of a given amount of income each year for a period specified in the annuity contract. Annuities are sold with or without insurance features. It is possible to purchase an annuity which calls for the payment of a definite sum each year for a specified number of years. Or it is possible to purchase a life annuity, which guarantees the payment of a definite sum each year beginning in a certain year and continuing for the entire life of the annuitant. If the annuitant desires, the payments may be made monthly, quarterly, or semi-annually instead of in a single yearly payment. Life annuities really are life insurance contracts worked backward. They insure the individual or the family of an income as long as the annuitant lives, while life insurance as ordinarily written insures income to survivors in case of the death of the insured.

Annuities and life insurance policies may be purchased with regular payments spread over many years. Or they may be purchased with a single payment. The single payment may be used to buy an annuity upon which payments will begin at once—that is, at the end of one year, one quarter, or one month—or it may be used to purchase a deferred annuity, upon which payments will begin when the annuitant reaches a stated age.

Annuities are primarily savings contracts. Usually they include the provision that in case the annuitant dies before the date upon which the insurance company is to begin payment of the annuity, the company will return to the estate of the annuitant the amount paid in to date together with interest compounded at a stated rate, for the years during which the contract has been in force. In some cases annuities are written on five-year or ten-year certain bases. These contracts pay a smaller amount per year, but guarantee the payment of not less than five or not less than ten payments to the annuitant. In case the annuitant dies before the specified number of payments has been completed, the balance of the guaranteed payments will be paid to his estate.

The cost of an annuity purchased with a single payment is determined by the age of the annuitant at the time he begins to receive his guaranteed annual income. He must pay into the insurance company the amount which, invested at compound interest, will be needed to pay him the stated income for his life expectancy. Obviously, the older the individual, the shorter is his life expectancy, and the lower is the cost of guaranteeing him a given amount of life income.

The cost of a deferred annuity depends in part upon the age at which the annuitant is to begin to receive payments under his contract. It depends also upon the length of time the annuity is to be deferred, and upon the number of years over which the payments are spread. The annuitant must pay to the insurance company whatever amounts are required to accumulate at compound interest the fund needed to buy the desired annuity. The earlier the payments to the insurance company are begun, and the longer the payment of the annuity is deferred, the lower is the cost of a given life income.

Many annuities are flexible contracts. The annuitant agrees to pay a stated yearly premium to the insurance company writing the annuity contract. He continues as long as his earning power justifies the saving. When he retires he receives as an annuity whatever monthly or yearly payment his accumulation will purchase for a man of his then attained age.

It is possible for the family to purchase one annuity for the husband and another for the wife. Or it is possible to purchase a combined annuity which will pay a stated sum as long as both husband and wife are alive and the same or another stated sum to the survivor.

Annuities are designed primarily to insure against the hazard of a penniless old age. They are generally popular in periods of declining prices. As prices fall, the purchase of an annuity gains in the increased amount which each dollar of his contract will buy. In periods of rising prices, they are less desirable. They are contracts which pay a fixed-dollar income. As prices rise, these dollars lose in purchasing power. Annuities may be used by families of moderate means to supplement income from invested savings, or they may be used to provide the entire income for man and wife after retirement. Deferred annuities are especially attractive to the family without dependents, the childless couple, or the family which has reared its children and is concentrating upon its savings for old age. For most families they are not a substitute for, but a supplement to, life insurance.

Health and accident insurance. As it is written at present, health and accident insurance is a form of income insurance. It is designed to guarantee a certain income for a specified period in case the policy holder is disabled from certain stated causes. In addition to payments for time lost by the policy holder, many policies provide for the payment of stated amounts for medical care in the case of non-disabling accidents. Some policies provide additional payments for the period in which a policy holder is confined to a hospital.

Health insurance provides protection against temporary disability only. Most policies provide for the payment of claims for a stated number of weeks, usually not more than a year in the case of each disability. Because the great majority of accidents and minor illnesses involve only a few days of lost time, first day coverage—that is, payment for every day of disability—makes this insurance expensive. In order to reduce the cost of providing the insurance, most policies provide for a seven- or fourteen-day waiting period during which no benefits are paid. Some policies pay for accidents from the first day and for illness from the eighth day. Some policies, designed to provide insurance against loss of income from serious accident or serious illness only, pay no claims during the first month of the disability, but continue to pay for a somewhat longer period. Other policies specifically rule out any claims for time lost from chronic illness.

Because of the temptation to stay at home and be paid for doing nothing, many health and accident insurance policies limit their payments to the period in which the policy holder is actually confined to the house. Other policies, which naturally are more expensive, pay for the entire period of convalescence, assuring the policy holder of an income until he is able to return to work. To discourage malingering, most companies write insurance for not more than 80 per cent of the regular income of the insured.

There is no standard health and accident policy. For this reason it is important to read each policy carefully, and to select the type of policy which gives most nearly the protection desired. If the family wants protection against loss of income from minor accidents and minor illness, it will pay a high premium and obtain protection beginning with the first day of the disability. If it is able to set up its own reserves against the loss of a few days now and then, it may prefer to insure only against major accidents and serious illness. In this case it will buy a policy providing for a long waiting period, but paying regular instalments for a long period of disability. If the family is chiefly concerned with protection against permanent disability, instead of taking out a regular health and accident policy it may add a total and permanent disability clause to its life insurance policies.

The rate charged for health and accident insurance varies with the accidents and diseases covered, with the length of waiting period, and with the maximum number of payments for each separate disability. Policy provisions vary greatly. Some seem to say one thing in the large type on the face of the policy, but actually say something entirely different in the fine print on the inside pages. It is highly important, therefore, for a family to read carefully every health and accident policy submitted to it. It must know just what it is buying.

It must decide whether or not to carry health and accident insurance in part on the basis of its cost and in part on the suitability of available coverage. It must be suspicious of any policy that seems to give a great deal of protection at low cost. For in buying insurance it is never possible to get something for nothing.

Fire insurance. In contrast to the health and accident insurance companies, fire insurance companies offer a highly standardized policy, the terms of which have been well interpreted during the years by many court decisions. As is often the case with legal documents, the standard policy does not always mean exactly what the layman might think it says. But the meaning of each clause is definite, nevertheless, and a well-informed insurance agent can explain the meaning of the policy to his customer.

Since fire insurance companies offer a standard form of coverage, rates depend upon the hazard involved in the individual property covered by the policy. There are a number of factors which influence the rate. The location and construction of a building, the use of a building and the nature of the contents, the construction and use of other buildings in the neighborhood, the amount of fire protection which is available, and the protective devices in the building itself— these and many more are taken into account in determining the risk which is involved in insuring either a building or its contents. A family can frequently reduce considerably the cost of its fire insurance by learning what is necessary to secure more favorable classification and so a lower rate.

It is important to understand that a fire insurance policy is a limited contract. It covers losses resulting from fire only. It does not cover fires which occur as a result of invasion, insurrection, riot, or civil war; nor does it cover the destruction of property by the act of civil authority to prevent a fire from spreading. It does not cover losses from theft, even though the theft occurs as a result of a fire. It does not cover losses due solely to explosion or lightning. It covers only fire losses caused by the explosion or the lightning. It does not cover fire losses to properties if illuminating gas is generated on the premises, or if there are present on the property any explosives or any petroleum products of greater inflammability than kerosene. It does not cover losses from earthquake, for it specifically provides that if a building falls for any reason other than as the result of a fire, the fire policy is automatically canceled. A fire insurance policy covers loss from smoke damage from a fire. But it does not cover smoke losses from a "friendly" fire. To protect against smoky furnaces or a smoking oil burner, it is necessary to take out smudge insurance.

Because of the hazards which are covered by fire insurance under the standard policy, many families carry some supplementary insurance protecting against loss from windstorm, lightning, explosion, hail, earthquake, and even damage from falling aircraft. A family may carry loss-of-use insurance which will compensate it in part at least for the rent it must pay in case it must vacate its home for a time following a fire. If the family owns rental property, it may carry insurance which will compensate it for the loss of rents due to a fire.

How much fire insurance a family should carry upon its house and its household goods and other personal property depends upon their value, and upon the chance of partial or total loss. In most cases, if fire protection in the community is at all adequate, rates are so low that most families feel they cannot afford to do without some fire protection.

Which and how many of these supplementary policies a family should carry depends upon the hazard to which the family property is subjected. Property located in an earthquake zone should be protected by earthquake insurance. Property located near an airport may need coverage protecting against damage from falling aircraft. In a home equipped with an oil burner, it may be wise to carry smudge insurance. The family must decide in each case whether or not the risk is heavy enough to demand insurance, and whether the rates are low enough to make it worth while to carry the supplementary policy.

Automobile insurance. The general introduction of the automobile has led to the development of a number of types of automobile insurance which are available to the family to protect it from the hazards involved in the ownership and operation of the family car. The family needs two types of coverage: protection against loss or damage to the car itself, and protection against any liability which may result from injury to the person or damage to the property of others.

The automobile insurance policy as it is usually written is really a composite of a number of different kinds of insurance policies. Sometimes they are all written by one company. Sometimes they are written by one agent who distributes the risks among a number of companies.

Most automobile insurance policies provide for the protection of the car against losses from fire. To the standard fire insurance policy is usually added an endorsement insuring the owner against loss from theft, and in some cases other endorsements to cover losses from windstorm, hail, explosion, and water damage, as in the case of any fire insurance policy.

Collision insurance is usually written by a company specializing in automobile risks. Collision insurance covers damage to the car from collision with either moving or stationary objects. It does not, as is sometimes assumed, cover all possible types of damage to the car. For example, if a car is parked by the side of the street and boys playing in the street throw a ball through a window, the damage will not be covered. Most collision policies specifically exclude any damage to tires. Some pay for damage to tires in case of a collision which causes other damage to the car.

Because some people have been dissatisfied with the coverage which the usual type of collision insurance provides, a few companies issue a more expensive type of policy which covers all damage to the car from whatever cause. They even include damage to the finish by boys at play. This policy obviously is more expensive than the usual collision policy.

More than they need protection against possible loss from damage to the automobile itself, families need protection against possible claims for damages arising from the ownership and use of the family car.

Public liability insurance is written to cover any losses to the automobile owner from injury to persons outside the immediate family of the insured. Property damage insurance covers any losses from damage to the property of others. Because there is no way to predict the possible size of such claims, most public liability policies limit the responsibility of the insurance company to $5,000 in the case of injury to a single person, and $10,000 in the case of a single accident. In the case of liability for property damage, the usual limit is $1,000 for each accident. It is possible to secure more protection by paying an additional premium. Families of considerable means, who may be subject to excessive claims because of their social prominence, often carry a policy with $25,000, $50,000 or even higher limits. They may carry property damage insurance up to $5,000 for a single accident.

Public liability, property damage, and collision insurance may be written to provide for complete coverage, or they may be written on a $35, $50, or $100 deductible basis. This means that if the insured has complete coverage he is protected against any damage, no matter how small, which may come under the provisions of the policy. In the case of a minor collision, in which a fender is dented or the paint scratched, he is entitled to compensation for the cost of repairs. In case of minor damage to another car, he is fully protected. Under the deductible type of policy, the policy holder agrees to stand part of every loss. He must pay the first $25 of every repair bill. He must pay $25, or $50, or $100 of every liability claim. The cost of complete coverage is much greater than the cost of a deductible type of policy, because of the large total cost of a great many minor accidents, because of the cost of settling many minor claims, and because of the greater moral hazard which complete coverage always involves. If insurance companies had their way they would write only deductible policies. The public, however, demands and is willing to pay for complete coverage, and therefore has it.

The chief objection of families of moderate means to the deductible type of policy lies in the fact that they have no way of knowing in advance just what the cost of their insurance may be. If they have no accidents during the year, it will, of course, be low. But if they have two or three accidents in close succession, each of which involves a payment of even so comparatively small a sum as $25, they may find it very inconvenient to raise the money needed to meet their part of the loss. To meet the need for a policy which will remove most of the moral hazard of complete coverage, and at the same time will definitely limit the loss to the individual policy holder, insurance companies have developed the retention type of collision policy. Under this policy, the insured is quoted a rate which covers the entire cost of protection for a year. He pays a stated portion of the premium, usually 40 or 50 per cent, when he takes out the policy. He retains the balance. In case he makes no claims during the period the policy is in force, he makes no further payments. If, however, his car is damaged to such an extent that it becomes worth his while to pay the balance of the premium, the policy holder is completely covered for the rest of the year. Under both deductible and retention policies, the careful driver can get protection against a serious accident at moderate cost. The retention type of policy appeals especially to the family that is able to pay part of one loss, but that needs to know the maximum amount of risk it must personally assume in any one year.

The rate charged for automobile insurance depends upon a number of factors. One is the type of car. Cars are classified in three groups according to the risk which they have been found to involve. Another is the territory in which the car is used. Experience has shown that there is a greater hazard involved in insuring a car used in city traffic than in insuring a car which will be used most of the time in a small town or in the open country. Usually an extra premium is charged if the automobile is to be driven outside of the United States and Canada.

The cost of coverage for public liability and property damage depends not only upon physical traffic hazards, but upon the state laws regulating legal liability. Contrary to common belief, liability insurance does not provide protection for every person who is injured in an automobile accident. It protects only against claims which can be established in the courts. And the law of the various states varies greatly in regard to legal liability. For example, if the state recognizes the defense of contributory negligence, if the injured person did anything whatever to contribute to the accident, in some cases if he even failed to do everything in his power to avoid the accident, he is held to be equally liable with the owner of the car, and so can recover no damages for injuries received. If, on the other hand, the courts determine liability on the basis of the relative amount of negligence involved, it is much easier for an injured person to establish a legal claim for damages. The cost of public liability insurance, like the cost of any other insurance, depends upon the probable amount of claims which the insurance company must pay. As a result, in states in which it is difficult to prove legal liability, rates tend to be low. In states in which it is comparatively easy to establish such liability, rates must be high enough to reimburse the insurance company for all its losses on public liability policies.

Under the ordinary public liability policy, protection goes with the car. The owner of a car is insured against liability only so long as he is driving the car against which the policy is issued. The policy holder can, however, for an additional premium, secure protection against liability in case he is driving in other cars, which are not owned, hired, or leased by him.

The family must decide for itself whether or not to protect its own property by fire, theft, or collision insurance. It must be sure to secure adequate protection against public liability. Now that many states are requiring the owner of an automobile to demonstrate his financial responsibility, it is no longer safe for the family of moderate means to be without some means of meeting the judgments which may be brought against it. Ordinarily, the safest way to insure the family's required financial responsibility is through the purchase of a public liability or property damage policy in a strong insurance company.

There is as yet no standard automobile insurance contract. The family must, therefore, read carefully every policy submitted for its consideration. It must inquire as to the exact meaning of the clauses which each policy contains. It must select the policy which gives most nearly the type of protection it needs.

The family should pay special attention to any provisions or conditions which may void the policy. Some of these provisions are easy to overlook, but failure to understand and observe all the provisions of the policy it selects is likely to leave the family without protection when it needs it most.

The family insurance program. If a family is to get the maximum return for the money it spends for insurance it must have a carefully worked out insurance plan. It must buy insurance with the idea of protecting against specific risks. It must select the types of policies which exactly fit the family's needs. Because insurance does not and should not compensate completely for any loss, a family must set up additional reserves for whatever part of each risk it is impossible or unwise to cover by insurance. Because the family needs insurance during most of its life, because it must supplement its insurance coverage with its own reserves, it is obvious that the family's insurance program must be worked out as an integral part of the family's long-time spending and savings plan.

Economic security and the improvement of living. Every effort which a family makes to provide for the future is grounded in a deep and fundamental desire for security. Its purpose is to insure in so far as possible the maintenance of a desirable manner of living. There is, of course, no such thing as absolute security. But each family wants to be able to continue to live as it is now living, or a little better, if possible, as the years go by, without danger of loss of income from unemployment or default of investments, without the danger that its income may be rendered inadequate by rising prices, with the assurance that its standard of living will not be reduced by increasing demands at the peak of the family's needs, or by the contingencies of ill-health, accident, or death.

There seems to be no common conception of what is involved in family security. In most discussions the term is used in one of two ways. The individual family is usually inclined to think in terms of what we may for want of a better term call *economic security*. Economic security implies that the family will be able to maintain its present standard of living out of its own resources throughout the entire life of the family.

The concept of economic security is purely relative. What economic security includes varies from family to family, depending upon what each individual family feels is essential to assure the maintenance of its present position in the economic and social scale.

On the other hand, *social security* seems to mean the insurance of socially desirable minimum living standards for every individual and every family in a social group. In a social security program, there is no intention of providing by collective action more than this socially desirable minimum. Personal preferences of individuals are only incidental. Social security is desired by the group for the good of the group. Social insurance is a term which has come to be applied to a number of measures like unemployment insurance, group payment for medical care, and old-age pensions, designed to provide social security. Social insurance assumes that certain minimum standards are so desirable, not from the point of view of the individuals who live upon them, but from the point of view of the group as a whole, that it is worth while for the group to compel the universal maintenance of these minimum standards, even at some cost to itself.

There are two principal types of social insurance. One type is set up as an economical means of providing families in need with a minimum of relief from common funds at the least possible cost in dollars to society, and in social stigma to the recipient. The other type is set up as a system of compulsory savings, designed to protect the group against the cost of caring for individuals or families who because of misfortune or lack of foresight fail to make adequate provision for loss of income from unemployment, accident, illness, or old age.

For families in the lower income groups, social insurance of some sort may be desirable. But social insurance cannot provide for these families more than they can provide for themselves, unless funds are taken from the incomes of other families farther up the economic scale. If social insurance means only compulsory saving, it will provide for the future needs of these low-income families at the expense of present living standards which are already generally considered to be too low.

If families are to plan for their own future intelligently, they must take account of any compulsory plans for social insurance to which they may be subject either as contributors or as recipients, and adjust their own savings program to conform to the requirements of these plans. If families in the lower income groups are to be required to provide for their own future out of already inadequate incomes, they should be told that they are going to be required to save. They should not be led to believe that they are going to get something for nothing. They must understand that they will not be able to live as well on their present income minus these compulsory savings as they can on the whole of their present income.

If, on the other hand, in order to insure for everyone a minimum of protection against the hazards of unemployment, accident, illness, and old age, it is necessary to subsidize the families in the lower income groups, this subsidy should be frankly recognized for what it is. Families in the lower income groups should count upon such subsidies as part of their income, and families farther up the income scale should understand exactly what their share of the common social responsibility for less fortunate families is to be. Families living above the minimum, all of them, must make provision not only for their own future, but for their share in the compulsory provision for the future of others.

Large-scale attempts to provide social security by such devices as social insurance suffer from one inevitable disadvantage. They call for contributions convenient to the average family. Benefits must be devised to meet the needs of the average family. And there is no average family. In individual families, the peak of family expenses may come at different ages. The maximum earning power of the head of the family may come at different times. It is, however, impossible to set up any large-scale scheme on any other basis.

Social insurance, therefore, cannot be a complete substitute for personal saving. Unemployment insurance offers a good example of this. It seems as if unemployment ought to be an insurable risk. There is much to be said for the compulsory accumulation of reserves during employment out of which to pay families some income during periods of unemployment.

Unemployment insurance guarantees a minimum of income to workers who are unemployed more than the average amount for their trade. It requires, however, that the man who is steadily employed turn in part of his earnings to care for his less fortunate fellow worker. Organized on a social security basis, unemployment insurance will provide for minimum needs, but it alone will not provide economic security for the family living above the subsistence level. Even if such a family is eligible to participate in the benefits of unemployment insurance, it can maintain its usual level of living only if it supplements these benefits with personal savings. And it must make these savings out of its usual earnings minus its contributions to the unemployment insurance plan.

In the same way, compulsory old-age pension laws will provide families living to the retirement age with a minimum of income upon which to fall back in their old age. But if any family wants anything more than this minimum of social security, it must continue its own savings for old age. If it wants more than a mother's pension for the family in case of the death of the family wage earner, it must continue to carry its own life insurance.

Under the provisions of recent social security legislation, every worker must contribute to an old-age pension fund by a tax upon his earnings. This tax must be paid every year of his working life. Under this plan he is required to save a specified portion of his income each year for his old age, regardless of his present needs. Levied upon families in the lower income groups, such a tax forces families at the peak of the life cycle still farther below the modest standard they try hard to maintain, making it necessary for them to rear children in poverty in order to provide for a possible old age that at least half the parents will never attain. Levied upon families in the middle classes, such a tax does not decrease the amount which they must save during their early years in order to provide for the peaks of family expenditure. It forces these families to make savings for old age early in life, which they might much better make after they have fulfilled the obligations involved in bringing up their children.

Social insurance may be a necessary and economical way to provide the unfortunate, the inefficient, and the infirm with a minimum of relief. It may be an effective means of requiring the improvident to save for the future. But we must remember that, from the long-time viewpoint, some of the apparently improvident in the lower income groups who are investing their income in their children are not so improvident as we may be inclined to think.

If it is to attain more than the minimum which social security requires, every family must work out for itself its own economic security, having in mind its own needs, its own resources, its own limitations, and even its own life expectancies. It can attain economic security for its members only by making personal provision for its needs throughout its whole life as a family.

There is no security for anyone in promises of pension laws which may soon be repealed. There is no security for anyone in any political action which can be revised at any time by changes in the will of a majority. In recent years there has been no security to be had even in lending savings to governments which can default upon their obligations at will. In the years since the World War almost every Western nation has defaulted upon at least part of its obligations either openly or indirectly by debasement of the currency.

There is, however, a definite part for the government to play in helping families everywhere to attain to a higher degree of economic security. Even if there is no one to make a government live up to its contracts, the government has the power to force private individuals and private corporations to do as they have agreed. The government can make its most immediately effective contribution to individual security by insisting upon the observance of private contracts, by regulating banks and insurance companies, by supervising securities issues, and by safeguarding individual investments by insisting that every individual or corporation that borrows money shall to the full extent of its ability repay that money as and when it has agreed.

There is no easy way of mass progress toward higher levels of living. It is possible to raise the general level of living only by raising the level upon which each individual family lives. Raising living levels is only in part a problem of increasing family incomes. It is even more a problem of the development and wise use of existing family resources.

Genuine progress toward better living can come only as each individual family learns to look down the years, and to see in detail both present and future problems in their proper perspective in the whole life of the family. Genuine progress can be made only by families that are willing to accept the conditions under which they must live, to order their daily lives intelligently, to live in the present courageously, and to face the future fearlessly, making such wise use of all their financial, social, and personal resources that the family's life will continue to unfold on higher and higher levels, in this generation and in the next and in the next. To provide the knowledge necessary to such wise use of all the family's varied resources, together with the perspective and sense of direction which will enable families everywhere to go forward to better living, is the purpose underlying both the development of the science and the practice of the art of family finance.

QUESTIONS

1. For what purposes are families of your acquaintance saving?
2. Against what specific contingencies is your family maintaining reserves? Are these reserves adequate to their needs? How do you tell?
3. Suppose your family has $1,000 to invest. What sort of an investment would you advise? On what basis do you make your decision?
4. In your community at the present time what are generally considered to be suitable investment opportunities for family savings? Evaluate each.

5. Give some original examples of profitable investment of family funds in family working capital.

6. Secure a number of sample policies for each of the more common kinds of insurance a family carries. Analyze carefully the provisions of the policies in each group. Then draw up a new policy which it seems to you best covers the needs of families for the type of protection it is designed to provide. Why did you include each provision in your ideal policy? Consult an insurance agent to determine what such a policy would probably cost. Check each of your sample policies against your ideal policy. Which seems to you to provide most nearly the type of protection a family should have? Compare the cost of these sample policies, considering both coverage and cost. Which policy do you consider to be the best buy in each group?

7. In what ways can a family reduce its losses from insurable hazards? In what ways can it reduce the cost of its insurance? Explain in considerable detail.

8. What are the relative advantages of mutual and stock insurance companies? Of participating and non-participating policies?

9. Consult an insurance agent of your acquaintance. (a) Work out, on the basis of the rates he quotes you, the cost of the various types of life insurance policies for a man 25 years old, a woman 25, a man 40, a woman 40, a man 60, a woman 60. (b) Find out the cost of providing a life annuity of $100 a month purchased in a single payment when a man is 65, 70, 75, years old. Compare the cost of the life annuity with a ten-year-certain annuity of the same amount. How much would it cost to provide such an annuity for himself and his wife, two years younger, which will provide an income of $100 a month as long as either of them shall live?

10. Work out a complete savings, investment, and insurance program for each of the families described in question 10, page 81. Compare the amounts and the purposes for which each family should be saving. In what sorts of securities should each family invest its funds? What risks should they insure? What will such insurance cost in your community? Indicate the changes which each family should be prepared to make in its savings and investment program in order to adjust to changes in business conditions in future years. What changes will possible social security legislation make in the savings program of each of these families?

11. Analyze current proposals for social insurance from the point of view of the family which is interested in making certain and adequate provision for the future of the parents without sacrificing unduly the present needs of the children.

REFERENCES

Abel, M. H., *Successful Family Life on the Moderate Income*, Revised Edition, Ch. XV, pp. 175-183. J. B. Lippincott Co., Chicago, 1927.

A realistic discussion of the problem of savings and investment faced by families with moderate incomes. Special consideration is given to the adjustment of the savings program to the changing demands upon the family income.

Ackerman, S. B., *Insurance*. The Ronald Press Co., New York, 1928.

A brief description of the problem of insurance. This book presents briefly a number of fundamental principles involved in insurance and then describes in considerable detail the principal types of insurance contracts.

Andrews, B. R., *Economics of the Household*, Revised Edition, Chs. VIII and IX, pp. 163-220. The Macmillan Co., New York, 1935.

These chapters are packed with a great deal of interesting information, including estimates of the value of family property and how it is acquired, trends in savings, the usual facilities for saving and investment, and a detailed discussion of relative advantages of various types of life insurance policies.

Davis, H. W., *Money Sense*. McGraw-Hill Book Co., Inc., New York, 1934.

A discussion of savings, investment, and insurance problems in their relation to the family's lifetime economic program.

Donham, S. A., *Spending the Family Income*, Revised Edition, Ch. IV, pp. 30-39. Little, Brown and Co., Boston, 1933.

A concise and practical discussion of standards for savings.

Hubbard, Clarence T., *Where Fire Insurance Leaves Off*. F. S. Crofts and Co., New York, 1930.

A concise but comprehensive description of what the standard fire insurance contract does not do and the various types of special covers which have been written to supplement the fire insurance policy. Written in terms the layman can understand.

Kyrk, Hazel, *Economic Problems of the Family*, Chs. XIII, XIV, and XV, pp. 228-293. Harper and Bros., New York, 1933.

An excellent discussion of the risks of disability, unemployment, and old age, together with an analysis of the ways in which a family may make personal provision for protection against the uncertainties of the future, the extent to which such provision is possible, and the problems involved in supplementing family savings with various forms of social insurance.

Nystrom, P. H., *Economic Principles of Consumption*, Ch. XIX, pp. 484-507. The Ronald Press Co., New York, 1929.

An analysis of the conditions favoring family savings, a description of the forms these savings take, and significant statistics showing the trend in family savings during the first three decades of the twentieth century.

Schnedler, William A., *How to Get Ahead Financially*. Harper and Bros., New York, 1926.

A book which sticks to its subject. It includes both the philosophy and practice of savings and investments. Ch. XII, "Life Insurance," is a discussion written from the point of view of what the family wants to know. Chs. VIII and IX, "Investing Savings Wisely" and "Re-Investing Dividends and Interest," discuss briefly a few of the problems the family faces in putting its money to work. See also Ch. V, "How Much Should I Save?", and Ch. VI, "Funding Unusual Expenses."

INDEX